Cahokia and the
Archaeology of Power

ISBN
0-8173-0888-1

Cahokia and the Archaeology of Power

Thomas E. Emerson

The University of Alabama Press
Tuscaloosa and London

Library of Congress Cataloging-in-Publication Data

Emerson, Thomas E., 1945–
    Cahokia and the archaeology of power / Thomas E. Emerson.
      p.   cm.
    Includes bibliographical references and index.
    ISBN 0-8173-0888-1 (alk. paper)
    1. Cahokia Site (East Saint Louis, Ill.) 2. Indians of North America—Illinois—
American Bottom—Antiquities. 3. Mississippi culture—Illinois—American Bottom.
4. Social archaeology—Illinois—American Bottom. 5. American Bottom (Ill.)—
Antiquities.
    I. Title.
E78.I3.E45 1997
977.3'89—dc21   97-13085

British Library Cataloguing-in-Publication Data available

To Jo

Contents

Figures and Tables

FIGURES

TABLES

Acknowledgments

A lengthy research project such as this creates debts to many that can never be fully repaid or recognized since over the years the project was carried out with the unending assistance and support of family and friends; constructed upon the data, interpretations, and inspirations of multitudinous colleagues; partially subsidized by public agencies and assisted by cooperation from their staffs; and allowed to continue by the patience of all. Primarily, however, this work is the result of the affection, patience, and support in thousands of ways from my wife, Jo, and our children, Samuel, Frederick, Andrew, Nils, Kjersti, and Hans.

My route to the discipline of archaeology has been circuitous. Human interaction in the past has always fascinated me because of its apparent self-revealed clarity and its obliviousness to the nuances and restrictions of the present. This fascination led me to the literary realm of history, politics, and sociology. It was only after completing undergraduate degrees in sociology and political science, interspersed with occasional interludes in plastic factories and paper mills as a machine operator, in house construction with my uncles, and after returning from two tours in Vietnam, that I discovered the fascination of anthropology and eventually pursued graduate degrees in archaeology at the University of Wisconsin-Madison (UW).

My early training at UW was under the late Dr. David A. Baerreis, truly a gentleman and a scholar. It was he who focused my initial interests in environmentally oriented research of human behavior. He also impressed in me a healthy regard for the essential relationship of a strong data base to the creation of strong interpretations.

The impetus for the completion of this particular study was provided by two individuals. The first was Dr. James B. Griffin, who explained to me, in an amazingly short, succinct lecture, using no uncertain terms, why its completion was necessary. The remaining shove was provided by Dr. Timothy Pauketat who sent me small innocent-sounding tidbits of "post-processualist" thought. Before I knew it I was hooked, and consequently, this work didn't turn out to be about Mississippian rural settlement as a reflection of floodplain environments but, instead, about elite-nonelite relations, power, and ideology.

My introduction in the early 1970s to field archaeology came in the birthplace of Midwestern archaeology, Fulton County, Illinois, with Larry Conrad who was then a graduate student at UW. Only Larry would have had the audacity to believe the massive, multicomponent Orendorf site could be salvaged from strip-mining by a handful of volunteers and students. Four seasons of 6-day weeks, 10-hour days in the central Illinois heat, often to the accompanying roar of bulldozers and road graders, the excavations of nearly 200 structures and 1,300 pits with little equipment beyond shovels and trowels, often funded from Larry's personal bank account—all carried out with virtually no support from the established archaeological community—have left an indelible impression on me. Those four years, especially the 1973 and 1974 seasons when I was field director, allowed me to do more archaeology than many professionals do in a lifetime. I owe Larry a lasting debt for allowing me to be part of this unique project.

The primary data used in this research have been generated, to a large degree, during my participation in the FAI-270 Archaeological Mitigation Project coordinated by Professor Charles J. Bareis, University of Illinois at Urbana-Champaign, and overseen by Dr. John A. Walthall, Illinois Department of Transportation. Chuck and John provided me with the opportunity to work in the field and lab, access to the collections and to unpublished records and data, various logistical and material support, and just plain, old-fashioned moral support. A large part of my gratitude to John and Chuck comes from their unstinting belief in publication. The University of Illinois Press FAI-270 publication series they fostered and supported provided me with wide-ranging experience in the analysis of primary site data and in report preparation.

My fellow site directors on the FAI-270 Project, Andrew Fortier, John Kelly, Dale McElrath, and George Milner, made the experience especially rewarding through both their professional and their personal interactions. They were extremely forthcoming in their opinions on such topics as archaeological field methods, theory, culture history, and ceramic and lithic typology. Also willing to share their ideas were the numerous people involved in the fieldwork, analysis, and publication on the project. Friends and colleagues such as Carolyn McElrath, Ned Hanenberger, Joyce Williams, Douglas Jackson, Mark Mehrer, Sissel Johannessen, Alison Towers, and Lise Marx provided much-needed support. Often that support has continued in later years and is appreciated. The FAI-270 Project was an experience that, I am sure, none of us will easily forget.

One cannot do Middle Mississippian research in the American Bottom without acknowledging the contributions of such individuals as Drs. James B. Griffin, Melvin Fowler, and Robert Hall in setting the stage for all future studies in chronology, settlement, and symbolism. Drs. Griffin and Hall have been especially helpful in this regard. The work I have done was possible only because of their previous endeavors. Dr. George Milner has been generous in his assistance throughout the years and in providing me with access to unpublished site information. George has been especially cooperative and helpful in advancing our mutual knowledge and understanding of Mississippian settlement. Dr. William Woods has provided insights into Mississippian agriculture and American Bottom physiography; Drs. George Holley and John Kelly both have waxed poetic on ceramics; Dale McElrath has lectured me on Mississippian lithics; Dr. Timothy Pauketat has expounded on elites and political economy; Drs. Fortier and Mehrer and Mr. Ned Hanenberger provided essential unpublished primary data; and others such as Chuck Bareis, James Brown, Douglas Jackson, Kenneth Farnsworth, John Walthall, R. Barry Lewis, Larry Conrad, Duane Esarey, John Richards, James Stoltman, Fred Finney, Mike Conner, Brad Koldehoff, Bob Salzer, Rinita Dalan, Roland Rodell, Clark Dobbs, Tom Wolforth, Guy Gibbon, and Alan Harn have assisted me in trying to comprehend the Mississippian world. They can judge how well it has worked by reading this volume.

A special thanks is also due to Judith Knight and the University of Alabama Press staff for their efforts to make this work available to a wider audience in its present handsome format. (Little did I think when I started the publication process that the hardest task would be to find a title for this volume.) Their work was eased by the outstanding efforts of Michael Lewis, Production Manager, and Linda Alexander, Graphic Designer, Production Office, Illinois Transportation Archaeological Research Program. Mike formatted and structured the text and figures while Linda provided new photographs of many of the figurines. The graphics and technical production of this volume are largely a result of their expertise. Permission to use one of the striking murals by Lloyd K. Townsend for the cover art was graciously provided by the Cahokia Mounds State Historic Site. Portions of these data have been published previously by the University of Nebraska Press and have been incorporated into this work with their permission. Dr. John Kelly, Dr. Timothy Pauketat, and an anonymous UAP reviewer asked some very difficult questions and made extremely cogent observations on an earlier draft of this volume. I am indebted to them for helping me create more focused and explicit versions of my arguments.

Cahokia and the
Archaeology of Power

1

Introduction

One day several blind men encountered an elephant in their path. One man
surrounded the elephant's leg with his arms and exclaimed, "An elephant is
like a tree!" Another man grasped the animal's hairy tail and pulled, saying,
"No, an elephant is like a rope." The last blind man, as he was encircled by the
beast's trunk, shouted, "Help! The elephant is as a snake and it is crushing
me!"

—An old fable

Robert Hall (1975a: 25) once equated the efforts of archaeologists to understand Cahokia with the blind men and the elephant, each archaeologist
gazing intently into his or her own small part of the beast, seeking to comprehend this extinct megalopolis. Cahokia has been labeled both a state and
a chiefdom, perceived as an economic giant and as economically inconsequential, as a regional military power and as a polity only in partial control
of its own immediate hinterlands. How do we reconcile such divergent
views? I believe comprehension is possible and that, as Hall alluded, what
has been missing is perspective. Perhaps to understand Cahokia we must,
perforce, leave it.

To gain that perspective I examined a series of rural Middle Mississippian
sites that existed in the American Bottom between about A.D. 1050 and
A.D. 1375 (cf. Hall's calibrated chronology 1991), i.e., the full span of
Cahokian existence. Many of these sites have been excavated within the last
decade using similar approaches and techniques, and in a majority of cases I
directed, participated in, or observed the excavation process. It was during
the excavation of these sites that I perceived their possible differential func-

tions and the potential patterning of architectural and material culture within site types.

Furthermore, it seemed the examination of these relatively short-term rural sites might provide a series of synchronic snapshots of the diachronically oriented transformation of Cahokia. These data provide a unique opportunity to study, for the first time, the rural evidence for the establishment of hegemonic, centralized power at Cahokia during the eleventh and twelfth centuries after Christ. This goal, I believe, has been accomplished.

In order to understand Cahokia, we must not only leave it spatially and temporally, but we must break with it conceptually as well. The traditional ways of understanding the past have not provided keys into those areas of Cahokia's past that I am interested in exploring. Recent research has been extensive and insightful in elucidating Cahokian subsistence, chronology, material culture, and external relationships but has made few inroads into the complex issues involved in its internal organization (with the notable exception of Timothy Pauketat's recent work). Yet I am specifically concerned with the political and ideological mechanisms that articulated the greater Cahokian polity. Perhaps we can approach such topics through a different way of seeing the past.

The search for a different way of perceiving the past has grown out of my increasing disenchantment with positivist approaches—a disenchantment shared by numerous other archaeologists. My major concern has been that the past has been dehumanized; mechanistic societies have been created that operate with functionally motivated, clockwork precision and that respond, necessarily, only to external environmental stimuli. Human society appears to have disappeared from much of the archaeological literature. I believe that it is possible for archaeology to have a rapprochement with the human past through concepts now common in what is referred to as "postprocessual archaeology" (cf. Hodder 1985). Such archaeologies provide theoretical and methodological ways to gain insights into the social, political, and ideological past. In this specific research I am interested in revealing aspects of Cahokian ideology, power, and political and religious organization as materialized in its rural countryside. However, I have no intention of throwing the baby out with the bath water—human society does live within a natural environment that is an important parameter of its existence, reproduction, and transformation. Consequently, I have included the broad parameters set by the natural landscape in my discussions of settlement.

What is a "postprocessual" approach to the past? A number of reviewers (cf. Leone 1986; Conkey 1989; Shennan 1986; Watson and Fotiadis 1990) have divided this diverse theoretical and methodological perspective into two major "schools," one with a specific Marxian bent and the other a combination of symbolic, structuralist, and cognitive leanings. I find that Watson (Watson and Fotiadis 1990: 614), in her recent critique, has usefully categorized this latter school as broadly accepting "material culture as 'text,' an encoding of the symbol systems that ordered the lives of those people who created the material culture" and as concerned with "the recursive or interactive quality of culture—the interplay between and among people, their symbolic systems, and each other; the daily and moment-by-moment creation of systems of meaning." This is a focus that both challenges and intrigues me.

I have begun this work with a brief reexamination of the role of individuals in human society. Why concern ourselves with the individual in a discipline that seeks broad patterning in material culture and often, of necessity, subsumes the person in the masses? Simply because an individual's actions are, via a theory of *praxis,* the crucial locus of cultural reproduction and transformation (Gibbon 1989: 107–110; Hodder 1982: 5, 1984, 1985: 7–9; Ortner 1984; Tilley 1982: 26–27). Yet *praxis* must perform in a wider social milieu that I find provided in the concept of structuralism. In his specific conceptualization of human society Giddens (1979: 59–95) has recognized "a structured totality" based on a deep-lying structure that serves as principles for the process of "structuration" that mediates between *praxis* and structure; it is the process of "structuring structure" (similar to the *habitus* of Bourdieu [1977]). I find this concept of structure, as have others (e.g., Hodder, ed. 1982; Wylie 1982), to provide a heuristic for an archaeological study of material patterning since it is focused on recognition of *recurrent social practices.*

These recurrent social practices are part of the human social order that also results in the material world being "made orderly and intersubjectively meaningful through the imposition of . . . established 'models of intelligibility' or 'innate logics of classifications'" (Wylie 1982: 40) or, more simply, patterned in a culturally understandable manner. Artifacts, and the material world in general, are part of a "symbolic, active communicative field" (Shanks and Tilley 1987: 95). As Hodder (1992) argues, recognizing the communicative potential of the material world redirects our attention from analysis focused on form and function toward a focus on culture and context. In this study I strongly emphasize the role of material goods in understanding the formation and continuance of social inequality, power, and ideology, following the lead of Douglas and Isherwood (1979: 97) who argue convincingly that the partitioning of material goods reflects the underlying partitioning of power and status within a society. Therefore, from this perspective, the material world can be studied in its own right as a valid reflection of society (i.e., Douglas and Isherwood 1979: 74-76; Shanks and Tilley 1987: 112-113; Miller 1985: 202-203).

Since this is the study of a specific type of human society (i.e., one that is hierarchically organized), I also examined relevant questions of human equality and stratification. In this process I find the conceptualization of equality, as it exists in both anthropological and Western thought, to be a chimera. Personal and institutional human inequality is the reality of human society. Having eliminated the false dichotomy between egalitarian and nonegalitarian societies, the fascinating question then becomes one that attempts to recognize the critical emergence of "institutionalized inequality" (i.e., stratification), and seeks the processes that created those institutions.

The creation of institutionalized inequality bespeaks such issues as power and ideology. These sources of inequality play a unified central role in hierarchical societies through Gramsci's concept of hegemony (i.e., domination through both ideological manipulation and physical coercion). A significant focus of this work is on the role of ideology as a force of social control and power for the Cahokian elite. Yet ideology, just like power, is not solely the property of the elite, and as we will see, ideology also is an important resource among the Mississippian commoners in both earlier and later periods of Cahokia's existence.

The issue, of course, is one of how one studies such idealistic matters as ideology and power. It is in this role that the patterning of the material world becomes crucial to advancing our understanding of the past. The acquisition and loss of ideological and political power can be seen reflected in the material world through the study of what I have called an *architecture of power, artifacts of power,* and *sacred landscapes* (cf. Earle 1987, 1991; Lightfoot 1984; Helms 1979). There is little doubt that virtually all hierarchically organized societies have sumptuary rules that restrict the distribution of certain material goods. Similarly, certain architectures and artifacts are marked by the controlling elite as signifiers of political and religious power. I propose that such architectures and artifact assemblages can be recognized at Cahokia and their context, appearance, ubiquity, and disappearance can be used to trace the rise and fall of centralized Cahokian power.

To ensure that the contextual parameters are secured for this study, chapter 3 establishes the cultural and historical background for the reader. This chapter details the chronological sequence, material culture, and conventional American Bottom archaeological wisdom concerning Middle Mississippian culture at Cahokia and its environs. It also provides an opportunity to bring to the reader's attention some of the newest developments in the modeling of Cahokia's development. Discussions by Milner (1990), Emerson (1991b), and Pauketat (1991, 1992) now suggest that the Cahokian polity's hegemony was both short-lived and less empowered on a regional scale than some previous researchers believed. This research has also demonstrated with impressive archaeological evidence the coalescence, for a brief period, of extremely centralized Cahokian power in the eleventh and twelfth centuries. This new evidence is more in line with current theoretical knowledge of the organization and operation of hierarchical societies on a worldwide basis than previously held, economically derived models.

Chapter 4 sets the parameters for the study of the Cahokian Middle Mississippian polity by looking at settlement organization evidence from late prehistoric cultures across the eastern United States. This review examines broad models of Mississippian settlement and compares them to data recovered from regional Mississippian groups. On the basis of this comparison, I defined two forms of hierarchical settlement articulation, "direct" and "sequential," that were present in the prehistoric midcontinent. Each of these forms has distinct implications for understanding the complexity of the associated Mississippian political organization. Based on this understanding, I present a new model for interpreting the political and ideological aspects of Cahokian Mississippian rural hierarchical settlement.

Building on the early recognition of functional and chronological variation in the Cahokian rural areas (cf. Emerson and Milner 1981, 1982), I examine the archaeological evidence from various rural settlements within a chronological context. While there is little in terms of comparative information, it now appears that these *specific* functionally differentiated settlement types are confined to the Cahokia countryside, although the associated "sequential articulation" mode of organization may be more widespread. While the recognition of an American Bottom pattern of dispersed villages is shown to be part of a broader Eastern Woodlands pattern, it is clear that their political and religious organizational structure is unique.

Rural Cahokian sites are described in detail in chapter 5. This process demonstrates the archaeological evidence for the material patterns of architectures and artifacts of power and the creation of sacred landscapes in the countryside. A number of distinct settlement types are defined that include specialized political, religious, and mortuary forms. It is possible in the diachronic description of the rural settlements to recognize distinct events in the appearance and disappearance of these architectural and artifactual expressions that correlate with political and ideological changes at Cahokia.

In chapter 6 I look at the implications of these settlements for understanding the political and social organization of the countryside. Here I argue their organizational structure represents powerful hegemonic control exerted from the major political centers rather than being an imitative reflection engendered by an independent rural populace. This analysis indicates that for a brief one- to two-century period Cahokia served as the central place of power within the American Bottom. The evidence suggests that Cahokian control of the countryside was facilitated by the appointment of rural "functionaries." The purpose of this control was to expedite the intensification of agricultural production to provide subsistence support for the central elite, and that control and mobilization of comestibles was an important factor in Cahokian elite power. Furthermore I discuss the ramifications of identifying rural hierarchical diversity and functional differentiation among settlements and the implications of such diversity and differentiation for understanding political and religious complexity at Cahokia.

Ideology, religion, and ritual form the core of chapters 7 and 8, which use the symbolic and ritual material culture from the rural temples to create an image of eleventh- through thirteenth-century Cahokian cosmology. Their symbolic content and context are explored using Eastern North American Indian ethnohistory and ethnography to provide a guide for their comprehension. The iconographic evidence put forward in chapter 7 suggests the presence of a fertility, world-renewal, mortuary complex that dominated rural Cahokian religious beliefs and rituals. That this was some form of what came into history as the Green Corn or Busk Ceremony is, I believe, virtually certain.

Furthermore, it seems probable that the Cahokian elite manipulated this community-centered ideology to increase their power base and, perhaps, create a divine chieftainship during the climax of centralized elite power in the late eleventh and early twelfth centuries A.D. This manipulation is manifestly evidenced in the countryside by the presence of Stirling phase religious architecture and associated artifacts in temples and mortuary facilities that I believe represent a fertility-based cult controlled by the elite. As with the specialized political facilities described earlier, the appearance of the religious facilities, iconography, and sacred artifacts and landscapes provides evidence for the power and domination of the rural populace by the central Cahokian elite.

In the final summary chapter I provide a diachronic perspective of the rise and fall of the hegemonic power of the Cahokian elite as manifested in the material remains of the countryside. These sites show there was a clear pattern of elite political consolidation and ideological appropriation during the Stirling phase that was a distinct break with previous patterns of the earlier Lohmann community and religious-based leadership. However, such consolidation of power was fragile and collapsed during Moorehead times, leading to a disintegration of the system during the Sand Prairie phase. Such a perspective on the rise and fall of Cahokia provides strong corroborative evidence for these prehistoric political and religious events as well as strong support for the utility of this theoretical approach to the study of hegemonic power, political centralization, and domination.

2

The Conceptual Parameters

It is impossible to conceive of a theory of society without a conception of
human nature.

—Tom Campbell 1981: 18

Any study of ideology, religion, political power, dominance, or other expressions of Cahokian hegemony must first be based on a thorough understanding of the theoretical parameters involved. In order to create a model
for hegemonic-driven social change it is necessary to establish the concept
of cultural stability and transformation based on the principle of the individual as the locus of social variation (i.e., *"praxis"*). Such a model must be
enveloped in a theory of *practice* within a broader structural framework (a la
Giddens 1979) to provide a heuristic for cultural transformation. That type
of approach, based upon structuralist principles, argues for the recognition
of material culture as a patterned "text" interpretable in the archaeological
record.

The theoretical ramifications of hegemonic power (i.e., ideological persuasion and political coercion) are reflected in the material world. That power
is inherent in human inequality and is critical for the development of hierarchical political and social structures. It is possible, incorporating these principles, to investigate the idealist world of hegemonic forces.

THE INDIVIDUAL AND SOCIETY

The individual as a force in social theory is neither new nor unique, yet the
full understanding and elaboration of the individual's role as both actor and

initiator of social change are recent in anthropology and have only begun to impact regional archaeological research and studies (e.g., Pauketat 1991, 1992, 1994; Emerson 1995: 10-17). This new interest in the individual, now often called the *theory of practice,* can be traced (cf. Ortner 1984) through Marxist approaches, focusing on social structures, to such important calls to action as Bourdieu's (1977) *Outline of a Theory of Practice* in the 1970s.

Individual action provides the catalyst for both stability and change within the broader cultural system, for it is by multiple individuals' actions that the system is reproduced. In fact, Sahlins (1981: 67) questions "whether the continuity of a system ever occurs without its alteration, or alteration without continuity." For those who adopt a theory of practice, individual action and the intended results must be considered, among many other factors, "in respect of unconscious motives, operating or 'outside' the range of the self-understanding of the agent." Even more critical are the "unintentioned consequences of intentional conduct" (Giddens 1979: 59). Yet the individual is part of a social group, and "social systems are produced as transactions between agents . . . but they are the outcome of action only in so far as they are also involved as the medium of its production . . . [And] the 'collective' is bound to the very phenomenon of action" (Giddens 1979: 95).

Practice must perform within a greater social milieu that we have yet to identify. In this particular instance I am interested in examining the structure of Middle Mississippian Cahokian society, especially as it is reflected in the realm of ideology and domination. Structure provides a categorical, conceptual framework within which individuals act to create social form, reproduction, and transformation. Most important, it provides a framework within which the material and ideal worlds are linked, for they are both transformations of that underlying structure into other mediums. Structuralism has many guises, but here I will depend primarily on Gidden's (1979: 59-95) critique of structuralism and his elucidation of structuration as an alternative methodology of cultural reproduction and transformation, although occasionally I will use both Bourdieu (1977) and clarifications from Hodder (1982: 7-11, 1991: 73-79).

Giddens (1979: 63-65) comprehends a "structured totality" (i.e., a social system) on the basis of three terms: structure, system, and structuration (see figure 2.1). This structured totality takes into account "an implicit recognition of a syntagmatic dimension (patterning in time-space) and a paradigmatic dimension (continuity-producing, virtual order of elements) in social analysis" (Giddens 1979: 63). Structure has a *virtual existence* and refers to the rules that *bind* time and space in social systems (i.e., it possesses *structuring properties).* However, while structures do not actually exist in time-space (except in the theoretical moment of social constitution), Giddens (1979:

Cahokia and the Archaeology of Power

STRUCTURE:	Rules and resources, organized as properties of social systems. Structure only exists as "structural properties"
SYSTEM:	Reproduced relations between actors or collectivities, organized as regular social practices
STRUCTURATION:	Conditions governing the continuity or transformation of structures, and therefore the reproduction of systems

Figure 2.1 Structure, System, and Structuration (after Giddens 1979, Figure 2.2).

65) argues that "we can analyze how 'deeply layered' structures are in terms of historical duration of the practices they recursively organize, and the spatial 'breadth' of those practices; how widespread they are across a range of interactions."

Giddens's concept of structuration is critical in redressing a basic flaw in structuralist theory—perpetual synchrony. Without a theory of social action theorists are unable to generate change or even reproduction. Structuration mediates the recursive relationship between practice and structure. It includes the social means and modes of reproduction, it involves the process of *structuring structure,* and it allows for both unconscious *and* discursive, as well as practical, consciousness in social reproduction.

Habitus, a concept similar to structuration and developed by Bourdieu (1977), mediates between practice and structure through a series of dispositions. Like Giddens, Bourdieu stresses that the combination of practical logic, knowledge, and common strategies for action coalesces to create a common behavior. The passing of *habitus* to individuals through the process of enculturation ensures variation in the series of dispositions instilled in each actor. Especially important in this process is the role of the material world as a purveyor of culture. Structuration and *habitus* create actors who are neither ignorant participants in a mechanistic society nor skilled players who consciously produce specific actions. As Hodder (1991: 77) points out in these perspectives, "There is a duality of structure; the structure is both the medium and outcome of action. The individual plays a central role as self-monitoring, creative, and with degrees of competence." Most importantly, however, it is through these that structure is able to incorporate both synchrony and diachrony and enable generation. Systems play the role that social structure does in traditional definitions, although Giddens is careful to remind us that systems are "patterned in time as well as space, through continuities of social reproduction" (1979: 64).

Giddens (1979: 65-66) integrates the structural totality he defines as follows:

> Social systems involve regularized relations of interdependence between individuals or groups, that typically can best be analyzed as *recurrent social practices*. Social systems are systems of social interaction; as such they involve the situated activities of human subjects, and exist syntagmatically in the flow of time. Systems, in this terminology, have structures, or more accurately, have structural properties; they are not structures in themselves. Structures are necessarily (logically) properties of systems or collectivities, and *are characterized by the "absence of a subject."* To study the structuration of a social system is to study the ways in which that system, via the application of generative rules and resources, and in the context of unintended outcomes, is produced and reproduced in interaction.

Structure, as a heuristic, plays a critical role, via practice, in providing for a paradigm to portray the processes of social stability and transformation. Such a paradigm is necessary if one focuses on investigating the role of "idealist" factors such as ideology and domination in producing change in prehistoric societies.

HIERARCHICAL SOCIETIES

While practice may focus on any aspect of the cultural system, it has been especially congenial in exposing the inequalities, asymmetries, and domination that reside as central cores of all cultural systems (Ortner 1984: 149). Thus, practice provides a conceptually important base in pursuing the goals of this study for elucidating Middle Mississippian ideology, power, and domination within a paradigm of structural reproduction and transformation. It is not the presence or absence of inequality, status delineation, prestige, or hierarchical organization that differentiate "egalitarian" from "hierarchical" societies (a false dichotomy as I noted earlier), for these appear to be coterminous with human society (Emerson 1995: 18-20). Rather, it is the appearance of institutionalized forms of these relationships that marks the threshold. It is clear that egalitarian societies have "powerful leveling mechanisms" (often both social and environmental) and an "ideology of equality" (Service 1975: 71) that serve to reinforce social homogenization and suppress the accumulation and consolidation of power by individuals or select groups. Such leveling mechanisms have been overcome in the development of more complex and permanently organized hierarchical societies. As Durkheim (1933: 94) puts it, the *"equilibrium has been broken."*

There is no doubt that one can arrange societies along continua of complexity, permanence, and power regarding the hierarchical organization of their leadership. It is also apparent that a key variable is the relative ability of those possessing status or prestige in hierarchically organized societies to utilize *power over* (a la Miller and Tilley 1984). In egalitarian societies leaders persuade and manipulate; in hierarchical societies they simply command. Based on these reflections, it would seem appropriate to conclude that inequality and hierarchy are, in fact, definitional aspects of human society.

What subterfuge translates the powerful leveling mechanisms of segmental or egalitarian societies into conveyers of inequality and hierarchy? Why do the many allow the few to rule? More important, how do the institutions of inequality come into existence? To understand the relationships of groups within socially differentiated hierarchical societies requires a comprehension of origins. Wright (1984: 48; a la Sahlins 1963, 1977, 1981) derives the classic pattern of chiefly ranked elite and commoners out of earlier forms of ascribed, big-man societies. Ongoing community fissioning and increased elite intercommunity relations create an elite-commoner dichotomy that is supported by ideological and mythological sanctions, thus leading to the institutionalization of inequality. Such a scenario tells only part of the story and privileges differentiation and elite power over social unity. On the other hand, other recent origin stories have proposed that elite-commoner relations are one of communal unity (cf. Saitta 1994). Such an approach denies the existence of intragroup power relations, promotes a vision of intragroup harmony, and denies the very nature of elites (i.e., the unequal access to *power over*). Such a vision is not supportable from the ethnographic, ethnohistoric, or archaeological record.

I believe a more balanced vision of elite-commoner interaction can be produced by reexamining the origins of institutionalized hierarchical societies. I begin with the assertion that inequality and hierarchy are definitional aspects of human societies (cf. Fallers 1973; Fried 1967; Service 1975; Emerson 1995) and, important, that such hierarchies are built on a consensual basis. The consensual nature of hierarchies is grounded in the social perception of "communitas" (cf. Turner 1969; Helms 1996; also Pauketat and Emerson 1996) that promotes a model of society as unsegmented, homogenous, and unstructured and that encapsulates the communal aspects of society. Perceptions of communitas are supported in all societies by a Durkheimian "solidarity" that invokes the recognition of the "in-group/out-group" differentiation. Such consensual feelings support the emergence of big-man societies and are equally important in the rise of chiefly hierarchies. They emerge from the world of intercommunity competition, in which communities (not individual big-men or chiefs) strive to better themselves vis-a-vis the "others" (i.e., outside communities). Scholars have focused on the role of feasting, public ceremonials, giveaways, construction of monumental architecture, and other expressions of group power as if they are the sole property of the elite. Yet I suspect that these efforts are best characterized as symbolic expressions of communitas and group solidarity rather than of elite coercive power.

But the public expressions of communitas that promote society also carry the seeds of elite alienation. Elevation of the elite in the promotion of community prosperity increasingly distances those elevated from the community. This distance is created by the ongoing association of the elite with the symbols of the cosmos and sacred universe. The correlation of eliteness with sacredness removes the elites from communitas even as they are promoted by it. Elite alienation is the product of communal efforts. The elite become inhabitants of a sacred landscape and a cosmic society at the virtual insistence and for the communal good of their society. At the point of alienation one can speak with assurity of the institutionalization of inequality—a point that may only be manifested with the emergence of the state. Consequently it is more appropriate to speak of hierarchies as resulting from communal activities and the elite as being the recipients of a consensual power rather than expropriators of such power. Perhaps the process is best conceived in Foucaultian terms as the expression of communal power in which "the logic is perfectly clear, the aims decipherable, and yet . . . no one . . . invented them, and few . . . can be said to have formulated them: an implicit characteristic of the great anonymous, almost unspoken strategies . . . whose 'inventors' or decision makers (and participants) are often without hypocrisy" (Foucault 1978: 95).

This process is not an elite duping of the commoners nor is it an imposition of a dominant ideology on the unsuspecting masses. It comprises specific actions with unseen ramifications, an intentional process with unintentioned results, for while "people know what they do; they frequently know why they do what they do; but what they do not know is what what they do does" (Foucault, personal communication, cited in Dreyfus and Rabinow 1983: 187). It is a process that may appear both directionless and intentionless, lacking exploiters or exploited, *but* it is not a process without power, power resident both in the elite and in the communitas.

Recognizing the presence of communitas and solidarity as essential factors in community formation and elite emergence is not synonymous with recognizing communalism (e.g., Saitta 1994). While Saitta's (1994) exposition on communalism in chiefly societies is phrased in terms of a useful critique of overly prescriptive models of prestige-good economies and elite dominance, I do not find it captures the essence of Mississippian hierarchical societies (i.e., operationalized hegemonic processes). His focus on identifying "exploitative" versus "nonexploitative" relationships is hardly susceptible to archaeological investigation, yet is crucial to his argument that elite domination does not exist at Cahokia. It is this very need to pigeonhole Mississippian society as "nonclass/class," as "a way to expand archaeological inference in the social realm," that is at the heart of my concern with Saitta's postulates (1994: 219). His categorization of subsumed classes within a framework of communalism recasts the elite-commoner dichotomy as unity while it ignores that individuals are often partners and full participants in their own subordination (and superordination a la Foucault). This categorization obscures rather than elucidates critical elite-nonelite power relationships. It is the operation of social networks, economic pathways, and political and religious actions that is important in establishing hegemonic order in both hierarchical and nonhierarchical societies.

Who were the Cahokian elites? Such a question must first consider the more general question of "eliteness" in any society. It is apparent from the literature (e.g., papers in Marcus, ed. 1983 and D. Chase and A. Chase, eds. 1992) that "eliteness" is in danger of becoming a meaningless category, both in present-day and in archaeological studies, because of its catchall use and lack of definition. Indiscriminate use is producing a loss of theoretical meaning.

Research into the nature of elites in Southeastern late prehistoric societies has been limited (although see papers in Barker and Pauketat, eds. 1992 for some interesting beginnings); however in neighboring Mesoamerican societies it has been a persistent and controversial topic. D. Chase and A. Chase's (eds. 1992) recent volume on the topic raises many issues relevant to this study. Essentially all discussions of elites reflect a basic dichotomy in their perceived definitions and functions. Elites are commonly identified as the rich and powerful in a society and thus can be correlated archaeologically with material remains that evoke similar "rich and powerful" associations. In general, as in Mesoamerica, I believe this is the tacit definition used by most Southeastern archaeologists. An equally valid view, and one that I subscribe to, defines elites as those that "run" society (i.e., who have power and control over a society's institutions [Marcus 1983: 12–13]). A. Chase and D. Chase (1992: 3) conclude that such a definition must "concern itself with the concepts of power and control . . . abstract notions that are difficult to identify concretely in the archaeological record" and focus their primary attention toward elites as the rich and powerful.

Models of elite definition in Mesoamerican archaeology, ethnohistory, and ethnography are characterized by a basic division common to all who study elites (A. Chase and D. Chase 1992: 9-10). Traditional approaches have visualized two-tiered reconstructions in which society is composed only of elites and commoners. Elites are hereditary nobles who rule society, while the vast remainder of the population are simply commoners who till the fields (i.e., society's producers). Some more recent models have begun to interject layers into this elite-commoner dichotomy by introducing concepts such as middlemen, specialists, secondary elite, even bourgeoisie. These models make the point that while the "elite" may have controlled society, they were aided and assisted by a large number of individuals who had access to varying levels of elite symbols and rights (i.e., sharers in "eliteness").

George Marcus (1992), in a review of the papers in D. Chase and A. Chase (1992), rightly assesses the difficulties in the archaeological identification of elites and, in fact, the limited utility of most current elite or stratification theory to effectively further our understanding of the functioning of prehistoric societies. He suggests that a more fruitful avenue of investigation involves the theoretically innovative work of Foucault and Bourdieu on domination and power. That is the goal of this research, and I will demonstrate that the archaeological record can be used to elicit concepts of power and to identify those members of Cahokian society who can be considered among the elite.

By any definition, elites existed at Cahokia. North American ethnohistoric and ethnographic data are rich (e.g., sources on the political and social offices of such groups as the Caddo, Natchez, Omaha, Apalachee, and Winnebago; for several excellent discussions of this issue see Scarry 1992; Wyckoff and Baugh 1980; Knight 1986, 1990) in documenting the presence of diverse political and religious offices to indicate that a strict two-tier system did not dominate the region's hierarchically organized societies. Based on such analogies it seems appropriate to visualize a gradation of "elites" within the Cahokian polity that ranged from the paramount chief as the highest of the high to the low-ranking political and religious functionaries who, I propose in this study, managed the rural areas.

I have chosen specifically to use the term "elite" to refer to that segment of the Cahokian population that exercises hegemonic control over some portion of the general population (i.e., those who control society). Thus, in this context I consider "eliteness" as related to political and religious *power over* a kin group, rather than solely as a function of restricted membership in that group.

The study of hierarchical societies has become one of the central foci of archaeological research (cf. Drennan and Uribe 1987) in this era of "postprocessual" concerns. Overwhelmingly, the current archaeological dialogue (e.g., Drennan and Uribe, eds. 1987) concentrates on "origins," categorizing schemes, correlations with cultural and environmental variables, their evolutionary relationships, and ultimately, their value as heuristic devices.

One factor emphasized in this debate is the tendency of typological approaches to make definitional phenomena unavailable to investigation (Plog and Upham 1983); i.e., it is impossible to investigate the relationship of an "independent" variable (e.g., population or settlement size) to the chiefdom or state, if that variable is used to define the society. Noting the range of variation has led some researchers to reject "chiefdoms" in favor of more amorphous labels such as "middle-range societies" (Feinman and Neitzel 1984; Upham 1987). While I will use the more traditional term "chiefdoms" in this study, the Feinman, Neitzel, and Upham papers make a critical point that research aimed at "labeling" societies leads us to no new understanding of their development. Our elucidation of variation rather than typological classification should be the goal of archaeological research.

The conceptualization of chiefdoms has moved far from its early Service-generated redistributive paradigm (Service 1962) toward a political model that stresses political and social differentiation (Earle 1987: 281). The archaeological and ethnographic record for chiefdoms seems to provide evidence of extensive variation within a wide set of boundary conditions (Drennan and Uribe 1987: xi). The point is clear—chiefdoms are a complex and varied concatenation of characteristics, each of which must be studied in its own specific context.

Most current definitions of chiefdoms derive from Wright's discussions (1977, 1984) that emphasize the political organizational nature of such societies. It is "a socio-political entity in which overall social control activities are vested in a subsystem which is externally specialized vis a vis other activities, but not internally specialized in terms of different aspects of the control process (e.g., observing, deciding, coercing); there is, in short, one generalized sort of political control" (Wright 1984: 42). Chiefdoms have institutionalized social status differentiating an elite group who fill formal offices within a political structure representing a *"permanent, centralized, decision-making authority"* (Spencer 1987: 371). The necessary correlation of institutionalized office and status differentiation is seen by some as essential to chiefly development (Johnson 1978).

Chiefly leadership is best characterized as generalized. Wright (1977) points out that the decision-making authority within a chiefly society is centralized at both the community and regional scales, but that these offices show little evidence of internal differentiation or specialization. While there is tremendous difference in scale, there is little difference in the types of duties performed or responsibilities held by the paramount chief versus the local village headman. This generalized leadership role also highlights one of the weaknesses of the chiefly system—any delegation of power by the paramount chief to a subordinate was a total delegation (Earle 1987: 289). Leadership strategies in chiefdoms strive to create a homogeneous authority and de-emphasize any tendency to subdivide that authority (Wright 1984: 50).

Having said that, we can immediately identify variations in leadership form between simple and complex chiefdoms. "Simple chiefdoms are those in which . . . control is exercised by figures drawn from an ascribed local elite subgroup; these chiefdoms characteristically have only one level of control hierarchy above the local community" (Wright 1984: 42). By contrast, in complex chiefdoms "control is exercised by figures drawn from a class of people that cross-cuts many local subgroups, a 'class' being defined as a ranked group whose members compete with each other for access to controlling positions and stand together in opposition to other people. Complex chiefdoms characteristically cycle between one and two levels of control hierarchy above the local level" (Wright 1984: 42-43).

Chiefly political organizations are synonymous with long-term instability, which is epitomized in the classic pattern of "chiefly cycling" of complex chiefdoms (cf. Anderson 1990a, 1990b, 1994; Scarry, ed. 1996). Because of the undifferentiated nature of authority within this political structure, any stress in the system may immediately translate into subversion and division. Consequently, an examination of long-term political structure within a chiefdom will reveal a continually shifting pattern of consolidation and diffusion. This means that chiefly development is one of punctuated change, not continual evolution (Earle 1987: 281). Perhaps the key elements of chiefly political reality are best summarized by Earle's description of chiefdoms as "fragile, negotiated institutions held together by economic interdependence, ideology, and force" (1989: 87).

POWER AND IDEOLOGY

The discussions of hierarchical societies, of human inequality, of social stratification, of group domination and subordination are dependent on concepts of power and hegemony. Power is a critical precursor of hegemony, yet one that seldom, until recently, entered consciously into archaeological discourse. With the freedom offered to archaeological studies based on a rejection of strict positivist theory and methodology, subjects such as power, hegemony, domination, and subordination have taken on increased interest as topics worthy of investigation. Such research becomes possible when it is acknowledged that material remains of prehistoric societies are "creations by peoples in accordance with their representations of the natural and social world . . .

the social production of reality. This represents a radical shift in perspective in the direction of making the past *human*" (Miller and Tilley 1984: 2).

Power

Power seems a commonsense term, easy to comprehend; however, even in its simple dictionary definition, we can see two very distinct facets. This dichotomy is also representative of the scholarly debate over power. Power can be seen as simply the "ability to act, to do something, freewill," or it can be presumed to be the "coercive ability to control others' actions, i.e., to prevent action." It can be a property of the many or the one, of institutions or the individual. It can signal conflict or communication, be negative or positive.

Foucault (e.g., 1978, 1979) has had the most effect on archaeological concepts of power through his studies of social history (e.g., Hodder 1991; Miller and Tilley, eds. 1984). Foucault, rather than position power outside of society as an amoral unitary force of negation, places power in society; it is distributed throughout society and among individuals. Foucault recognizes that every interaction contains power. In a similar line of reasoning, Miller and Tilley (1984: 7) argue that power "can be regarded as a dispositional capability, neither possessed nor exercised or controlled by any particular agent or collectivity, but as a structural feature of social systems, which is only manifested through its effects on individuals, groups, and institutions." Power in this format is an intrinsically active part of every individual in a theory of practice and can be thought of as an "empowering" force in processes such as structuration.

The fullest elucidation of power in an archaeological sense has been pursued by Miller and Tilley (1984). They follow Benton (1981: 176) in recognizing only two aspects of power, the *power to* and the *power over*: "By *power to* we refer to power as an integral and recursive element in all aspects of social life. *Power over*, by contrast, can be specifically related to forms of social control. While *power to* can be logically disconnected from coercion and asymmetrical forms of social domination and does not, therefore, imply *power over*, the latter sense of the noun power must always involve *power to*" (Miller and Tilley 1984: 5).

While they do not adhere to Foucault's complete thesis of power, there are many ramifications of his perspective that have value in understanding power. A primary contribution is the imbuing of individual and social interactions with power and through its manifestations as attributions to social categories. Power is resource bounded, but it is not dependent merely on coercive force; it may as easily be expressed as knowledge resources. Its expression is, however, "dependent upon access to an asymmetrical distribution of resources" (Miller and Tilley 1984: 7). Its ability to be expressed as *power over* does require coercive force as well as an agent. Since the expression of *power over* creates a recursive relationship between the coercive agent and those over whom power is being exerted, such situations are always dynamic. It is in attempts to reduce social stress in such situations, through "the active production of a normative consensus naturalizing and misrepresenting the extant nature of asymmetrical social relations" (Miller and Tilley 1984: 7), that ideology and power meld.

Power, while defined partially as a mentalist construct, here, is manifest in social actions and material remnants. One of those most powerful manifestations of power is the built environment. Foucault (1979, 1986; Tilley 1991; Dreyfus and Rabinow 1983) shows us the intimate relationship between power and the built world. The built world, he argues is "a generalizable model of functioning: a way of defining power relations in terms of everyday life of men. . . . It is the diagram of a mechanism of power deduced to its ideal form" (Foucault 1979: 205). The built world is an exercise of power through space, but it is not a model that represents power; rather it is a means where power is operationalized in space (Foucault 1979: 190). In Foucaultian concepts of power one must continually remember that power is inherent throughout the system, and the built environment represents only one of many "nodes" where interconnecting lines of power are manifested. The operation of power through the constructed form is a constant and subtle expression of power that "works" directly on individuals—it is this subtlety that makes it so effective (Tilley 1991: 206).

It is such material manifestations of power, especially in the built environment, that are critical to our future exploration of archaeological ideology and domination. It is important, then, that the assumptions concerning power be clarified (following Miller and Tilley 1984: 8):

1) *Power to* is an integral element in social life, a component of all social practices, an existential part of human existence and can be disassociated from social control and domination, characterized by *power over.*

2) Power may have some of its conditions of existence in the economic base, e.g., systems of labour exploitation but is not simply an affect of the economic.

3) Power is both productive of knowledge and non-material resources, and a negative repressive element bolstering social inequalities.

4) Power is dialectically related to resources, to operate it draws on these resources and in turn reproduces them.

5) Power is not unitary, it cannot be tied down to a single essence or form.

6) At one level power is neither possessed nor exercised but is a structural feature of the social totality only manifested at its point of constitution in social action and interaction through its effects.

7) Power is attributable to individuals, groups, etc., not as possession but in terms of the effect of its exercise producing a structured asymmetry of resources.

Hegemony

How are the dual attributes of coercion and persuasion in power conceptually operationalized? Commonly, scholars (e.g., Ortner 1984: 149; Pauketat 1991: 19; Williams 1977: 108-110) have adopted the concept of "hegemony" from Antonio Gramsci (1971) to specify a cultural milieu that is characterized by the privileged role of dominance in the systemic interdigitation of power, domination, ideology, and society. Gramsci's specific contribution to our understanding of the exercise of domination between groups has stemmed from his linking ideology and force as twin attributes of power. Williams (1977: 108-110, as cited in Ortner 1984: 149) contends that Gramsci's "hegemony" broadly incorporates "culture as social process" and "ideology" to signify culture at its broadest sense, but especially inclusive of "the lived dominance and subordination" of subgroups. While hegemony implies power and control over subalternate groups, this does not automatically restrict its methods to force and coercion. Gramsci (1971: 57) recognizes that an elite may (must) maintain its supremacy through both "domination" and "intellectual and moral leadership" (i.e., the power of leadership stems from *both* physical repression and ideological persuasion).

Does such ideological persuasion translate into a Gramscian "dominant ideology theory"? Abercrombie, et al. (1980: 14) note that Gramsci does not depict subaltern groups as helpless victims duped by the dominant ideology. In fact, Gramsci's concepts have as much to do with resistance by subalternate groups to hegemony as domination. He suggests that the masses have a dual consciousness. The alternate consciousness of the subalternate groups is "common sense," that which is "fragmentary, incoherent and inconsequential, in conformity with the social and cultural position of those masses whose philosophy it is" (Gramsci 1971: 419). Such a perspective is in keeping with Gramsci's (1971: 333) vision of humans as active interveners in the production of structure in that "[t]he active man-in-the-mass has a practical activity, but has no clear theoretical consciousness of his practical activity, which nonetheless involves understanding the world in so far as it transforms it. His theoretical consciousness can indeed be historically in opposition to his activity."

Hegemony can also represent a mechanism to resist domination. Miller et al. (1989: 11-13) stress that aspect of hegemony as a force of social change in the ability of subaltern groups to form associations and gather hegemonic power with which to overthrow a dominant group. Hegemony, although often used in that manner, is not confined to dominant groups but represents the potential of all groups in society. Thus hegemony can be a significant force in historic transformations and is especially useful in understanding intergroup conflict in societies. Here I shall use "hegemony" to refer to that exercise of power by a dominant *or* subaltern group through coercion and consent in the social and political system manifested in the interplay of practice, power, domination, and social/historical change.

Ideology

Power expressions within hierarchical societies result in asymmetry, domination, constraint, subordination, inequality, restriction, and limits; but essentially the previous discussions have demonstrated that such ends do not require expressions of coercive force. Instead, numerous scholars recognize that the discriminating force may be the "persuasion" of ideology. This introduces the concept of "ideology" into the structure of power.

All recent discussions and elaborations of ideology spring from a Marxian base (Abercrombie et al. 1980: 7-29; Giddens 1979: 165-197; Larrain 1979: 13-34; Sumner 1979: 1-56). For Marx and Engels, a precept of ideology was the "false consciousness" of a dominant ideology, a creation of the ruling classes, arising from the inequality of economic relations in order to mystify the masses, serving to naturalize inequality, to engage the masses in their own domination (Marx and Engels 1989; Larrain 1979: 35-67). Marx's and Engels's portrayal of ideology has been so important in the development of the concept that I have quoted it here at length:

> The ideas of the ruling class are in every epoch the ruling ideas, i.e., the class which is the ruling *material* force of society, is at the same time the ruling *intellectual* force. The class that has the means of material production at its disposal, has control at the same time over the means of mental production, so that thereby, generally speaking, the ideas of those who lack the means of mental production are subject to it. The ruling ideas are nothing more than the ideal expression of the dominant ruling material relationships, the dominant material relationships grasped as ideas; hence of the relationships which make the one class the ruling one; therefore, the ideas of its dominance. The individuals composing the ruling class possess among other things consciousness, and therefore think. Insofar, therefore, as they rule as a class

and determine the extent and compass of an epoch, it is self-evident that they do this in its whole range, hence among other things rule also as thinkers, as producers of ideas, and regulate the production and distribution of the ideas of their age: thus their ideas are the ruling ideas of the epoch. (Marx and Engels 1989: 64-65)

The subsequent emergence of what is referred to as "dominant ideology theory" as a major focus of theoretical expansion and debate by later Marxist and non-Marxist writers has been detailed in Sumner (1979) and Abercrombie et al. (1980). Much of the debate has concentrated on just how "dominant" the "dominant ideology" actually is. Are subalternate groups really completely bamboozled? Are there no competing subgroup ideologies? Are the ruling classes also duped by their own ideology or do they consciously manipulate it to control subordinate groups? Is ideology a tool for domination or the essence of everyday life?

Today few theorists would advocate the idea of a social wholeness encapsulated within a dominant ideology but would speak rather of multiple ideologies within a society (e.g., Abercrombie et al. 1980; Bloch 1989; Giddens 1979). Subaltern groups often preserve ideologies that clearly differ or may even be in conflict with the dominant ideology expounded by the ruling elite, yet this does not denigrate the importance of the dominant ideology. Ideology creates the social and natural world for humans, explaining and naturalizing it—no member of a society can escape the influence of its dominant ideology. As Pauketat (1991: 19) neatly summarized it, the "dominant ideology appropriates the consciousness of individuals." Yet the elite cannot totally suppress subaltern ideologies. Consequently, the role of a dominant ideology in "managing" subordinate groups is one fraught with problems, conflict, and contradictions. It is the interplay of these unresolved contradictions that may serve as a major source of transformation within society.

In traditional Marxian thought, ideology arises out of the necessity to conceal the reality of material inequality between the dominant and the subordinate groups; consequently, it is always negation of reality. It also serves, however, as "a condition for the functioning and reproduction of the system of class domination . . . by hiding the true relations between classes, by explaining away the relations of domination and subordination. Thus, social relations appear harmonious and individuals carry out their reproductive practices without disruption" (Larrain 1979: 47). This implies the opposition of reality by ideology; yet as I note above, ideology is critical in the creation of individual knowledge. If our knowledge is created by ideology, if ideology masks reality, how can we recognize reality? We come again to the persistent idealist-materialist dichotomy. It is clear that we need to work toward an understanding of ideology from a different perspective.

How then do we understand ideology? In interpreting Marx, two very different threads of theory have emerged: one (traditional Marxism) perceives ideology "on the level of discourse, as a barrier to the production of knowledge," and the other, following Althusser (1977), regards "ideology as incorporated within the practical conduct of social life" (Giddens 1979). Here I will avoid the Althusserian vision of ideology because I am specifically interested in the manifestation of ideology in its more traditional aspects in Mississippian society. For that approach it is appropriate to follow Giddens (1979: 187) who argues that to sidestep the ideal versus the real dilemma we need to see the primary value of the ideological concept as a "critique of domination." In a similar vein, Shanks and Tilley (1982: 131) regard ideology "as a mode(s) of intervention in social relations, carried on through practice, which secures the *reproduction* rather than the *transformation* of the social formation in the presence of contradictions between structural principles at the level of structure, and of clashes of interest between actors and groups at the level of system." Such definitions are in keeping with the view that ideology involves the manipulation of ideas and material and "provides the framework within which, from a particular standpoint, resources are given value, inequalities are defined, and power is legitimated" (Hodder 1991: 72).

The above discussion includes the implication that the ideology of domination "functions" within social formations—these parameters have been delineated by Giddens (1979: 193-196) as the: (1) representation of a specific group's interest as those of all society's members; (2) denial or shift to a different social sphere of contradictions within a social system; and (3) reification or naturalization of the status quo to support its permanence and durability and disguise its susceptibility to change. It is clear that these aspects of ideological functions intermesh in the complex weave of society. Within such a context ideology interacts with power through practice and is manifested in the material world.

The role of ideology has come to the fore in studies of chiefly hierarchical societies as a recognized and formidable power base when operationalized in conjunction with the more traditional areas of economic and military control (Earle 1989: 86). Often derived from a Marxist orientation, such new studies of inequality focus on points of conflict and stress within societies such as elite-commoner friction and elite and intercommunity competition.

Earle (1987: 298-300, 1991: 6-10), in his review of ideological elements of chiefly societies, has suggested ideology may be manifested in several ways. Perhaps first and foremost are "ceremonies of place associated with the creation of a sacred landscape." Such communally constructed landscapes are the homes of the elites who mediate society's relationship with the cosmos and serve, in addition, as a spatial materialization of that cosmos. Second, there are "symbols of individual power" that encompass the exotic, ritual objects associated with elite positions and that are often part of an extensive trade/exchange network that involves distant places and foreign elite interaction. Such objects, categorized as part of an "international style," symbolize social distance and esoteric power (cf. Helms 1979) and indicate the elites' participation in the wider world. Finally, "symbols of warrior might" indicate the physical dominance of the elite class as part of the natural order.

It is clear that archaeologists can now identify the material manifestations of ideology with some assurity. There is an increasing acceptance of cosmology, religion, and symbolism as important factors in hierarchical societies. Yet on one of the central issues, researchers remain divided (i.e., the role of ideology as a "prime mover" in the equation of inequality). Is ideology simply the balm that soothes the pain of inequality and conflict, or does it have a deeper, insidious role as a creator of those very features? It should be no surprise that I support a strong role for ideology in the structuring of hierarchical societies, and the depiction of that role will be a focus of much of my later discussion.

IMPLEMENTING A STUDY OF HEGEMONY

Practitioners of archaeological structuralism have made convincing demonstrations in Hodder (ed. 1982) of its specific potential, and both Hodder (1982) and Wylie (1982) argue convincingly for its acceptance. In fact, Wylie (1982) has argued at length that since material culture is "meaning determined" and central to archaeology, structuralism has become a requisite paradigm for the discipline.

It is necessary to establish the foundations for a structural understanding of material cultural. The essence of the argument is straightforward. Cultural items represent:

> meaningful constructs inasmuch as they often represent a definable tradition whose structures of articulation (i.e. of the elements comprising the constructs in the field) embody a set of intuitions about what constitutes a well-formed construct comparable to the intuitions identified in linguistics as a governing competence or body of structuring principles. They represent, that is, various aspects of material reality that have been "made cultural," appropriated by a

cultural system and, in this, transformed, made orderly and intersubjectively meaningful through the imposition (or objectification) of established "models of intelligibility" or "innate logics of classification." (Wylie 1982: 40)

The implications of this concept provide archaeologists with an entirely new way of defining material culture.

The realm of material goods provides the essential matrix of archaeological study and thought—archaeologists are the conveyors of the material past, in both deed and thought. From such evidence, the reconstructions of the totality of past cultural lifeways may be attempted. Yet the connections of the material and nonmaterial worlds have often seemed of marginal concern to researchers. When such relationships have been approached, traditional archaeological interpretation has focused on the correlations of ethnic or social groups with specific artifact forms or patterns while more recent positivist archaeology has envisioned the functional aspects of material goods in the greater realm of human adaptation. Both approaches emphasize the restrictions and limitations of the material world. Neither of these approaches is conducive to the study of ideology and hegemony within a hierarchically arranged prehistoric society that I wish to undertake here.

Instead, I will follow the lead of certain researchers (especially Douglas and Isherwood 1979; Shanks and Tilley 1987: 95-117) in emphasizing the "potentialities" of material culture within societies where the material world is viewed primarily "as constituting a symbolic, active communicative field" (1987: 95). In such an approach, we understand assemblages of goods as presenting a set of coherent, intentional meanings aimed at knowledgeable actors able to read those messages (Douglas and Isherwood 1979: 5). If we perceive material items in this light then we must step back from understanding "[m]aterial culture . . . merely [as] a *reflection* of cognitive systems and social practices but [see it as] actively involved in the formation and structuring of such practices" (Shanks and Tilley 1987: 85). Goods are mediators in social practice—not simply "objectified thoughts."

The implications of this concept are twofold (Hodder 1992). First, this concept strongly emphasizes the *cultural* and *contextual* aspects of "material culture," thus redirecting our approach from functional and physical form. More important, it brings to the fore the often weak relationship between an object's meaning and its physical properties within and between societies. This downplays the importance, and in fact, even the validity, of any broad cross-cultural analysis. Also, when objects are perceived as active, flexible social mediators, one must be aware of the multivocality of meaning in their interpretation. A second implication of this concept is that it correctly stresses the importance of cultural, social, and historical context within the archaeological interpretation of meaning. The search for, and the identification and interpretation of, such context is a particular strong suit of the structural analysis advocated in this research.

How does material culture "communicate"? Shanks and Tilley present (1987: 96) this communication as framed within the bounds of perception, based on "three fundamental factors: (1) common media framing and facilitating the act of perception; (2) the senses themselves . . . structuring the subject as embodied receiver; and (3) epistemic or cognitive presuppositions ordering the content of that perceived. . . . From such a perspective we can view material culture as being involved actively in the process of perception and as media framing and facilitating the act of perception and gaining knowledge of the world."

Material culture can be viewed as a medium of discourse. One important aspect of this discourse is the social or "ritual" activity of consumption which "make(s) sense of the inchoate flux of events" (Douglas and Isherwood 1979: 65). This role was even more important in "oral" societies that lacked the written word, those in which material culture in general might be expected to play a similar role by creating a greater unity of forms of discourse (Shanks and Tilley 1987: 97).

I noted earlier the importance of the individual in prehistory, the individual as actor, as an initiator of change; yet when we move to material culture as discourse, we find ourselves resubmerging the individual into the social milieu. What is the role of the individual in material culture production? In my earlier conceptualization of the individual as actor, I argued for the role of society in creating parameters within which the actor performs. The role of the actor in material discourse is no different. There must be an insistence on the "logical priority of the social and the structuring of social relations in accounting for all social practices including material culture production" (Shanks and Tilley 1987: 97). Individuals do not create the structure of the language or the social relations within which they operate any more than they create the patterns of their material culture. As with language and social relationships, however, they interact, manipulate, and transform the discourse of the material world. It is this link with the individual, the requirement of human interaction in the production, reproduction, and transformation of material that brings material goods within the purview of practice. It is through practice that the material world is reified.

Like society, material culture is structured, and this structure is discernible through the patterning in the archaeological record. This is not a unique insight of structural archaeology but a reality of the discipline, virtually since its inception. The insights that now emerge from the patterned record relate to the perceptions of the deeper structural nature of society. It is a "structured record, structured in relation to the social construction of reality and in relation to social strategies of interest and power and ideology as a form of power" (Shanks and Tilley 1987: 98). It is the structuring that allows goods to act as "a structured sign system."

What are the implications for such a perspective on the study of material culture? First and foremost is the emphasis on contextual position of material goods, in time, place, and association—goods as tangible signs of structure require such treatment. It also mandates that the material world be treated as a meaningfully structured mediator within the realm of social relationships. In such an active role, material goods have value in helping researchers understand the formation and continuance of social relations, especially in the context of inequality, power, and ideology. This is especially apparent in the social consumption of material goods. The "partitioning among goods" reflected in the archaeological record should be related to the "underlying partitioning in society" (Douglas and Isherwood 1979: 97), and such distinctions of inequality or status should be emphasized even more by sets of material goods (1979: 118). Douglas and Isherwood (1979: 88 ff., 131-146) have focused on delineating the importance of material goods as communicative devices of "exclusion" by those in power to establish material boundaries of status. In this context they stress "luxuries as weapons of exclusion" within a status consumptive information system.

This perspective downplays the material aspects of adaptation, function, and ethnicity in favor of social relationships but still allows for inclusion of these aspects in the wider spectrum of context. We must not fall prey to the "Cartesian" misconception that there is some innate qualitative difference in meaning between goods judged to be "necessities" for the body, such as food, and "luxuries" for the mind, such as religious paraphernalia (Douglas and Isherwood 1979: 72). Perhaps most important (Douglas and Isherwood 1979: 74-76; Shanks and Tilley 1987: 112-113; Miller 1985: 202-203), such a view of material culture means that the material world is *not* a reinterpretation or representation of another social reality. All aspects of society stem from and are independent but interacting manifestations of structure; consequently, each is knowable in its own terms. Thus, material culture is not the weak reflection of some other truer version of social reality and can be studied in its own right. But it also means that there may be many readings of material discourse. I intend to present some of those readings in this work.

Within such a framework Wylie (1982: 42-45) contends that Pettit's (1977: 96) characterization of structuralist method as "hardly more than a license for the free exercise of imagination" can be countered effectively. Structural models that seek to organize our understanding of the past are constrained by "(a) plausibility considerations introduced by the analytic model . . . and mediated by background knowledge of how such phenomena could have been generated, and (b) empirical constraints on what may reasonably be claimed about the cultural past adduced from the material record of conditions and processes that actually existed in the past" (Wylie 1982: 42-43).

The raw material for the construction of models consists of evaluating and winnowing comparable data from analogous situations to create guides to understand the phenomena under study. Unless the past can be demonstrated to have been radically different from the period of study, a uniformitarian approach to the importance of past forces and mechanisms in the present is simply logical. It is the abuse of analogical data by researchers who fail to define the portions of the analogue that are valid and who fail to use sufficient discrimination in the formation of their models that has led to its eclipse in archaeological research.

I have already dealt with the issue of the synchrony of structure by examining above the theory of practice as outlined by Giddens and Bourdieu. The theory of practice also provides, in fact demands, a place for the individual in society. The individual provides the critical interface between structure and practice. It is the actor who is the initiator, the mover, of the dialectic in this instance. Specifically, the duality of structure that results from the dialectic between practice and structure interjects the potential of social reproduction and transformation. Consequently, structuration or *habitus* provides the critical connection to culture history that allows the archaeological study of structure.

Past uses of structural paradigms have revealed a tendency to ignore historical and cultural context to provide synchronic "snapshots" of society. Hodder (1991: 77-78) contends (in fact, cites his own 1982 edited volume as an example) that such approaches seem inherently incapable of addressing such issues as historical development, specific context of symbols, the function of ideology, or dealing "with the questions of where the style, structure, or ideology comes from."

Yet is it necessary that structure be antithetical to history? I have shown that the conceptual framework exists within a theory of practice to enable the diachronic examination of structural reproduction and transformation. Perhaps an even more cogent argument lies in the elegant demonstration of Marshall Sahlins (1981, 1985) that history and structure are inseparable in understanding the reproduction and transformation of eighteenth-century Hawaiian society. Using the meeting of Captain Cook with the Hawaiians, he demonstrates the process that led to the transformation of structures of "longue duree" related to *mana* via the "structure of the conjuncture" (i.e., the relations of practice).

The essential outcome of this process is social change or transformation that is, in his terms, "failed reproduction." The transformation of structures of "longue duree" occurs due to the recursive nature of practice. In this specific case, the inability of traditional Hawaiian societal practices to comprehend adequately British culture and actions led to new interpretations of those practices. Such new interpretations or meanings, because of the duality of structure and its recursive relationship with practice, ultimately transformed the structural basis of traditional Hawaiian society. Sahlins notes that while cultural reproduction is inherent in transformation, its effects on structuration "are maximally distinguishable in situations of culture contact" (1981: 68). In such a context the potential for variation in the *"revaluation of the sign in practice"* is maximized. This model of change is especially attractive because it provides explanations in which social changes are generated by social factors.

The question of whether this model is relevant to history still arises. The relationship is straightforward—such a transformation of structure can be studied only in a diachronic framework (i.e., history). In fact, the essence of Sahlins's argument (1981: 72) is that history *is* structure: "The dialectics of history, then, are structured throughout. Powered by disconformities between conventional values and intentional values, between intersubjective meanings and subjective interests, between symbolic sense and symbolic reference, the historical process unfolded as a continuous and reciprocal movement between the practice of the structure and the structure of the practice."

RESEARCH GOALS

The goal of this study is to utilize the archaeological record to elucidate the relationship of elites, power, and ideology within a prehistoric hierarchical society in the heartland of the Eastern Woodlands. A basic assumption of my work has been that all human societies are inherently comprised of structures of domination and subordination, although such structures may range in expression from covert to direct. The rise of elites as a force within societies is recognized by the "institutionalization" of forms of subordination. Furthermore, in initiating this research, I have argued for the recognition of the individual as the key heuristic to social reproduction and transformation through *praxis,* thus redirecting past focuses and emphasizing *societal relations as reflected in archaeological change.*

A study such as this is possible because material culture is conceived of as a medium that reflects the recursive relationship between the individual and society. The material world as a medium of discourse is even more heavily stressed in the world of "oral" societies—artifacts are the words in the text of communication. I accept the premise that the partitioning of society is reflected in the partitioning of material goods (i.e., the structures of the social and material worlds are correlates). This study is further strengthened by the introduction of the concept of "structuration" that isolates the recognition of recurrent social practices—again reflected in patterning in the material record. This is the backdrop against which patterns of change and stability are played out in the text of material culture.

Our understanding of power and ideology is through the intermeshing of their essence in the Gramscian concept of hegemony: physical coercion and ideological persuasion. Power is reflected in differential access to material culture as well as in the material manifestations of force. Ideology is the tool with which to naturalize inequality while power is the force to maintain it. I recognize, however, that power emanates from below as well as from above and that this phenomenon is reflected in the past. The material record, as a primary conveyor for elite messages, should ably reflect the hegemonic uses of ideology to mask the exercise of *power over* and elucidate the role of ideology in elite formation in hierarchical societies.

Our understanding of hierarchical sociopolitical organizations and their posited relationships to settlement hierarchies has been greatly expanded by the application of informational and organizational theory to archaeological data sets by Johnson (1973, 1978) and Wright (1969, 1977; Wright and Johnson 1975). Essentially, such models correlate increasing variation and levels of settlement with increasing sociopolitical complexity. If this correlation is reflective of reality, it provides settlement studies with strong sociopolitical insights specifically into Mississippian administrative complexity, decision making, and overall hierarchical organization.

Moreover, the recognition of the settlement-hierarchy relationship allows us to track variations in the sociopolitical realm through shifting modes of settlement articulation (e.g., a la Wright). How is this done? Lightfoot and Upham (1989:20) utilize three axes to characterize variation in political systems including (1) a vertical axis that consists of "the number of vertical tiers in the decision-making organization," (2) a horizontal axis that describes "the structure of decision-making at any specific tier of the hierarchy," and (3) the power axis that "refers to the power and authority that are manifest at any specific tier of decision-making." In this last axis, authority is measured by the ability of the elite to make decisions for and manipulate those of lower status, often with mechanisms such as ritualism and economic control, while power is the ability of elites to enforce their decisions.

The question, of course, is how does the archaeologist translate this organizational management model and these political characteristics into one readable in the material record? This issue has been addressed in some detail by scholars in the Southwestern United States attempting to sort egalitarian from hierarchical societies (Lightfoot 1984: 42-49; Lightfoot and Upham 1989: 22-29; Upham et al., eds. 1989). First, however, it is necessary to define one of the basic concepts that I will use throughout this discussion: "hierarchy." Like the earlier discussion of elites, hierarchy is in danger of becoming a catchall term for differing organizational forms having little to do with one another. In this study, the concept of "hierarchy" will refer specifically to decision-making hierarchies that are "separate administrative organizations that specialize in different aspects of policy making and activity regulation" (Lightfoot 1984: 22). Such hierarchical organizations can be characterized by vertical differentiation into distinct administration levels in which the higher ones integrate and coordinate the activities of lower levels and by horizontal diversification of decision making in which managers at the same horizontal level have distinct tasks and duties (Lightfoot 1984: 22-23).

Specifically addressing archaeological evidence of hierarchical organization present within the settlement system, Lightfoot notes that hierarchical systems should be characterized by clear hierarchical (vertical) variation in settlement sizes, locational centrality for centers of power, functional (horizontal) variation among the tiers of the settlement hierarchy, and variations of burial treatment (1984: 43-47). It should be noted that within the Cahokian polity the large-scale spatial organization conditions that allow for the recognition of a multitiered, vertical hierarchical organization have been satisfied by the present evidence of the archaeological record (e.g., Fowler 1978; Milner 1990). What is sought here are insights into horizontal variation within that broad organizational structure.

Since this study is focused on the lowest levels of the Cahokian settlement system, it is on that aspect that I will concentrate my attention. Again, Lightfoot's model for the study (1984) of sociopolitical change in the Southwest provides a guide for my examination of the Cahokian polity's hierarchical system. He provides an outline of sociopolitical assumptions about power and leadership (Lightfoot 1984: 46-47) that should have measurable archaeological manifestations at each tier in the political hierarchy. Lightfoot uses identified differences *between* settlement tiers to demonstrate the existence of a vertical hierarchical sociopolitical system within certain prehistoric Southwestern native groups. Adapting from that concept, it is clear that such markers should also have validity for identifying both synchronic and diachronic sociopolitical variation *within* (i.e., horizontal) a settlement tier. These archaeological manifestations focus on markers of political and religious administrative authority within a settlement tier that includes (1) easier access to and greater accumulation of valued goods such as are often associated with elite prestige economies, (2) greater facilities for the accumulation and storage of both valued goods and comestibles, (3) centralized spatial location with regard to the administered group, (4) both "architecture of power" and (5) "artifacts of power" that are limited to either/or religious and political leadership and authority and, finally, (6) evidence of differential postmortem treatment of individuals within the tier.

What are these archaeological markers in the Cahokian sociopolitical realm? Can we distinguish sociopolitical variation (i.e., sort the leaders from the followers) within the rural Cahokian settlement system? As I will demonstrate in the following chapters, we can recognize these markers of sociopolitical and ideological differentiation within the Fourth-Line Communities and, moreover, use this evidence to understand variations in elite power within and around Cahokia. Ideology is most commonly manifested in the material world in the form of religious and status paraphernalia and architecture. In chiefly societies (cf. Earle 1987: 298-300, 1991: 6-10), as discussed previously, ideology can be "materialized" in communally constructed "sacred landscapes," "symbols of individual power," and "symbols of warrior might."

In investigating the material world, however, we find that the simple tasks of identifying those material symbols of eliteness and power are not as straightforward as one might hope. It has become a truism that Mississippian societies are categorized as prestige-good economies by current researchers (e.g., Peregrine 1992; Welch 1991; Pauketat 1992; Peebles 1987; Brown et al. 1990). These prestige goods, or "symbols of individual power" (Earle 1987, 1991), most often are characterized as exotic, ritually charged durable materials (associated with elite positions) that circulate through extensive trade/exchange networks that touch distant places and foreign elites (e.g., Helms 1979, 1988). In prestige-goods economies, ruling elites emphasize the control and acquisition of prestige goods because they serve as critical links in carrying out social transactions and paying debts (Frankenstein and Rowlands 1978). It is through this system of "payments" and "rewards" that prestige items passed down the social ladder where they served as markers of status in hierarchical societies (Friedman and Rowlands 1977; Feinman and Neitzel 1984; Lesure 1996; Peregrine 1992; Dalton 1977; Eckholm 1977; Dupre and Rey 1973).

However, the simple dichotomy of prestige versus utilitarian goods has been seriously questioned (i.e., Hirth 1992; Lesure 1996) and found wanting. Essentially, the "prestige goods" network is the expression of social, political, and religious relationships through the medium of material goods. Hirth (1992), for example, identifies at least two relationships inherent in prestige-goods use: (1) status markers or badges of authority that symbolize office or rank and thus are restricted in distribution, and (2) wealth items that are used to meet social obligations such as marriage alliances, initiation fees, and death payments and that are more widely disbursed in the community. Additionally, Lesure (1996) raises the issue of the complexity of assigning "value" to goods and questions how this value is constituted since it may shift through time and place. At the very least, archaeologists must recognize gradations of value that are reflected in various types of social interactions. As an example, Lesure (1996) outlines the potential use of valuables in social-reproductive payments, as inalienable wealth, and as ornaments for display.

Pauketat (1992) has firmly placed Cahokia within the broader pattern of Mississippian prestige-goods economies. Attempts to categorize the economies of other Mississippian polities have had mixed results. Pauketat (1992) identifies as prestige goods such items as exotic cherts, marine shell, copper, mica, galena, quartz and fluorite crystals, silicified sediments, hematite, nonlocal pottery, St. Francois Mountain igneous rocks, and flint clay. (Also see Trubitt 1996: 187-200 for an in-depth discussion of this topic at Cahokia.) I suspect, from the earlier discussion, a diversity of social relations is likely hidden within that list of Cahokian prestige goods. For example, shell beads were most likely used for wealth exchanges, as in the rest of the Southeast (Prentice 1987; Trubitt 1996), while status markers might be represented by items such as ear ornaments, copper artifacts, or shell cups (Brown et al. 1990).

Cahokia, as an example of a prestige economy, however, presents problems of interpretation compared to other Mississippian examples. At Moundville, Welch (1991) observed that prestige goods did not move downward to lower-order settlements in the system. Blitz (1993: 176-178), on the other hand, found the widespread distribution of some "elite" goods throughout the Lubbub Creek polity. At Cahokia it has been extremely difficult to isolate and interpret the "prestige goods" and to understand their distribution. Items such as minerals, crystals, and nonlocal pottery, for example, seem to have flowed throughout the system and are found at the smallest settlements. In fact, the patterned diachronic distribution of Cahokian prestige goods in rural areas seems to contradict the theoretical basis of a prestige-goods economy (i.e., it appears that as elite control increases, the movement of prestige goods decreases; and, when that control decreases, the flow of goods increases [see Pauketat 1992: 38-39; Milner with Williams 1984: 196; Emerson 1995: 288-290; Trubitt 1996]). This pattern is diametrically opposed to that theorized for prestige economies by Frankenstein and Rowlands (1978). It has also been very difficult to identify categories of items that represented "status" versus "wealth" goods. In fact, it seems likely that these categories are not useful in examining the issue at Cahokia (cf. Lesure 1996). It is possible that fairly mundane items may have had significant meaning attached to them via their transmittal through elite individuals or localities that were imbued with power (cf. Pauketat 1992, 1996; Pauketat and Emerson 1991; Emerson 1989). As Lesure has argued (1996), it is a matter of ascertaining how "value" is constituted and assigned. At Cahokia that is a difficult task since little research has been done on identifying elite material culture per se. Consequently, I will use the terms prestige goods, wealth items, and status items interchangeably to refer to the minerals, exotic ceramics, foreign cherts, and other such items brought into the countryside through a centrally controlled distribution system.

In the Mississippian world, ideology was most often seen as part of cults closely associated with segments of society and, perhaps, even as actively engaged in the realm of internal conflicts between social groups (cf. Brown 1985; Knight 1986). Yet it was clearly associated with the establishment and maintenance of the elite dominance and in the naturalization of the social order as Earle has suggested for other areas. Within Mississippian society, however, ideology was also manifested by representations across a wide social spectrum of depictions of fertility in its broadest sense. Fertility iconography is one of the major manifestations of elite ideology in the Cahokian world. The archaeological context of such fertility symbolism, its material manifestation among both the elite and the nonelite, its relationship to social and political change, and its correlation with the rise and fall of elite power are all aspects of this study that will contribute to our comprehension of the role of ideology within hierarchical societies.

The role of hegemony in the rise of the Cahokian polity has been documented within the great center of Cahokia by the recent efforts of Pauketat (1991, 1994). In brief, his reconstruction suggests that during the Lohmann phase, elite formation in the American Bottom occurred in a series of collaborative chiefdoms that lacked a paramount leader. Centralized elite power came to the fore with the advent of the Stirling phase and the creation of a sacralized elite ruled by a divine chief. This was followed by either a diminution of centralized power or, at least, its loss of blatant divinity. In the final moments of the polity there was little centralized elite control or power manifested, and the polity finally faded into obscurity in the fourteenth century.

This study approaches the identification of hegemony within the Cahokian chiefdom through its presence in the material record. The goal of this study is to examine the interrelationship of power and ideology in the formation, rise, and consolidation of elite political control in the Cahokia chiefdom-level polity. I do this by examining two major manifestations in the archaeological record—rural architecture and settlement, and religious architecture and symbolism. These two material manifestations seem, to me, to represent the primary correlates of two related aspects of Gramscian hegemony. The variation and nature of political control in rural settlements reflect the coercive, physical, *power over* aspect, while the religious sphere is indicative of the ideological forces of the Cahokian polity. As one might suspect, however, these spheres are not mutually exclusive, and as I will demonstrate in later discussions, there is significant overlap between the two.

To understand the relationship between the development of an elite hierarchy, the relative exercise of power, and the role of ideology, it is necessary first to determine the material parameters of each; second, to recognize and isolate internal changes and variations; and, third, to establish the valid correlation of these changes. Quite simply, we must establish the synchronism of changes in the material manifestations of elites, ideology, and power. Only in this manner can we perceive possible correlations and define the mutual dependence or independence of these factors. This approach, combined with a diachronic perspective, is our best opportunity to elucidate variations in the roles of power.

I intend to examine the role of hegemony in the rise and collapse of the Cahokian polity through the medium of its periphery: the rural countryside. It is through that waxing and waning that Cahokia's political and ideological power will be most starkly manifested. If the emergence of an elite is correlated with the establishment of an ideological system to "naturalize" the inherent inequality and the creation of a pattern of political control to encourage popular support, then these attributes should appear in the archaeological record.

Based on the previous discussions, we should be able to observe the expression of Cahokian hegemony by examining the following patterns of material culture in the rural countryside (see figure 2.2 for the proposed relationship of material culture, settlement, and hierarchy).

I. Manifestations of Political (i.e., Coercive) Power

(1) *Patterns of an Architecture of Power.* As noted by various scholars, elite political power is often visibly manifested in the realm of architecture (especially a la Foucault). Such architecture may emphasize elite status in the form of elaborate domestic structures, storage facilities associated with the elite accumulation of comestibles and goods, or ritual facilities that indicate access to supernatural power. This study will examine, in detail, rural Mississippian settlements about Cahokia to document the presence or absence of

---

Manifestations of Political (Coercive) Power

Architectural Patterns
    elaborate and large structural facilities
    ritual facilities
    specialized storage facilities
    recreation of sacred landscapes

Status and Wealth
    Concentrations of prestige/wealth goods

Mortuary Practices
    Mortuary patterns that are differentiated from those of commoners

Manifestations of Religious (Ideological) Power

Architectural Patterns
    temples and charnel houses
    specialized ritual structures
    recreation of sacred landscapes

Artifacts, Symbols, and Cults of Power
    Concentrations of religious and symbolic artifacts
        and ritual plants

Mortuary Practices
    Mortuary patterns that are differentiated from those of commoners

---

Figure 2.2 Proposed Manifestations of Cahokian Elite Hegemony.

such architectural patterns. I postulate that periods of increased political control from Cahokia should have resulted in the appearance within rural settlements of specialized architectural facilities associated with political dominance and control. Such facilities might have included storage buildings or granaries, meetinghouses, sweat lodges, or status domiciles and, in general, would reflect significant variation and differentiation in forms of rural architecture. Such political centers may have indicated the existence of political specialists, should have been centrally located, and should have served as organizational nodal points for the surrounding populace.

Conversely, periods of little centralized political control from Cahokia should have seen an absence of specialized facilities of power and control in the countryside. Evidence for local political specialists should not be present. Rural architectural differentiation should have been limited, and most buildings should have been domestic structures or small-scale community structures. No structures associated with the large-scale storage of comestibles or goods should have been present. Decreased political control should also have allowed the population to occupy more dispersed settlements spread across the landscape, with few, if any, obvious centralized nodes.

I wish to evaluate an assumption of this study: that is, the rural settlement architectural patterns and periods of elite dominance from Cahokia covary. How does one evaluate this assumption? It is clearly necessary to have an independent measure of Cahokia's political, social, religious, and economic power against which the fluctuations of rural organization can be measured. In this instance, recent innovative research by Pauketat (1991, 1994) has established a series of independent measures that chart the waxing and waning of power at the Cahokia site. If the assumptions I have proposed hold true, the evidence, as predicted above, for periods of centralized and decentralized power should covary at Cahokia and in the rural countryside.

(2) *Patterns of Eliteness, Prestige and Wealth Items, and Mortuary Practices.* It is generally believed by researchers that the distribution of exotic items or other goods described as prestige-related is controlled by the elite within hierarchically organized societies such as chiefdoms. Consequently, the ubiquity of such goods at rural sites should reflect the relative "eliteness" and power of the occupants. In Mississippian times such items would have included exotic and status ceramics; minerals and crystals; or status artifacts such as earplugs, beads, or discoidals. Such prestige/wealth items may also be correlated with the appearance of patterns of mortuary treatment of rural elites that differentiate them from the local populace. Based on our general knowledge of hierarchical societies, the rural sites in periods during which the maximum exertion of Cahokian power in the countryside occurred should be marked by the presence of concentrations of prestige/wealth goods, structures of power, and elite mortuary practices.

According to current theory on the patterns of prestige-goods distribution, a lack of centralized Cahokian control of and *power over* the countryside should have deprived the rural population of access to prestige and/or exotic items since such materials are assumed to move as part of the elite-prestige economy. This should result in few prestige goods being present in rural sites. With a decreased influence from Cahokia, we should see a general decrease in other markers of status differentiation, such as architecture and mortuary practices, as lineage groups gained more control at the local

Cahokia and the Archaeology of Power

level. The pattern that was observed in the Cahokia data calls many of these theoretical preconceptions about elite goods distribution into question.

II. Manifestations of Religious (i.e., Ideological) Power

(1) *Patterns of an Architecture of Ideological Power.* Control of ideological power by the elite may best be summarized in the presence of an architecture of ideology (i.e., such buildings as temples, priest houses, and specialized elite mortuary facilities). Such facilities were manifest mostly at the large elite centers with their temple mound and plaza complexes that contain temples, sweat houses, charnel houses, and other related religious architecture. With the exercise of elite ideological control over rural populations, such architectural facilities would appear in the countryside. The identification of specialized religious facilities will be especially important in our attempt to determine the presence or absence of elite religious specialists. Depending on the organizational structure of elite power, these specialists may or may not have been associated with centers of political control. If there were specialized political and religious practitioners, then their relative centers of power may be distinct. However, if political and religious power were simply facets of the same individual's control, we should see rural centers that reflected this political–religious integration.

The presence of specialized rural architectural facilities also will provide insights into the presence of organized cults. The existence of elite-sponsored cults (for example, the twelfth-century Cahokian fertility cult as Pauketat and I (Pauketat and Emerson 1991) have suggested, would be strengthened by the demonstration of rural temples dedicated to their service. Furthermore, the identification of rural cult facilities will provide an excellent opportunity to examine the symbolism present in the material goods associated with them and increase our understanding of Mississippian ideology.

(2) *Artifacts, Symbols, and Cults of Power.* Ideological power in the material world is most often displayed in exclusive, or at least, differential access to exotic and/or religiously "charged" objects (i.e., *sacra*). Such items in the Cahokian countryside might include pigments, minerals, symbolic ceramics, ritual ethnobotanical items, figurines, and pipes, as well as ritual structures and mortuary patterns. A critical first step in the interpretation of such *sacra*, subsequent to their identification, is to determine patterns of symbolic congruence that may be understood in ideological terms with reference to existing information on Midwestern and Southeastern Indian mythology and religion. Once one has established the presence of such a symbolic pattern, it is possible to examine its role in Middle Mississippian power relations.

During periods of Cahokian maximal power, such ideologically empowered items and practices should have been under the control of centralized elites. The elite centralization of ideology should have resulted in the creation of an organizational structure for its manipulation and to ensure its continued reproduction. This organizational structure would be reflected in social terms in a "cult." Such cults have previously been postulated to explain Mississippian ideology (i.e., Knight 1986), and I have argued for the presence of a fertility cult as a primary force in the Cahokian world (Emerson 1989, 1995; Pauketat and Emerson 1991). The strongest evidence of cults is reflected in the archaeological record through a homogenization of symbolic referents and the presence of religious specialists. Consequently, the existence of a unified symbolic pattern combined with evidence of *power over* indicates that one is seeing an example of elite manipulation of ideological power.

In instances of elite decline and power loss, the associated ideological organizational structure would collapse and may have disappeared from the rural areas. Certainly all architectural manifestations of elite-controlled cults would presumably be gone. This should have resulted in the loss of access by rural populations to elite-related sacra and possibly either a shift in emphasis or general increase in heterogeneity of the symbolic referents. It is also possible that elite-cult symbolism disappeared completely from the material record.

(3) *Structure of Power.* As Earle (1987, 1991) noted earlier, the communal making of a sacred landscape is a well-recognized elite strategy for naturalizing the association between elite and cosmic power (i.e., the mirroring of the macrocosm in the microcosm of the constructed architectural form [Tilley 1991: 309]). The elite rule with a supernatural mandate. Such an association is possible because of the shared "structure" of the social and cosmic worlds. Can such a structure be identified in the material record? I will argue it can, through the recognition of congruent patterning within the material world of mythology, space, politics, and symbols. Using evidence from the ethnohistoric and ethnographic record in conjunction with the spatial and mythological patterning within the elite centers, an essence of the structure of the Mississippian world can be distilled. Once identified, its utilization within Mississippian society can provide insights into power relationships. As related by a number of scholars, elite exercises of power are most often linked to the manipulation of symbols of the normalized world. The underlying structure of society, because it is basic to all aspects of the social consciousness, is one of the most potent symbols. In the Mississippian world, a powerful element of structuration was the cosmic four-cornered world and

its translation into the elite temple mound and plaza complex (cf. Knight 1989b).

For Foucault (1986), the congruence of structure, the built environment, and power forms a certain type of space that he refers to as "heterotopia." He has argued that such spaces, i.e., the actualized space of a mythic reality (or as others have expressed it, a "sacred landscape"), are constants in human societies. They serve to define the "other space" (where people live); to represent privileged or forbidden space where individuals reside who have a special relationship to society (e.g., elites, priests); to break the link with regular time in that they are timeless (i.e., "slices of time" [a la Eliade 1954]); and to represent the power to juxtapose real space with other incompatible spaces such as the world navel, fertility ceremonies, and public and secret ceremonies.

It is clear that the built environment of Mississippian world structuring carried many of the attributes of Foucault's heterotopias, especially in its penultimate expression of the mound-plaza complex. From the ethnohistoric and archaeological record, I suggest that such spaces were associated with mythic time, sacred and liminal space, special individuals, and other worlds. Foucault's insights (e.g., 1986) provide a broader window for viewing Mississippian space.

Fluctuations in elite ideological power should be reflected by variations in the presence and absence of the elites' symbols in the rural countryside—those that represented their relationship with the structure of society. Consequently, during periods of centralized elite dominance, as defined at Cahokia (cf. Pauketat 1991, 1994), the countryside should have been "remade" to reflect such patterns. During these periods of central dominance we should see artifacts and symbols symbolizing the elite view of world structure appear in the rural power centers. Even more important, however, we should see the elite reorganization of the countryside to reflect its special relationship with the cosmos (i.e., the creation of rural elite sacred landscapes filled with the symbolic referents from the material world). In the archaeological record this will be indicated by the presence of symbols of the four-cornered world, both in artifactual remains and spatial organization.

3

The Cultural-Historical Contexts

When I arrived at the foot of the principal mound, I was struck with a degree
of astonishment, not unlike that which is experienced in contemplating the
Egyptian pyramids. What a stupendous pile of earth!
—Comment of Henry Brackenridge [1814: 187]
upon viewing Cahokia's Monks Mound.

MISSISSIPPIAN CULTURE AND CAHOKIA

The prehistoric Mississippian cultures of the eastern United States represent
the epitome of social, political, and religious development of the area's aboriginal inhabitants. While there is near universal acceptance of Mississippian as the premier cultural "climax," vigorous debates continue on "what is
Mississippian?" James B. Griffin (1985) has extensively documented the
changing archaeological concepts from the early ceramic definition of Holmes
(1903) to the more ecologically oriented definition proposed by Smith (1978a,
1984). Griffin (1985: 62-63) concludes his overview by portraying Mississippian in a broad new light—one that is not tied to artifact types, construction techniques, arbitrary categories of cultural evolution, specific habitats,
or even geographic regions. Instead, Mississippian societies (Griffin 1985:
63) are characterized as those that (1) participated in a series of new cultural
innovations between A.D. 700 and 900; (2) incorporated those disparate
innovations into their culture through contacts with other groups; (3) con-

structed planned permanent ceremonial centers, towns, and associated settlement hierarchy; (4) possessed various forms of a hierarchical social, political, and religious system; (5) participated in a religious system that emphasized the interaction of spirit world and man with a rich iconography expressed in marine shell, copper, ceramics, and stone; (6) participated in extensive trade networks; and (7) reached a cultural "crest" between A.D. 1200 and 1500.

Cahokia

One of the earliest and most dominant centers of Mississippian cultural development was in the Central Mississippi River Valley at Cahokia in the American Bottom (Fowler 1974; Pauketat 1994: 40-107; Milner 1990; Emerson and Lewis 1991; Stoltman 1991). The section of the American Bottom area that figured so importantly in Mississippian times was the northern floodplain zone containing about 450 km^2 of the Mississippi River Valley just south of the confluence of that river with the Missouri and Illinois Rivers. Recent research has provided a detailed description of the Late Woodland and Emergent Mississippian cultural development (Kelly et al. 1984a, 1984b; Kelly 1987, 1990a, 1990b; Emerson and Jackson 1987a) that preceded the appearance of the Middle Mississippian groups in the area. While it is clear that many of the traits that later were important in the Mississippian cultural matrix appeared about A.D. 600 (Emerson and Jackson 1987a; Fortier et al. 1991; Kelly 1990a), the period from about A.D. 925 to 1050 was one of intense transformations of the social, political, religious, and economic organizations of the indigenous Late Woodland peoples (Kelly 1987). In the American Bottom, that period saw the full-scale adoption of maize horticulture, nucleated villages, and many material traits that would coalesce to form the Middle Mississippian culture.

The greatest development and elaboration of prehistoric culture in the American Bottom occurred about A.D. 1050 with the appearance of Middle Mississippian societies. The period was marked by the proliferation of Mississippian peoples and their settlements up and down the valley bottoms and the associated bluffs. One of those temple mound centers, Cahokia, far exceeded the rest in size and presumed complexity, covering more than 13 km^2 (Fowler 1989). Estimates place about 120 mounds within the site boundaries, which also included approximately 1.8 km^2 of available residential and agricultural space (cf. Pauketat and Lopinot 1997). The dominant feature of this site was Monks Mound, a large, multiterraced platform mound located within the central ceremonial precinct. That massive mound and a number of smaller mounds and plazas, along with about 120 ha of the ceremonial areas, were surrounded by a bastioned palisade for at least part of the site's history.

In addition to Cahokia, which was the major ceremonial or perhaps even urban center in the American Bottom, there were four other significant multimound centers (figure 3.1). These centers each included several hundred acres of habitation and ceremonial zones in addition to several associated mounds. There was such a center in the present location of St. Louis, one in East St. Louis, one to the north at Mitchell, and one at Pulcher to the south near Columbia. Pauketat (1994: 80–92) has most usefully visualized the central portion of this massive concentration of monuments and habita-

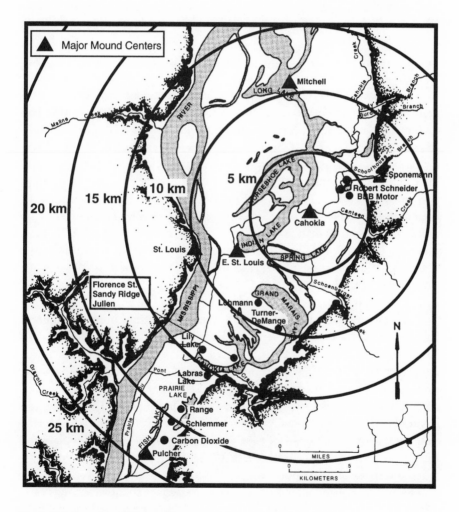

Figure 3.1 Location of Sites in Text.

tion areas as Cahokia's Central Political-Administrative Complex, noting the extreme difficulty of archaeologically separating the Cahokia, East St. Louis, and, perhaps, even the St. Louis "sites."

A number of single temple mound towns and numerous small villages, hamlets, farmsteads, and camps were scattered throughout the area. The picture of a densely populated floodplain appears, with a subsistence base of corn in addition to heavy utilization of the wild floral and faunal resources. Archaeological research at Cahokia and the surrounding area suggests the presence of a highly stratified society with a developed religious and political leadership. The presence of large-scale retainer sacrifice and differential distribution of status goods suggest that we are dealing with at least a chiefdom level of political organization, although some (e.g., Gibbon 1974; O'Brien 1989, 1993) have argued that it may represent an actual example of the state.

Chronology and Taxonomy

In the summer of 1971, the Cahokia Ceramic Conference was held to integrate and interpret more than one-half century of information that had accumulated since W. K. Moorehead's first excavations took place in 1921 (Fowler and Hall 1972, 1975; Hall 1972b). A sequence of eight phases was established, incorporating ceramic, architectural, and social information in their definitions. Considering the size of Cahokia, the intensity of occupation in the American Bottom, and the obvious cultural pluralism that existed in the area, these phases were proposed as representing the current state of knowledge rather than as definitive. The phases included a Patrick phase, pre-A.D. 600-800; an Unnamed phase, A.D. 800-900; Fairmount phase, A.D. 900-1050; Stirling phase, A.D. 1050-1150; Moorehead phase, A.D. 1150-1250; Sand Prairie phase, A.D. 1250-1500; and a final Unnamed phase, A.D. 1500-1700.

This sequence has survived intact for the most part, although refinements have been added by subsequent research, especially that of the FAI-270 Archaeological Mitigation Project (Bareis and Porter, eds. 1984). The initial attempt to clarify the Cahokia ceramic sequence was by Gregg (1975a) who, on the basis of his work at the Horseshoe Lake site, suggested that the Unnamed phase (A.D. 800-900) be defined as the Jarrot phase. This suggestion has not been accepted generally. Later research by Kelly (1980) on the Merrell Tract in Cahokia provided evidence that the Lloyd phase should replace the Unnamed phase and, furthermore, that the Fairmount phase should be divided into early and late portions.

The most dramatic alteration of the phase sequence, however, was produced by the FAI-270 research. Kelly et al. (1984b) suggested the delineation of an Emergent Mississippian period that subsumed all of the phases between A.D. 800 and 1000. In addition, they were able to define northern and southern American Bottom cultural variations within this time frame to create two sets of phases. Kelly (1987, 1990a) formalized this north-south division as the northern Late Bluff and the southern Pulcher co-traditions. The Lloyd (A.D. 800-900), Merrell (A.D. 900-950), and Edelhardt (A.D. 950-1000) phases are in the north, while the Dohack (A.D. 800-850), Range (A.D. 850-900), George Reeves (A.D. 900-950), and Lindeman (A.D. 950-1000) phases are in the south. In the American Bottom, the concept of an Emergent Mississippian period is appropriate to describe the series of cultural transformations that led to the emergence of a fully Mississippian culture at about A.D. 1000 (cf. Kelly 1987).

Most recently, Fortier et al. (1991: 5-10) have put forward a number of additional modifications to the sequence, suggesting a new Sponemann phase (ca. A.D. 750-800) and a subsequent Collinsville phase (ca. A.D. 800-850) in the Late Bluff Emergent Mississippian Tradition. Kelly (1990a: 117-124), on the other hand, assigns Sponemann to the Late Woodland period and dates it ca. A.D. 700-750. At question in this discussion is the relative importance of various defining traits—Fortier emphasizes those that resemble the Emergent Mississippian period, Kelly those of the Late Woodland period.

The FAI-270-related research can be seen as a refining rather than an altering influence on the Mississippian sequence. When the concept of the Emergent Mississippian was actually implemented, it subsumed the "early" Fairmount phase that had been proposed previously by Kelly (1980). Once this clarification was made, it became evident that the "late" Fairmount was essentially Mississippian in content, and it was redefined as the Lohmann phase (A.D. 1000-1050). A somewhat similar event occurred on the opposite end of the chronology with the recovery of Oneota structures and features on FAI-270 sites. The Sand Prairie phase was shortened from A.D. 1500 to A.D. 1400, and a Vulcan phase, representing an Oneota cultural presence, was placed at A.D. 1400 to A.D. 1600. The remainder of the Mississippian phases remained intact and were strengthened by the addition of further information gained from excavation and analysis.

A description of the Mississippian cultural phases now extant in the American Bottom area are selectively outlined here, based on the original data presented in Fowler and Hall (1972, 1975) as modified by Milner et al. (1984) and other, more recent work by regional scholars (for a fuller treatment see Emerson 1995: 66-70). The chronology has been adjusted here to take into account the modifications suggested by Robert Hall (1991) to bring the previous arbitrary cultural time line into closer conjunction with calendar years.

Lohmann Phase—A.D. 1050-1100. The Lohmann phase represents the first Middle Mississippian phase in the American Bottom. This phase, which represents the later portion of the Fairmount phase as originally defined in Fowler and Hall (1972) and which equates with Hall's (1966) Pre-Ramey or Pulcher phase, was delineated by the research of the FAI-270 project (Milner et al. 1984). Kelly (1990b: 77) has proposed a southern contemporary of the Lohmann phase that he has named Lindhorst and views as the terminal phase of the Pulcher Tradition.

The most important phenomenon during this time period is the implied transformation that took place in the political, religious, and social aspects of life during the late Emergent Mississippian period and the early Lohmann phase. Since the more detailed definition of the transitional phases has been of recent origin, it has not been possible to determine how this change is reflected in the Cahokia internal sequence. Consequently, the events discussed here could date to either the Late Emergent Mississippian Edelhardt phase or the following Lohmann phase.

The ceramic assemblage most frequently includes jars, but seed jars and bowls are common, with beakers, bottles, hooded water bottles, juice presses, and stumpware also present. Diagnostic jar rim forms were most typically angled and everted rims with angled shoulders. The majority of the ceramics were shell tempered although grog, grit, and limestone were sometimes used. Surface colors on slipped or polished vessels are predominantly light-slipped reds and tans, but brown or black does appear. Monks Mound Red (a ceramic type originating in the southern American Bottom Pulcher Tradition sites) is common in Lohmann phase assemblages. The lithic assemblages include frequent microdrills, corner- or side-notched, triangular points, hoes, discoidals, and the more common flake tools.

It was during this period that the construction of Monks Mound began (Reed, et al. 1968; Collins and Chalfant 1993; Skele 1988; Emerson and Woods 1990), and the alignment of the civic and religious center of Cahokia was laid out. By the late Lohmann phase, the sun circles or woodhenges were being constructed (Pauketat 1991; Wittry 1969; Smith 1992). The evidence for a stratified society appeared in the form of elaborate status burials and retainer sacrifice in Mound 72 (Fowler 1991). Also contained with these burials were exotic items, which suggested to Fowler (1972: 88) a high degree of control over the exchange of exotic resources. This material was present in raw form (i.e., a roll of unworked sheet copper and sheets of unmodified mica). Caches of foreign projectile points also were found with the burials, indicating contacts with both the Caddoan and the Great Lakes regions. The utilization of Mound 72 apparently was confined entirely to the Lohmann period and may have represented the mortuary complex of a specific elite lineage.

The increased house size, the beginning of large public construction projects (e.g., mounds), as well as the presumed appearance of large Emergent Mississippian-Early Mississippian towns suggest to some that there were quantum increases in population (from an Edelhardt population of 1,300 to 2,700 to a Lohmann population of 10,000 to 15,000 at Cahokia [Pauketat and Lopinot 1997]) and in the degree of social and political control. Harn (1971: 34-35) identified six outlying towns, each with a minimum of one temple mound, as dating from this transitional period. These towns may have developed in situ out of previous Emergent Mississippian settlements or may have represented the actual movement of people out from Cahokia proper. There is no doubt that by the Lohmann phase these temple towns were a permanent part of the American Bottom scene.

This phase also was the transition from single-post to wall-trench house construction, with both forms occurring, and an increase in the overall size of the residential structures. This gradual increase in size is a phenomenon that continued throughout the Mississippian sequence, and it has been documented by research of the FAI-270 Project for small sites outside of Cahokia proper (Milner et al. 1984, figure 61). These outlying small sites are important sources of information on change in the American Bottom, and Yerkes (1983) has argued for evidence of at least household specialization during the Lohmann phase.

There is some evidence that at least minimal contacts to the north were established during this phase. Early Mississippian traits have been identified at the Rench site in Central Illinois (McConaughy 1991), the Collins site in northeastern Illinois (Douglas 1976), the Trempealeau site in southwestern Wisconsin (Green and Rodell 1994), and the Chapman site in northwestern Illinois (Emerson 1991a).

Stirling Phase—A.D. 1100-1200. This phase is the time of major Cahokian expansion. Stirling influences, to various degrees, were present at the East St. Louis, Mitchell, Divers, and Pulcher sites in the American Bottom, north into the Lower Illinois River Valley and the Spoon River sites of the Central Illinois River Valley, the Apple River sites of northwestern Illinois, and as far north as Aztalan (cf. articles in Emerson and Lewis 1991; Stoltman 1991). An interesting phenomenon that may be associated with the Stirling phase seems to be the establishment of large nucleated towns at some distance from Cahokia and, at the same time, the apparent abandonment and absorption of closer towns. Both Harn (1971: 36-38) and Munson (1971: 14-16) posited a reduction of larger sites during this time period, based on the evidence from surface collections. This apparent reduction, however, clearly reflected an increasing population nucleation into fewer centers rather than any absolute population decreases (cf. Milner 1986). The nucleation of population had begun during the Emergent Mississippian and Lohmann phases with the appearance of small temple towns and their associated hamlets (cf. Kelly 1992). The desertion of these small towns during the Stirling phase, while Cahokia expanded, suggests that this was due to a population shift from the satellites to the major population center.

Winters (in Harn 1971: 36) points out that this nucleation of population and abandonment of the surrounding area was a common pattern in the process of urbanization. Previous population estimates computed for the Cahokia site suggest that from 10,000 to 43,000 people occupied the location during the Stirling and Moorehead phases (cf. Gregg 1975b; O'Brien 1972a; Reed et al. 1968). Recent new population calculations by Pauketat and Lopinot (1997) suggest Stirling Cahokia populations of 5,000 to 7,000. This means a density of 2,800 to 4,000 people per km². Fowler tends to accept the higher figures, given the large amount of public construction that occurred at this time (1972: 91).

Milner (1986) has explored the question of American Bottom Mississippian population density outside the main Cahokia site, based on the extensive excavations of the FAI-270 Project. In his sample areas to the south of Cahokia, he found that relative population density was greatest during the Lohmann and Stirling phases, decreased during Moorehead times, and sharply declined in the Sand Prairie phase. Lohmann and Stirling phase population density estimates ranged from 9 to 23 individuals per km². The Moorehead figures were from 5 to 9 individuals per km², while the Sand Prairie density varied between 1.5 and 3 per km². It is evident that the rural portions of the American Bottom, as represented in Milner's data, contained a small, very dispersed, portion of the population.

Unfortunately, while we have fairly reliable information for the areas outside of the main towns, we still have little for the actual towns themselves. Of all the outlying satellites in the American Bottom, it is only about Mitchell that we have archaeological evidence to indicate that the site flourished at this time. Porter (1969: 151-152) has postulated that this is due to the town's critical position at the mouth of the Missouri River, which allowed it to control this area. However, recent limited excavations at the East St. Louis Mound Group by John Kelly (personal communication 1994) did reveal what appears to be an active utilization of several mounds during the Stirling phase.

It appears, however, that there is some resistance to any form of "assimilation" or "consolidation" because, during this period, stockades began to be erected around the central precinct at Cahokia. The earliest palisades seem to have been started about A.D. 1200 and possessed circular bastions along the strongly built wall. This was followed by at least two additional rebuildings, including a palisade with square, closed-back bastions and a final fortification, including square bastions with an open back (Anderson 1969; Iseminger et al. 1990).

I have argued in other contexts (Emerson 1991b) that this early period of American Bottom Mississippian political consolidation was inherently unstable as various elite groups vied with one another for control of resources and power. That the eleventh century is marked by the dramatic appearance of cultural homogeneity in the American Bottom suggests the probable political and cultural dominance of a single polity. To achieve such a dominance must have entailed a previous period of political strife and internecine warfare characterized by and encouraging population and settlement disruptions, elite migrations, and general instability in the locality.

At Cahokia itself, a flurry of construction activities dated to the Stirling phase. Monks Mound was completed, and extensive mound building occurred in other parts of the site. Sun circles were still present, as well as large circular components in Tract 15B. The first accepted evidence for craft specialization on the site seems to be from this time period. Mason and Perino (1961) suggest, on the basis of the association of microdrills and marine shell, that an area to the west of the Kunnemann Mound Group may have been a center for the production of shell beads. This concentration of microdrills has been confirmed by recent extensive surface collections from the Kunnemann Tract (Holley 1995) and the elite manufacture of shell beads identified at the Kunnemann Mounds by Pauketat (1993). In addition, through microwear analysis, Yerkes (1983) has demonstrated the close association of microdrills and shell working at a number of other American Bottom sites.

Stirling phase structures were larger than those of the previous phase and were almost all constructed using the wall-trench method. For the first time, different functional types of Middle Mississippian structures can be recognized at the outlying sites, including sweat lodges, storage structures, and perhaps seasonally specific residences (cf. Emerson 1995).

Virtually all of the ceramic assemblage is shell tempered, although other materials appear infrequently. The typical jar forms have angled rims, with everted and rolled shapes becoming common. Shoulders are still mostly angular. Plain surface treatments are usual, although black and brown filming often occurs. Ramey Incised jar forms appear for the first time in the assemblage. Forms such as bottles, hooded bottles, and seed jars continue. Stumpware declined and disappeared before the end of this phase. By the end of the phase Tippets Bean Pots, Cahokia Cordmarked, and globular juice presses are found in the assemblage, but fabric-impressed pans have not been recovered. Lithic items continue virtually without change from the preceding Lohmann phase.

Limited contacts to the south are indicated by the presence of exotic ceramics and represent a continuation of this contact from earlier periods. Southern Cult motifs in the form of the forked eye/weeping eye motif are common. Exotic materials such as red ocher, galena, quartz crystals, marine shell, mica, and flint clay are often recovered from Stirling contexts. Frequent evidence for fertility symbolism is associated with this phase, as are large stone figures and pipes and symbolic ceramics (Emerson 1982, 1989; Pauketat and Emerson 1991).

Moorehead Phase—A.D. 1200-1275. Although changes occurred in the ceramic assemblage, the basic pattern of life at Cahokia seemed unchanged. The site, according to Fowler (1972: 89), became more "urbanized," and by the end of the Moorehead phase, Cahokia is seen by some as a city of approximately six square miles in area (Brandt 1972: 65). Pauketat and Lopinot (1997), however, document a dramatic drop in Cahokia Moorehead populations to 3,000-4,500 people. In addition, some architectural changes occurred: circular compounds were replaced by rectangular forms; wall-trench houses were enlarged, perhaps indicating larger families or different household units; and single-post houses and rectangular pits disappeared. Structures tended to be nearly square; special functional forms tended to be present. Lithic assemblages continued unchanged, and exotic materials continued to be present.

Limestone tempering, common in earlier phases, was now completely gone. This may suggest a change in the relationship of Cahokia with areas to the south where limestone tempering was prevalent, it may reflect some technological changes, or it simply may reflect the giving up of old habits. Porter (1964) has pointed out that, technologically, the switch from one carbonate (limestone) to another (shell) would represent no difficulty. Shell tempering dominated the scene. Cahokia Cordmarked, with its cordmarked surface and shell tempering, replaced the earlier grit- and grog-tempered, cordmarked types. The shell-tempered bean pot with handles, called Tippets Bean Pot, became more common and more plentiful than a previous form with limestone tempering. Juice presses and crucibles with grog temper continued. Wells Broad-Trailed plates, with their highly polished black surfaces, narrow rims, and broad-trailed decorations, were present. The Cahokia version of Mounds Place Incised was common; however, it appeared as early as A.D. 1125 on Tract 15B (Hall 1972a). A new form, the narrow-necked, medium-high water bottle made its first appearance. Both low and rolled rims declined in popularity at the expense of the higher and everted rim forms. While angled shoulders were still common, the majority of the jar forms had curved shoulders. Ramey Incised and Powell Plain disappeared by the end of this phase. Red slip, so popular previously, was replaced to a large extent by black surface finishes.

Sand Prairie Phase—A.D. 1275-1350. Current data suggest that this was a period of minimal activity at the site of Cahokia. Mantles may have been added to some of the mounds, but there is little evidence of elite activity at the site. Evidence for the presence of the Southeastern Ceremonial Complex (SECC), or at least contact with groups who practiced it, is indicated by the find of a sandstone tablet with a falcon(?) dancer on it, associated with the east lobe of Monks Mound (Williams 1972: 75-77, figure 7). Evidence for the presence of SECC materials at Cahokia has been unusually limited, so this find within a somewhat debatable context is interesting, to say the least. Other evidence indicates that the American Bottom area very likely participated to some degree in the SECC as early as the Stirling phase and continued as late as the early Sand Prairie phase (see Brown and Kelly 1996). The absence of SECC material at Cahokia itself is probably a result of the vagaries of sampling the large site, especially the absence of data from the mounds of the central precinct area.

As noted previously, the Sand Prairie phase is marked by the absence of Powell Plain and Ramey Incised ceramics. Common ceramic forms are Cahokia Cordmarked; plain jars; deep, wide bowls; effigy bowls in the form of conch shells or with effigy attachments; the fabric-impressed "salt" pans; vertical-sided pans; the Tippets Bean Pot; and the Wells Incised Plate possessing medium-high rims and fine incising.

House structures also reached their maximum size during this phase. Two structures from Tract 15B were each more than 450 square feet. This is a considerable increase over the "Fairmount" period houses from the Merrell Tract 15A, which were from 75 to 150 square feet in size (Hall 1966: 5-6). It generally can be said that from earliest to latest there was a consistent increase in the size of houses at Cahokia and the American Bottom (Vogel 1975; Milner et al. 1984). Sand Prairie phase structures were of wall-trench construction and generally square. No specialized structures are known. For the first time, we found mortuary activity associated with the small outlying residential sites. A number of small rural sites, such as Julien-Florence, were associated with charnel houses and stone-box graves.

Some suggest that the nucleation of population that began earlier continued into this phase. Brandt (1972: 65) has pointed out that in the entire American Bottom, only eight sites outside of Cahokia are known to have Sand Prairie materials. In fact, of these eight, four were probably part of the "city" of Cahokia. More commonly, however, researchers believe that this phase was marked by the dispersal of Mississippian populations out of the Bottom and into the surrounding secondary drainages and uplands (e.g., Koldehoff 1989; Woods and Holley 1991).

Oneota Culture—A.D. 1300?-1600? At the original Cahokia Conference there was a controversy regarding the nature of the cultural components present in the American Bottom and at Cahokia at this time. The period between A.D. 1500 and 1700 was labeled the "Unnamed phase." Oneota ceramics were recognized as being present in areas of Cahokia and the surrounding areas of the American Bottom (Hall 1966: 4-5). The problem was one of whether these represented Oneota-Late Mississippian interaction or a later occupation of the American Bottom by Oneota people. That there was some form of Oneota-Mississippian interaction seems to be indicated by the earlier presence of Ramey Incised pottery on which curvilinear designs are bordered by Oneota type punctates and a Ramey Incised rim with a chevron design including punctates. Hall (1973: 4-5) believes both indicate early Oneota influence.

The FAI-270 Project investigations have contributed some information toward resolving this question. Some structures and a number of pit features associated with Oneota ceramics were recovered from the Range site (Milner et al. 1984; Hanenberger and Mehrer 1998). More recently, a small Oneota component was excavated at the Sponemann site to the north of Cahokia (Jackson et al. 1991). It appears that there was an actual Oneota presence in the American Bottom, but that presence was, at best, represented by the intrusion of a few isolated family groups. This evidence led Jackson (1992: 383-391) to reevaluate and reclassify the known Oneota materials from the American Bottom. The results of his efforts produced a sequential scheme of three Oneota "complexes." These have been designated a Bold Counselor complex, related to the phase of that name in the Central Illinois River Valley, and a Groves complex and a Vulcan complex, both related to the later Oneota phases of Iowa and Minnesota.

MODELING CAHOKIAN DEVELOPMENT

Previous Models

The presence of the massive Mississippian cultural development in the American Bottom has captured the imagination of a number of scholars who have sought insights into its genesis and the reasons for its existence. Past models resulting from these efforts have been discussed and summarized by Kelly (1980) and Hall (1991). They fall primarily into three categories that can be seen as representing in-situ evolutionary development, development stimulated by migration and contact, or a composite model stressing broad regional interaction. The writings of Fowler (e.g., 1974) and his students (Benchley 1974; Gregg 1975a) generally represent the in-situ school of thought that proposes the emergence of Cahokia Mississippian culture out of the previous Late Woodland base with a minimum of outside contact and stimulus. However, one should not overstress the "isolationist" aspect of Fowler's perspective. While he (1974) attributed the development of Cahokia in its local context as resulting from a series of technological innovations, including maize agriculture, he also noted the importance of outside contacts to this process.

A diametrically opposed view of Mississippian origins in the American Bottom is presented by Donald Lathrap (as summarized in Hall 1991) and his students at the University of Illinois-Urbana. Lathrap argued for strong Mesoamerican and Caddoan influences as the prime movers in Cahokian origins. Lathrap, O'Brien (1972a, 1972b), and Freimuth (1974) were all strong advocates for the actual movement of fully developed "Mississippian" concepts and, perhaps, actual people into the American Bottom. Somewhat more moderate views of the migration-contact perspective are taken by Vogel (1975) and Porter (1974). Vogel proposes a two-century period of American Bottom Late Woodland peoples' interaction with some "outside" Mississippian groups to explain local ceramic change. Porter (1974, 1969) favors the migration-contact perspective with a strong economic flavor and brings "pochteca" traders out of the south as one of the possible contact mechanisms.

Kelly (1980) proposes a middle-of-the-road model that he calls an integration model since it emphasizes the American Bottom development as part of the broader cultural processes that occurred over much of the Mississippi River Valley. It should be noted that this model also contains a fairly strong dependence on contact with the Central Mississippi River Valley as an impetus to local Mississippian cultural origins. The primary factor in the emergence of Cahokia per se, however, is seen as an internal phenomenon resulting from its economic role as a possible market and redistribution center.

While the details may differ, Hall (1991) has demonstrated that the interaction concept has been a major paradigm of Middle Mississippian studies in the Midwest for quite some time. Interestingly enough, Hall attributes the origins of this approach to Caldwell (much better known for his "Hopewell Interaction" model) who, in 1961, argued for the need to understand the nature and direction of Cahokia interactions with contemporaneous groups. Numerous scholars have found the interaction approach to contribute to their understanding of regional Mississippian cultures (for example, Brown 1965; Harn 1975; Moffat 1991; Conrad 1991; Emerson 1991a). R. L. Hall, especially (e.g., 1966, 1967, 1975a, 1975b), has advocated the value of the interaction approach, and it forms the theoretical basis for his most recent synthetic statement on Cahokia (1991).

The recent research in the American Bottom (summarized in Bareis and Porter, eds. 1984) has amply demonstrated that the four centuries preceding the A.D. 1050 appearance of "Middle Mississippian culture" are marked by the introduction of nucleated villages with courtyards, the bow and arrow, large-scale maize horticulture, new ceramic traits, presumably concomitant increases in population, and more complex social and political structures. With the Late Woodland and Emergent Mississippian peoples so thoroughly setting the stage for the entrance of the Mississippian culture, it is now clear that there can no longer be any serious consideration of large population movements of outside groups into the American Bottom to explain Mississippian origins. The origins of Cahokia are tied to the wider development of complex societies throughout the Mississippi River Valley and the Southeast at this time (Steponaitis 1986; Smith 1986), and the processes are reflected in the Emergent Mississippian cultures and their eventual transformation into fully Mississippian groups. In general, the factors that can be linked to the emergence of Cahokia are the presence of a substantial population density supported by indigenous crops and maize within an environmentally diverse area, concurrent with the development of political, social, and economic complexity.

Cahokia: A Recent Consensus?

Researchers who evaluate the newly published and unpublished archaeological data from Mississippian research in the American Bottom and at Cahokia itself are beginning to reach a consensus on the diachronic development of Cahokia as a political, economic, and social entity. Summaries by Milner (1990), Emerson (1991b), and Pauketat (1991, 1992, 1994), emerging from varying perspectives and differing theoretical bases, and using divergent data bases, are remarkably similar in telling the tale of prehistoric Cahokia's cultural history. The interpretation of that development has increasingly diverged.

One emphasis that pervades this tale is a perception of American Bottom Mississippian as emanating from a "more decentralized, dynamic, and less populous sociocultural system" peopled by "politically quasiautonomous, economically self-sufficient, town-and-mound centers" (Milner 1990: 21). Mehrer (1995) has supported this view in his research, emphasizing the independence of the Cahokian rural populations. While not completely opposed to this scenario, other analyses have focused on the political and symbolic realms and subsequently de-emphasized ecofunctional and economic factors. These interpretations tend to visualize a period of Cahokia centralization and power that united much of the American Bottom in a single polity. Pauketat (1991, 1992, 1994; Pauketat and Emerson, eds. 1997; also Emerson 1995, 1997a, 1997b) especially has been in the forefront of documenting and modeling the dynamism of Cahokian elite social and political emergence. His work has been critical in delineating the potential inherent instability in the Cahokian political and ideological power structure.

How have these concepts been incorporated into our latest perspective on Cahokia? To some extent they have re-emphasized the importance of the late Emergent Mississippian period because it is clear that some of the critical political transformations that marked the Lohmann phase must have had their genesis in the earlier period. In the American Bottom there is extensive evidence for the Emergent Mississippian period cultural transformations (Kelly et al. 1984b; Kelly 1987; Emerson and Jackson 1987a; Fortier et al. 1991).

Unfortunately, evidence for the appearance of one of the essential markers of clearly Mississippian hierarchical society—the temple mound *and* plaza organization—is missing at present. There are a few tantalizing clues that some centers may have had their origins in the Emergent Mississippian era (cf. Wilson 1994; the Morrison site). Griffin (Griffin and Jones 1977) argues for a pre-Middle Mississippian construction of at least some of the six major mounds at the Pulcher site. Excavations at the single-mound centers of Horseshoe Lake (Gregg 1975a) and Lohmann (Esarey and Pauketat 1992) demonstrate pre-Mississippian utilization and occupation. Despite Porter's arguments (1974) to the contrary, there is evidence that the large Mitchell center with its eleven mounds had at least some use before its heyday in Stirling times.

Recent work at Monks Mound (cf. Emerson and Woods 1990; Skele 1988) confirms that the major portions of the mound were in place by A.D. 1000–1100, while radiocarbon dates indicate a post-A.D. 850–900 date for the beginning of construction (Reed et al. 1968). Presumably, construction was under way during the latter portion of the Emergent Mississippian period. Although data until recently have been scarce for the East St. Louis Metro group of forty-five mounds, excavations by John Kelly (1988, 1994, 1997), for the Illinois Department of Transportation, near the former location of the Cemetery Mound have revealed an extensive, fully developed, Stirling phase ceremonial zone. The complexity of these deposits certainly suggests the existence of antecedent ceremonial precursors. A similar Emergent Mississippian origin seems likely for the St. Louis complex of twenty-six mounds.

By A.D. 1000, the American Bottom may have been the setting for a minimum of a half-dozen civic-ceremonial centers that supported simple chiefdoms. Although there is no supporting evidence at present, several of those centers (e.g., Pulcher, Cahokia, or East St. Louis) may already have incorporated some of their smaller neighbors to form small-scale complex chiefdoms. There is some evidence that even parts of the uplands (cf. Emerald Mounds site, Pauketat and Koldehoff 1983) may have been involved in this process. The emergence of chiefdoms, once begun in the area, would have tended to have a snowball effect (Service 1962; Carneiro 1981) because of the adaptive advantage of this organizational pattern in dealing with other such groups in the region.

Until recently little discussion has focused on the role of models of chiefdom-level sociopolitical development in understanding American Bottom Mississippian societies. Given the widespread successful application of such studies to comparable prehistoric societies in the Southeast, this absence is puzzling.

Chiefdoms have been the subject of extensive ethnographic and ethnohistoric research (e.g., Fried 1967; DePratter 1983; Goldman 1970; Sahlins 1958; Service 1962) and archaeological studies (e.g., Anderson 1990a, 1990b, 1994; Cordy 1981; Drennan and Uribe, eds. 1987; Helms 1979; Peebles and Kus 1977; Steponaitis 1983; Pauketat 1991, 1994). There is little doubt that chiefdom-level societies existed throughout the Southeast during the Mississippian period (DePratter 1983; Hudson 1976; Swanton 1946). Smith has characterized the sociopolitical pattern of that time as "being loosely woven and consisting of small shifting networks of conflict and alliance. . . . Through time, each of these shifting networks and their constituent polities traced a unique developmental trajectory along a possibility bounded on one end by minimal organization (fragmented segmentary tribes) and on the other by maximum sociopolitical complexity (large complex or regional-level chiefdoms)" (1986: 58).

David Anderson (1986: i, 1990a, 1990b, 1994) has outlined a number of factors critical in promoting stability or change in chiefdoms. These include (1) strength of ideologies that sanctify chiefly authority; (2) effectiveness of social mechanisms to deal with chiefly succession, population growth, territorial maintenance, or expansion; (3) ability of chiefly organizational structures to maintain stability in the face of stress; (4) degree of control over status goods and the position of individual polities in elite goods exchange networks; and (5) impacts from other surrounding societies. These factors need to be taken into account when modeling Mississippian sociopolitical development in the American Bottom.

It is an axiom of chiefdoms that they are unstable and subject to "cycling" behavior. This characteristic results in patterns of emergence, expansion, collapse, and reconstitution or total dissolution (Anderson 1990a, 1994). The concept of chiefly cycling is critical to understanding Mississippian cultural development. If one envisions the tenth-century American Bottom as occupied by at least several emerging, competing chiefdoms—some rising in power, some declining—it places Cahokia's eventual rise as a paramount center in a reasonable context.

The late tenth and early eleventh centuries in the American Bottom were marked by extreme cultural variation between localities, perhaps encouraged by local and regional competition, trade patterns, and social interaction. By the end of this period, Cahokia had become the paramount civic-ceremonial center in the Bottom, probably via an increasing sacralization of elite power (cf. Pauketat 1991, 1992, 1994). This rise to dominance was reflected in the trend toward increasing homogeneity of the cultural assemblages during the Lohmann phase and culminated in the Stirling phase. The period from about A.D. 1050 to 1150 reflected a time of internal and external consolidation for the dominant elite of Cahokia. This latter century also marked the first appearance of large-scale defensive palisades with bastions at Cahokia (Anderson 1969; William Iseminger, personal communication 1987). In addition, it represented the period of fullest expression of the fertility iconography (Emerson 1982, 1984, 1989, 1995, 1997b; Pauketat and Emerson 1991; Pauketat 1992) that was central to legitimizing and symbolizing the dominant religious and chiefly elite. It may also have been a period of increasing political stress even further exacerbated by increasing environmental degradation (Lopinot and Woods 1993) and population densities (Milner 1986; Pauketat and Lopinot 1997).

I tend to see the late eleventh- and early twelfth-century Mississippian political situation in the American Bottom as potentially unstable, as various elite factions vied for power during Cahokia's rise as a paramount center (Emerson 1991b; also cf. Pauketat 1992). This political and social instability was reflected in the construction of the massive, bastioned palisades around the central precinct of Cahokia. Such a dominance could not have been achieved without opposition from established elites at other centers. Those groups had several options that ranged from successful resistance to group destruction, from political incorporation and/or cultural assimilation into the Cahokia sphere to escape through emigration. I have suggested that one contributing factor to the outflowing of Stirling phase Mississippians was the social and political instability that must have accompanied the consolidation of power at this time by the Cahokian elite as they achieved economic, political, and/or religious domination in the American Bottom (Emerson 1991b).

There is good reason to believe that between A.D. 900 and 1350 a number of competing chiefdoms existed in the American Bottom area, sometimes splintered and warring, occasionally consolidated into a powerful complex paramount chiefdom. Between A.D. 1050 and 1200 there may have been a period of consolidation when the ruling elite at such a center as Cahokia held sway over much of the American Bottom. This consolidation was a short-term affair and disintegrated by the 1300s. The northern Mississippian expansion, about A.D. 1050, is seen as an outgrowth of these local conflicts, environmental deterioration, and increasing population density in the American Bottom.

In the remainder of this work, I will show how these complex patterns of Cahokian religious and political domination are reflected and demonstrated in the archaeological materials recovered from the surrounding rural sites. I will argue that the rise of centralized Cahokian political power forever altered the form of the surrounding rural settlement organization. Briefly, I will show that the end of the Emergent Mississippian period was marked by the sweeping away of the rural villages and their populations. The onset of the Lohmann phase was marked by the appearance of a Cahokian-organized rural political organization that can be seen in the initial presence of specialized religious and political structures (i.e., an "architecture of power"). This rural political organization became even more specialized and dominant in the Stirling phase, rapidly collapsed during the following Moorehead phase, and disappeared completely by the Sand Prairie phase. The archaeological evidence for the presence of an architecture of power and patterns of elite status, prestige goods, and cult and mortuary practices to support these interpretations are presented in detail in the following chapters.

4

Mississippian Rural Settlement

Settlement . . . is almost a uniquely powerful data category, a virtual material isomorph of infrastructure and political economy which records and preserves the most significant features of energy production and flow. Since Darwinian adaptation is by definition operationalized in terms of population numbers and distributions, the paradigmatic mandate is direct and overwhelming. Despite the customary strictures concerning the use of negative evidence, one can say that what is not observable or reliably recoverable from this class of data was probably of negligible systemic importance.

—(Price 1981, cited in Willey 1983: 462)

The purpose of this research is to shed light on the hierarchical organization, ideology, structuring, and patterns of power and domination in the Cahokian polity a millennium ago. The earlier chapters have created a theoretical and cultural-historical context within which to examine these issues and have provided a methodology to identify political and social forces within the Mississippian hierarchical framework. The context for that discussion can be broadened by examining a series of small, subordinate sites that surrounded Cahokia and that provided essential insights into the hierarchical, political, and ideological organization of that Middle Mississippian polity.

However, it is important to establish a regional context within which to interpret these sites and to look at them within the broader parameters of Mississippian settlement models. An examination of regional settlement patterns demonstrates that there are two very different ways that Mississippian site hierarchies can be organized. These variations in hierarchy center on the relationship between mound centers and their subalternate settlements. If past American Bottom settlement models are reviewed with these insights, it is possible to discern a new model of American Bottom rural settlement building on those previously developed (cf. Emerson and Milner 1981, 1982; Emerson 1992, 1995).

In order to constrain geographical and chronological variation, this study has emphasized Lohmann and Stirling phase sites (ca. A.D. 1050-1200) from the northern locality of the American Bottom near the site of Cahokia, although all periods will be considered to document diachronic shifts in paramount political centralization. This evidence from recently excavated sites allows the definition of the nature of lower-level sites and their place within the settlement system. Furthermore, it allows the construction of a model that explains the articulation of these various settlement units into a larger political, social, and religious unit—the dispersed village within the context of the Cahokian Mississippian political hierarchy. Such patterns of architecture and artifactual material reflect political and religious power and can be used subsequently to interpret the nature of the Cahokian political domination in the countryside.

SETTLEMENT STUDIES

The importance of the human-land interaction has been acknowledged since the beginnings of anthropological inquiry (e.g., H. L. Morgan, *Houses and House Life of the American Aborigines* 1881). The recent concentration on settlement studies has come into its own only since the early 1950s with the work of Gordon Willey (1953, 1956, ed. 1956; cf. Parsons 1972; Ford 1974; Butler 1977; Green 1977; Smith, ed. 1978). An integral assumption of such studies is that there is a correlation between the organization of societies, their geographical setting, and their built environment. The attraction of settlement studies is the potential they hold by being "a more direct reflection of social and economic activities than are most other aspects of material culture available to the archaeologist" (Parsons 1972: 127-128).

Settlement patterns are interpreted as reflecting a culture's adaptation to its "environment," with the environment understood (a la White 1959: 8) as including both natural and societal aspects. These two aspects of the environment, the ecological versus the social, have formed distinct avenues of research in settlement studies (Trigger 1968: 54; Green 1977: 16; Butler 1977: 6). Some early studies tended to overstress one aspect at the expense of the other (for example, Coe and Flannery 1964; Sears 1961, 1962), leading to a distorted interpretation of the past. Settlement studies obviously must incorporate both ecological and social factors into their research designs and models. Just as clearly, however, the relative importance of social and ecological variables can be affected by many factors, such as environmental degradation or the technological level of the society.

From an anthropological standpoint, the greatest potential of settlement-related research has been associated with the study of social organization. To a large degree this has resulted from the richness of the available ethnographic record and the elaboration by anthropologists and other social scientists of the necessary theory and methodology to deal with social organization, ideology, and economy (e.g., Chisholm 1962; E. Hall 1966, 1968; Eliade 1954; Levi-Strauss 1963). Social theorists have also been swift to recognize that the structural organization of a society is often reflected in its spatial configuration. It is instructive that ethnographers have been involved in the study of archaeological settlement almost from its inception (e.g., Vogt 1956). Vogt (1956, 1968, 1983) has consistently argued for the potential of settlement studies as an integrative force in anthropological research and as the logical meeting ground for archaeology and ethnology. Archaeologists have also been active in seeking to deal with the social, ideological, and political implications of settlement information (e.g., K. C. Chang 1958, 1967, ed. 1968; Parsons 1972; Sears 1961, 1962, 1968; Trigger 1968; Struever 1968; Winters 1969).

One of the more important conceptual changes introduced into the study of settlements has been this idea of the "settlement system." While typologically oriented models of settlement patterns are often static, those of settlement systems are dynamic—"refer[ing] to the functional relationships among the sites contained within the settlement pattern . . . the functional relationship among a contemporaneous group of sites within a single culture" (Winters 1969: 110). It is the all-encompassing nature of the settlement system concept that is so attractive. In such a system it is necessary to recognize seasonal and functional variations in sites in order to understand the associated subsistence strategies, artifact use and meaning, and the correlation between material, social, and ideological attributes. The settlement system serves as an integrating and interpretive mechanism that provides for the ecological and social aspects of settlements to be reunited into a synthetic whole. It provides an important linchpin in this study for our understanding of rural domination and ideology via the creation of sacred landscapes and an architecture of power.

MIDDLE MISSISSIPPIAN SETTLEMENT

It has been nearly two decades since *Mississippian Settlement Patterns* (Bruce Smith, ed. 1978) was published. In this work Smith created a model of Mississippian settlement patterning that relied heavily on environmental and adaptive factors. He argued that Mississippian was best defined as "a cultural adaptation to a specific habitat situation" (1978a: 480) that included the linear bands of circumscribed agricultural land and concentrated biotic resources found in the meander-belt zone of the floodplains of major rivers. Within this habitat, Mississippian settlement patterning was explicable in relation to well-drained, natural levee soils suitable for agricultural fields and access to plant and animal resources of the oxbow lakes.

The sites that would have shown the greatest response to these environmental criteria should have been the small farmsteads that Smith (1978b: 489) has characterized as "representing the minimum economic unit, [that] would be occupied by a single to several nuclear-extended family groups on a year-round basis. The number of individuals occupying these small settlements would . . . be largely a function of the number of hectares of high-quality soil available within close proximity." If this environmental variable was the prime determinant of settlement patterning, then the optimal settlement pattern in meander-belt environs would have been one of dispersed households. Historically, such a pattern seemed common among Indian groups across much of the Eastern Woodlands (for extensive references see Woods 1987).

Yet as Smith (1978a: 489) examined the settlement data, he concluded: "Since such a dispersed pattern of small settlements has rarely been observed in pure form in a Mississippian context, it is obvious that factors additional to energy efficiency influenced the distribution of Mississippian populations."

The factors that countered dispersal were the needs for internal organization in order to successfully compete with other groups and to successfully defend and maintain their borders. Mississippian settlement became a continuum between fortified, nucleated, defensible villages on one end and economically efficient, dispersed households on the other (Smith 1978a: 490). The commonly accepted Mississippian settlement model of a large, fortified, centrally located village surrounded by dispersed farmsteads is a compromise between defense and economic efficiency. These local centers are visualized as being located near both agricultural lands and oxbow lakes with the farmstead population within easy walking or boating distance. The functions of the center were to maintain social cohesiveness and to serve as the location of the public ceremonial areas and the residences of the elite. Populations of such centers would be mainly the elite, but the centers would be capable of housing the farmstead populations during ceremonial events, for social obligations, and during periods of conflict.

Scholars face many research problems, for example variations of time, space, and sociopolitical complexity, when they attempt to study Mississippian settlement systems at the local center level (Smith 1978a: 491-502). Time variations may include seasonal occupations of farmsteads due to recurring hostilities, farming practices, or political alliances. To control for such variation, tight chronological parameters are required. If Mississippian settlement was closely related to environmental factors, variation in the environment should be reflected in the resultant patterning. Sociopolitical complexity was clearly a factor in the patterning of the large Mississippian centers' placement across the landscape. In the case of complex chiefdoms, it would also have created a settlement hierarchy of centers. The primary effect of increased sociopolitical complexity in Mississippian organization, though concentrated in the upper levels of the settlement systems, should be reflected *throughout* the system—a topic considered in more detail later in this study.

REGIONAL MISSISSIPPIAN SETTLEMENT VARIATION

As Smith's (ed. 1978) volume on Mississippian settlement demonstrated, there is great variability in the way these people distributed themselves across the landscape and in the way groups articulated with one another. Consequently, in attempting to understand the settlement in the American Bottom it is useful to look at insights gained by researchers of Mississippian groups in other Midwestern areas. Three regional studies are especially suitable: the Powers phase populations of the Western Lowlands of Missouri and Arkansas, the Kincaid groups in the Black Bottom along the Ohio River in southern Illinois, and the Spoon River peoples in the Central Illinois River Valley. Each of these areas has been subjected to extensive investigations specifically aimed at delineating settlement patterns, and each suggests a slightly different pattern with implications for variations in the associated system. Following the discussion of these groups I will present and contrast the data from American Bottom rural settlements.

The Western Lowlands Settlements

The Western Lowlands of southeastern Missouri and northeastern Arkansas have been the location of extensive research by James Price (1978). Excavations and surveys in the sand ridges and floodplain of the Little Black River have revealed in great detail Mississippian settlement patterns and systems of the fourteenth-century Powers phase.

Price's research has delineated four levels of Mississippian sites, including a civic-ceremonial center, villages, hamlets, and limited-activity sites. Powers Fort, which represents the ceremonial center, covered 4.6 ha; village sites had a bimodal size distribution, with some about 0.6 ha and some about 1.0 ha; hamlets were 0.1 ha in size; and limited-activity sites were small, containing only one to three structures.

Excavations in the Powers phase sites have yielded some information on the composition of these sites. Powers Fort was a multimound center that contained a large residential area and perhaps a cemetery. The Turner and Snodgrass village sites have been completely excavated (Price and Griffin 1979). These excavations resulted in the definitions of large cemeteries, public buildings on courtyards, and moderate residential areas with high- and low-status zones within the villages. Hamlets have not been excavated but are thought to contain 9 to 12 structures. As far as presently known, these hamlets do not contain any high-status ceramics, materials, or public architecture. The limited-activity sites represent the farmstead or household-level sites defined by other Mississippian researchers. Such sites occasionally yield small cemeteries.

Price (1978), based on the current state of knowledge, has suggested how those various sites may have articulated to form a system. Although there has been a fairly intensive investigation of some village and limited-activity sites of the Powers phase (cf. Price and Griffin 1979; Smith 1978b), little is known about the ceremonial center or the hamlets. There is some evidence for variation in the function of the limited-activity sites. Smith's (1978b) detailed study of Gypsy Joint indicates that it fulfilled the traditional role of a year-round "farmstead" occupied by an extended family. Price (1978: 227) noted, however, that the Big Beaver and Old Helgoth Farm sites, both located near the ceremonial center, differ from Gypsy Joint. Big Beaver, for example, had no subsurface storage pits, and Old Helgoth Farm had a small cemetery. That variation may be accounted for by the closeness of the latter two sites to the ceremonial center. These three sites are important, however, in pointing out the variation that existed within the limited-activity site category.

The role of hamlets within the Powers phase system is speculative, but Price indicated that they probably resembled the farmsteads in function. He (Price 1978: 227) specifically stated that he "doubt[s] that they contain any public structures, fortifications, or courtyards" which are usually associated with the villages.

Powers phase excavations have focused on the two large Turner and Snodgrass villages (Price and Griffin 1979). These two adjoining, presumably contemporaneous villages, appeared to serve differing needs of the Mississippian peoples who utilized them. Turner contained 48 structures (some of which were clearly public in nature), high-status and low-status residence zones, a large mortuary area, and maize storage facilities. The

Cahokia and the Archaeology of Power

Snodgrass site contained 94 structures, with an interior high-status area of substantial houses surrounded by less well built houses in the outer site areas. Price (1978: 228) argued that while such paired villages were probably associated with the Powers Fort ceremonial center, they likely were economically independent and represented the central point for the surrounding hamlets and farmsteads. In fact, he suggested that such villages may have been the part-time residences of many of the people who also lived in the limited-activity sites. In this model the villages would have always maintained a core population, but perhaps the less substantial houses were occupied for only part of the year. In such a system, "social, political, and economic organization [would] ... have centered around paired villages on sand ridges, [with] each village serving different functions in annual ceremonial scheduling. The divisions among and within the villages were probably along sociopolitical lines. The core versus peripheral divisions of the villages was probably along status or rank lines" (Price 1978: 228). The villages served as the basic level of social and political integration in the short-lived Powers phase settlement system.

Powers Fort, with its four large mounds, massive palisades, and large residential population, would have served as the major ceremonial and political force along the Little Black River and was, as the paramount center, the supreme level of overall integration for this Mississippian system.

The Black Bottom Settlements

The Black Bottom is a small floodplain locality along the Ohio River, in Pope and Massac Counties, Illinois. This bottom reaches a maximum of 5 km in width and 16 km in length and is characterized by a ridge-and-swale topography. Centered in this area is the large multimound Kincaid site. The Kincaid site and Mississippian archaeology in the Black Bottom were the focus of extensive excavations in the 1930s by the University of Chicago (Cole et al. 1951) and, more recently, by Jon Muller, Southern Illinois University-Carbondale, who began a systematic survey in this area in the 1960s (Muller 1978). As a result of this research, the Mississippian settlement patterns and systems of this area are some of the most thoroughly modeled in the Midwest and Midsouth.

Muller (1978) and his students have recorded more than 100 Mississippian sites in the Black Bottom. The pattern reveals three distinct sizes of sites as reflected in surface scatter. There are small sites less than 0.01 ha in area that seem to have represented temporary camps or extractive stations. A second group is composed of sites that are approximately 0.3 ha in area. These sites were the residential units of the Mississippian peoples. The smaller sites usually contained one to several houses that were the year-round living quarters of family groups. The larger of these sites reached 0.9 to 1.0 ha in size and included a cluster of the residence groups. Muller (1978: 276) characterized these "hamlets," which may have contained from 10 to 15 structures, as made up of a clustering of smaller "farmsteads."

The final Mississippian settlement unit is that of the massive Kincaid site. The multimound, palisaded site represents the maximum population centralization in the Bottom. Muller (1978: 276) noted, however, that while the palisaded area at Kincaid covered about 70 ha, only about 6 ha showed any evidence of actual occupation. In fact, Muller emphasized that the internal organization of the occupation inside of the palisaded area was identical to that observed at the other smaller sites in the Bottom—it consisted of small farmsteads, along with some hamlets.

Their various studies have led the Southern Illinois University-Carbondale researchers to envision a "building block" system as operating in the Mississippian settlement patterning in the Black Bottom. The basic unit consisted of the small farmsteads that included 1 to 3 structures organized in a L- or U-shaped layout in association with ramadas or corn cribs (Muller 1978: 280). When several of these farmsteads clustered together, they formed a hamlet of 8 to 15 structures. Kincaid has been interpreted as a group of hamlets with mounds and a palisade, although this has yet to be substantiated by excavations.

It is the modeling of the Kincaid settlement system by Muller (1978), Butler (1977), and Riordan (1975) that is important to this discussion. In this model, the individual farmstead unit is the minimal settlement. Such farmsteads are the basic economic unit, self-sufficient, and occupied year around. The hamlet is a cluster of farmsteads and appears to represent the same economic patterning as the farmsteads. Muller (1978: 285) did not see any evidence for specialization, either economic or political, in these clusters. Riordan (1975: 137-138) has argued that some of these hamlets serve as "nodal" points, and the presence of exotic goods, fine ceramics, and burial plots seems to bolster this suggestion. The overall conclusions, however, were that "if there were some individuals in these nodal sites who did perform social functions as redistributors, these roles were not so highly ranked nor involved so much time as to relieve their households of basic productive tasks. 'Leadership' on the hamlet level appears to have been added to the other functions of the household, rather than replacing them" (Muller 1978: 285).

Butler (1977) has argued that these farmsteads and hamlets were organized into "dispersed villages." The typical village would consist of a hamlet with a surrounding group of farmsteads. While it is possible to recognize nine such dispersed villages on the basis of surface material distribution in the Black Bottom, Muller has pointed out that the validity of such dispersed villages as social and political entities has not yet been proven. The major difficulty (Muller 1978: 285-286) in delineating such villages in the archaeological record is the inability to establish the contemporaneity of the seemingly associated farmsteads and hamlets (for a similar dilemma in the American Bottom see Milner 1981). Yet, given the narrow time span of many Mississippian phases, it is possible that the observed patterning in rural settlements may reflect their contemporaneous utilization. The role of Kincaid in such a system as portrayed above has not been clearly defined. Presumably, the population was somewhat involved in production, distribution, administration, and religious activities. That such a pattern was the result of chiefdom-level political organization is likely.

Central Illinois River Valley Settlements

One of the early centers of Mississippian research in the Midwest was the Illinois River Valley. Pioneer excavations by the Dickson family (Harn 1967) and slightly later by the University of Chicago (Cole and Deuel 1937) were followed in the last few decades by extensive research by Alan Harn, Illinois State Museum, and Lawrence Conrad, Western Illinois University. Based on these investigations, a large body of data has been recovered that has provided interesting insights into Mississippian settlement in this area.

The Mississippian occupation and utilization of the Central Illinois River Valley consisted of seven major temple towns and their associated satellite settlements. Such towns usually included a single mound on a plaza, with 4 to 8 ha of residential area surrounded by a palisade. One such town, Larson, and its settlements have been studied in detail by Harn (1978, 1994). The Larson town site central area covered about 8 ha, with a single mound on a plaza. The site may have contained more than 200 structures in its prime. About 6 ha of the occupation were surrounded by a palisade. The town had large cemeteries just outside the wall. Harn (1978) has argued that the occupation of Larson was in large part seasonal, with an emphasis on the winter months.

Seven hamlets are delineated within the Larson settlement system. Hamlets, as defined by Harn (1978: 252-254), were those sites that ranged from 1.5 to 6 ha in area, contained houses and large public structures arranged in rows around a central plaza, and often had large cemeteries (including as many as several hundred burials). Such sites were placed at the juncture points of major environmental zones and may have been seasonally occupied.

More than 30 camps have been located among the Larson settlements. Such camps were usually near the hamlets and presumably were associated with them. These camps varied in size and may have included from 1 to as many as 15 structures. Some of the camps may have functioned simply as the locus of temporary daily activities. Harn (1978: 254-257) suggests that the camps were primarily for the purpose of food procurement.

Under the Larson settlement system as proposed by Harn (1978, 1994), the major occupation of the central town occurred during the winter months, and the population generally dispersed to the hamlets in the summer. The camps were occupied on a temporary basis to exploit the specific microenvironments.

Harn's model is based primarily on the evidence from the thirteenth-century Larson phase sites with which he is most familiar. Conrad (1991), in looking at the evidence from Mississippian sites that fall chronologically earlier than the Larson phase, has argued for the existence of a different settlement system. He suggests that the initial Mississippian intrusions into the valley were similar to the dispersed village systems found in comparable time periods in the American Bottom and the Black Bottom. Such a system would have consisted of nodal hamlets and their associated farmsteads. The large fortified villages, in Conrad's opinion, were a later development.

MODELS OF LOWER-LEVEL MISSISSIPPIAN SETTLEMENT

An examination of the proposed settlement systems from the regional studies detailed above reveals some diversity in the nature of lower-order sites, such as farmsteads and hamlets, in the overall settlement hierarchy. In the Powers phase, Price notes that there may have been variation in the function of the limited activity sites (i.e., farmsteads). In some instances they seem to have functioned as year-round farmsteads for family groups; in others their purpose is less clear. He specifically equates hamlets with farmsteads in function and denies them any ceremonial or public role. The hamlets and farmsteads depended on the village for their ceremonial, social, and political integration.

Muller and his associates in the Black Bottom recognize the farmstead as the basic unit for the family. They do not appear to see any variation in such small sites. The hamlets were simply clusters of farmsteads; however, some researchers have argued that such hamlets may have served as "nodal" centers, but such a function seems to have been weakly developed, if present. Butler proposes that those farmsteads and hamlets were organized into dispersed villages. How the dispersed villages articulated with each other and the mound center is unknown.

Harn's terminology makes correlations with other models somewhat difficult since what he referred to as hamlets would be considered villages by most other researchers, and his camps included both farmsteads and hamlets. The description of "hamlets" as containing large cemeteries, public structures, and plazas reinforces the view that these sites were villages. The Larson phase model differs significantly from those proposed for the Powers phase or the Black Bottom. The small camps are suggested to have been the primary agricultural/subsistence-oriented units, probably occupied by family groups. Hamlets may have had a similar function. Both the camps and the hamlets, however, are suggested to have been only seasonally utilized in the summer, with the entire population withdrawing to the large fortified village in the winter.

Prior to the FAI-270 Project (Bareis and Porter, eds. 1984), little excavation had focused on the lower-level sites in the American Bottom (with the notable exception of Bareis's [1976] work at the Knoebel site). Due to this lack of data, Fowler (1974, 1978) and Harn (1980) were forced to lump the farmsteads, hamlets, and villages without mounds together as fourth-line communities. While a function was not proposed for such sites, the assumption of most archaeologists working in the area seems to be that they represented small farming settlements. It is not clear whether these sites were occupied year around or seasonally. These settlements, which included a single nuclear family to a moderate number of such families, were apparently tied to the larger second- and third-level mound centers that, in turn, were linked to Cahokia. Neither Fowler's nor Harn's discussions included any suggestions of differential function for sites within the fourth-line communities.

FAI-270 researchers (Emerson and Milner 1981; Emerson 1992, 1995) argued for a different picture of the place of rural sites in the overall settlement system. It was suggested that farmsteads represent year-round occupations by family groups and that these farmsteads were tied together by "nodal" sites to form a dispersed village. Possibly a small number of those dispersed villages were integrated through the common use of a rural ceremonial site. Such dispersed village systems were ultimately united through the mechanism of the mound centers.

From the above cited studies, it is clear that the sociopolitical articulation of lower-level sites within a hierarchical system could take several paths:

(1) The *Direct-Articulation* model argues that farmsteads and hamlets were basically food-producing units directly tied to a mound center (figure 4.1a). The key interpretive factor lies in the view that these sites are conceived of

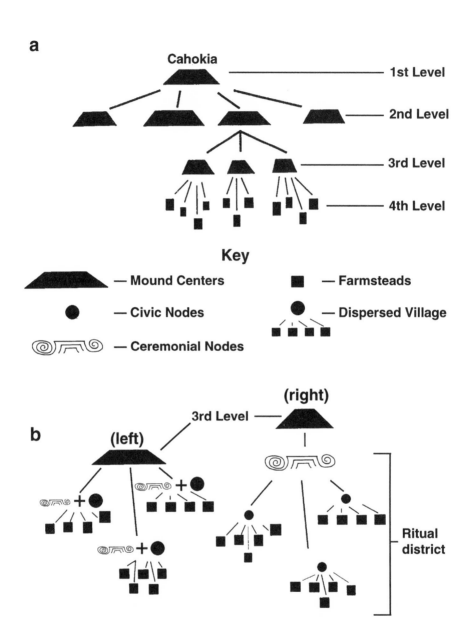

Figure 4.1 Models of Settlement Articulation; (a) direct and (b) sequential (left) dispersed villages with associated ceremonial nodes tied to mound centers via civic nodes and (right) dispersed villages and civic nodes tied to mound center through a ceremonial node to form a ritual district (after Emerson 1995, Figure 3).

as independent entities unrelated to one another except through the center (i.e., the point of sociopolitical articulation). Therefore, such sites should have been functionally uniform, and any differences should have been directly related to group size or variations in the resources being exploited. Status differences should have been minimal, and there should not have been evidence in those sites indicating they had political, religious, or community functions. Suggested examples of such systems (with some variations) are the Powers Phase sites, the Larson phase sites, and Fowler's model for the American Bottom.

(2) The *Sequential-Articulation* model (figure 4.1b) suggests that lower-level sites were functionally differentiated and may have included a number of different types, such as farmsteads, civic nodal sites, and ceremonial nodes. This model also suggests that small sites may have been integrated in a "sequential" fashion through the mechanism of dispersed villages. Therefore, at the lowest level of community organization one might recognize, at a minimum, two facets—the farmstead and the civic nodal site (figure 4.1b, left). Such nodal sites contained evidence of community functions and suggestions of political and status differences. It is possible that those nodal centers may have been linked through ceremonial nodes to form a ritual district (figure 4.1b, right) of multiple dispersed villages. It was those dispersed villages that articulated with the mound center. Such systems are thought to have been operational in the Black Bottom, the American Bottom, and for the earlier settlements in the Central Illinois River Valley.

While the identification of these two modes of articulation are important in and of themselves in demonstrating settlement variation between Mississippian groups, they also have broader implications for interpreting the nature of the hierarchical sociopolitical systems of which they are an integral portion.

AMERICAN BOTTOM SETTLEMENTS

The most comprehensive attempt to propose models of Mississippian settlement systems in the American Bottom was that of Melvin Fowler (1974: 27-33). Diachronically, he envisioned the Mississippian settlement systems as having progressed through a series of developmental stages beginning during the Late Woodland Patrick phase. Fowler developed an elaborate scenario for the Mississippian settlement systems of this locality. His major arguments can be characterized as the "community stratification" model in which all settlements are categorized with regard to their "functional" role in the overall system.

The "First-Line Community" was a unique category represented by the massive site of Cahokia. Fowler described it as controlling the location of all other sites within the American Bottom in that all other "communities were supportive to it and were strategically located to control various resources, transportation, and communication within the American Bottoms and out-side areas" (1974: 27). "Second-Line Communities" were represented by the four major, heavily populated temple towns of Pulcher, East St. Louis, St. Louis, and Mitchell. Those towns were placed at critical points on the major waterways to control communications, as well as to act as collection and redistribution centers for regional resources. Single mound centers formed the "Third-Line Communities," which are thought to be located near spe-cific resource zones to collect them for Cahokia. Around the larger commu-nities were clustered the "Fourth-Line Communities," the hamlets, villages, and farmsteads.

Fowler (1974: 32) notes that this "community stratification" model re-quired many of the Mississippian sites in the American Bottom to be con-temporaneous—but data are not yet sufficient to demonstrate the validity of such an assumption. Harn (1971, 1980) has, in fact, suggested that this is not the case. Working with data based on scattered surveys of the American Bottom (Harn 1971; Munson 1971), he has argued that a "population nucle-ation" model of Mississippian settlement is more appropriate to explain his observations.

The population nucleation model suggests that the paucity of surface material dating from the Stirling phase in the American Bottom reflects the actual paucity of occupation rather than the fragility of the period ceramics (Harn 1980: 20). Harn's survey data suggested that the primary occupation and utilization of the third- and fourth-line communities occurred during the•Fairmount phase (Emergent Mississippian), but these were abandoned by Stirling times. This abandonment of the smaller sites coincides with the centralization of power at Cahokia and may be attributable to it. Harn indi-cates the increase of political power, depletion of resources, and the need for defense as some of the possible factors. Population numbers may not have decreased, but the clustering of all this population into the central Cahokia core area (possibly including East St. Louis and St. Louis Mound Groups) would have dramatically increased relative densities. As both Harn and Fowler point out, the nucleation of population is one of the attributes that scholars have associated with the urbanization of some major Mesoamerican sites (cf. Parsons 1971; Sanders 1972).

Fowler's (1978) settlement model is based on perceived site size and com-plexity. The site size variable is derived from nonsystematic surface collec-tions and the number of mounds, while site complexity and importance seem directly measured by the number and size of mounds. The lower end of the settlement hierarchy consists of fourth-line communities. These communities were characterized as being farmsteads, hamlets, or small villages that did not have mounds associated with them and did not extend beyond a few hectares in area (Fowler 1978: 471). While a function is not clearly proposed for such communities, the assumption appears to be that they represented small farming settlements. Those settlements, which may have ranged from a single nuclear family, to an extended family, to a moderate number of such families, are seen as tied to the larger mound communities of the second and third levels that, in turn, were tied to Cahokia. These fourth-line sites are often viewed as seasonal occupations, existing only to produce food for consumption for the larger sites. There had been no suggestion that there were any differential functions for sites within the fourth-line category—they were viewed simply as food-producing units of varying size.

Although never directly acknowledged, it is apparent that many of the relationships and preconditions postulated in Fowler's model are derived from aspects of Service's (1971) redistributive chiefdom. Service argued (1971: 133-134) that chiefdoms arose in areas of discontinuous resources and were characterized "by specialization in production and redistribution of produce from a controlling center. . . . Chiefdoms are *redistributional societies* with a permanent central agency of coordination." Fowler stresses the placement of secondary and tertiary centers to control resources—presumably with Cahokia acting as the redistributive force in the polity. As we now know, the existence of a redistributive economy in chiefly societies is more problematic than suggested by Service and certainly is open to a variety of criticisms and alternative models (cf. Earle 1987: 291-298; Welch 1991).

AN ALTERNATIVE AMERICAN BOTTOM MODEL

An alternative Mississippian settlement model has been offered by researchers associated with the FAI-270 Archaeological Mitigation Project (Emerson and Milner 1981; Emerson 1992, 1995). This project involved the survey, testing, and mitigation of the archaeological resources from well over a thousand acres of highway alignment stretching for 34 km north-south in the American Bottom, as well as hundreds of acres of upland borrow pits. The history and impact of this massive project have been documented by a number of authors (Bareis 1981; Bareis and Porter, eds. 1984; Porter 1981, 1984; Griffin 1984) and will probably continue to be evaluated in the coming years. One of the central foci of this project was "the nature of the Late Woodland and Mississippian community plans and what this represented in the cultural evolution to complex society" and "how the rise and fall of Cahokia was reflected in sites on the American Bottom outside of Cahokia proper" (Bareis and Porter 1984: 7). This interest was a primary motivation in dictating the FAI-270 site excavation approach of total site stripping to expose all subsurface features. As Porter (1981) noted, this approach was also supported by the positive experience of researchers using similar techniques at sites such as Knoebel (Bareis 1976), Conrad and my (cf. Conrad and Emerson 1974) massive excavations in the 1970s at Orendorf, the Powers phase sites (Price and Griffin 1979), and his own work at Mitchell (Porter 1974). The concentration on large-scale exposures of sites dictated many of the field decisions and analysis approaches on the FAI-270 Project, and this is important to understand in evaluating the results of this research.

The FAI-270 Project concern with settlement has been outlined in a number of places (Porter 1981, 1984; Bareis and Porter 1984), and this discussion is based on those sources. The general premise was that there was no solid foundation for Mississippian settlement studies, that such models as Fowler's (1978 and elsewhere) were based on limited surface collections data and, therefore, subject to inherent limitations. The basic relationship between the surface data and the subsurface features had never been established and, consequently, had questionable interpretive value. With a few exceptions there had been no effort to study the internal structure of large portions of settlements or the correlation between such sites. Therefore, based on the positive results of other researchers and the glaring absence of information in the American Bottom, "it was decided that a major focus of the FAI-270 Project work would be to obtain information on architectural features and their internal arrangement within sites" (Bareis and Porter 1984: 14).

In terms of the FAI-270 Project this meant an approach based on the theoretical stance of Trigger (1968, 1978). His three settlement levels were to be implemented as follows: "1. The types of structures and related pits at one site should be defined. 2. The way in which these structures and pits are spatially arranged within a site area reveals the community plan. 3. The way in which these community plans and their settlement area are distributed over the geographic area under study forms the settlement pattern" (Bareis and Porter 1984: 14).

The social correlations of these archaeological features were seen as (1) single households representing family groups; (2) clusters of structures that were the remains of a social group (i.e., of a "community" that interacted on a daily basis); while (3) the community and its area of activity formed the settlement. The distribution of communities across the landscape created the settlement pattern.

AMERICAN BOTTOM DISPERSED VILLAGE

The excavations by the FAI-270 Project in the late 1970s and early 1980s provided the data to question the validity of the previous views of fourth-line communities. During that period, George Milner and the author were involved in the excavations of a number of so-called fourth-line Mississippian sites. Milner's excavations were focused on a number of farmsteads and a nodal site (Julien, Turner, DeMange), while I was involved with farmsteads and a unique temple-mortuary site (Julien, Marcus, Florence Street, Sandy Ridge Farms, BBB Motor). As a result of our interaction and discussions on these sites, we collaborated on a number of papers (Milner and Emerson 1981; Emerson and Milner 1981, 1982, 1988) that outlined our views of Mississippian farmsteads, small site functional variation, and dispersed villages in the American Bottom. While Milner's interest was primarily on the farmsteads and their relationship to mortuary and health factors, I was concerned with developing a model for the dispersed village and further defining the component units.

At the time the model was proposed there was substantial new information on the widespread occurrence of the small, fourth-line community type in the American Bottom. Known examples of such communities had been tested and/or excavated at a number of locations in the area (see figure 3.1). Such communities, or segments thereof, were present at seven sites in St. Clair County: Julien (11-S-63), Schlemmer (11-S-3), Sandy Ridge Farm (11-S-660), Lilly Lake (11-S-341), Labras Lake (11-S-299), Range (11-S-47), and Turner/DeMange (11-S-50/447). These sites provided the clues to suggest a model for Mississippian fourth-line community articulation and interaction that I first presented in draft form in the analysis of the BBB Motor site in 1981.

The American Bottom data appeared to resemble closely that recovered from the Kincaid locality. It was clear that the elemental unit of the Mississippian settlement pattern, the farmstead, was relatively abundant throughout the American Bottom. Julien and Turner/DeMange presented a clear picture of such sites. They conformed to the pattern that has emerged in other areas of Mississippian culture: small units consisting of from one to three structures and associated pit features. Such structures, for the most part, did not seem to be differentiated and, as suggested by many, the sites probably functioned as farmsteads for nuclear or extended family groups on a year-round basis. These farmsteads generally were scattered along the ridgetops (especially the sand ridges) within the ridge-and-swale topography of the American Bottom floodplain.

It is possible to observe clustering of household units in certain areas that were of sufficient size to be considered central places or "nodal sites." The term "nodal" is intended to reflect the integrative aspect proposed for such sites. It is common to observe small clusters of from four to six structures at sites such as Labras Lake, Range, and Julien. In this area sweat houses were associated with these centralized clusters. The best examples may be at Labras Lake, with its three rectangular structures and two sweat houses. Sweat houses also were present at Range and Julien in areas of similar topography. Similar sweat houses have not been reported from the Kincaid area; however, whether this reflects the lack of excavated evidence and the general reliance on surface materials to delineate site function or the absence of such site structures is not clear.

The presence of sweat houses at central locations and, in many instances, in association with a clustering of structures, suggests that such areas may well have functioned as nodal sites for the surrounding household units. It would not be surprising, considering the importance of ritual purity in the Southeast, to find a sweat house in conjunction with the household of a local leader (Swanton 1946: 386 ff.). Pauketat (1993: 141-142), in fact, noted the correlation of sweat houses and elite structures with mounds at Cahokia, reinforcing the correlation in the countryside of sweat houses with local leaders. Such nodal site sweat houses can also be interpreted as having been community-centered in nature and may have functioned as an integrative device for the surrounding dispersed households. The presence of dispersed villages seems likely in the American Bottom, based on the available evidence. The best example of a segment of dispersed village may be the Sandy Ridge Farm-Julien-Florence sites that stretched along a ridge near the modern city of Cahokia.

An American Bottom dispersed village (during the clearest demarcation in the Stirling period) can be thought of as consisting of a central nodal site, with a nucleated cluster of domestic and general-purpose structures associated with a specialized structure such as a sweat house, and surrounded by a number of associated households spread along the nearby ridge systems. These nodal sites were distinguished from small to medium clusters of domestic structures, often referred to as "hamlets" in other Mississippian systems (but apparently rare or absent in the American Bottom), through the presence of ritual- and/or community-centered architecture. Such a nodal site usually was placed on a topographically high, centrally located spot on a ridge system. Together the nodal site and its associated farmsteads could be thought of socially as a community and spatially as a contiguous group.

Based on the evidence collected from the excavated small sites in the American Bottom, it is clear that dispersed village settlements were recognizable and formed a coherent pattern. There was one type of small site, however, that appeared unique. This was the isolated ceremonial node documented at the BBB Motor site. It is not self-evident how such ceremonial sites articulated with the surrounding settlements. I suggested, however, that this ceremonial node may have served as the local religious center and charnel house for one or more dispersed villages.

The basis for this model was the visual patterning obvious in the excavated fourth-line sites and the similarity to the settlement pattern of the Black Bottom. No attempt beyond the phase level was made to control for contemporaneity of structures, to demonstrate specific functional differentiation between proposed site types, to thoroughly present a model of the settlement system that dealt with the method of articulation of such sites, or to place these proposed dispersed villages in their cultural and chronological context. As tentative and preliminary as the model was, it did create an opportunity to reexamine our assumptions about lower-order Mississippian settlement.

Subsequently, new information and expanded analyses have provided essential data to build on our previous Stirling phase model of rural settlement and expand its implications for a diachronic understanding of Cahokian Mississippian political and religious domination. This settlement model was an important foundation on which to base my examination (Emerson 1995) of these rural sites to provide greater understanding of the politics and religion of the Cahokian polity. This research demonstrated that these rural sites could be used to trace the rise of Cahokian centralized political and religious domination. These insights were achieved by focusing on the evidence for an "architecture" and "artifactual assemblage" of power and observing diachronic changes in their intensities and manifestations.

5

Cahokian Rural Nodes: The Archaeological Evidence

I am primarily interested in the definition and explication of rural settlement units that suggest the presence of a politically and/or ideologically based hierarchical system. Such settlements should, consequently, contain indicators of special status, such as having community-centered functions, occupancy by elite, unique architecture, "sacred landscapes," high frequencies of exotic or ritual materials, or other such features normally associated with power in Mississippian lifeways. To accomplish that definition and explication we can examine the archaeological evidence behind an "architecture of power" and artifactual assemblage. Obviously, to clarify the "distinction" of such hierarchical nodes one must have a general perspective on the form of the typical rural settlement unit.

A recent typological study by Mark Mehrer (1988, 1995) provides those data. He explored some of the previously identified segments of American Bottom dispersed rural settlements in terms of spatial patterning of debris deposition and the formal typology and distribution of architecture and pit features. While providing a broad perspective on rural Mississippian housecluster patterning, his details must be viewed with caution. A number of his examples of Stirling phase houseclusters have now been identified as Lohmann phase by myself and others, and further analysis has eliminated some clusters, such as at the Range site, for example. At the Julien site I have argued for the reassignment of a Moorehead phase cluster to the Lohmann phase, and there is the strong possibility that the clusters assigned to Moorehead and Sand Prairie components at Julien and Florence may need reassessment.

Chronologically, Mehrer's study covered components from the late Emergent Mississippian Edelhardt phase through the Middle Mississippian Sand Prairie phase. This work included 91 structures and more than 700 features from seven sites (figure 3.1), including Carbon Dioxide (Finney 1985), Range (Mehrer 1982), Julien (Milner with Williams 1984), Turner-DeMange (Milner with Williams 1983), BBB Motor (Emerson and Jackson 1984), Florence Street (Emerson et al. 1983), and Robert Schneider (Fortier 1985). While the primary focus of the research treated the recognition of formal "types" of feature and structure morphology and the specific dispositional patterns of debris within and between structures and features, Mehrer (1988: 87–126) also provided researchers with an essential summary of American Bottom Mississippian rural building styles, household clusters, and feature patterning. However, he relied on extant reports and did not include any detailed discussion or justification for the specific feature inclusion and composition of each household cluster.

I have attempted to include such discussions in the following analysis. The quantification and examination of these defined household cluster patterns support those identified by previous researchers and allow one to see the nature of the chronological changes that characterize the rural settlement milieu. In the following analysis I will use Mehrer's summary information combined with recent excavations and analysis and a reexamination of notes and materials from previously excavated sites to develop and expand my earlier concepts to present a more refined model of rural Mississippian settlement.

One of the most difficult issues in the analysis of such house clusters is assigning specific functions to structures. Rarely do such structures have any functionally diagnostic evidence directly associated with their archaeological remains. In my discussion of these many archaeological features I have generally followed the functional assignment of structures as presented by the original analysts. In cases where my interpretations have differed, I have made this clear and presented evidence to justify my argument.

In this chapter I will present a chronologically ordered description of the archaeological evidence to define a number of specialized settlement forms. These forms include *nodal households, civic nodes,* and *ceremonial nodes.* In each instance I have included a detailed description of the associated architecture, spatial patterning, artifact assemblage, and ethnobotanical and faunal materials. The data presented will show that each of these settlement forms had a distinct material signature that allows its identification (compare this data with figure 2.2). *Nodal households* are represented by single-family house clusters that have indications of community food storage, prestige/wealth items, and ceramic inventories suggesting community feasting. *Civic nodes* are marked by specialized ritual architecture (e.g., sweat houses), a number of residence and storage structures, and a high density of status goods, including ritual ceramics. The *ceremonial nodes* are associated with fertility and religious activities and include mortuary features, temples, specialized storage and activity buildings, and many exotic religious artifacts. In the subsequent chapter I present an interpretive discussion of a posited function and hierarchical organization for these settlements and their implications for understanding Cahokian domination of the countryside.

LOHMANN RURAL SETTLEMENT

The Lohmann phase represented the first truly Middle Mississippian cultural expression in the American Bottom. Three distinct Lohmann phase household (i.e., non-nodal) organizational patterns were recognized (Mehrer 1988: 108-113) based on an analysis of six households from the Carbon Dioxide, Range, and Turner-DeMange sites. Mehrer's patterns, labeled LA, LB, and LC, were identified on the basis of the types and distribution of pit features. These households typically included one to three buildings: some (LA) have only a few exterior large pits with a high density of debris and small scattered exterior pits, while others (LB) have a pattern of widely dispersed pits.

The third and most unusual household pattern (LC), which contained only structures, was recognized only at the Range site Lohmann component and can now be considered invalid for reasons that will be discussed in more detail below. Generally, Lohmann households were relatively widely spaced across the landscape and marked by the "dispersed nature of exterior pits with their work spaces, the lack of substantial interior pits, few tools ... few exotics, and a tendency for a few exterior pits to contain the main portion of the household material. The recurrent patterned arrangement of exterior pits around a small open area is also found in later phases" (Mehrer 1988: 113).

Julien Nodal Household

Another form of Lohmann site organizational pattern not identified by Mehrer appeared at the Julien site centered on Structure 267 (figure 5.1), and I believe it represents a nodal household (table 5.1). This structure was identified as a Stirling phase household (Mehrer 1988: 114, figure 26A, JUL-3) overlain by a later Moorehead set of unique features (Mehrer 1988: 121, figure 28E, JUL-9). This is presumably based on Milner's (Milner with Williams 1984: 186) tentative identification of Feature 289 as Moorehead(?)

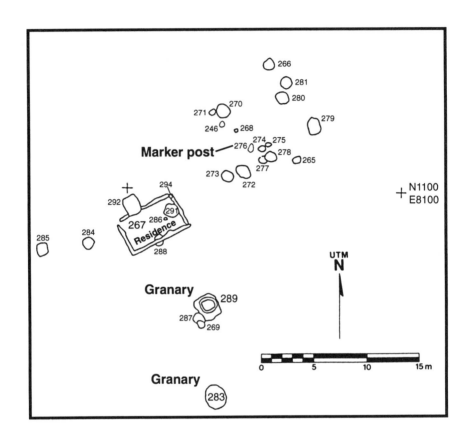

Figure 5.1 Lohmann Phase Julien Nodal Household (after Milner with Williams 1984, Pocket Map).

Cahokia and the Archaeology of Power

Table 5.1 Lohmann Phase Julien Nodal Household (JUL-3)

Buildings

Residential: 1 WT (F267)
                    Area - 16.4 m^2

Storage: 1 Circ. WT (F289)
                    Dia. 1.04, Area - .85 m^2
                    Limestone Floor

                    1 Circ., No WTs observed (F283)
                    Dia. 2.08, Area - 3.4 m^2
                    Limestone Floor

Ceremonial: None

Facilities

Pit Count: 24   Pit Volume: 5.7266 m^3

Marker Post: 1 (F276)

Ceremonial: 0

Caches: 1 Hoe in pit (F246)
                    1 WT Cache of Galena, Red and
                          Yellow Ocher, Limonite, Fire
                          Clay Earspool (SW wall)

Materials

Exotics: Galena 1 (1.3 g)
                    Red Ocher (field observation)
                    Yellow Ocher (field observation)
                    Limonite (field observation)
                    Flint Clay Earspool (13.1 g)
                    Beads - 4 (3 ceramic & 1 crinoid, ca. 9.4 g)

Ceramics: Jars   12
                    Bowls   11
                    <u>Seed Jar   1</u>
                    Total vessels 24

Status/Ritual Ceramics: None

---

and the superimposition of Feature 292 on the wall trench of Structure 267. There is reason to question a number of these assumptions.

Reexamination of the ceramics from the Julien Structure 267 feature cluster provided good evidence that they represented a late Lohmann phase occupation. Twelve jars, eleven bowls, and one seed jar were recovered from the cluster. The bowls are predominantly red or plain surfaced and roughly one-half shell tempered and one-half limestone tempered. The dozen jars, with one exception, have an incurved neck between the rim and shoulder. Nine are shell tempered and three limestone tempered. One-third of the jars have unmodified rims, one-third everted, and one-third extruded. Most of the vessels have plain surfaces. The Rim Protrusion Ratio (RPR, see Holley 1989: 20-26) for the assemblage was 0.609, virtually identical with the Lohmann assemblage mean from the ICT-II of 0.623 (Holley 1989: 44). The absence of Ramey Incised ceramics, while not conclusive, is also supportive of an earlier date. The limestone temper, the unmodified and extruded rim forms, the RPR value, and the plain surfaces all strongly indicate a Lohmann affiliation for the complex.

The issue of the "Moorehead" component within this structure cluster is more difficult to resolve; however, there are credible circumstances to reject it and move these features into the Lohmann component. Features 284, 292, 269, 287, and 289 were classed as part of a Moorehead component in Mehrer's study. Features 284, 269, and 287 are pits that contained no internal evidence or diagnostics; therefore, their affiliation was presumably based on association. The rectangular Feature 292 "overlays" the north wall trench of Structure 267; however, it too contained no Moorehead diagnostics. I worked on the excavation of this specific set of superpositionings and, more than most, am aware how tenuous was the assignment of cultural affiliation. The other proposition that we considered was that the Feature 292 pit was dug alongside the standing wall of Structure 267 and was contemporaneous—an interpretation that I now favor.

The Feature 289 complex was a subrectangular basin (2.3 m x 2.01 m) that contained a substantial circular wall trench with a diameter of 1.04 m enclosing a limestone floor. The nature of the feature itself, a limestone-floored basin, bespeaks an earlier time line (Kelly et al. 1987, 1990). Unlike the other features attributed to the Moorehead component, this complex contained a single, potentially diagnostic, everted, shell-tempered, cord-marked rim sherd. This thin, finely cordmarked vessel appears similar to those somewhat rare, aberrant cordmarked vessels that appeared in Lohmann (Timothy Pauketat, personal communication 1995) and early Stirling phase components. It is clearly not what one would type as Cahokia Cordmarked and would associate with the later Moorehead or Sand Prairie components.

There were no other items in this isolated cluster of features that suggested any association of this area with the Moorehead phase. In addition, the closest Moorehead cluster of features, consisting only of a single structure and a few pits, is over 70 m to the northeast of the Structure 267 cluster. Simply on the basis of propinquity, a very "Mississippian" characteristic, the features should be associated with Structure 267. Consequently, I have interpreted this isolated cluster of features as a Lohmann phase facility.

The Structure 267 cluster consists of a single wall-trench structure measuring 5.42 m x 3.02 m (16.37 m²) with a single interior deep pit. The structure is marked by the presence of galena, red and yellow ocher, limonite, and a flint clay earspool which were cached in the southwest wall trench. Abutting the exterior northwest wall trench is the rectangular Feature 292, which is another deep pit. About fifteen small and large pits cluster off the northern corner of the structure. The shallow pits may represent various cache pits (e.g., Feature 246, which measured 50 cm x 46 cm x 19 cm deep, contained only a massive hoe). These features also included three ceramic beads and one crinoid bead. There is a single marker post, Feature 276, in the midst of the feature cluster. The post mold is 79 cm x 45 cm and 43.5 cm deep, with an extraction ramp up one side. Such a marker post with an ordinary structure cluster would be unusual.

To the southeast of Structure 267, at about 6 m, is the circular, limestone-floored Feature 289 previously discussed. Another 5-6 m south of that feature is Feature 283, which was a shallow (14 cm) circular depression roughly 2.08 m in diameter (3.4 m²). The bottom of the pit appeared covered by numerous limestone slabs. In the field it was suspected that the feature might be identical to Feature 289; however, rodent disturbance was so extensive that no wall trenches or posts were found. I am inclined to think that Feature 283 represents a facility similar, if not identical, to Feature 289. Supportive of a specialized function of limestone-floored features is Kelly's (1990b; Kelly et al. 1987, 1990) observation that such pits occurred in ceremonial contexts as early as the Patrick phase at the Range site and became especially prevalent in the later Emergent Mississippian period.

How does this complex compare with the standard Lohmann household cluster as defined by Mehrer? It is marked as different from the more usual Lohmann phase structure/feature clusters by the presence of a single wall-trench structure in association with two specialized, limestone-floored (storage[?]) facilities, the presence of a marker post, a large number of bowls (about 50% of the vessel assemblage), crinoid and ceramic beads, and a number of cached exotics (i.e., pigments and earspool) in the structural wall trenches. While not overwhelming evidence, there is the suggestion that this complex was occupied by residents of a higher status and a more community-centered (i.e., food storage) function than other household clusters of this phase.

Range Civic–Ceremonial Node

The Range site (11-S-47) was one of the more complex sites excavated within the FAI-270 Project. With its more than 5,000 features and extensive superpositioning, the simple definition and association of a component's features were often difficult tasks. In Mehrer's study (1988: 109-113) he identified a superimposed set of buildings, an isolated structure with prepared hearths, and an absence of pits as defining a possible Lohmann household pattern (LC). Subsequent reanalysis of all of the Range site Lohmann and Stirling features by Hanenberger (Hanenberger and Mehrer 1998), while indicating that the earlier associations posed by Mehrer were inappropriate, did delineate four apparently separate Lohmann structure clusters, ML-1 through ML-4 (*contra* Kelly 1990b: 105-107, who categorized them as Lindhorst Phase). ML-3 and ML-4 clearly are typical Lohmann residential complexes or "farmsteads" consisting of several structures and their associated pits. ML-1 (figure 5.2) is suggested to be a "community center" and ML-2 (figure 5.3) is tentatively suggested to have some community-centered function of uncertain association. These two clusters are separated by only about 45 m and sit on the highest section of the Range site ridge. Both are dramatically different from the typical Lohmann households and from one another, and I would suggest that they are most likely contemporaneous portions of a Lohmann nodal civic–ceremonial site.

RML-1 (figure 5.2, table 5.2) contains two adjacent, large, rebuilt wall-trench structures, Structure 19 and Structure 32 (plus Structure 33 and Structure 51). These structures are separated by a 12 m cleared area from Feature 631, which is a massive, multiwalled, single-post structure. Structure 19 measures 5.25 m x 2.3 m (12.1 m²) and has a rebuilt end and side. It contains one interior storage pit, and its floor area is internally segmented by posts, including one large post or mortar adjacent to the wall. Material recovered included debitage, hoe flakes, abraders, five bowls, five jars, a celt, a clay discoidal, one projectile point, and miscellaneous debris. Its adjoining structure, Structure 32, consists of three superimposed wall-trench buildings. The smallest, Structure 33, is 3.2 m x 1.8 m (5.76 m²); the middle, Structure 51, is 4.07 m x 2.2 m (8.95 m²); and the largest, Structure 32, is 5.38 m x 2.88 m (15.5 m²). Hanenberger suggests that Structures 33 and 51 were specialized structures (perhaps storage), given their extremely small size. The only interior feature was a shallow basin. The material contents of the multiple structures were minimal, including only three jars and a bowl, some

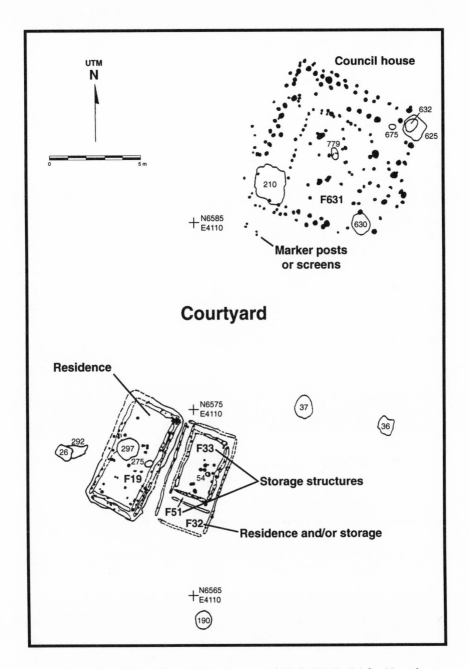

UTM
N

0   5 m

Council house

632
675
625

779

210

N6585
E4110

F631

630

Marker posts
or screens

Courtyard

Residence

N6575
E4110

37

36

292
26

297
275

F33

54

Storage structures

F19

F51
F32

Residence and/or storage

N6565
E4110

190

Figure 5.2 Lohmann Phase Range Civic–Ceremonial Node (RML-1) (after Hanenberger and Mehrer 1998).

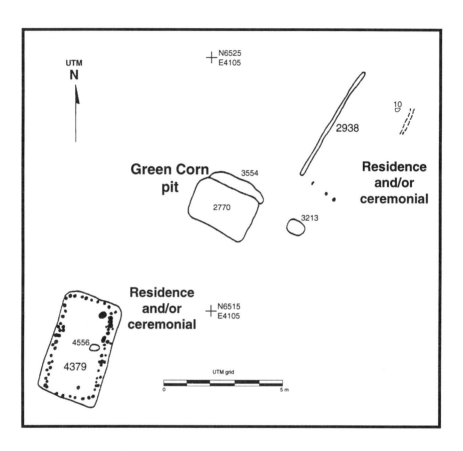

Figure 5.3 Lohmann Phase Range Civic–Ceremonial Node (RML-2) (after Hanenberger and Mehrer 1998).

Cahokia and the Archaeology of Power

Table 5.2   Lohmann Phase Range Civic–Ceremonial Node (RML-1)

Buildings

Residential: 1 WT rebuilt (F19)
                  Area - 12.1 m^2

Storage: 3 Sequential Buildings
                  1 WT (F33)   1 WT (F51)   1 WT (F32)
                  Area - 5.76 m^2 Area - 8.95 m^2 Area - 15.5 m^2

Communal: Multiwalled SP (F631) w/benches
                  Area - 57.8 m^2

Facilities

Pit Count: 12   Pit Volume: 3.83 m^3

Marker Posts: 4

Ceremonial: 0

Caches: 0

Materials

Exotics: Galena - 5 (6.4 g)
                  Red Ocher - 2 (.4 g)
                  Limonite - 72 (58.8 g)
                  Clay Discoidal - 1 (4.5 g)

Ceramics: Jars   23
                  Bowls   10
                  Pan   1
                  Bottle   1
                  Total vessels 35

Status/Ritual Ceramics: None

---

debitage, a few points, a flat abrader, and two microdrills; however, they contained all the galena, hematite, and limonite recovered in RML-1. Five storage/processing pits were scattered about the exterior of the Structures 19 and 32 complex.

To the northeast of the two structures is a unique, large, multiwalled, single-post "community structure." Hanenberger suggests, based on analogies with the Creek (Hudson 1976: 218-219), that it may have served as a Lohmann phase "town house" where the community's elite gathered to discuss and plan activities, to feast, and to socialize. Its architectural layout suggests a large open-roofed shelter with interior floor dimensions that are exactly square, measuring 7.6 m on each axis, with a floor area of 57.8 m². The structure has large wall and central posts and was built with open corners that may have served as entryways. There are rows of interior posts along the north, west, and, less clearly defined, east walls that mark the edges of benches or storage shelves. Intermixed with these bench supports are larger posts that must have assisted in supporting the roof. Features occur in the east, south, and west corners of the building. In general, these pits are marked by burning, limestone, and bone, suggesting food preparation functions. Four single posts are also present just outside the southwest corner of the structure and may represent some form of screen or perhaps marker posts. Material associated with the structure included a diversified vessel assemblage of 11 jars, 1 pan, 1 bottle, and 3 bowls. Other items recovered were points, debitage, a few stone tools, and a bone shuttle.

The RML-1 complex, with its unusual large community structure, the large wall-trench structures, and the two uniquely small storage structures, stands in stark contrast to the known residential household patterns defined by Mehrer. The virtual absence of associated storage and/or processing pits is unusual given the large number of buildings. Some of the recovered material assemblage is also notable for its mundane nature, and there is only a moderate amount of unique or exotic items present. The material assemblage does not appear to suggest large, community-centered activities, as does the architecture. For example, only 35 vessels are present, including 23 jars, 10 bowls, 1 pan and 1 bottle. The material assemblage of tools consists of 7 points, 2 hoe fragments, 2 microdrills, 4 bifacial tools, flakes, cores, 5 abraders, and 1 celt, with only a clay discoidal being somewhat unusual. Limestone was plentiful with over sixteen hundred pieces recovered. Botanical remains include corn, squash, sunflower, nuts, and starchy seed assemblage; morning glory seeds were recovered that might have ritual connotations. Exotic minerals were the one material category that occurred in moderate amounts, with 2 pieces of Red ocher, 72 of limonite, and 5 of galena. These minerals were restricted to the Structure 19 and 32 area.

RML-2 (figure 5.3, table 5.3) is another architecturally and artifactually unusual complex in the Lohmann component at the Range site. Hanenberger (Hanenberger and Mehrer 1998) suggests that this may be the earliest Lohmann component at Range, perhaps even filling that transitional niche between the Lindeman and Lohmann phases. It is located about 45 m south of RML-1 and includes two rectangular structures. Structure 4379 is a small rectangular single-post structure with interior dimensions of 3.8 m x 1.85 m (7.03 m²) with a single interior post or mortar. Just over 8 m to the northeast lies Structure 2938, which represents a partially eroded wall-trench structure measuring 4.82 m x 2.52 m (12.15 m²) and has a small smudge pit near one corner. Neither structure had interior posts which might indicate the presence of roof, bench, or shelf supports. Between the two buildings is a large rectangular pit (Feature 2770) measuring 2.65 m x 1.7 m x 1.2 m in depth (4.43 m³ in volume) with 24 fill zones. Hanenberger (Hanenberger

Table 5.3 Lohmann Phase Range Civic–Ceremonial Node (RML-2)

Buildings		
Residential/ Ceremonial:	1 SP (F4379) Area - 7.03 m²	1 WT (F2938) Area - 12.15 m²
Facilities		
Pit Count:	2 Pit Volume: .16 m³	
Marker Post:	0	
Ceremonial:	1 Green Corn Pit (F2770) Volume: 4.43 m³	
Caches: 0		
Materials		
Exotics:	Red Ocher - 1 (85.9 g) Marble Discoidal - 1 (338 g) Shell Beads - 2 Engraved Sherds - 1 (8.5 g) Shell Disks - present	
Ceramics:	Jars 40 Bowls 24 Seed Jar 4 Stumpware 3 Total vessels 71	Status/Ritual Ceramics: No. of vessels ceremonially killed 4 decorated or effigy vessels
Botanical :	Red Cedar Tobacco	

and Mehrer 1998) notes that this pit is four times larger than any other Lohmann pit feature. Adjacent to Feature 2770 is a small roasting pit. Only one other exterior multipurpose pit is thought to be associated with this feature cluster.

The RML-2 cluster includes a total of 71 vessels, including 40 jars, 24 bowls, 4 seed jars, and 3 stumpware. Among nonceramic items were 3 points, 3 stone tools, debitage and cores, 6 abraders, 4 hammerstones, a metate, and discoidal. It also contained a large hematite slot abrader. Shell hoes and beads were an unusual addition to this cluster, as were 2 possible trade vessels. Botanical remains were common and included maize, squash, and nuts. Other specimens of interest for their potential ritual use are tobacco and red cedar, both confined to Feature 2770.

The material content of the three major features is very different. No material could be confidently associated with the wall-trench structure. Structure 4379 had a large assemblage of vessels (some apparently ceremonially killed), but few other items (3 abraders, debitage, cores, bone awl, etc.). The vessels included 18 jars (2 with notched lips and 1 whole grog-tempered jar), 17 bowls (5 red-slipped), 2 decorated seed jars, and 1 stumpware vessel.

Feature 2770, however, contained massive amounts of Lohmann debris. The recovered vessels (some ceremonially killed) included 22 jars, 2 decorated seed jars, 5 bowls (1 effigy), 2 stumpware vessels, and some decorated body sherds. Other artifacts in the pit were a discoidal, 7 shell hoes, 4 abraders, 2 manos and a metate, a large hematite "abrader," 2 shell beads, shell disks, stone cutting, scraping, and boring tools, debitage, and other miscellaneous items. Hanenberger (Hanenberger and Mehrer 1998) notes that this feature was the only Lohmann phase feature that contained red cedar. The association of cedar, tobacco, effigy bowls, a discoidal, several ceremonially killed vessels (both in this pit and in Structure 4379), shell disks and beads, and engraved sherd disks may argue for a ceremonial function. The similarity of this type of repository feature to the "world renewal" or Green Corn-related Feature 183 at the Sponemann site (to be discussed later in this section) should be noted (cf. Fortier 1991a).

As with RML-1, the primary argument for the special nature of RML-2 is the unique architectural pattern of the cluster and the linking of wall-trench and single-post structures with a probable community-centered repository feature and the virtual absence of other features. This special status is reinforced by the presence of such artifact classes as ceremonially killed vessels, discoidals, shell beads and disks, hematite, effigy bowls, tobacco, and red cedar. As in the other instances I will examine, it is the association rather than the presence or absence of items or feature types that is critical to identifying such feature complexes.

BBB Motor Lohmann Priest–Mortuary Ceremonial Node

The BBB Motor site (11-Ms-595) is located on a small ridge about 3.4 km east of Monks Mound at Cahokia (Emerson 1982, 1984). Prehistorically, the site area may have been an "island" surrounded by open water and marsh. The topography consists of a number of low-lying ridges surrounded by marshes, sloughs, ponds, and lakes.

The Lohmann component that I have interpreted as a Priest–Mortuary ceremonial node (Emerson 1989, 1995) included 52 features laid out in a linear pattern along the ridge and consisted of a small cluster of wall trenches, pits, and posts and, to the south, a larger cluster of structures and pits (figure 5.4, table 5.4). The larger cluster contained 2 wall trench structures with 7 internal pits, 1 post pit, 8 burials and associated pits, and 23 pits. The smaller group of features contained 7 wall trenches, 1 post mold, and 4 pit features. These areas are discussed separately in the following section. (A detailed re-analysis and presentation of Lohmann feature and artifact data were published in Emerson 1995, appendices I-III.)

Structure 176 (figure 5.5) is the northernmost of the two structures in the component. In plan view it is a rectangular, wall-trench structure with no basin; it measured 4.24 m by 2.5 m yielding a floor area of 10.6 m². Only a sandstone abrader and a little burned clay and chert were recovered from its interior. On the structure's ends and northwestern side the walls were formed by single trenches. A set of double wall trenches was present on the southeastern side, presumably due to the rebuilding of this wall. Three features are associated with Structure 176.

Feature 174 is a shallow depression representing a possible entryway into the structure. Features 171 and 212 are typical internal storage pits, which contained a number of vessels (8 jars), 3 microdrills, a Hayes point, a small ceramic pipe(?) fragment, lithic tools, and general debris.

A little over 17 m separates Structure 16 from Structure 176 to the north. Structure 16 is rectangular, with wall-trench construction (figure 5.5). It has an internal area of 15.8 m² and measures 5.0 m by 3.16 m. Despite the absence of basin fill, the structure floor and wall trenches yielded hematite, a sandstone abrader, two chert tools, and general debris. In addition, a massive quartz crystal was eventually recovered from the west wall trench where it had been cached. An intriguing aspect of this structure is a series of internal post molds that are present along the end wall trenches. Possible inter-

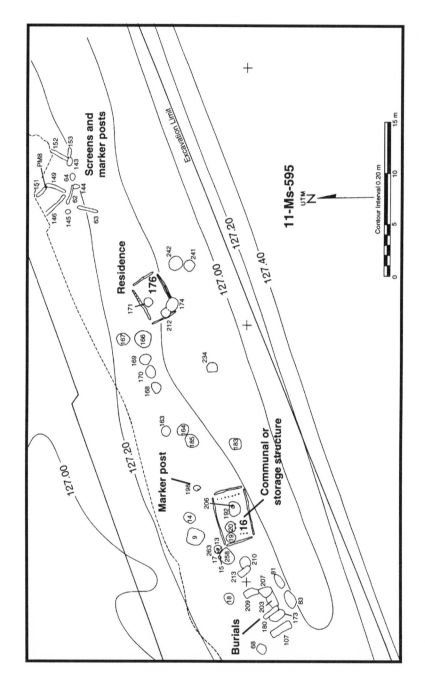

Figure 5.4 Lohmann Phase BBB Motor Priest–Mortuary Ceremonial Node (after Emerson 1984, Figure 59).

Cahokia and the Archaeology of Power

Table 5.4 Lohmann Phase BBB Motor Priest–Mortuary Ceremonial Node (BBBLCN)

Buildings			
Residential:	1 WT (F176) Area - 10.6 m^2		
Communal:	1 WT (F16) w/benches Area - 15.8 m^2		
Facilities			
Pit Count:	28 Pit Volume: 13.3 m^3		
Marker Posts:	2 Isolated WT: 7		
Ceremonial:	8 burials		
Caches:	0		
Materials			
Exotics:	Galena - 2 (19 g) Hematite - 3 (.6 g) Quartz Crystals - 3 (289.5 g) Limonite - 1 (.7 g)		
Ceramics:	Jars	71	Status/Ritual Ceramics: None
	Bowls	21	
	Seed Jars	2	
	Stumpware	3	
	Funnels	3	
	Total vessels	100	
Botanical:	Red Cedar		

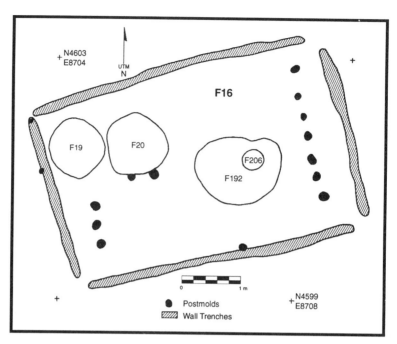

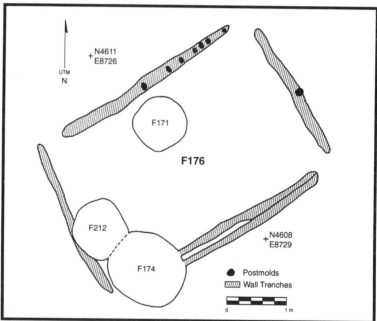

Figure 5.5 BBB Motor Site Structures 16 (Top; Emerson 1984, Figure 61) and 176 (Bottom; Emerson 1984, Figure 60).

pretations of these rows of posts include interior partitions, supports for benches, or supports for the structure's superstructure.

Four internal features are associated with Structure 16. Features 19, 20, and 192 all appear to be of the usual internal storage pit type, with moderate amounts of lithic and ceramic debris in their fills. They also contained a galena fragment, limonite, stone tools, microdrills, and a number of vessels (seven jars and two bowls) including a large (50 cm in diameter) straight-sided bowl and two jars with small "jug-like" vertical necks. Feature 206 may be interpreted as either a post or a wooden mortar. If Feature 206 is a central support post and the interior posts also served a similar function, Structure 16 must have had a substantial superstructure and/or was in use for a lengthy time period. Structure 16 was also distinguished by the placement of a marker post a little over 1 m north of its northeast corner.

A group of eight burials lies 2.5 m to the west of Structure 16. They fall into two plan view shapes: rectangular and oval. One-half of these pits contain human remains, but the remainder are "empty." The latter pits are assigned to the "burial" category based on their location and morphology. Milner (1984b: 396) reported three of the features, Features 81, 107, and 173, contained permanent tooth enamel. Feature 209 contained fragmentary long bones, including portions of a femur and two tibiae.

The fill of the burial pits contained a moderate to large amount of cultural debris. Only in one case, a clay discoidal in Feature 81, is there a clear example of the inclusion of an item as a grave good. Other possible grave goods included a denticulate, an abrader, and a core, each with a separate burial. Based on the plan shapes, arrangement, and orientation of the burials, two definable groups with two diametrically opposed orientations appear to be present. One set of five features (Features 107, 173, 180, 209, and 213) runs in a southwest-northeast direction, basically, paralleling the shoreline. Three other burials were recognized that include Features 203, 81, and 83. The first of these features is actually in the row formed by the previously discussed burials, while the latter two features are aligned in a row just to their south. They are approximately perpendicular (94.10 degrees) to the first burial set. The burial pits in the first row, with one exception, are all rectangular, while the pits in the second group are all oval.

Twenty-three pit features and a small post pit make up the remainder of the features in the component. The majority of these pit features are spread linearly to the northwest of Structures 16 and 176, between them and the lake shore. A few pits are located to the south of the structures. Just seven (or 33%) of the pits (Features 9, 68, 163, 166, 167, 242, and 258) contained 52% of the recovered ceramic vessels and much of the other debris from the site. The primary disposal area seemed to be Feature 9, which contained 21 vessels. Spatially, those heavily used pits stretched from one end of the component to the other.

The artifact assemblage from the Priest–Mortuary complex included 100 vessels identified as to type. Jars constituted 71%, bowls 21%, funnels 3%, stumpware 3%, and seed jars 2% of the vessel assemblage. Included among these vessels were a decorated miniature jar with trailed lines, punctates, and a polished red slip finish; a red-slipped bowl with an indentation where an effigy head had been attached; and a single example of a small "bird" head that was likely attached to a bowl. Several decorated body sherds were recovered. A lone example of a noded, shell-tempered, red-slipped body sherd was present. The most interesting sherd had an engraved design on both its interior and its exterior surfaces. The sherd was a fragment of a shell-tempered vessel with a polished, dark-slipped exterior and plain interior. It was recovered from Feature 9. A profile of a human or falconoid human head was engraved on its outer surface, while on the interior surface another profile of a human head (more difficult to discern) was scratched (Emerson 1989).

Two small triangular points were recovered. One is of the Hayes type (Suhm and Jelks 1962: 277), made of a white silicified sediment. This point was recovered from Feature 171, which is an internal pit of Structure 176. Within the lithic assemblage, artifacts in the abrader class made up the largest number of nonchert tools. A total of 20 abrading tools were recovered from the Lohmann features. Another ground stone tool is a crudely pointed butt end of a broken celt made of a coarse-grained basalt.

Three crystals were found in the Lohmann component; a small one in Feature 9 (6.5 g), another in Feature 149 (4.6 g), and a massive crystal (weighing 278.4 g) in the southwestern wall trench of Structure 16. This latter crystal is the only one found which has retained its crystalline structure. Both ends show evidence of smashing. On one face, an interior area of red impurities is visible. Two ground galena specimens (12.9 g and 6.1 g) were recovered from Features 14 and 20, respectively. Three fragments of ground hematite (0.1 to 0.3 g) and a single piece of limonite weighing 0.7 g were found.

As expected at Mississippian sites, Whalley (1984: 333-334), noted that "plant remains . . . conformed to the . . . pattern found at other Mississippian components in the American Bottom. . . . Maize, nutshell, seeds of the starchy seed complex, and oak and hickory wood were ubiquitous, while seeds of sunflower, various grasses, wild bean, black nightshade and prickly mallow occurred frequently. The only, and perhaps significant, exception to this pattern at the BBB Motor site was the . . . red cedar recovered."

The isolated northern area Lohmann component contained seven wall trenches, four pits, and a single post mold (figure 5.4) located eight meters to the northeast of Structure 176. One set of three features represented a shallow post pit extraction/insertion ramp complex. The pits contained few sherds and/or lithic items. A single quartz crystal was recovered from the fill of the wall trench, Feature 149. It is clear that features do not represent the remains of structures or other more conventional features; rather, they served as foundation trenches to hold "screens" designed to create walled, private zones. They do not seem to represent activity or work loci associated with everyday activities since almost no cultural debris was found in association. Given the placement of the features, the lack of utilitarian debris, and the religious nature of the Lohmann component, the screens may have been erected to shield the performance of certain activities of a special nature from the casual observer. Such screens may have been the precursors to the isolated wall-trench screens that appeared in the following Stirling phase rural civic and ceremonial centers.

One feature distinguishing the Lohmann countryside from that of previous periods is the appearance of specialized mortuary facilities, such as those recognized at the BBB Motor site. The site, located on a isolated island, consisted of a number of burials laid out in specific groupings associated with two structures interpreted as representing a "guardian's" domicile and a community-centered and/or storage structure with benches. To the northeast of the main cluster of features was an aggregation of wall trenches and posts, perhaps representing a screened or special-use area.

The assemblage of artifacts with the Lohmann priest-mortuary complex was not heavily weighted toward exotic items, although it did contain engraved "falcon dancer" sherds, galena, hematite, quartz crystals, and limonite. Important to confirming the area's ritual nature was the presence of red cedar. The ceramic vessels associated with the component were generally plain, utilitarian forms, including a moderate number of bowls. Functionally, the ceramics appeared to have been for food preparation and serving—a use that correlates well with the interpretation of the area as hosting community-centered activities. This is also supported by the large number of storage pits at the site.

STIRLING RURAL SETTLEMENT

The Stirling phase is acknowledged by all American Bottom researchers to represent the climax of Mississippian culture, both at the local and regional scales. It is also one of the best known manifestations, with extensive excavations providing a wide range of data. In keeping with that trend, Stirling phase rural settlements have been thoroughly investigated by the FAI-270 Project as well as by earlier and more recent investigations. Mehrer's study (1988: 113-120) included 15 Stirling phase houseclusters from the Range, Julien, Turner-DeMange, BBB Motor, and Robert Schneider sites. He recognized three household patterns (SA, SB, and SC) for the Stirling phase. SA households consisted of a single building surrounded by about 15 to 20 pit features, often arranged in several clusters around a cleared space. The second household pattern, SB, included two adjacent buildings with "several exterior pits clustered near the outside walls." The final type, SC, had a single structure with one isolated exterior pit located at a distance of 15 to 20 m. In his overall assessment of this patterning, Mehrer (1988: 118) notes that "a standard number of buildings was consistently matched with a particular arrangement of exterior pits"; however, "household types did not consistently incorporate one or another of the building types defined," nor was the debris distributed in any obvious patterns among pit features or structures.

Mehrer's typological examination of household patterns also reconfirmed the Stirling phase nodal sites at Range, Julien, and BBB Motor that we had distinguished earlier (cf. Emerson and Milner 1981), thus reinforcing our previous characterizations. Two forms of nodal sites can be recognized: the civic nodes, as manifested at Range, Julien, and Labras Lake (not included in Mehrer's analysis), and the ceremonial nodes, as exemplified by BBB Motor and Sponemann. In the following discussion I will elaborate on my understanding of these nodal forms.

Labras Lake Civic Node

A Stirling phase occupation from the Labras Lake site (11-S-299) has been excavated and reported by Yerkes (1980: 143-257, 1987: 84-94) and represents one of the clearest examples of a civic node (figure 5.6, table 5.5). Six rectangular wall-trench structures (varying in size from 8.5 to 18 m²) and two small circular wall-trench structures were excavated in addition to 85 deep and shallow storage-processing pits, 11 hearths, 85 post molds, 1 smudge pit, and 1 isolated wall trench. The central area of the Labras Lake site includes three rectangular wall-trenches (Houses 1-3) and two circular structures (Structures 39 and 400), arranged about a small westward-opening courtyard (9 m EW x 9 m NS), that were seen (Emerson and Milner 1981, 1982) as representative of the core element of a Stirling civic node. Ceramic and lithic evidence indicate that these clustered structures were contemporary, while their association with the outlying Houses 4-6 is uncertain (Yerkes 1987: 88-89).

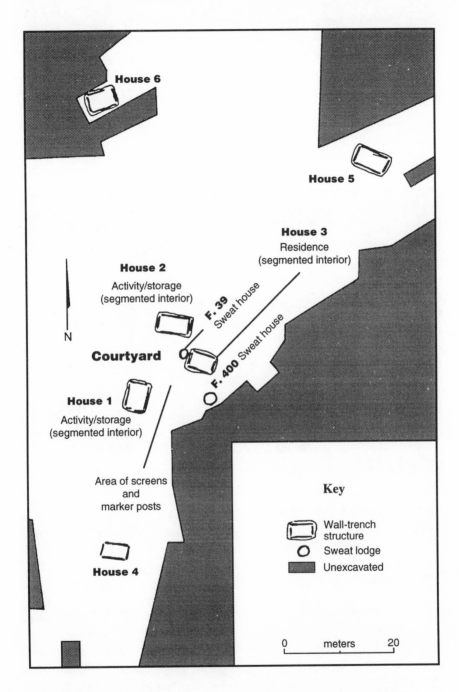

House 6

House 5

House 3
Residence
(segmented interior)

House 2
Activity/storage
(segmented interior)

F. 39
Sweat house

F. 400 Sweat house

N

Courtyard

House 1
Activity/storage
(segmented interior)

Area of screens
and
marker posts

House 4

Key

⬜ Wall-trench
structure
O Sweat lodge
▨ Unexcavated

0   meters   20

Figure 5.6 Stirling Phase Labras Lake Civic Node (after Emerson 1992, Figure 7.2).

Table 5.5 Stirling Phase Labras Lake Civic Node (LLCN)

Buildings

Residential:	2 Sequential Buildings	
	1WT (H3)	1WT (H3)
	Area - 11.3 m²	Area - 11.3 m²
Storage or Activity:	Both w/ benches or partitions	
	1WT (H1)	1WT (H2)
	Area - 18 m²	Area - 15.4 m²
Ceremonial:	1 Circ. WT (F400)	1 Circ. WT (F39)
	Dia. - 1.62 m	Dia. - 1.73 m
	Area - 2.06 m²	Area - 2.35 m²

Facilities

Pit Count: ca. 34   Pit Volume: Not Available

Marker Posts: Numerous   Isolated WT: 1

Ceremonial: Courtyard (9 m x 9 m [81 m²], opens to west)

Materials

Exotics:	Hematite - ? (at least 74 g)		
	Ramey Knife - 1		
Ceramics:	Jars	17	Status/Ritual Ceramics:
	Bowls	7	1 lobed effigy jar
	Seed jars	1	2 bowls (engraved/incised)
	Bottles	1	1 Ramey Incised jar
	Beakers	2	1 LMV incised jar
Total vessels		28	5

The three central structures display extensive rebuilding and reuse in two instances. House 1, on the south side of the courtyard, is of single wall-trench construction measuring 4.8 m by 3.76 (18 m²). Numerous small post molds parallel the interior walls and may have been benches or storage facilities. House 1 possesses a central burned hearth, three storage pits, and four shallow pits. One narrow, deep pit (diameter 85 cm and depth 80 cm) just off center may represent a central post. An effigy (duck?) bowl, a lobed (squash) effigy jar, a grog-tempered engraved bowl, and a number of plain or smudged jars and red bowls were associated with the structure complex (Richard Yerkes, personnel communication 1985). Lithics included multiple hoe flakes, points, scrapers, and knives, but few abraders. Four grams of hematite were found. Hickory nuts, chenopods, and maize were common.

House 2, across the courtyard to the north, shows evidence of at least two or perhaps three rebuildings of its walls. It is a long, narrow, rectangular building of wall-trench construction measuring 5.7 m by 2.7 m (14.2–15.4 m^2). The central area of the structure is densely packed with post molds that roughly divide it into three segments. It contained a large storage pit and a central post. Multiple stone tools (such as scrapers, knives, and microdrills), including a broken hoe, were recovered from the building. The only exotic material was 59 g of hematite/ocher. Among the more typical plant remains were numerous acorn and maize remains and the only sunflower seed from the site. In addition to a number of jars, notable vessels included a Ramey Incised jar, a red-filmed effigy bowl, and a beaker.

The complex labeled House 3 represents two complete rebuilding episodes. The first structure was a small, rectangular, wall-trench building 4.1 m x 2.75 m (11.3 m^2) superimposed on a sequential building with an identical floor area. Both structures contain a small number of interior pits and depressions and numerous interior posts. A Ramey knife, celt, 11 g of hematite, and 9 g of Missouri river clinker represented unusual items among the more typical Mississippian flake tool assemblage. This complex also contained an extensive amount of limestone (over 3.5 kg). While the ceramics were limited, they were unusual, consisting of a beaker, a fine-grog incised and punctated jar, and a red-filmed bottle, along with several plain jars.

Two circular structures are present: Feature 39, on the eastern end of the courtyard next to House 3, and Structure 400, which is the easternmost structure in the node. The circular wall-trench structure, Structure 400, has an interior diameter of 1.62 m (2.06 m^2) and contains a shallow central hearth. The structure's wall trench is C-shaped in plan with a small opening, presumably an entrance, facing directly east. Only moderate amounts of sandstone, debitage, and potsherds were found in the fill. The other circular structure, Structure 39, measured 1.73 m (2.35 m^2) across the interior with a shallow interior wall trench encircled by single posts on its exterior. Its floor contains evidence of burned earth and charcoal, but little cultural material. Both structures are similar in form to what has been identified as sweat houses in the American Bottom (e.g., Mehrer 1988; Hanenberger and Mehrer 1998).

There appears to be at least some pattern of site organization with the three rectangular structures laid out about the courtyard. The courtyard is relatively clear of other features, with the notable exception that one of the sweat houses is on its eastern end. Another area, enclosed by House 3 on the north, House 1 on the west, and the sweat house (Structure 400) on the east, is just southeast of the courtyard. That area, rather than being marked by the absence of features, contains numerous pits, random and linear arrangements of post molds, and a single northeast-southwest trending isolated wall trench. The wall trench placement may have served to block the view of the sweat house from the courtyard. The post molds and wall trench occupy the central part of the area and may have served as screens or marker posts associated with the sweat house.

The information presented by Hall (1980: 366-406), by Yerkes (personal communication 1985), and gathered through my personal examination of the ceramics indicates a placement for this node in the Stirling phase, based on vessel types, rim forms, and surface finishes. The ceramic assemblage contains several Stirling types such as Powell Plain, some Ramey Incised, and a few beakers, as well as several non-Stirling forms such as Cahokia Cordmarked (a single example which I have not been able to locate for examination) and Monks Mound Red.

The organizational structure of the site and the presence of two sweat houses suggest that this was a nodal site that served some community function. The courtyard layout, the sweat houses, the wall trench, and post mold screens generally conformed to what appear to be Mississippian markers for special and/or ritual areas. However, the site content in terms of status or exotic items appeared fairly low. The only items of notice in this regard at the site consisted of red ocher, Ramey Incised jars, several "imported"(?) vessels, a Ramey knife, a squash effigy jar and effigy bowls, beakers, microdrills, and a water bottle. That limited inventory of goods again emphasizes that only by examining the full range of architecture, spatial organization, and material culture can we recognize the critical markers of Mississippian rural hierarchy.

Yerkes (1987: 184) has interpreted this community as a possible nodal point or homestead cluster with a year-round occupation. He believes that this occupation was a self-sufficient community living on a diversified subsistence base of farming, gathering, and hunting. In addressing our previous identification (Emerson and Milner 1982) of this area as a nodal site, he notes that "the concentration of storage pits near the central houses, the presence of sweat lodges, and the restricted distribution of shell drills may be the legacy of that kind of control" (Yerkes 1987: 184).

Range Civic Node

RMS-1 is one of two Stirling phase components recognized at the Range site and represents a nodal site located on the apex of the ridge overlying the previous Lohmann RML-1 complex. RMS-2 is a small Stirling phase homestead consisting of two superimposed wall-trench structures and five exterior pits much to the south of RMS-1. Both are described in detail in Hanenberger and Mehrer (1998).

The RMS-1 complex (figure 5.7, table 5.6) contains 10 structures and 31 features and is interpreted by Hanenberger (Hanenberger and Mehrer 1998) as a community center for a number of dispersed farmsteads within the Prairie Lake area. There are five rectangular wall-trench structures, one rectangular single-post structure, and four circular, single-post structures clustered into a northern and southern group.

The southern group consisted of three structures, Structures 171, 174, and 316, around a 9 m x 9 m square courtyard which is open to the south. Structures 171 and 174 are single wall-trench structures measuring 4.64 m x 2.25 m (10.44 m^2) and 5.14 m x 3.3 m (17 m^2), respectively. Structure 171, on the western edge of the courtyard, contains a large storage pit in one end (Feature 323), a post or mortar pit along the western wall, an irregular basin along the eastern wall (Features 358 and 333), a small smudge pit in the southern corner, and a shallow depression in the central floor area. Structure 174, to the north, has multiple post molds throughout the floor area as well as a partial double wall trench along the eastern wall. These may have served as support for benches or storage. The structure had no interior pits or hearths. Extensive portions of the floor and basin show evidence of burning. Structure 316 is a small (3.5 m x 2 m; 7 m^2) rectangular single-post structure on the east side of the courtyard. It was constructed in a sandy soil, making it difficult to locate its archaeological traces, and only three post molds are visible. It has a deep storage pit (containing a stored cache of tobacco seeds) at its western end, which is immediately adjacent to a small roasting pit densely filled with burned limestone. A shallow pit is located on the eastern end of the floor. Three pits are associated with this cluster and are located about the edges of the courtyard. Two are deep storage pits, while the other, Feature 320, is a large shallow pit feature.

The feature and structure contents represent a wide spectrum of Stirling phase materials. The 26 recovered vessels represent 3 Ramey Incised jars, 14 jars, 5 bowls, 2 stumpware, and 1 pinch pot. Materials also included cores, flakes, stone tools for perforating and cutting, hoe fragments, some points, abraders, and two sherd disks. More exotic materials included hematite and quartz crystals.

The northern cluster at RMS-1 contains four circular buildings (Structures 50, 64, 28, and 46), three single wall-trench rectangular structures (Structures 16, 38, and 218), and three exterior storage pits (Features 47, 56, and 523)—all strung in linear fashion just off the ridge crest. The group lies about 5 m north of the southern group. The wall-trench structures are extremely diverse in morphology. Structure 38 is a small (3.18 m x 1.88 m;

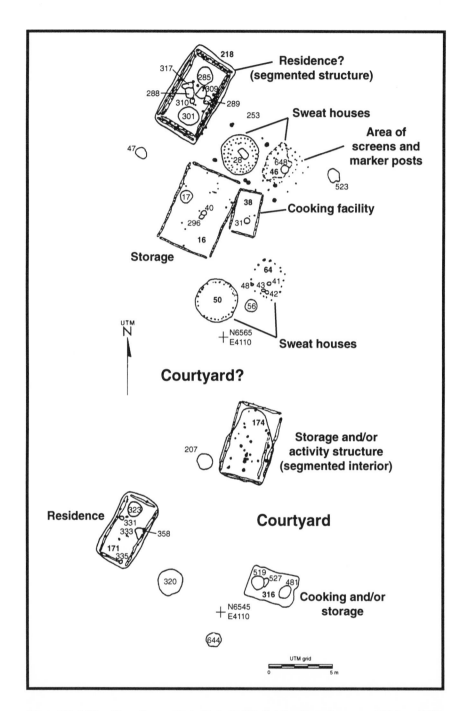

Figure 5.7 Stirling Phase Range Civic Node (RMS-1) (after Hanenberger and Mehrer 1998).

Table 5.6 Stirling Phase Range Civic Node (RMS-1)

Buildings

Residential:	1WT (F171)	1WT (F218)
	Area – 10.44 m^2	Area – 17.6 m^2 w/partitions

Storage or Activity:

1WT (F174)	1SP (F316)	1WT (F38)	1WT(F16)
Area – 17 m^2	Area – 7 m^2	Area – 5.98 m^2	Area – 24.6 m^2
w/benches	Cooking?	Cooking?	Limestone pit

Ceremonial:

1SP Circ. (F50)	1SP Circ. (F64)	1SP Circ.(F28)	1SP Circ. (F46)
Dia. – 2.9 m	Dia. – 2.3 m	Dia. – 2.5 m	Dia. – 3 m
Area – 6.6 m^2	Area – 4.13 m^2	Area – 4.91 m^2	Area – 7.21 m^2
Limestone Floor		w/benches	w/benches

Facilities

Pit Count: 23   Pit Volume: 7.3 m^3

Marker Post:: Several

Ceremonial: Courtyard (9 m x 9 m [81 m^2], opens to south)

Caches: Tobacco seeds (F519)

Materials

Exotics:	Galena – 10 (263.5 g)	Botanical: Tobacco Cache
	Hematite – 9 (21.7 g)	
	Quartz Crystals – 4 (9.1 g)	
	Limonite – 2 (81.2 g)	
	Copper – 1 (.8 g)	
	Modeled clay objects – 6	

Ceramics:	Jars	66	Status/Ritual Ceramics:	5 Ramey Incised
	Bowls	26		3 seed jars
	Bottles	3		(engraved/incised)
	Pans	3		8
	Stumpware	4		
	Seed Jars	4		
	Funnel	1		
	Pinch Pots	7		
	Total vessels	114		

5.98 m²) building with a single intensely fired hearth near the center of the building. It is immediately adjacent to and may be superimposed by Structure 16, which is a massive single wall-trench structure measuring 6.04 m x 4.07 m, with an interior area of 24.58 m². It is the largest Stirling building at Range. The structure, despite its large size, contains only three interior features. Two of these (Features 40 and 296) are large central post pits that must have served as roof supports. The only pit feature, Feature 17, was a specialized (cf. Kelly 1990b; Kelly et al. 1987, 1990) limestone-floored pit roughly one meter in diameter and one meter deep. That structure burned, and the carbonized remains collected included many charred timbers, as well as maize, sunflower seeds, and squash, suggesting that many food items may have been stored there.

Structure 218 (5.5 m x 3.2 m; 17.6 m²) was the northernmost structure in that group and was a complex double wall-trench building, which suggested a rebuilding and a long use life. It contained a number of internal posts, and one row across its floor suggested an internal partition isolating about one-third of the northern end. There are numerous internal features, including two large storage pits (Features 285 and 301), one at each end of the floor. The central floor area has multiple shallow pits plus several depressions. Several lithic tools, including hammerstones, a celt, a mano, and a limestone hoe, were found in these pits; thus, they may have served as tool caches. This structure also contained numerous exotics, including quartz crystals, hematite, and galena. A single large post or mortar (Feature 289) abuts the center of the interior eastern wall. The intensity of occupation, storage, and exotic items suggests that this was a high-status residential building.

Four circular, single-post structures were part of this group; two (Structures 50 and 64) lie just to the south of the Structures 16 to 38 group, and two (Structures 28 and 46) are just to the north. Structure 50 (2.9 m dia.; 6.6 m²) has a deep basin and a partially packed, limestone-covered floor, which is encircled by a single row of small posts. There was a central burned area on the floor. Immediately to the northeast of this building is Structure 64, which measured 2.3 m in diameter (4.13 m²) and is enclosed within a single row of small posts. No basin was present in this feature, nor was there any interior hearth; both absences may be due to erosion. The circular Structure 28 (2.5 m dia.; 4.91 m²) is the most complex of these buildings, with its double (and partially triple) set of wall posts. A number of the interior posts are interpreted as bench supports. The floor is partially limestone covered and lies within a deep basin. There is a central firepit. Just to the east is Structure 46, another partially eroded circular structure with a double set of encircling posts (3.0 dia.; 7.21 m²) in which the inner row probably represents bench supports. It has a deep, intensely fired, circular hearth. These four circular structures are interpreted to be sweat houses for purification. Given their apparent spatial pairing, it may be that they represented two sets of features of contemporaneous buildings. Although not extensively discussed, Hanenberger (Hanenberger and Mehrer 1998) noted the presence of 13 exterior posts in the areas of Features 28 (4 of which were clustered about Feature 28) and 46. It may be that these represent marker posts or screens for demarcating this area.

The northern portion of RMS-1 contained abundant material items. These included a large number of vessels (97): 2 Ramey Incised jars, 3 incised or lip-notched jars, 50 plain jars, 2 seed jars, 3 engraved or noded seed jars, 3 bottles, 6 pinch pots, 22 bowls, 3 pans, 2 stumpware, and 1 funnel. Lithic items included numerous cores, hoe flakes, debitage, and hammerstones, as well as bifaces, perforators, gravers, scrapers, and points. Abraders, manos, a celt, microdrills, a gouge, sherd disks, a limestone hoe, and other miscellaneous items were present. Exotic minerals included galena, hematite, copper, quartz crystals, and limonite.

The Range civic node represents the largest and most complex example of this type of rural settlement with its two distinct clusters and numerous specialized buildings. The southern portion of RMS-1 has one typical Stirling phase domicile (Structure 171) in conjunction with a large structure with interior benches that may have served as a storage and/or gathering place and a small flimsily built structure that may have been for storage. Across the central cleared space to the north was another, even more specialized, portion of the site that contained four sweat lodges, a large building with a specialized storage facility, a small specialized rectangular cooking facility(?), and an apparently high-status residence. The total vessel assemblage contained 66 jars, 26 bowls, 4 seed jars, 3 pans, 3 bottles, 1 funnel, 4 stumpware, and 7 pinch pots. Other materials of note beside the many bifacial stone tools were a gouge, celt, limestone hoe, 21 abraders, 6 modeled clay objects, and extensive limestone debris. Exotic minerals were plentiful with 9 pieces of hematite, 2 of limonite, 1 of copper, 4 quartz crystals, and 10 pieces of galena. Botanical remains from RMS-1 included wood charcoal, giant cane, the starchy seed cultigens, a large cluster of tobacco from a pit (Feature 519) in Structure 316, sunflower, morning glory, and maize.

Julien Civic Node

The Julien site, with its building sequence stretching from the Lohmann to the Sand Prairie phases, is an important link in disentangling rural settlement patterns. In Milner's original analysis (Milner with Williams 1984), the

primary focus was on establishing the relevance of the Cahokia chronology
to small-scale rural Mississippian sites. Consequently, he did not focus on
the identification and discussion of the phase association of individual features, although he did present tentative correlations for structures. Based on
that original analysis and subsequent reexamination of the ceramics by Milner
(personal communications 1990) and by me, it is possible to define a cluster
of Stirling phase rectangular wall-trench and circular structures that can be
identified as a nodal site (as predicted in Emerson and Milner 1981). It is
clear from the structure layout and superpositioning that the specific form
of the nodal site evolved through time. From my examination of the ceramic evidence, I believe this nodal site dates to the midpoint of the Stirling
phase. The chronological affiliation and association of exterior features in
this cluster with the Stirling phase is less certain.

The nodal site, which sits roughly on the highest crest of the ridge, can
be seen as two clusters of structures separated by an area 10 m wide that
contains a moderate cluster of pit features (figure 5.8, table 5.7). The three

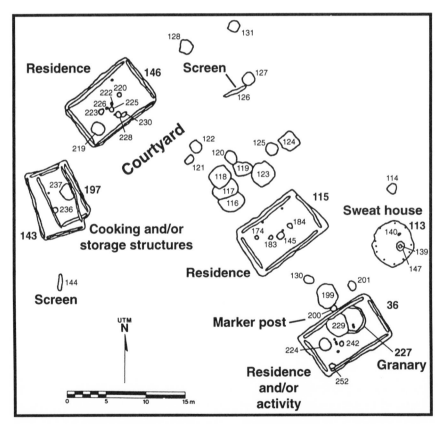

Figure 5.8 Stirling Phase Julien Civic Node (after Milner with Williams 1984, Pocket Map).

Cahokia and the Archaeology of Power

Table 5.7 Stirling Phase Julien Civic Node (JULCN)

Buildings

Residential:	1WT (F146)	1WT (F115)	1WT (F36)
	Area - 19.3 m²	Area - 17.6 m²	Area - 18 m²
			Prep. floor
Storage or	1WT Circ. (F227)	1WT (F197)	1WT (F143)
Activity:	Area - 3.06 m²	Area - 9.3 m²	Area - 15.48 m²
	Dia. - 1.75 m		

Ceremonial: 1SP Circ. (F113)
Dia. - 2.85 m
Area - 6.38 m²

Facilities

Pit Count: 28 Pit Volume: 6.63 m³

Marker Post: 1 Isolated WT: 2

Ceremonial: Courtyard (10 m, opens NE and SW)
Redug (World Renewal?) Pit (F224)

Caches: 0

Materials

Exotics: Galena - 7 (80.8 g)
Hematite – 38 (187 g)
Mica – 5 (.7 g)
Limonite – 1 (.1 g)

Ceramics:	Jars	41	Status/Ritual Ceramics:
	Bowls	14	7 Ramey Incised jars
	Bottles	1	1 trailed bowl
	Funnels	2	1 trailed plate
	Hooded		1 hooded water bottle
	Water Bottle	1	10 decorated
	Plate	1	
	Total vessels	60	

---

structures in the westernmost cluster are Structures 146, 143, and 197. Structure 146 is a single wall-trench building measuring 5.67 m x 3.4 m (19.28 m²) with a central hearth, five interior posts (perhaps acting as central roof supports), and four shallow pits in the southern quarter of the floor. Exotic material recovered by excavations in this structure included galena (80.8 g), mica (5 pieces), a tri-notched projectile point, a large ground hemisphere-shaped Missouri River clinker object, as well as more mundane items such as abraders, hammerstones, and bifacial tools. One of the seven jars present was a Ramey Incised vessel, while two bowls were also recovered.

Structure 197 is a small (4.06 m x 2.29 m; 9.3 m²) single wall-trench structure with no interior features. It is superimposed by a larger (4.9 m x 3.16 m; 15.48 m²) single wall-trench building containing a central hearth and a single shallow pit along one wall. Both Structures 143 and 197 are oriented at right angles (i.e., from northwest to southeast) to the other structures in the nodal point. They contained no vessels, except for a single bowl, and virtually no artifacts, although a knife fragment and some limonite were recovered.

The easternmost cluster contains two rectangular wall-trench structures (Structures 115 and 36) and two circular structures (Structures 227 and 113). Structure 115 is a single wall-trench building that measured 5.46 m x 3.22 m (17.58 m²), with one deep and three shallow interior pits. It also contained a center post. Among the material recovered from the structure were pieces of at least four hoes, a gouge, some abraders, and a large deposit of red ocher (187 g). With 21 vessels present, it had the second largest assemblage in the nodal site: 4 bowls and 17 jars, 3 of which were Ramey Incised, were present.

Structure 36 is a complex building with several unique aspects. It measured 5.63 m x 3.19 m (17.96 m²), with a large (ca. 1.6 m diameter and 0.89 m deep) storage pit along the center of a wall. Another pit feature, Feature 224, was located in the center of the southern half of the floor. It showed evidence of multiple reexcavations and reuse. In the southern corner a large intact Powell Plain vessel had been cached in the floor, in a pit just large enough to contain it. A single large post was located in the center of the floor, and four smaller posts were nearby. Two additional posts were in the northern half of the floor. These posts may have served as roof supports, as racks for hanging or storing items, or as partitions. The entire structure surface had a prepared floor, with the exception of Feature 229. Material items recovered included a microdrill, gravers, abraders, projectile points, and hoe fragments. It had the largest assemblage of vessels, with 25 recovered. These included 16 jars (3 of which were Ramey Incised), 5 bowls, 2 funnels, 1 bottle, and 1 hooded bottle. Feature 199, which abuts Structure 36, contained a trailed plate form.

The Structure 36 complex superimposes a circular wall-trench structure, Structure 227, measuring 1.75 m in diameter (3.06 m²). It contained no internal features and has been interpreted by Milner (Milner with Williams 1984: 30), partially because of its substantial construction, as an above-ground storage facility. The other circular structure, Feature 113, to the northeast of

Structures 115 and 36, is a clear example of a sweat house. A single row of posts forming the encircling wall provided an interior floor diameter of 2.85 m (6.38 m²). It had an intensely fired set of superimposed cylindrical hearths located just off center in the floor. One of the episodes of burning in these hearths represented a smudge fire and contained small twigs and corn cobs.

The Julien civic node contained at least 20 exterior features, 14 of which were located between Structures 115 and 146 and 4 between Structures 115 and 36. Two isolated wall trenches, Features 126 and 144, ca. 2 m and 1.5 m long, respectively, were located near the edges of the nodal site. Their function is unknown. A single large post abutted the exterior wall of Structure 36 and may have served as a marker post. The remainder of the features consisted of shallow to moderately deep pits, presumably used in storage and processing. The material found in the pits included sandstone abraders, projectile points, debitage, cores, hematite, hammerstones, and miscellaneous bifacial tools. Only three identifiable vessels were recovered from the exterior pits and included one jar, one trailed bowl, and one plain bowl.

The Julien civic node appears to represent a pattern similar to what we have seen at the Range and Labras Lake sites. At least two forms of specialized structures are present, an early community storage facility and a sweat house. The three rectangular wall-trench structures that are aligned in a roughly northwest-southeast row appeared to be similar in nature. They all contain large amounts of ceramics, exotic materials, and other general debris. Structure 36 is especially interesting with its reused pit, cached Powell Plain jar, packed floor, numerous and diverse ceramic vessels, and exterior marker post. The two superimposed structures, on the other hand, stand out in their virtual absence of material and variance in alignment. Structure 197, the smaller of the two and lacking any internal features, may have been a storage facility. Structure 143, which possesses only a central hearth and a shallow pit, may have served as a cooking area.

BBB Motor Temple-Mortuary Ceremonial Node

It is with the examination of the mortuary/temple/religious rural ceremonial nodes that we see the greatest elaboration of Stirling phase hierarchical specialization. Two examples are present, the BBB Motor temple-mortuary ceremonial node and the Sponemann temple ceremonial node, both in close proximity of Cahokia and to one another.

The BBB Motor Stirling temple-mortuary ceremonial node contains 64 features, including 2 single-post basin structures with 10 internal features, 2 isolated wall trenches, 3 post pits, 12 posts, 23 burials and associated pits, and 12 isolated pit features (figure 5.9, table 5.8). Their internal organization

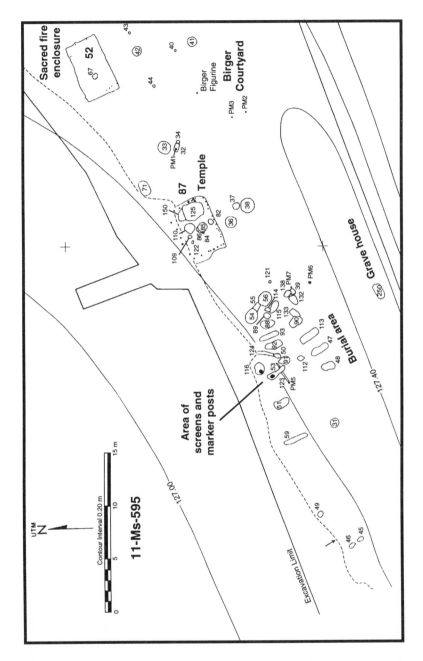

Figure 5.9 Stirling Phase BBB Motor Temple–Mortuary Ceremonial Node (after Emerson 1984, Figure 45).

Cahokia and the Archaeology of Power

Table 5.8 Stirling Phase BBB Motor Temple-Mortuary Ceremonial Node (BBBSCN)

Buildings		
Residential:	0	
Storage:	0	
Ceremonial:	1SP (F52) Area - 18.1 m^2 Sacred Fire	1SP (F87) Area - 16.5 m^2 Temple

Facilities		
Pit Count:	22 Pit Volume: 8.5 m^3	
Marker Posts:	15 Isolate WT: 2	
Ceremonial:	1 Redug (World Renewal?) Pit (F125) 12 Burial Pits 11 Burial Processing Pits 1 Grave House (F250) Birger Courtyard (4 m x 4 m; opens to south)	
Caches:	Birger Figurine	

Materials			
Exotics:	Galena - 4 (13.5 g) Hematite - 4 (11.1 g) Mica - 16 (1 g) Quartz Crystals - 2 (66.7 g) Figurines - 2 (3181 g)	Botanical:	Red Cedar Jimsonweed
Ceramics:	Jars 39 Bowls 5 Seed Jars 2 Beakers 4 Funnels 2 Total vessels 52	Status Ceramics:	7 Ramey Incised Jars 1 Trailed Jar 3 Lobed Jars 1 Effigy Bowl 1 Foreign Bowl 1 Cambered Jar 14 decorated

and association with a small courtyard indicates that all were part of a systematic layout of features at the site. (Feature and artifact information were published in Emerson 1995, appendices I-III; additional graphic and metric information was published in Emerson 1984.)

Structure 52, the northernmost building, is a rectangular-basin, single-post structure measuring 5.54 m northeast-southwest and 3.26 m northwest-southeast, with a floor area of about 18.1 m^2 (figure 5.10). A single subfloor hearth was found in the center of the southwestern portion of the

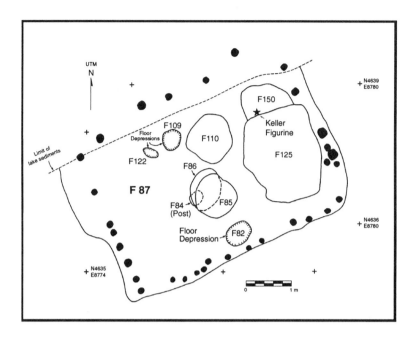

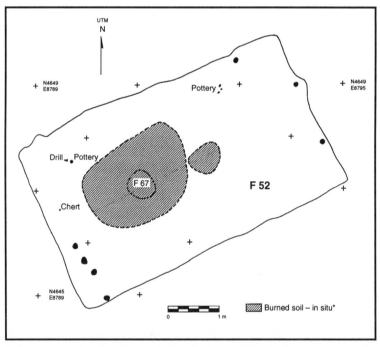

Figure 5.10 BBB Motor Site Structures 87 (Top; Emerson 1984, Figure 47) and 52 (Bottom; Emerson 1984, Figure 46).

structure. This hearth was surrounded by several distinct areas of burning, both on the floor and in the lower basin fill, covering a large portion of the structure. These fires represent a complex sequence of at least four different, sequential strata of burning, indicating numerous fires—perhaps for ceremonial cooking, medicine preparation, or even for the containment of a "sacred fire."

Structure 87, identified as a temple (figure 5.10), is located a little over 12 m to the southwest of Structure 52. The basin measured about 5.8 m northeast-southwest and exceeded 3.8 m in width. The single-post walls surrounded an interior area of 16.5 m². Nine interior features were distributed over the floor of the northeastern half of the building. These features consisted of three shallow depressions (Features 82, 109, and 122), two deep, large pits (Features 110 and 125), a shallow pit (Feature 150), and a central complex of two pits and a large support post (Features 85 and 86, and Post Mold 84).

Feature 150 was a shallow depression superimposed by the northern edge of Feature 125. It contained, however, the upper torso and head of the Keller figurine. Aside from the effigy, only a few flakes and bodysherds were recovered from the fill. Feature 125 was a large, irregular, deep rectangular pit measuring ca. 2 m x 1.7 m x 93 cm deep. This feature did not represent a single event but, rather, a number of prehistoric excavations, reexcavations, and subsequent filling episodes within a circumscribed area. It was similar in that regard to the "world renewal" pits encountered previously in some Lohmann phase nodal sites. It contained a large amount of material, much of it of an exotic nature. Feature 110 was another of the internal pits in Structure 87. It was a large circular pit that produced the only Cahokia trinotched point from the site.

Fifty-five percent of all the ceramic vessels (n = 30) in the temple-mortuary area came from Structure 87 and its internal features. Twenty vessels were recovered from Feature 125, consisting of 14 jars (including 3 Ramey Incised and 3 squash/pumpkin effigy jars), 3 beakers, 2 bowls, and a juice press. Feature 110 yielded 5 vessels, including 2 jars, a beaker, a seed jar, and a bowl. Five additional jars were found on the structure floor and depression (Feature 82). One of these was a Ramey Incised vessel.

Features 110 and 125 also contained the only mica recovered, consisting of 16 fragments, 9 of which were pierced for attachment to some covering. Feature 125 and Structure 87 also contained 3 pieces of galena that showed evidence of grinding for use as a pigment. The temple complex produced 10 abraders, several showing signs of use in pigment grinding, and 4 mano-metates.

An overall evaluation of the Structure 87 complex suggests the existence of a permanent, large, heavy, well-built superstructure requiring a central post. The internal layout of the subfloor features is interesting: the northeast half of the structure floor has been dug and redug, yet the southwestern floor is virtually clear of pits. That separation is clearly more than a coincidence and likely is associated with a functional or ritual division of the structure's interior space. That this division of the space had some longevity is documented by the obvious span of time involved in the multiple re-excavations of the Feature 125 complex.

Three features, located just to the southeast of Structure 87, appear closely tied to the structure's utilization and may have served as debris traps. The Structure 87 complex, in combination with the nearby Feature 71, Features 32-34, and Features 36-38, contained 48 vessels or 92% of all the vessels in the temple-mortuary complex. These vessels were concentrated in an area less than 10 m across. In addition, much of the remaining cultural debris was also concentrated in that area. Such a tight circumscription and high density of material is unusual in small sites.

Features 36, 37, and 38 contained six vessels, including a small cambered, noded jar and two Ramey Incised jars. Feature 38 contained a large number of items, including seven galena cubes, four abraders, a microdrill, and much burned clay and daub. It also held the base of the Keller figurine. It appears from the profile evidence that after the figurine was broken, it was deliberately inserted into the partially filled feature and then covered.

Approximately 6 m to the southwest of Structure 87 is a cluster of 30 features. Twelve of these pits were interpreted as burial features. All are oval or rectangular in plan view. A few of the features contained human skeletal remains, but most were "empty"—the bone having decayed. Milner (1984b: 396-397) has described the skeletal material from Features 88 and 113. Feature 88 contained only tooth enamel from permanent dentition. Feature 113 contained skeletal material, from at least three individuals, consisting of long bone and cranial fragments. At least one of the individuals buried in this feature was an infant. Numerous cut and scrape marks on the bones from this feature indicate postmortem mortuary processes that included the cutting of ligaments and muscle attachments and the removal of fat and flesh.

A few burials contained worked artifacts. In cases such as the whole Ramey Incised vessel in Feature 92 or the two quartz crystals in Feature 91, the items were clearly deliberate inclusions and can be considered grave goods. The single abraders found in Feature 55 and Feature 115, the piece of Missouri River clinker from Feature 51, and two decayed mussel fragments from Feature 88 are much more difficult to interpret. These latter items cannot be positively identified as grave goods, but given the general scarcity of cultural material in the grave fills, that is likely the best interpretation.

The orientation of the burials was fairly consistent. The layout of the majority of the burials consisted of two parallel rows running roughly northeast-southwest. One row of five burials lies close to the lakeshore, while one to two meters behind this row lies a second row consisting of four features. Two additional burials were located at the northeastern end of those two rows at a slightly skewed angle. It seems possible to recognize three groups of burials based on spatial organization and orientation; however, how they relate to one another is difficult to determine.

One burial feature deserves special attention. Feature 250 was located about seven meters to the southeast of the second row of burials. That specialized feature, with wall trenches on three sides, apparently possessed a superstructure. It appears to represent a "grave house" since similar features have been noted ethnohistorically in the Southeast (e.g., Lawson 1966[1709]). The exact function of this grave house is speculative, but Milner (1984b: 397) has noted evidence for postmortem processing in Feature 113. It is probable, then, that bodies were exposed, disarticulated, and cleaned at the site. In this context, Feature 250 may represent a processing location where bodies or disarticulated remains were stored prior to their final interment in a formal grave.

Eleven other pits were located in the burial cluster. Since they were spatially isolated from the rest of the temple/sacred fire zone and occurred within the confines of the burial area, they may have been associated with the burial complex and represent mortuary processing pits. Similar shaped pits with the same approximate dimensions were present in the Sand Prairie phase cemetery at the Florence Street site (Emerson et al. 1983). Such pits often included disarticulated human remains and grave goods, while others were emptied of their human remains but had clearly played a role during the processing of human remains. The majority of the BBB Motor site pits discussed here appear to have served a similar function.

A number of miscellaneous marker features were found in the northwestern part of the burial area between the burials and the lake shore. These included two wall trenches and three post pits with insertion/extraction ramps. Four post molds were also recorded. All these features seem to have served primarily as pole markers or as wall screens.

A number of features placed in an area created a "courtyard" surrounding the Birger figurine (figure 5.9). Three of these were pits (Features 33, 41, and 42), while the remainder were either posts (Features 40, 43, and 44, and Post Molds 2-3) or post pit/post combinations (Features 32 and 34, and Post Mold 1). Features 41 and 42 were both shallow pits that contained little material. Feature 33 contained numerous cultural items, especially rough rocks, burned clay, and 52 fragments of mud dauber nests. It also contained a number of ceramic fragments. Immediately to the south of Feature 33 is the Feature 32/Feature 34/PM 1 complex. This feature group appeared to have consisted of two paired posts with a shallow pit linking them. Feature 32 also contained a number of mud dauber nests. When taken together, Features 32-34 contained nine vessels, including six jars, a seed jar, a bowl, and a juice press. Although no Ramey Incised rims were found in this group, the only Ramey Incised bodysherds (six) recovered from the site were from Features 32 and 33 (deposited as offerings or, perhaps, reflecting the intense use of Ramey Incised vessels in this specific area?).

There is an intriguing pattern in the arrangement of the pits and posts around the Birger figurine. The figurine was buried in a small pit just large enough to contain it. For a distance of four meters in every direction about this pit a cleared area was created. However, at ca. 4 m in each cardinal direction, one finds either a post, a pit, or a post-pit combination. To the north is located a post (Feature 44), and in the opposite direction are two posts (Post Molds 2-3); to the east are a pit (Feature 41) and a post (Feature 40), and to the west are a group of posts and a pit (Features 32 and 34 and Post Mold 1). None of these placements is precise, either in terms of direction or distance. No astronomical or precise directional function is attributed to these items, yet their placement on the cardinal points did not seem random. It is significant that an area of a little over 50 m^2 about the Birger figurine was kept clear of all pits and posts. In addition, the loose arrangement, roughly along the cardinal directions, of some of these features seems more than coincidental. The pattern of a cleared ritual and/or courtyard area associated with multiple poles of ritual significance, from which ritual objects may have been suspended or which may have functioned to demarcate boundaries, was common among the Southeastern groups as well as being noted previously in American Bottom Emergent Mississippian and Mississippian sites.

The artifact assemblage from this ceremonial node is unique. Fifty-two vessels were present, with the dominant form being the jar. Jars constituted 74.9% of the recovered vessels with 39 examples (including 3 effigy jars [7.7%]). The 5 examples of bowls (including 1 effigy bowl) formed the next largest group at 9.6%. All other vessel forms occurred only in minor proportions: 4 beakers (7.7%), 2 juice presses (3.9%), and 2 seed jars (3.9%).

Other artifacts of note include a small clay pipe bowl fragment, a possible tubular pipe, and two flint clay figurines. The Birger figurine is large: 20 cm high and weighing 2,709 g. The broken Keller figurine's base was recovered from Feature 38 and its torso from Feature 150. It is 13 cm high and weighs 472 g. These figurines are illustrated and discussed in chapter 7.

Lucy Whalley's (1984: 321–335) ethnobotanical analysis generally confirmed the similarity of the site's assemblage of nuts, maize, and starchy seed complex with that recovered from other Mississippian sites. The most striking aspect of the assemblage, however, was the amazingly high recovery rate of Eastern red cedar (*Juniperus virginiana*). A full 25.6% of the identifiable wood charcoal was red cedar (compared to its virtual absence at contemporaneous sites such as Julien and Turner). Also of importance was the unique recovery of *Datura,* a possible hallucinogen, from the temple structure.

As summarized by Whalley (1984: 333–334):

> [These] plant remains . . . conformed to the Mississippian plant pattern found at other Mississippian components in the American Bottom. . . . Maize, nutshell, seeds of the starchy seed complex, and oak and hickory wood were ubiquitous, while seeds of sunflower, various grasses, wild bean, black nightshade . . . occurred frequently. The only, and perhaps significant, exception to this pattern at the BBB Motor site was the high percentage of red cedar recovered and the presence of two *Datura stramonium* (jimson weed) seeds. These plant remains are evocative since references can be found in the ethnohistoric literature to their use in the curative practices and rituals of eastern North American Indians.

The symbolic and ritual nature of these plants made an important contribution to understanding the nature of the site and will be discussed more fully later in this volume.

The BBB Motor site temple–mortuary node can be seen as a clear development out of the previous Lohmann priest–mortuary ceremonial node and, in fact, I have suggested that the two are sequential and intimately related symbolically and ritually. The early Stirling complex contained a temple structure with extensive ritual debris, including exotic minerals, ritual vessels, a reused pit feature, quartz crystals, pipes, hallucinogenic plants, red cedar, and a spectacular figurine; an enclosure for the "sacred fire"; a courtyard with a buried cult figurine; and numerous burials.

As in the Lohmann mortuary program, recognizable groups of burials may have represented social divisions. While mortuary goods were limited, one burial did contain a Ramey Incised vessel and another quartz crystals, perhaps indicating some special religious position and/or status. Burials were limited and seemed to indicate that only a segment of the society was interred there. A special feature present was a grave house near the edge of the site, supporting the idea that the mortuary program included exposure and defleshing of the body on site in some cases.

As similar as they are, significant shifts can be seen between the Lohmann and Stirling components at the BBB Motor site. The community-centered aspects of the Lohmann mortuary complex are now lacking, and the nature and the organizational complexity of the later component suggests to me the presence of religious and/or mortuary specialists. The Stirling temple complex suggests an increasingly restricted access to its mortuary and fertility rituals, which probably were confined to a small group of elite leaders and their families.

These trends of both elaboration and restriction blended with consolidation continued into the later parts of the Stirling phase, as seen at the Sponemann ceremonial center discussed in the following section. Sponemann has a number of buildings organized about a courtyard. These buildings include a temple, storage facility, sacred fire enclosure, renewal pits, isolated marker posts, and wall trenches. The complex is associated with another cluster of elite residential buildings organized about a courtyard to the south. The list of status items from the Sponemann site is similar to that at BBB Motor and includes items such as exotic minerals, stone figurines, quartz crystals, ritual vessels, and red cedar.

Sponemann Ceremonial Node

The Sponemann site is located on the outer bank ridge of the Edelhardt Lake meander scar, just a little over 1 km north of the BBB Motor site, and 4 km northeast of Cahokia's Monks Mound (figure 3.1). It contains 107 Stirling phase features, including 12 structures, that were analyzed and reported by Douglas K. Jackson, Andrew C. Fortier, and Joyce A. Williams (Jackson et al. 1991). Their report, as well as my examination of much of the original data, form the basis for the following summary, evaluation, and in some cases, reinterpretation of the site.

The general physiography and available resources were similar to those depicted for the BBB Motor site, although the Sponemann complex was located on a larger, higher land form, well above the adjacent Edelhardt Lake marsh. Excavated evidence of Stirling phase utilization consisted of two spatially distinct areas representing a ceremonial complex (figure 5.11) with special structures, pits, and exotic artifacts, including stone figurines and an adjacent residential area. My focus is on the ceremonial complex.

Fortier (1991a: 49-124) associated 63 features with the ceremonial complex, including 8 structures with 19 interior features, plus an additional 23 external pits, 5 isolated wall trenches, 6 post molds, and 1 hearth (figure 5.11, table 5.9).

The structures are organized in a U-shaped pattern demarcating a three-sided plaza or courtyard that is open to the northwest. On the north side of the plaza lies Structure 282, interpreted by the excavators as a "temple,"

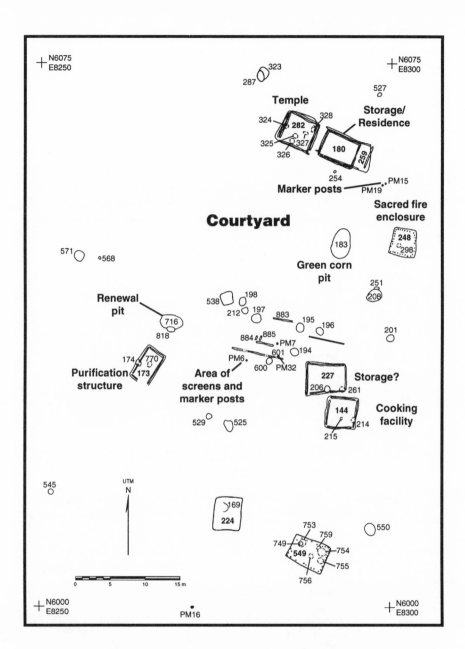

Figure 5.11 Stirling Phase Sponemann Ceremonial Node (Jackson et al. 1991, Figure 6.2).

Table 5.9 Stirling Phase Sponemann Ceremonial Node (SPCN)

Buildings

Residential/ Storage:	2 Sequential Buildings 1WT(F180/259) Area: 15.4 m^2	1WT(F180/259) Area: 21 m^2	
Storage/ Activity:	1WT(F173) Area: 10.9 m^2	1WT(F227) Area: 19.3 m^2	1WT(F144) Area: 14.1 m^2
Ceremonial:	1WT(F282) Area: 16.5 m^2 Temple	1SP(F248) Area: 10.9 m^2 Sacred Fire/Sweat Lodge?	

Facilities

Pits: 40   Volume: 15.5 m^3

Marker Posts: 6+   Isolated WT: 5

Ceremonial: Courtyard (23 m x 23 m [529 m^2], opens to west)
1 Redug (World Renewal) Pit (F716)
2 Green Corn Pits (F183 & 208)

Caches: Microdrill Cache (F571)

Materials

Exotics: Galena – 4 (314.7 g)   Botanical: Red Cedar
Hematite – 10 (76.2 g)   Tobacco
Quartz Crystals – 1 (.7 g)
Limonite – 16 (15.4 g)
Flint Clay Figurines 3+ (533 pieces, 1,524.8 g)
Crinoid Bead – 1

Ceramics:	Jars	104	Status/Ritual Ceramics:
	Bowls	23	21 Ramey Incised Jars
	Seed Jars	10	1 Effigy Jar
	Beakers	11	1 Effigy Bowl
	Pans	17	<u>4 Minibeakers and Bottles</u>
	Funnels	2	27 decorated
	Minibeakers	2	
	Long–Necked Bottle	1	
	Hooded Bottle	1	
	Carinated Bowl	1	
	<u>Lobed Jar</u>	<u>1</u>	
	Total vessels	173	

---

while immediately to the east is Structure 180/259, which appears to be a residence. The lone square, single-post structure (Feature 248) that marked the eastern end of the courtyard was interpreted as a "sweat house." The southern side of the courtyard was difficult to interpret since it included a number of structures and features. The westernmost rectangular wall-trench structure (Feature 173) was tentatively suggested by Fortier to be a "purification" house. To the east of this structure, separating it from Structures 144 and 227, are a series of single wall trenches generally paralleling the plaza's long axis. Structure 144 is an approximately square wall-trench structure on the southeastern corner of the plaza, interpreted as a "special food preparation household." Immediately north of Structure 144 is the rectangular wall-trench Structure 227 of unknown function. Forming a second row of structures farther south of the courtyard are Structures 224 (to the west) and 549 (to the east). Their association with the ceremonial complex is problematical.

The temple (Structure 282, figure 5.12) is a rectangular wall-trench building, on the northwest corner of the courtyard, measuring 16.5 m². The presence on three sides of double wall trenches, numerous interior support posts, three distinct floors, and a large central support post pit [similar to Feature 84 in the temple at the BBB Motor site] suggested rebuilding and a long use life. The structure included "three broken bauxite [flint clay]figurines, two miniature beakers, one unique miniature, white-slipped, noded applique jar [interpreted as an effigy conch dipper], an effigy hooded water bottle, a quartz crystal, a Mill Creek hoe-spade cache, and a Ramey Incised jar" (Fortier 1991a: 55), as well as numerous other ceramic vessels and lithic tools. The figurines appeared to have been shattered prior to their deposition in the structure and the subsequent fire. Similar figurine fragments were scattered throughout a number of features within the ceremonial complex. This situation appears analogous to the deposition pattern of the Keller figurine at BBB Motor. An internal prepared(?) hearth contained only charcoal from red cedar. Additional ethnobotanical remains recovered from the structure included a large number of sunflower seeds, cane, maize, black nightshade, wild bean, maygrass, chenopod, and tobacco seeds. The structure's utilization ended in an apparently intentional conflagration that destroyed it and its contexts.

Less than one meter to the east of the temple, on an identical orientation, is Structure 180/259, a rectangular, wall-trench building representing an original structure (15.34 m²) expanded to a larger one (21 m²). The structure contains no interior pits with the exception of a central post pit (figure 5.12). Debris recovered included primarily lithic materials, such as cores and flakes, hammerstones, a drill, a scraper, and a celt, although four jars,

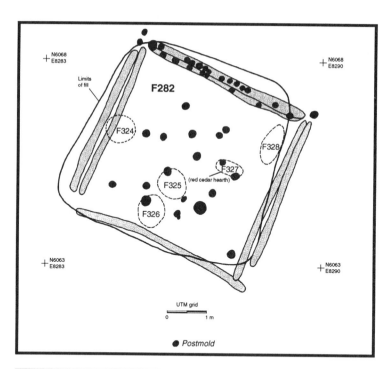

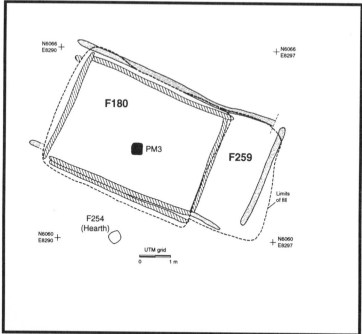

Figure 5.12 Sponemann Site Structures 282 (Top; Jackson et al. 1991,
Figure 6.3), 180, and 259 (Bottom; Jackson et al. 1991, Figure 6.6).

Cahokia and the Archaeology of Power

one pan and four bowls were present. The structure has been interpreted as either a residence for guardians of the temple or as a restricted entryway into the temple (Fortier 1991a: 70). It is possible it was a storage facility for the temple.

The unique, square, single-post building on the eastern end of the courtyard, Structure 248 (figure 5.13), has been suggested to be a "sweat or ritual purification house." Its small size, 3.4 m by 3.2 m (10.88 m²), and the presence of a single hearth as the only interior feature could be conducive to such an interpretation. Maize kernels were abundant in this structure. Red cedar was the predominant wood charcoal, although cane was also burned in the hearth. A single Ramey Incised vessel, a small amount of sandstone, and chert were recovered. I believe it is more likely a "sacred fire enclosure" since all other known sweat houses in the American Bottom were circular and devoid of artifacts.

Three buildings bordered the southern side of the courtyard. Structure 173 (figure 5.13) is of rectangular wall-trench construction and measured 10.91 m² with a single central hearth. This structure stands out from others because of the high density of red cedar remains in the hearth and as structural members. Cane was also present. Little material was present and appeared to be generalized midden debris, with the exception of a Ramey knife fragment. Emphasizing the "red" coloration of a number of items such as red cedar and pokeweed or "redweed," Fortier indicated this may have been a "red" cabin linked to purification in historic Green Corn analogies (1991a: 77), with the Structure 282 complex being the opposed "white" cabin.

Structures 227 and 144, in the southeastern corner of the courtyard, are separated by less than one meter. Structure 227 (figure 5.14), which abuts the courtyard, is oriented roughly parallel to the plaza. It was a large building, measuring 19.26 m², with only a single pit. Extensive material was recovered, including a dozen sandstone slot abraders, fragments of two flint clay figurines, some chert, and Ramey Incised and other vessels. Little evidence was present to indicate any ceremonial function. Noting that the building was not burned, Fortier (1991a: 81) commented that the structure is atypical of Stirling phase residential domiciles, and its function is problematical. Its adjoining Structure 144, on the other hand, was destroyed by fire. Since Structure 227, less than a meter away, was unburned, this indicates the two structures were not contemporaneous.

Structure 144 (figure 5.14) was a roughly square building 3.8 m by 3.71 m (14.1 m²) with a heavily burned hearth and an interior shallow basin. The structure's floor contained six grinding stones, a metate, two slot abraders, chert scrapers, and a biface. A Ramey Incised jar and an apparently ritually

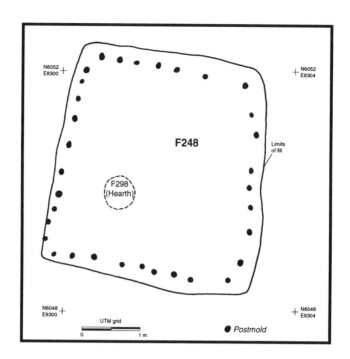

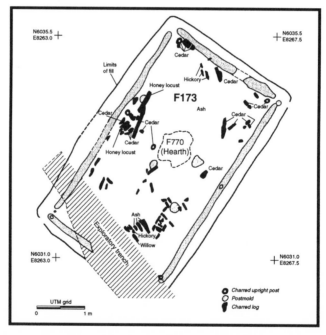

Figure 5.13 Sponemann Site Structures 248 (Top; Jackson et al. 1991, Figure 6.7) and 173 (Bottom; Jackson et al. 1991, Figure 6.8).

Cahokia and the Archaeology of Power

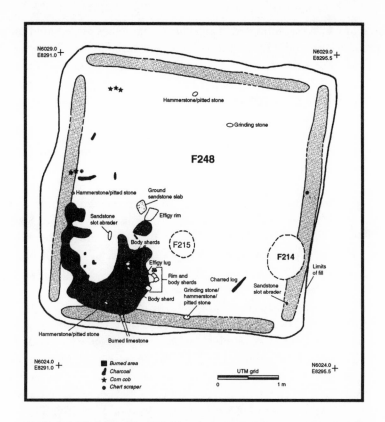

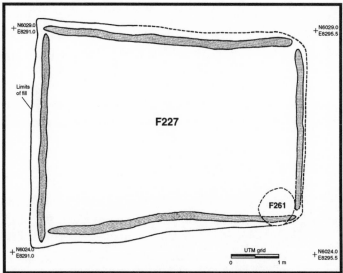

Figure 5.14 Sponemann Site Structures 144 (Jackson et al. 1991, Figure 6.9) and 227 (Jackson et al. 1991, Figure 6.10).

killed effigy bowl with inward facing "bear" effigy lugs represented the vessels present. Although not mentioned in the feature discussion, the building was shown (Fortier 1991b: 278, figure 9.1) as containing figurine fragments. Considering the grinding tools, Fortier (1991a: 81) suggested the structure was a specialized food preparation facility, although he notes the lack of maize and the absence of storage pits.

Three isolated wall trenches are aligned running east-west along the southern edge of the courtyard. Two short wall trenches run at right angles to the other trenches (see figure 5.11). Three isolated marker post molds were also present. As noted at the BBB Motor site, such isolated wall trenches and posts are difficult to interpret but may have represented screens or sheds associated with the plaza. Two posts are located just to the east of Structure 180/259, marking the northeast corner of the courtyard. Far to the south another large post pit with a diameter of 45 cm is located. The use of marker posts is common in southeastern ethnographic accounts and is assumed to have played a similar role in Mississippian spatial symbolism.

A single, unique, clay-lined, prepared hearth was placed immediately between Structure 180/259 and the courtyard and presumably was associated with the structures. A number of external pits were selected for individual discussion by Fortier (1991a: 89-98) because of their unusual size, placement, and contents. Feature 183 is a large, basin-shaped pit located centrally at the eastern end of the courtyard, about six meters to the west of Structure 248. It is 4.14 m x 2.5 m x 0.63 m deep (2582.5 dm^3). The artifact and ecofact contents were impressive, consisting of

> 17.2% of all material by weight recovered by the Ceremonial Complex. . . .
> 25% of all identifiable ceramic vessels . . . 23.8% of all the Ramey Incised
> vessels . . . two "bauxite" figurine fragments . . . the only gneiss . . . a single,
> unique crinoid stem bead . . . the only notched Cahokia type projectile point
> . . . A total of 47 vessels [were] identifiable and include[d] jars (59%), bowls,
> beakers, pans, seed jars, and one funnel. The five Ramey Incised vessels found
> were highly fragmented and dispersed. (Fortier 1991a: 94)

Jackson (1991: table 7.29) noted the presence of 29 jars, 5 bowls, 2 pans, 2 beakers, 3 seed jars, and 1 funnel. Massive amounts of carbonized maize cobs and acorns were identified, as well as red cedar, maygrass, sunflower, wild bean, tobacco, panicum, chenopodium, marsh elder, and black nightshade. Only the temple, Structure 282, contained an equal diversity of ecofactual material.

Feature 208, which lies south of Structure 248 and Feature 183, contained large amounts of carbonized maize kernels, some black nightshade, and five ceramic vessels. It was lacking in ceremonial-related ethnobotanical items such as red cedar. It did contain a one-of-a-kind white sand lens that Fortier (1991a: 97) noted seemed similar to ethnohistoric accounts of the use of white sand to seal off contaminated substances on floors and other surfaces and the general association of "white" with purity.

Feature 716 lies just to the north of Structure 173, between it and the plaza. It is a massive pit measuring 3.3 x 1.87 x 0.87 m (4565.9 dm³). Fourteen vessels were excavated, including 8 jars (3 Ramey Incised), 2 bowls, 1 pan, 1 beaker, 1 seed jar, and 1 funnel. Its fill suggests that the pit was reused in a manner similar to Feature 125 at BBB Motor. It had a minimum of three distinct episodes of use and was redug at least once.

Some of the site's uniqueness is reflected in its associated material assemblage. Jackson (1991) described a total of 173 identifiable vessels from the component, including 104 (60.1%) jars (21 of which were Ramey Incised), 23 (13.3%) bowls, 11 (6.4%) beakers, 17 (9.8%) pans, 10 (5.8%) seed jars, 2 (1.2%) funnels, 2 (1.2%) miniature beakers, and 1 (0.6%) example each of a long-neck bottle, hooded bottle, carinated bowl, and lobed "squash" effigy jar (Jackson 1991: table 7.12).

It is a telling comment on the special nature of this assemblage that flint clay (n=533) was the second most numerous nonchert lithic material recovered, accounting for 16.3% of the items by count (Williams 1991: 256). Other exotic lithics seem limited, however, with only a single quartz crystal recovered from the temple, Structure 282, and only a single galena fragment and a crinoid bead found. Sandstone abraders and metates were common, as were drills (14, 10 of which were microdrills); both may have been related to specialized activities. In such sites it is becoming clear that the ethnobotanical evidence is a critical factor in determining specialized ritual use of a Mississippian feature complex (cf. Whalley 1984; Parker 1991). Parker's (1991) analysis of the Sponemann ceremonial complex indicated that, like all of the other Stirling phase sites analyzed in the American Bottom, the complex contained a standard assemblage of Mississippian subsistence and other ethnobotanical materials, including domesticates (predominately maize), starchy and oily seeds, nuts, and wood charcoal. What sets ritual sites, such as BBB Motor and Sponemann, apart from other Stirling phase sites is the presence of special plants like red cedar and plant species with medicinal and/or narcotic value.

Sponemann, like BBB Motor, was marked by the high frequency of red cedar charcoal (27.4% and 12.2% of identified fragments), while Parker (1991: 310) notes other Mississippian sites "without archaeological evidence of ceremonial spaces or activities, including Turner, Robert Schneider, Julien, and Range sites, either had no identifiable red cedar or negligible amounts (<1% of wood fragments)." Several features at Sponemann contained unusual amounts of red cedar (Parker 1991: 310). Structure 173 enclosed a hearth (Feature 770) that contained a unique group of ethnobotanical remains, including red cedar, monocots stems, and maygrass. This structure was also remarkable in the extensive use of red cedar as construction members. Hearth Feature 298, located in Structure 248, also had a high concentration of red cedar charcoal.

The only other ritual plant remain recognized by Parker (1991: 316-317) was tobacco, which is extensively referenced in North American ethnohistoric and ethnographic accounts as having had both magicoreligious and social utilization by native peoples. Other plants identified at the site, such as sumac, black nightshade, sunflowers, and Kentucky coffee tree, may have medicinal or religious connotations in the ethnographic literature (cf. King 1984), but that use is much more difficult to verify in a prehistoric context.

The excavators' analyses (Jackson et al. 1991; most specifically Fortier 1991c: 339-348) stressed the similarity of ritual aspects of the Sponemann site Stirling component to Eastern Woodlands native Busk or Green Corn ceremonialism. To this end many of the structures and features of the defined ceremonial complex have been interpreted as having specific functions based on ethnohistoric analogies. Fortier (1991c: 339-348) focused his interpretation of this complex on aspects related to Busk ceremonialism and its role in Middle Mississippian religious activities. While he concentrated his interpretation most centrally on arguments of a direct connection between the Sponemann evidence and historic Busk ceremonialism, in general, his conclusions can be seen to affirm, as Prentice (1986a) and I (Emerson 1982, 1989) had earlier, that fertility symbolism had a strong presence in Cahokia Middle Mississippian cosmology. He specifically interpreted the complex as:

> a specialized ritual center that functioned primarily as a busk or annual purification-harvest nodal point. It is argued that many of the refuse and discarded artifacts recovered from this complex do not represent ordinary habitation debris, but the remains of activities directly associated with one or more episodes of the busk celebration. Most of these remains represent typical Stirling phase refuse, but some of the artifacts and the specialized nature of the features in this complex indicate ritual and not residential activity. It is also proposed that the same individuals may have lived in the nearby Residential Complex and in other associated household communities in this locality.

In size and complexity the Sponemann ceremonial node dwarfs the isolated BBB Motor nodes with its multiple specialized buildings and large residential areas. This node represents the epitome of rural Stirling religious and ceremonial elaboration. It contained many of the features we have seen in the previous example at the BBB Motor Stirling component, with the major exception of the mortuary complex. It appears that the fertility symbolism that first emerged at the BBB Motor site became the dominating ritualism at Sponemann to the exclusion of mortuary rituals. (Although, as John Kelly, personal communication 1996, has pointed out, life and death are intimately related aspects of life cycle/fertility symbolism.) What led to the separation of these two previously linked symbolic systems is not clear, although it may have signaled the increasing importance of elite linkage with fertility symbolism as a political expression of power.

MOOREHEAD RURAL SETTLEMENT

It was in the examination of Moorehead and Sand Prairie phase rural settlements that Mehrer (1988: 120-125) suggested there may have been a continuation of the nodal concept into those two later phases that had heretofore been poorly recognized. While our sample of rural Moorehead phase settlements was restricted to five examples at the Julien and Turner-DeMange sites, they showed a very distinctive pattern. The Moorehead phase typical households were simple indeed, usually consisting of a single structure with a few interior and exterior processing and storage pits. The Moorehead phase nodal site at Julien was identified as consisting of possibly two related clusters of structures, along the northeast-trending ridge, separated by about 70 m. The one structure cluster (figure 5.15), which Mehrer tentatively identified as JUL-6, is part of a superimposed complex of at least eight structures/rebuildings and several dozen pit features.

One superimposed set of features represents three fairly typical wall-trench structures. Another cluster has at least four structures of which several had only three sides, and one had no walls at all. Between these two clusters is a single wall-trench structure. Virtually all of those structures, including the three-sided and wall-less buildings (with the possible exception of Structure 45, which may have represented a Stirling building), belonged to the Moorehead phase.

By taking the final built structure in each cluster (i.e., essentially adopting a minimalist view), Mehrer was able to reduce it to two wall-trench structures (Structures 5 and 7) with a small accompanying rectangular basin (Structure[?] 231) without wall trenches or posts. Without a very detailed reanalysis of this entire complex, I do not believe we have sufficient information to reasonably define, in its entirety, the Moorehead component or to establish the contemporaneity of individual structures between clusters (this is not to say that Mehrer's first approximation is not correct). Consequently, I will not include it in any detail in this summary and analysis, although I do not

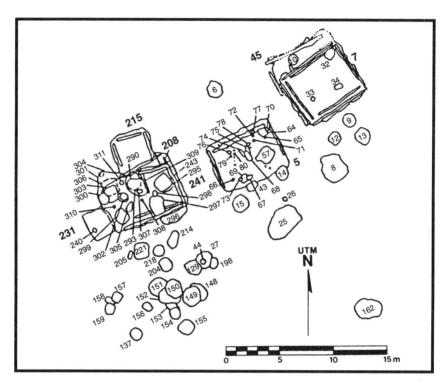

Figure 5.15 Moorehead Phase Julien Housecluster (after Milner with Williams 1984, Pocket Map).

want to dismiss this area because it presents important insights into the re-use of an area, imputing a special status to such a location and reinforcing the centrality aspect of the Structure 31 function as community-centered.

Julien Civic Node

The other possible nodal cluster (figure 5.16, table 5.10), identified by Mehrer as JUL-7, included Structure 3 and Structure 31 at the Julien site. However, in examining the available data, the evidence for the inclusion of Structure 3 in this Moorehead phase cluster appeared, at best, inconclusive. This small (4.52 m x 4.28 m; 19.35 m²), roughly square wall-trench structure has two small interior pits and one small exterior pit along a wall. The only ceramics recovered were two shell-tempered bowl rimsherds. The structure lies equi-distant between Stirling (Structure 36), Moorehead (Structure 31), and Moorehead/Sand Prairie (Structure 85) structures, so propinquity alone did not provide a phase identification.

Cahokia and the Archaeology of Power

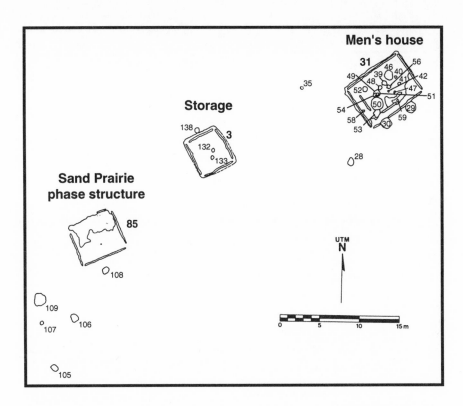

Men's house

Storage

Sand Prairie phase structure

Figure 5.16 Moorehead Phase Julien Civic Node (after Milner with Williams 1984, Pocket Map).

This situation led me to reexamine the ceramic, artifactual, locational, and structural nature of Structures 31, 3, and 85 since those three buildings shared a number of common attributes. They fell into a northeast-southwest trending line within 15 m of one another and were separated by at least 55 m from the closest other Moorehead features. All three structures were burned. All three contained or were associated with ceramic assemblages that may be considered related to the Moorehead phase. Structure 85 had no rims in it, but five pits (figure 5.16) to the south of it did contain ceramics that may have been associated. Only six vessels, three cordmarked jars, two plain jars, and a plain bowl, were recovered. Although only four jars could be measured, the mean RPR value of this assemblage was 0.355, somewhat low compared to other Moorehead components (i.e., 0.421 in Holley 1989: 202) and when compared to the mean RPR of 0.402 for the Structure 31 complex. This single wall-trench building was moderate in size (5.62 m x 5.24 m; 29.45 m²) with no internal pits.

Table 5.10 Moorehead Phase Julien Civic Node (JULMCN)

Buildings			
Residential:	0		
Storage or Activity:	1WT (F3) Area - 19.35 m^2		
Ceremonial and Communal:	1WT (F31) Area - 42 m^2 w/benches		

Facilities			
Pit Count:	13	Pit Volume: 3.47 m^3	
Marker Post:	0		
Ceremonial:	0		
Caches:	72 Projectile Points (F50)		

Materials			
Exotics:	Galena – 3 (26.7 g) Hematite – 8 (27.2 g)		
Ceramics:	Jars	15	Status/Ritual Ceramics:
	Bowls	7	2 decorated bowls
	Beaker	1	
	Pinch Pot	1	
	Total vessels	24	

Structure 85 had much less debris present than the other two structures but did include a large amount of limestone, a few flakes, and a single flake point. Feature 109, which was a moderate size exterior pit that appeared associated with the structure, contained whelk shell. The size, difference in debris density, the different RPR value, and the presence of exterior pits seemed to point to both a chronological and a functional difference from Structures 31 and 3. None of the above evidence is conclusive, but it does seem there is reasonable evidence *not to associate it with Structures 31 and 3* but to affirm it as a Sand Prairie structure.

The data support Mehrer's identification of a Moorehead cluster at Julien that consisted of Structures 31 and 3, with the latter building serving as an auxiliary feature to the complex Structure 31 facility. There was some support for this approach simply in terms of the contents of the structure. Structure 3 was laden with materials very similar in nature to Structure 31. It had a large number of bifacial tools, including hoe, knife, and biface fragments, sandstone abraders, hammerstones, Missouri River clinker, flakes, and projectile points. There were eight whole flake points and at least six point fragments present. Three pieces of hematite were recovered, along with an extensive amount of limestone, several pieces in slab form.

Structure 31 at Julien, on the other hand, is well documented and can be placed in the Moorehead phase with assurance. It is a single wall-trench structure well isolated from the other 10 possible Moorehead phase buildings at Julien and is placed just off the ridge crest east of the previously occupied Stirling nodal point. Only two exterior shallow pits lie within any distance of the building. This structure is one of the few described individually by Milner (Milner with Williams 1984: 40-44) because of its unusual nature. It is the largest building at Julien, measuring 7.5 m x 5.6 m (42 m^2), with seven interior pits, five interior hearths, four interior posts, and two interior wall trenches. The interior wall trenches, each about two meters long, stretched out from the southern corner of the structure and were clearly bench supports. The building floor contained numerous materials, including limestone (in one instance with red pigment rubbed on it), sandstone, flakes, abraders, hammerstones, four arrow points (one tri-notched with red pigment rubbed on it), two fragments of galena, and one of hematite.

Features 39, 40, 41, and 42 were restricted shallow surface hearths, while Feature 49 was ca. 82 cm in diameter and 15 cm deep. Three large (+30 cm diameter) deep post molds (Features 51, 54, and 56) clustered in the central area of the structure and may have served as central supports. These hearths and posts contained virtually no material except for one point in Feature 54. Another single large post (Feature 59), which contained a point fragment, was at the end of the bench support along the southeast wall. Also with little debris (with the exception of a single flake point) were Features 47, 48, and 58, which were shallow floor depressions. Features 46, 50, 52, and 53, however, were sizable storage pits, several being over 1 m in diameter. Three of these pits had few materials in them—Feature 46 contained rough rocks, flakes, cores, abraders, and a flake point; Feature 52, rough rock, and flakes; and Feature 53, limestone and flakes. Feature 50, located in the southern corner of the structure, was a different case. In its bottom layers it contained 72 flake points. It was also rich in other materials including abraders, hammerstones, metates, biface and hoe fragments, flakes, rough rocks, four pieces of hematite, and one fragment of galena.

Structure 31 and Feature 50 contained the majority of the recovered ceramic vessels (92%). Twenty-two identifiable vessels were present, including 15 plain jars (3 with cordmarked bodies), 5 bowls (1 trailed and 1 narrow-rimmed with decorated lip), 1 beaker, and 1 pinch pot. The jars provided a mean RPR value of 0.402, which was not unreasonable for a Moorehead assemblage.

The internal structure of the Moorehead phase node is different from those that preceded it. It appears to consist of a single specialized structure, apparently designed for community-centered use. I find Milner's suggestion that it was a "men's house" to be reasonable, if interpreted in a broad sense. Structure 3 seems to represent an auxiliary storage and/or work area. Structure 31 does differ from the other Moorehead buildings in its unique size and internal layout and features and in its bountiful supply of projectile points, exotic materials, and other items of material culture. To some extent Structure 3 shares in these attributes. There are no obvious, *directly associated* residential structures; instead a number of residential structures which appear roughly contemporaneous with the community building are scattered along the ridge. The importance of the superimposed cluster of eight structures, a number of which were unique or specialized facilities, discussed earlier certainly supports the special status given this locale. Whether these buildings should be considered as part of the "greater" nodal point is uncertain.

In passing, I should address the issue of the disappearance of the Stirling phase sweat house from the rural civic nodes. While we do not have extensive evidence of Moorehead nodal organization, what we do have suggests that the Stirling symbolism and ritualism associated with sweat houses was no longer relevant or had been transformed to some other sphere not visible in the archaeological record. Two sites, however, may call this into question. Limited testing of the Lawrence Primas site (Pauketat and Woods 1986) provided information on a complex rectangular wall-trench structure dating to a Moorehead period. A possible oval, single-post structure with a hearth was excavated at a distance of 36 m from this structure, but given the limited testing performed at the site, no direct evidence exists to associate it with the Moorehead component. Very limited testing of an area adjacent to the East St. Louis Stone Quarry mortuary assemblage also revealed portions of two circular structures (Esarey 1983). The work was very preliminary in nature and it was not possible to determine if these were associated with the mortuary complex. Consequently, until more conclusive evidence is presented, it appears that the rural sweat house was exclusively limited to the Stirling phase.

SAND PRAIRIE RURAL SETTLEMENT

Four Sand Prairie feature clusters were included in Mehrer's examination (1988: 123-125) of rural settlement—three from Julien and one from the Florence Street site. Two of the Julien households simply included a large structure with no interior pits and no or few exterior pits. The Structure 85 group of features discussed above in regard to the Moorehead Structure 31 complex represents such a household, as does Structure 91, a burned building with a moderate assemblage of vessels on the floor.

Julien Nodal Housecluster

A possible nodal housecluster, labeled JUL 11 by Mehrer, was recognizably different from the single Sand Prairie households by its inclusion of three structures and multiple pits. The group includes Structures 2, 17, and 82, roughly grouped about a small courtyard with three pits in its central area (figure 5.17, table 5.11). Structure 2 includes one rebuilding episode, when it was expanded from a moderate-sized wall-trench structure measuring 4.87 m x 3.77 m (18.36 m²) to a fairly large one of 6.28 m x 4.94 m (31.02 m²).

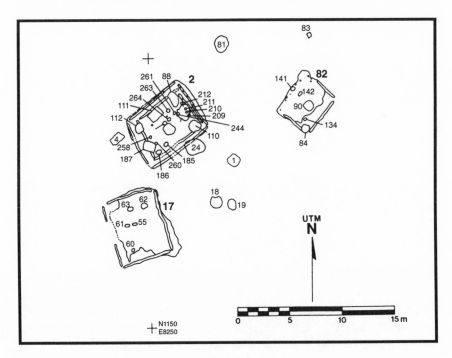

Figure 5.17 Sand Prairie Phase Julien Nodal Housecluster (after Milner with Williams 1984, Pocket Map).

Table 5.11 Sand Prairie Phase Julien Nodal Housecluster (JULSPNH)

Buildings				
Residential:	2 Sequential Buildings			
	1WT(F2)	1WT(F2)	1WT(F82)	1WT(F17)
	Area: 18.4 m^2	Area: 31 m^2	Area: 14.8 m^2	Area: 28.5 m^2
Ceremonial:	0			

Facilities		
Pits:	24	Volume: 6.47 m^3
Caches:	4 Ramey Knives, Adze – Floor Cache	
	Hickory Nuts – Floor Cache	
	5 Hoes, Abrader, Deer Mandible – F187	

Materials		
Exotics:	Galena – 6 (19.8 g)	
	Hematite – 18 (160.1 g)	
	Quartz Crystals – 1 (3.9 g)	
	Fire Clay Pendant – 1 (2 g)	
	Whelk Shell – Present	
	Galena Bead – 1	
Ceramics:	Jars 41	Ritual/Status Ceramics:
	Bowls 27	1 Decorated Plate
	Bottles 6	1 Effigy Bowl?
	Plate 1	
	Pan 1	
	Pinch Pots 4	
	Funnels 2	
	Total vessels 82	

The first wall-trench structure contained virtually no interior pits, but the
second had a large, deep storage pit in each corner (Features 88, 110, 112,
and 187) and one along the center of the northwest wall (Feature 111).
There were 10 small features representing posts ca. 30 cm in diameter, as
well as a number of smaller posts in the floor. Considering their disposition,
they probably represented multiple roof supports. The building, with large
portions of burned floor, shows evidence of having been destroyed by fire.

In the southwest corner of the floor there was a cache of four Ramey
knives and an adze as well as a floor cache of hickory nuts. Nineteen vessels
were recovered: they included nine plain and one cordmarked jars, two
bottles, six bowls, and one decorated plate. The large internal pits and their
fill were unusual, and Milner describes them in some detail (Milner with
Williams 1984: 50) because of their complex histories. Features 88 and 110

were partially open when the structure burned, creating complex fill zones, while Feature 88 also contained a cached hoe. Feature 187 had a large cache of items, including five hoes, a sandstone abrader, and a deer mandible. Twelve vessels were found in the interior pits. These consisted of four cordmarked jars (three from Feature 88) and one plain jar, two plain bowls, one pan, and two water bottles. Interestingly the RPR value for the vessels associated with Structure 2 was 0.307, somewhat in line with a late Moorehead assemblage (for example, the late Moorehead Primas site was 0.317; Holley 1989: 216). In fact, this assemblage may indicate a late Moorehead rather than a Sand Prairie horizon.

Material from the Structure 2 complex was extensive and consisted of large amounts of limestone, rough rock and sandstone, debitage, hammerstones, a microdrill, a deer mandible tool, 12 hoe fragments, 6 knives or fragments, cores, abraders, Missouri River clinker, 5 points, a celt, and such exotics as a quartz crystal, 11 hematite pieces, a pendant of flint clay, and a galena fragment.

Structure 82, to the east of Structure 2, is a single wall-trench building (4.18 m x 3.53 m; 14.76 m^2) with five internal pits. Feature 90 is a large central hearth, Feature 84 is a large storage pit in the south corner, while the remaining three are shallow pits. This complex included one cordmarked and three plain jars, one pinch pot, and a juice press or funnel. Also recovered was a duck effigy head from a jar or bowl. Other materials included four arrow points, flakes, abraders, two hoe fragments, hammerstones, a celt piece, hematite, and rough stone and limestone.

The Structure 17 complex included a large wall-trench building, measuring 5.88 m x 4.85 m (28.52 m^2), with three moderately deep pits and two large posts that may have been roof supports. Vessels present were three plain and two cordmarked jars, three bowls, one pinch pot, and two bottles. The structure contained a large amount of material goods. These included the usual limestone, sandstone, and rough rock, as well as flakes, hammerstones, debitage, cores, three hoe fragments, five points, abraders, a celt, five hematite pieces, and three galena fragments.

The seven possible pit features associated with the complex contained a number of ceramics: 16 bowls, 13 plain and 4 cordmarked jars, 2 pinch pots, and 1 juice press or funnel. These pits had limestone, sandstone, rough rock, flakes, biface fragments, points, abraders, hematite, a fossil, and a celt in their fill. Of note in Feature 87 was a galena bead and whelk shell.

The question of the dating of this cluster of structures has interesting ramifications for the understanding of rural settlement transformations surrounding Cahokia. Based on the ceramic and material inventory, it does not appear to conform to what I have considered to be Sand Prairie manifestations such as Structure 91 at Julien (Milner with Williams 1984: 44-48). Rather than discard the current phase assignment, which would be premature on the basis of my present overview, in this instance I believe that it would be most appropriate to classify this complex as extremely early in the Sand Prairie phase (or conversely, extremely late in the Moorehead). It is distinguishable from the previous Moorehead rural settlement discussed above that seems to be earlier and can be seen as representing an apparent development out of that earlier pattern of a community-centered "men's house" system. It is certainly distinguishable from apparently contemporaneous and later Sand Prairie single households, as noted above.

Florence Street Mortuary Ceremonial Node

The Florence Street Sand Prairie component consisting of three structures and a stone-box cemetery (figure 5.18) was excavated under my direction (Emerson et al. 1983). The habitation areas were analyzed by Jackson and Emerson (1983), while George Milner (1983b) provided the detailed overview of the Florence Street cemetery. Mehrer (1988: 123-124) suggested these might have represented part of a mortuary nodal complex.

At Florence Street, Structure 2 lies atop the ridge; it had been burned prehistorically and was heavily disturbed in historic times. It was a large (30.6 m²), rectangular (6 m x 5.1 m) wall-trench structure with only one shallow internal pit. Thirteen meters south of Structure 2 was a small (4.1 m x 3.16 m; 13 m²) rectangular single wall-trench building, Structure 60, containing one large pit that was virtually sterile. There was also a single post in the space where the two wall trenches came together in the northern corner.

This small building was superimposed by Structure 61, a large single wall-trench structure (5.4 m x 4.8 m; 25.9 m²) with two internal features. Feature 62 appeared to be a hearth, while Feature 63 was a shallow pit (which did, however, contain a miniature vessel). In the southern juncture of the wall trenches was a single post mold. Just over one meter away from the southern wall of this structure is another wall trench paralleling the building. Whether this represented some type of screen or porch is unknown. Buildings 60 and 61 were almost devoid of material, making their interpretation as to either function or chronological placement difficult. On the basis of propinquity, we placed them with the Sand Prairie component. It is possible that they were related in function to the Florence Street cemetery located only a little over 20 meters to the northeast. O'Brien (O'Brien and McHugh 1987), in fact, argues that these structures represent a Cahokian solstice shrine associated with astronomical and agricultural rites. The function of these early

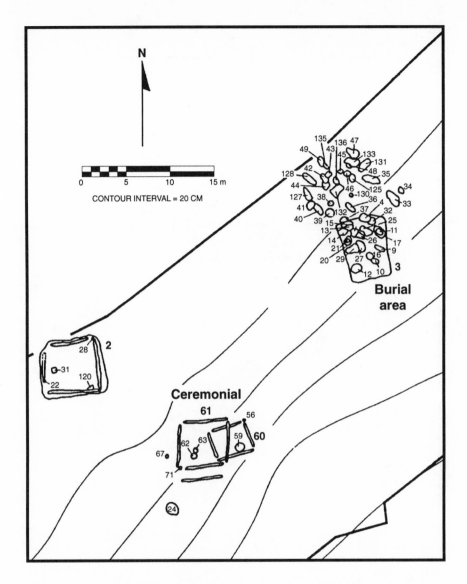

Figure 5.18 Sand Prairie Phase Florence Street Site Mortuary Node (after Jackson and Emerson 1983, Figure 76).

Sand Prairie structures is ambiguous and their association with the burial complex is difficult is demonstrate conclusively.

The Florence Street cemetery (figure 5.19, table 5.12) stands as a rela-tively isolated burial zone near the end of the ridge and is fairly well sepa-rated from most of the Sand Prairie structures. It contained 42 mortuary pits

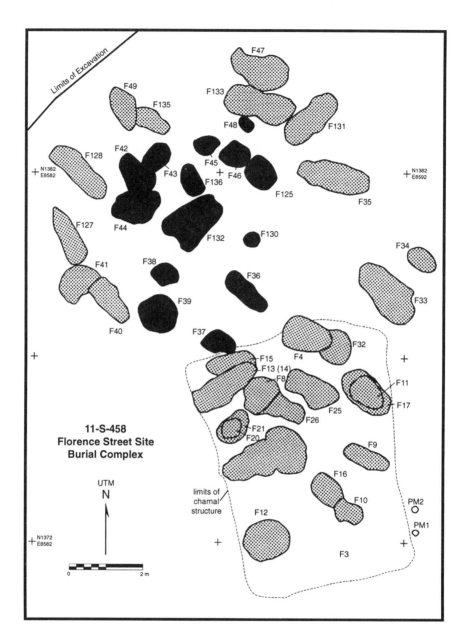

Figure 5.19 Sand Prairie Phase Florence Street Site Burial Area (Jackson and Emerson 1983, Figure 108).

Cahokia and the Archaeology of Power

Table 5.12 Sand Prairie Phase Florence Street Mortuary Node (SPMN)

Buildings		
Ceremonial/ Storage:	2 Sequential Buildings 1WT(F60) Area: 13 m^2 Isolated Corner Post	1WT(F61) Area: 26 m^2 Isolated Corner Post & Wall Screen
Facilities		
Pits:	4 Pit Volume: 5.2 m^2	
Marker Post:	At least 2	
Ceremonial:	Marked Charnal Area (7 m x 4.7 m; 33 m^2) 42 Burial and Processing Pits (48 individuals including adults and juveniles, male and female)	
Materials		
Grave Offerings:	Galena Bead – 1 (14 g) Quartz Crystals – 1 (19.8 g) Worked Copper – 1 (4 g) Abraders – 4 Projectile Points – 2 Chert Flakes – 23 Tools of Bone (7) and Antler (2)	

Ceramics:	Jars	10	mortuary	Status/Ritual Ceramics:
	Bowls	10		6 Effigy bowls
	Bottles	4		4 Bottles (1 long-necked)
	Plate	1		10
	Total vessels	25		

and a roughly rectangular stained area that presumably formed a rectangular cemetery plot, within and around which a minimum of 48 individuals were buried. This rectangular burial plot may represent the remains of a charnel area. Burials included males and females, adults and children, indicating that it truly was a "community" cemetery, and unlike some earlier Mississippian rural cemeteries (e.g., my interpretation of the BBB Motor burial program), did not represent a selected segment of the population. The cemetery contained numerous effigy bowls, jars, water bottles, plates and other small vessels, projectile points, grinding tools, a small embossed copper plate, a galena bead, worked bones, and a quartz crystal as grave offerings. Milner was able to distinguish some internal structure to the cemetery; it seemed to contain a central core of burials (shown in black, figure 5.19) surrounded by a larger number of peripheral inhumations; various burial configurations, including extended, bundled, and scattered forms; and burial programs that included burial, exhumation, and reinterment.

Milner has also excavated and analyzed comparable burial areas at sites such as East St. Louis Stone Quarry (1983a) and the Range site cemetery (Milner et al. 1998) and reviewed Mississippian burial patterns in general (1982, 1984a). It was in the context of that work that he first suggested such floodplain cemeteries represented a period of "social segmentation and community autonomy . . . [and] perhaps each Sand Prairie phase community maintained its own cemetery, with the cemeteries situated on the same series of ridges where the domestic structures and fields were located" (Milner 1983b: 298). The pattern seems supported by subsequent work. However, the specific Florence Street pattern of a cemetery and two possibly associated structures (i.e., Structures 60 and 61) is still unique.

SUMMARY

As has been demonstrated in this chapter, the rural Mississippian settlements near Cahokia were a far cry from a simple mass of undifferentiated rural subsistence settlements that may have typified earlier periods. At approximately A.D. 1050, the rural pattern of subsistence households was overlain by a complex system of hierarchically organized rural sites whose inhabitants' goals appeared to have been directed at "organizing" and "dominating" the countryside. These influences can be recognized in the appearance of specialized political and religious structures that I have argued represented an "architecture of power" and were associated with the appearance of some status/wealth items.

In the Lohmann phase I have demonstrated the appearance of nodal households, a civic/ceremonial node that possessed both political and religious attributes, and a community-centered mortuary center. During the Stirling phase the differentiation of religious and political responsibilities proceeded to the point that these activities were performed by different specialists at distinctive civic and ceremonial nodes. The development of fertility symbolism and attendant ceremonialism reached a high point during this phase.

The subsequent Moorehead phase was marked by the disappearance of this complex set of specialized, hierarchical sites and the return to a pattern of nodal households and community-centered political civic nodes. Sand Prairie phase sites showed no evidence for political activities of either a community-centered or elite nature; instead, the focus was on community-centered mortuary ceremonialism. There is some evidence for Sand Prairie nodal households.

In the next chapter I will explore some of the factors that facilitated these developments in the Cahokian rural settlement system and propose a number of interpretations about Cahokian political and religious life that can be derived from the data.

6

Interpreting Cahokian
Rural Settlements

A series of factors must be examined to arrive at a full understanding of rural settlement patterns and systems in the American Bottom around Cahokia during the Middle Mississippian period. These factors include the local physiography, the subsistence economy, and the social and political milieu. No single set of these variables can provide complete insights into the complex pattern observed in the archaeological record. Only by taking them all into account can we achieve a balanced perspective on the past.

PHYSIOGRAPHY AND ECONOMY

A dispersed rural settlement pattern articulates well with the known physiography of the American Bottom. As Smith (1978a) has discussed, the bottomland environment of major rivers is rich in self-perpetuating zones that have great potential for horticultural exploitation through a dispersed settlement pattern. However, such zones are extremely unstable and shifting in composition. The effect of flooding and high water levels on the American Bottom has been documented by Chmurny (1973). The point was made more directly by Charles Dickens in a trip across the American Bottom; he described it as an "unbroken slough of black mud and water . . . thick bush; and everywhere was stagnant, slimy, rotten, filthy water" (Dickens 1893: 154). Even today, with extensive levees and drainage ditches, in many places the land is wet and swampy. This has created a pattern in which land suitable enough for occupation and horticulture is keyed to subtle variation in elevation, and such lands occur mainly in widely scattered, small areas across the Cahokia locality.

While no data exist for the American Bottom, Muller (1978: 277) has calculated that each household/farmstead in the Black Bottom must have had at least 2 to 3 ha of associated agricultural land. This requirement limited the areas that could have been occupied by Mississippian farmers and dictated the relative density of rural populations. In Milner's study (1986: 229) of population for a section of the American Bottom he found that within his study area of 128.5 km² only 37.3% of the land was actually habitable. The greatest danger in the American Bottom was the overabundance of water in the form of floods, rain, or high water tables. The distribution of ground suitable for horticulture and settlement *and* also free from frequent seasonal inundations limited the distribution and density of household clusters and the size of population nucleations.

Woods (1987) reviewed the evidence for patterns of maize horticulture and agriculture in the Eastern Woodlands and concluded that, during the Middle Mississippian occupation of the American Bottom, agricultural-related factors also encouraged settlement dispersion. He argued for a pattern in which "maize was cultivated in large agricultural fields and small mixed-horticultural gardens . . . with primary production focused on lower-order farmsteads and hamlets dispersed to maximize the exploitation of fertile, readily tilled bottomland soils. . . . Agricultural fields were situated in alluvium on non-acid, silt loam soils of high natural fertility that was periodically renewed by flooding, but that did not have high water regimes after mid-May. Gardens were proximal to habitations, often on soils that had received cultural enrichment as a result of prior occupation" (Woods 1987: 285).

The effect of these practices was to create an agricultural landscape in which small, horticultural plots located near the houses on the ridges were fairly secure from flooding. As Smith (1978a) has observed, such a pattern was also the most effective approach to an energy-efficient utilization of the floodplain environment. Any larger community fields in the lower-lying silt loams, however, would have been susceptible to fluctuations in water levels and could easily have been devastated by unseasonable flooding. To a considerable degree, the physical dispersion of both residential and agricultural activities was a direct result of the physiography of the landscape.

Another factor that has not been given sufficient consideration in understanding the utilization and duration of dispersed households is the potential inadequacy of floodplain fields for permanent horticulture (cf. Wolforth 1989) due to invader weed species or soil deterioration. Wolforth made the point that mobility was a "fact of life" for farmstead occupants who may have been forced to move several times within a generation. Civic nodes and other community-centered facilities, on the other hand, may have increased permanence of location because of a shift in the inhabitants' economic and political relationships. This pattern was reflected in the implied reuse and longer occupations at some identified nodal sites such as Range or Julien (cf. Pauketat 1989). This occupancy and reuse of identical building sites may have indicated actual patterns of land tenure in nodal site placement. Taking into account farmstead movement because of environmental constraints produced a dispersed village pattern consisting of a relatively fixed civic node, probably having defined territorial parameters, surrounded by numbers of continually relocating farmsteads. As Wolforth (1989) noted, such a scenario has serious implications for the archaeological interpretation of prehistoric population density, elite-commoner proportions, burial practices, agricultural risk dispersement, and political and social organization.

Dispersion may have been encouraged by changes in local physiography. Evidence indicates that during the Mississippian utilization of the American Bottom, problems of fluctuating water tables (Emerson 1995: 242–248) and increased susceptibility to unseasonable flooding took place (Emerson and Milner 1988; Lopinot and Woods 1993; Milner 1987; Milner and Emerson 1981; Woods and Meyer 1988). Such changes would have played a role in settlement patterning during the Mississippian occupation. The chronological relationship between elevation and the placement of structures affiliated with various Mississippian phases can be documented at a number of sites (Emerson 1995: figure 29; Julien [Milner with Williams 1984]; Turner [Milner with Williams 1983]; Lohmann [Esarey and Pauketat 1992]; BBB Motor [Emerson and Jackson 1984]). This suggests that prior to A.D. 1000 water levels could have been considerably lower than at later times in the northern American Bottom area.

Recently, additional data have been brought forward by Lopinot and Woods (1993) to lend credence to this proposal. The authors carried out an intensive study and evaluation of the possibility that deforestation was a significant problem during the Mississippian occupation of Cahokia and the surrounding bottom and bluffs. They document changes in the record that indicated an increased exploitation of localized woods during Stirling times that may have led to extensive clearing of forest within 10 to 15 km of Cahokia. For purposes of transportation, trees near streams may have been the first to go, leading to increasing erosion and "the potential for more frequent, severe, and unpredictable local floods." Such a pattern would have been exacerbated during the advent of increased upland farming and clearing that began in the Moorehead phase, "thus perpetuating the risks of crop loss from local floods in the American Bottom." Consequently, it is possible that the appearance of increased flooding was the direct product of human degradation of the forested areas through overexploitation.

The Mississippian era in the American Bottom appears to have been marked by the increasing diminution of available arable and habitable lands, especially within the local ridge-and-swale systems, as these lands were increasingly utilized for monument construction and living areas, and as the local populations increased. A number of responses to these conditions were possible. One may have been the encouragement of population nucleation and dramatic increases in relative population density in favorable locales (i.e., higher elevations). The size of such nucleated centers would have been dependent on access to food resources—either locally grown on surrounding fields or obtained from dispersed rural producers. If the centers were able to effectively supply subsistence needs via a widely dispersed population of producers, then they may have grown to a considerable size. Fluctuating water tables, unseasonable floods, less available crop lands, a more widely dispersed support population, and increased population density at centers may have provided a social milieu conducive to considerable increases in political and social complexity, as well as stress.

Several possible social and/or economic factors may have created the dispersed pattern rather than its being a direct response to physiographic conditions per se. Cahokians had a number of alternatives to dispersion open to them, including large-scale land modification (cf. Dalan 1992, 1997), agricultural intensification via ridge field systems (cf. Fowler 1969), or social and/or political modifications to favor nucleation over dispersion. Consequently, it is premature to give priority to either cultural complexity *or* environmental changes as prime movers in creating this settlement pattern.

Bruce Smith (1978b), however, has argued that the explanation of the Mississippian dispersed farmstead pattern was its simple efficiency in exploiting the natural physiography of floodplains. Farmstead and population dispersion can be seen as a straightforward adaptation to the local environmental conditions, with no motivating force beyond efficiency.

It is possible though, with the increasing complexity of late Emergent Mississippian and early Mississippian culture, that dispersion may have been a result of the increased elite need for foodstuffs. New calculations of population and carrying capacity by Pauketat and Lopinot (1997), based on the data from large tracts recently analyzed at Cahokia, have provided additional insights into the issue of Cahokian subsistence and resource mobilization. Based on a projected 5 km catchment area, they estimated that Cahokian agricultural output could not have adequately nourished more than 7,500 to 12,000 persons. Given that they estimated Cahokian populations during the Lohmann phase in the range of 10,000 to 15,000 people, there could have been a shortage of subsistence staples.

The model of Mississippian dispersed farming generally stressed this approach as an extensive, low-energy system for the exploitation of the landscape. It is possible, however, to view this system in a very different light and to suggest that dispersed farming was actually the result of the implementation of an *intensive* system of agriculture. Such a perspective is borne out by Drennan's (1988) review of Mesoamerican farming systems. He noted that in a system that did not focus on large-scale communal land modifications (e.g., in canal systems) agricultural intensification required continued labor investment by farmers in their individual house plots. Such a system, if faced with increased output requirements, encouraged dispersion and focused on intensified local efforts to increase household crop production. This approach did not encourage community-centered activities or concentrated settlements. Thus dispersion can be interpreted as a reflection of agricultural intensification as well as signifying an extensive, low-effort system.

Given our current information on the limits of the Cahokian catchment area crop production and the synchrony of Cahokia's intense population nucleation with the initiation of the American Bottom dispersed settlement system, it seems likely that the latter was an outgrowth of the Cahokian elites' requirement for increased subsistence staples. The creation of a tightly controlled dispersed rural farming population to feed the nucleated population of Cahokia can be seen as a reflection of the intensification and modification of a previously existing Emergent Mississippian system to meet the new needs of Cahokia.

It is clear from the archaeological data that the Cahokians chose to disperse a portion of their population over the American Bottom's variegated landscape. Thus, they followed a well-known pattern present in many late prehistoric agricultural societies of the Eastern Woodlands. Where they differed, however, from every other known contemporary native North American group was the way in which they created a social, political, and religious organizational structure to manage that population. It is the evidence for this organization that I will discuss in the next section.

RURAL SETTLEMENT FORMS

Prefacing the Mississippian period at A.D. 1000 were rural settlement patterns (Kelly 1990a: 130-136) that provided the context for later development. During late Emergent Mississippian times, settlements focused on nucleation within villages or on small farmsteads or hamlets. Village sites revealed a formal organization pattern of structures and courtyards grouped around a central plaza. Kelly reported that the George Reeves phase village at Range appeared to be a coalescence of a number of smaller settlement units into a larger social group, and he interpreted it as representing "the best evidence of social ranking at this time" (Kelly 1990a: 131). This consolidation and elaboration of larger village organization continued through the Emergent Mississippian period although there was a trend at some locations during the Lindeman phase for size reduction that "may indicate the dispersal of village population into small social units, such as the numerous farmsteads recorded for this time period" (Kelly 1990a: 134).

The other segments of the settlement system operational during the Emergent Mississippian period were farmsteads and hamlets. There appears to have been some variety in size and form with examples such as the Marcus site (Emerson and Jackson 1987b), consisting of two structures and a few pits; a small courtyard cluster of four structures, such as at the Schlemmer site (Berres 1984; Szuter 1979); or a long linear distribution of 16 structures along the lake shore, as at the BBB Motor site (Emerson and Jackson 1984). What did appear consistent, however, was the lack of any evidence *within* these small hamlets and farmsteads of status differentiation, ranking, or community-centered activities. There was no concentration of exotic prestige/wealth items, specialized ceremonial goods or architecture, differential presence of storage facilities, or other items suggestive of anything other than an egalitarian atmosphere at the small Emergent Mississippian rural sites. That is not to suggest that the late Emergent Mississippian population was socially undifferentiated, but that high-status individuals and the markers of their status, along with the community-centered activities so important to social solidarity, were apparently confined to the emerging villages and mound centers. It is likely at this time that the farmsteads and hamlets were directly articulated with the larger villages and lacked any internal organizational mode.

It is against that backdrop that we see the development of the Cahokian Mississippian rural settlements. Past research has demonstrated the presence of small household clusters (throughout this volume I view the terms *household/household cluster/housecluster* as synonymous), usually perceived as *farmsteads* (cf. figure 6.1, table 6.1), across the American Bottom floodplain. Recently, Finney (1993) has suggested that we can distinguish a set of *special purpose structures* within this larger group of farmsteads. In this study I have been able to document at least three new forms of rural settlements. These include *nodal houseclusters, civic nodes,* and *ceremonial nodes* (cf. figure 6.1). The architectural and artifactual data for these settlement forms are presented individually in tables 5.1–5.12 and in summary form in tables 6.1 and 6.2 and figure 6.1.

Briefly, *nodal households* (figure 6.1) can be conceived of as the residences of rural, low-ranking elite families that had some community leadership

Generalized Characteristics of Rural Settlement Forms

Nodal Houseclusters: residences of rural, low–level functionaries and their families that may have some community leadership role and whose residences serve as a central place for rural community leaders; characterized by the presence of artifacts and architecture that suggest suprafamily activities and community functions

Civic Nodes: distinct locations for the exercise of political and social power by the rural functionaries and contain special–function architecture that may reflect either communal or centralized power

Ceremonial Nodes: rural religious and mortuary sites that, depending on their specific nature, may serve as the residence of religious functionaries, be associated with the community at large or be restricted to the elite, and/or serve as a mortuary facility or temple

Lohmann Phase

Nodal Households: one or two domestic residences and refuse; some caching of status/wealth objects, marker posts; specialized limestone-floored storage facilities, high bowl to jar ratio suggesting communal feasting; high storage ratio to living capacity

Linked Civic–Ceremonial Nodes: multiple domestic residences and refuse; large community center with cooking and seating arrangements; courtyard organiza-tion; high bowl to jar ratio; debris, artifacts, and renewal pits associated with Green Corn ceremonialism such as killed vessels, ritual plants, and pigments

Priest–Mortuary Ceremonial Nodes: charnel house; cemetery; communal structure; physically separated from residential areas as sacred space; special mortuary treatment of subset of population; possible priest residence; high bowl to jar ratio and storage capabilities

Stirling Phase

Civic Nodes: large number of domestic/storage structures and debris; internally segmented buildings; courtyard organization; ritual sweat lodges; low pit–structure storage capacity ratios; low bowl–jar ratios; status vessels, pigments, and minerals; marker posts; wall screens.

Ceremonial Nodes: diverse structures with domestic debris and including specialized cooking facilities, sacred fire enclosures, temples, possible priest residences and charnel houses; elaborate stone fertility goddesses; sacred and exotic vessels, pigments, minerals; cemeteries; set off from habitation areas; special mortuary treatment of subset of population; courtyard organization; marker posts and wall screens; low pit to structure and bowl to jar ratios; Green Corn ceremonialism and renewal pits.

Figure 6.1 Generalized Characteristics of Rural Settlement Forms.

Moorehead Phase

Nodal Housecluster: a grouping not adequately defined but may include a cluster of structures with many storage pits and a few specialized buildings

Civic Node: site that includes specialized communal structure, outbuilding and associated male artifacts interpreted as men's house; low pit to structure ratio but higher bowl–jar ratio suggests some communal feasting

Sand Prairie Phase

Nodal Housecluster: cluster of domestic and other structures; plentiful pigments, crystals and other wealth items; high bowl–jar ratio; few prestige vessels

Ceremonial Mortuary Node: marked cemetery, charnel house; numerous stone–box burials, extensive mortuary processing of burials; extensive grave goods especially in the form of effigy mortuary vessels; possible residences nearby

Figure 6.1 Generalized Characteristics of Rural Settlement Forms, continued.

Table 6.1 American Bottom Middle Mississippian Farmsteads Characteristics*

	Lohmann	Stirling	Moorehead/Sand Prairie
Sample #s	12	12	14
Contemp. Structs.	14	15	16
Range #s	1–2	1–2	1–2
Mode #	1	1	1
Mean #s	1.2	1.2	1.2
Mean M^2	11.2	16.2	18.2
Feature Range #s	0–29	3–24	0–14
Mean #s	4.7	11	5.5
Mean M^3	1.87	2.8	.75
Vessels Range #s	0–32	0–48	0–5
Mean #s	8.8	13.6	1.9

*Sample farmsteads are drawn from households excavated at the Turner, Radic, Sandy Ridge, 78th Street, DeMange, Robert Schneider, Lab Woofie, Labras Lake, George Reeves, and Carbon Dioxide sites in the American Bottom.

Table 6.2 Summary Data for Rural Nodal Settlement Forms

Nodes	JS Rat	Jars	SV	PS Rat	SA	PV	Bowls	JB Rat	Posts	Screens	Courtyard
JUL-3	0	12	0	0.3476	16.4	5.7	11	0.917	1	0	0
RML-1	0	23	0	0.0445	85.4	3.8	10	0.435	4	0	0
LLCN	0.294	17	5	-	-	-	7	0.412	many	1	81
RMS-1	0.121	66	8	0.0883	82.7	7.3	26	0.394	several	0	81
JULCN	0.244	41	10	0.0828	79.7	6.6	14	0.341	1	2	100
JULMCN	0.133	15	2	0.0224	170	3.5	7	0.467	0	0	0
JULSPNH	0.049	41	2	0.0875	74.3	6.5	27	0.659	0	0	0
RML-2	0.1	40	4	0.2292	19.2	4.4	24	0.600	0	0	0
BBBLCN	0	71	0	0.5038	26.4	13.3	21	0.296	2	7	0
BBBSCN	0.359	39	14	0.2464	34.5	8.5	5	0.128	15	2	16
SPCN	0.260	104	27	0.1434	108.1	15.5	23	0.221	many	5	529
SPMN	1	10	10	0.2	26	5.2	10	1.000	2+	0	0

Nodes	Segment Bldg	Communal	Granary	Storage	Sweat	Green Corn/World Renewal	Burials	Plants
JUL-3	0	0	2-4.25	0	0	0	0	0
RML-1	0	57.8	-	15.5	0	0	0	0
LLCN	2	2-33.4	-	33.4	2-4.41	0	0	0
RMS-1	1	17.2	-	24.6	4-22.85	0	0	Tobacco
JULCN	0	0	3.06	24.78	1-6.380	yes	0	0
JULMCN	0	42	-	19.35	0	0	0	0
JULSPNH	0	0	-	0	0	0	0	0
RML-2	0	0	-	0	0	yes	0	Cedar-Tobacco
BBBLCN	0	15.8	-	0	0	0	8	Cedar
BBBSCN	0	0	-	0	0	yes	12	Cedar-Jimsonweed
SPCN	0	0	-	44.3	0	3	0	Cedar-Tobacco
SPMN	0	0	-	26	0	-	42	0

Key

JS Rat - Ratio of status jars to all jars
Jars - # present
SV - # of status vessels
PS Rat - Ratio of pit volume to structure area
SA - m^2 of contemporaneous structure area
PV - dm^3 of possible storage pit volume
Granary - #$_o$ of buildings - m^2 of area
Storage - m^2 of area in possible storage buildings (does not include granaries) [Storage - m^2 of contemporaneous storage buildings (does not include granaries)]
Sweat houses - m^2 of area
Communal - m^2 of area
Segment bldg - Interior segmented buildings
JB Rat - Ratio of bowls to jars
Courtyard - m^2 of area

role and whose residences may have served as a central place for the community leaders. *Civic nodes* (figure 6.1) were distinct locations for the exercise of political and social power by the rural resident elite and contained special-function architecture (e.g., sweat houses and storage/cooking/residential buildings). Such *civic nodes* (figure 6.1) may have been designated as displaying either community or centralized power, depending on their architectural evidence. *Ceremonial nodes* (figure 6.1) were rural religious and mortuary sites that, depending on their specific nature, may have served as the residences of religious specialists, were associated with either the elite or the community at large, or served as mortuary facilities or temples. They were easily recognized on the basis of their specialized architecture (sacred fire, temple, cooking, feasting, charnel structures) and elaborate artifactual assemblage of such items as exotic ceramics, figurines, plants, or minerals. It is the specific content and context of these site forms, their appearance and disappearance, and their variation and change through time that provide us with insights into the political and social power of Cahokia and to shifting patterns of power and ideology.

Farmsteads

The bases of the rural Middle Mississippian settlements were the small, isolated *farmsteads* that were scattered along the ridges of the American Bottom floodplain. Such farmsteads consisted of one or two structures and a small number of associated pit features (table 6.1). Archaeological reports describing these farmsteads are plentiful (e.g., Jackson and Hanenberger 1990; Milner et al. 1984; Mehrer 1988, 1995; Trubitt 1996; and references therein). The diverse assemblage of floral, faunal, and artifactual materials has led regional archaeologists to interpret them as family residences occupied on a year-round basis by subsistence farmers. Typologically, these small sites have been described by Mehrer (1988) and appear to remain fairly consistent in form and function throughout the Middle Mississippian occupation of the American Bottom.

Recently, an additional form of small Mississippian site was recognized by Finney (1993). He has demonstrated that a series of *special-purpose sites* was commonly present in the rural area. These small, ephemeral sites with a low density of artifactual, floral, and faunal material were most likely field houses associated with agricultural activities. Such farmsteads and special-purpose sites have been recovered archaeologically throughout the Southeast and Midwest (e.g., articles and references in Smith, ed. 1978, 1990; Blitz 1993).

A remarkable characteristic of many of these small American Bottom farmsteads was the frequent presence of material considered "prestige goods" or "wealth items" (i.e., foreign/decorated pottery, minerals and pigments, exotic cherts, and other such materials). It is obvious that the residents of farmstead sites had access to these materials, although the social, political, or religious mechanisms that provided them are not clear. The presence of such items, however, should not deter us from distinguishing, in the Mississippian countryside, between such small family residences and the large multibuilding, nodal and religious centers (compare table 6.2 with table 6.1 regarding sheer size, functional variation, storage capacities, and other factors). While there was variation among farmsteads, none of them reached the size or complexity of the nodal centers described here.

Nodal Households

A *nodal household* was characterized by the presence of artifactual and architectural evidence that suggested suprafamily level activities and community functions (figure 6.1 and table 6.2). At Julien, the Lohmann phase Structure 267 nodal household included a single residential building with two specialized external, limestone-floored, ritual/storage facilities. The material assemblage did not appear greatly different from other Lohmann phase rural households, although the caching of artifacts (pigments, hoe, and an earspool) in or near the wall trench was unusual. To some extent it contained the traditional remains of a rural farmstead and, no doubt, was occupied by a family from a low-ranking elite lineage with some civil authority.

Material evidence suggests the inhabitants carried on normal subsistence activities, but there are indications that accumulated minor prestige goods were present and community-centered feasting practiced. This latter assumption is based on the bowl to jar ratio (0.92, figure 6.2) that is the highest for any of the rural non-mortuary nodal sites. The interpretation of a Lohmann nodal household as a centralized location for the accumulation of materials is also supported by the high ratio of storage area to structure area (0.35, figure 6.3). However, the most obvious evidence of this latter assumption is the presence of two granaries.

Another structure complex that bears some similarity to the Julien example is Structure 51 at the Turner site (Milner with Williams 1983, Feature Cluster 2). That complex contains a single-post structure with more than two dozen external pit features and an unusually large material assemblage, including several caches of artifacts. While it lacked any indication of community-centered activities, it stood out from the other Lohmann residential households and was another indication of the development of status and ranking differences that were beginning to develop in the rural areas.

The Lohmann phase nodal household represents the clearest example of a suprafamily residence with community authority and power. The evidence from subsequent time periods is more ambiguous. Although I have not attempted to disentangle the Julien site Moorehead residential compounds, the extensive reuse of a building site and the presence of large structures with ancillary buildings may have indicated the presence of high-status individuals near the community-centered men's building. It is possible that high-status houseclusters such as JUL-11 may represent late Moorehead-early Sand Prairie nodal households. If so, they most closely resemble the pattern reflected in the Moorehead houseclusters and reflect the continuance of a trend of high-status houseclusters toward increasing complexity.

Bowl to Jar Ratios at Ceremonial Nodes

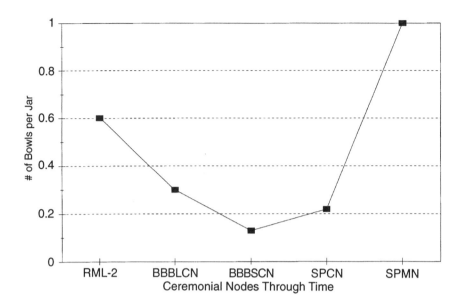

Bowl to Jar Ratios at Civic Nodes

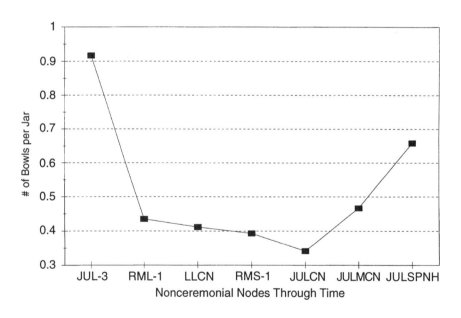

Figure 6.2 Bowl to Jar Ratios.

Cahokia and the Archaeology of Power

Pit Volume to Structure Area Ratios at Ceremonial Nodes

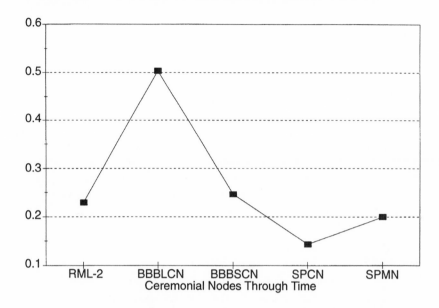

Pit Volume to Structure Area Ratios at Nonceremonial Nodes

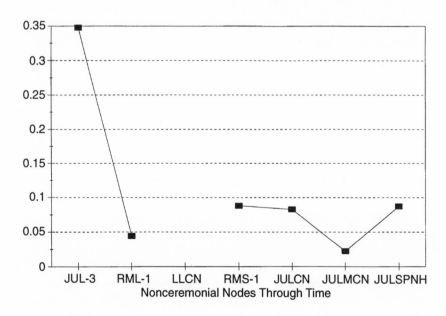

Figure 6.3 Pit Volume to Structure Area Ratios.

Civic Nodes

Civic nodes represented the specialized material expressions of community or centralized political and social power in the rural areas. This power was expressed in the presence of centralized ridge-top locations, ritual architecture, multiple storage, residential and special activity buildings, and high-status artifacts. These forms reached their most specialized expression in the Stirling phase (cf. figure 6.1 and table 6.2).

The Range RML-1 and RML-2 complexes provide an example of an early *civic/ceremonial node*. During the Lohmann phase, as I will discuss below, the functions of the *civic node* were partly linked to those of the *ceremonial node*. The early placement of RML-2 marks the appearance of specialized architectural facilities and community-centered ceremonial activities and provides evidence for the presence of Green Corn ceremonialism.

It is possible that RML-2 was contemporaneous with RML-1 just to the north; however, there was no hint from feature orientations or arrangement to prove such an association. RML-1 continued the community-centered theme of Lohmann nodal facilities with the presence of a massive (almost 60 m^2) square, single-post, open-sided, roofed community center containing benches and cooking facilities. In this case, the emphasis may have been on the political and social aspects of community-centered power. Such meeting places were commonly referenced in the southeastern ethnohistoric record (see Hudson 1976; Swanton 1946 for numerous accounts) as serving for daily meetings of adult males to take "council," gossip, imbibe "black drink" or the local equivalent, and generally socialize. Such locations were also often the centers for community-centered feasting and food distribution. Despite the "community-centered" appearance of RML-1 there was not extensive debris. This may reinforce the argument for its co-use with RML-2, which has extensive debris but no real community-centered architecture. Again, one can note the high ratio of bowls to jars in RML-2 and RML-1 (0.60 and 0.44, figure 6.2). While the ratio of storage pits to structure area does not suggest the presence of many stored goods, this ratio does not reflect the potential use of the numerous buildings present as storage facilities. RML-2 may represent the ceremonial and religious activities balanced against the civic function of RML-1 to make a unified complex.

The Stirling florescence was reflected in the countryside as well as in the major mound centers and at the regional level. This phase was marked by the creation of numerous specialized facilities and the appearance of their attendant functionaries throughout the rural areas. Since our original recognition of "nodal points" and "temple–mortuary complexes" (Emerson and Milner 1981), additional excavations and analysis have refined our understanding and revealed the variation that was concealed within these two simple forms of settlement. Three distinct examples of Stirling phase *civic nodes* have been analyzed in reports, and I have had the opportunity to reexamine them. These include the Labras Lake (Yerkes 1980, 1987), Range (Hanenberger and Mehrer 1998), and Julien (Milner with Williams 1984) *civic nodes.*

Stirling phase *civic nodes* characteristically contained three to five rectangular wall-trench structures and one to four circular sweat houses clustered about a small courtyard. The rectangular structures likely served as residences with additional storage or cooking functions. Occasionally, there were unique structures that were clearly associated with specialized large-scale storage or cooking. Above-ground storage at these civic nodes averaged 28 m² while the pit to structure ratio was fairly low (ca. 0.08, figure 6.3). Usually at least one of the rectangular structures had multiple interior walls dividing the space into multiple storage and/or activity areas. Such internally segmented buildings were primarily limited to Stirling nodes. Exterior space may have been segregated through the use of marker posts and/or wall-trench screens, as well as the placement of buildings and courtyards. As opposed to the Lohmann nodal sites that contained no status ceramics (i.e., decorated, exotic, or fineware vessels), such vessels were not uncommon in Stirling nodes (ratios of status vessels to jars range from 0.12 to 0.29, mean 0.22, figure 6.4). Other status and exotic items such as crystals, pigments, and minerals were present (tables 5.5-5.7).

The Range RMS-1 component seemed to represent the Stirling *civic node* played out on a grand scale with several possible residential units, multiple cooking facilities, a large community storage and meeting structure, and possible paired sweat houses. This organizational structure, however, did not differ dramatically from what was observed at the other sites. Labras Lake was the simplest form, with a single group of sweat houses and structures organized about a single courtyard; Julien was slightly more complex, with two groups of structures around a courtyard; while Range was simply a more complex version of that pattern. I believe it is critical to demonstrate the similarity of the rural patterns, but not to lose sight of, or too lightly dismiss, the observed variation that may have important implications for understanding specific developments in differing localities.

Rural nodal forms during the subsequent Moorehead and Sand Prairie phases are poorly represented in the rural areas. The Moorehead community at Julien contained a number of residential and ancillary structures associated with a *civic node* that has been interpreted as a community "men's house." The structure, with 42 m² of interior space, benches along two walls, multiple hearths, and extensive material debris such as exotic minerals, arrow-

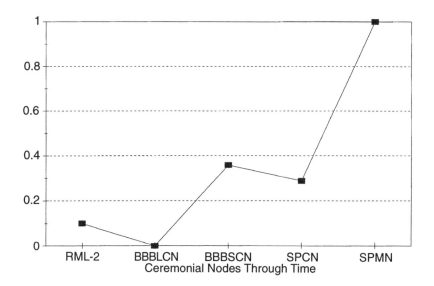

Status Vessels to Jars Ratios at Ceremonial Nodes

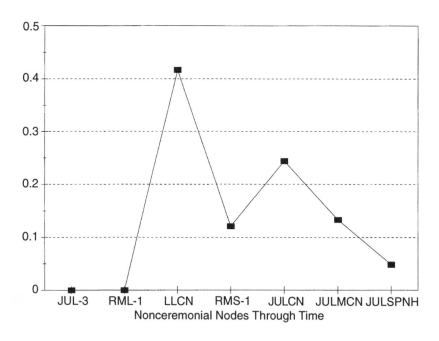

Status Vessels to Jars Ratios at Nonceremonial Nodes

Figure 6.4 Status Vessels to Plain Jars Ratios.

head caches, chipped stone tools, abraders, and domestic ceramic vessels provides a convincing picture of a community-used building. The bowl to jar ratio was 0.47 (figure 6.2) and could be interpreted as supporting a moderate pattern of community food distribution. Pit storage facilities were limited at the node (with a pit-structure ratio of 0.022, figure 6.3). If storage was an important function of the facility, it must have taken place in the men's house or the ancillary building. While the ancillary building may have served a more restricted use for storage (19.35 m^2 of available space) or special activities, it contained a debris assemblage similar to the community structure.

Ceremonial Nodes

Ceremonial nodes formed a newly recognized rural settlement form in the American Bottom. It is my contention that especially during the Stirling phase such sites were similar organizationally and symbolically to the specialized ritual edifices of the historic Southeast often described in the archaeological and ethnohistoric record as religious buildings (e.g., charnel houses and/or temples) (cf. figure 6.1 and table 6.2). Consequently, in this section I will discuss at length the evidence for interpreting these previously undocumented site types at four American Bottom sites. Early forms of *ceremonial nodes* were present in the Lohmann components (i.e., RML-2) at Range (Hanenberger and Mehrer 1998) and BBB Motor sites, the Stirling components at BBB Motor and Sponemann (Jackson et al. 1991), and the mortuary component at the Sand Prairie phase Florence Street site (Emerson et al. 1983).

The elaborate religious, associated ritual, and charnel and temple structures of southeastern chiefly societies, as reported by the early Spanish and French, have provided a rich source of information that has continued to fascinate historians and archaeologists working in the Southeast. Various scholars (e.g., Black 1967; DePratter 1983: 111-153; Swanton 1946: 778-781; Neitzel 1965; Waring 1968; Waring and Holder 1945; Brown 1975) have perused these documents and utilized these data for understanding the archaeological record. Attempts to use specific southeastern analogues to interpret American Bottom Mississippian cultural phenomena are enlightening experiences. It becomes obvious that while these sites are conceptually similar to those of the Southeast special-purpose structures, there are no direct or equivalent analogues. Yet many of the thematic attributes of these components so resemble those of the Southeast that they can be readily seen to fulfill the functions of a temple/priest-mortuary/Green Corn complex.

Benchley has presented a general summary of public structures based on an examination of the ethnohistoric data gathered from the Southeast. Her summary is reproduced here (1974: 270-273):

> The most often noted special building throughout the Southeast was called the temple. The building did not actually function as a temple in the sense of a place where the community worshipped and witnessed ceremonial manipulations of the priests. The temple was a sacred building elevated on a mound which housed both the bones of the deceased community leaders and the eternal fire (cf. Swanton 1911: 158, 159, 162, 167, 260, 269). The temple was a charnel house. The eternal fire was placed in a front room where an attendant watched to make sure that it never went out. The bones of the ancestors and their attendants were stored in baskets or boxes within the building or were sometimes temporarily buried in pits in the temple floor. Attendant burials were also interred outside the building. Sacred objects and treasures were housed in the temple and included stone and wood figurines of humans, animals, and mythical creatures; rock crystals; pearls; copper; pipes; and finely made ceramic dishes. Furniture within the buildings included benches, tables, mats, and baskets, as well as the fire basin. Structures outside the building could have included a small building for the keeper of the fire and an encircling fence. The wall mats on the temple were replaced annually. Emptying and rebuilding the temple, however, took place after longer intervals and evidently occurred when it was full of bones (Bartram 1958: 328). Renewal of the temple and its mound may have actually occurred at precise intervals set by a calendric system or at times when political power shifted from one lineage to another. Ethnohistorical observations, however, were too short lived to have recorded evidence for either of these possibilities.

Native populations of the ethnohistoric Eastern Woodlands made no clear distinction between structural complexes that various authors label as "temples" versus those considered "charnel houses." Seeman (1979: 43-45) has collated many ethnohistoric sources on historically known charnel structures, concentrating heavily on those from the Southeast and the Atlantic coast. His summary (table 6.3) provides additional evidence for multiple usage and ritual in the context of structures associated with mortuary programs; in addition to "their function as repositories for the dead,. . . [they also] housed important idols, ritual objects, weapons, war trophies, the sacred fire, and masses of capital" (Seeman 1979: 43). A more extensive study by DePratter (1983: table 5) supports Seeman's summary and expands the repertory and functions associated with such edifices. In the following discussion I will use the term "temple" to refer to the various manifestations of these multifunctional structures.

Table 6.3 Characteristic Functions of Historic Southeastern Charnel Houses (From Seeman 1979, Table 7.1).

	A	B	C	D	E	F	G	H
Powhatan	0	X	0	0	0	0	0	0
Algonquian	0	X	0	0	0	0	0	0
Siouan	0	0	0	0	0	0	0	0
Tocobaga	0	0	0	0	0	0	0	0
Choctaw	X	0	0	0	X	0	X	X
Biloxi	0	0	0	X	0	0	X	0
Chitimacha	X	0	0	X	X	0	0	X
Natchez–Taensa	0	X	X	X	X	0	X	0
Bayogoula	X	X	X	X	X	X	0	0
Acolapissa	X	X	0	X	0	0	0	0
Houma	0	X	0	X	X	0	0	0
Tunica	0	X	0	X	0	0	0	0
Creek	X	X	X	0	X	X	0	X
Grigra	0	0	0	X	0	0	0	0

KEY

A – Commoners buried in temples
B – Idols and ritual objects present
C – War trophies and weapons
D – Sacred fire
E – Priests
F – Storage of capital
G – Food offerings or feasts
H – Hierarchy of temples
O – Trait not recorded
X – Trait recorded

In examining the various discussion of temples given above, it becomes clear that a number of specific traits, which are said to be typical of these temple structures, were either not present or present in a different form at the Range, BBB Motor, Sponemann, and Florence Street sites. However, it should be patently clear from those same documents that extreme variation existed among historic examples. Composite pictures of temples such as those presented by Benchley, Waring, Swanton, and others represent an artificial ideal and not a standard met by all or even most documented historic examples.

In common parlance, temples were associated with platform mounds; however, many known examples are reported as located on the plaza or physically separated from a village (DePratter 1983: 117 and table 5). The key factor in temple placement is the identification of a ritual space and the restriction of the temple to that area. It is less critical whether that ritual space was defined by a plaza edge, a mound, or a separate, isolated location. There is sufficient documentation to indicate that temple–mortuary complexes (e.g., as among the Choctaw [Adair 1930: 192] or the Powhatan [Smith 1819: 139]) were occasionally clearly separated from the habitation areas. This was also true of some later square grounds. For example, as John Howard Payne (in Witthoft 1949: 64) noted, the Creek square he observed was far removed from dwelling areas. This separation may very well have stemmed from beliefs such as those recorded by Adair (1930: 84) concerning the "Mushohge" view of the temple, where "none of the laity dared to approach that sacred place, for fear of particular damage to themselves, and general hurt to the people, from the supposed divinity of the place."

The American Bottom ceremonial nodes' buildings were not, for example, raised on humanly constructed mounds. Commonly cited historic records or archaeological examples emphasize temples described on plazas in towns one might envision at such mound centers as Cahokia, East St. Louis, or Mitchell. The temple mound and plaza, however, were large-scale, public constructions associated with religious, political, and population centers in which spatial separation was used to bespeak social, political, and religious distance between the masses and the elite. While not identical, a similar pattern may have been present in outlying ceremonial nodes. One purpose of such organizational spatial constructs may have been to separate physically and conceptually the ritual zone from the general populace. For example, I have argued that the BBB Motor temple location was similar in concept to the temple mound-plaza arrangement since it was, in fact, spatially isolated by the surrounding lake and marsh, raised above the surrounding landscape on the small ridge, and geographically separated from residential areas—it was ritual space. A similar context was present at Sponemann, with the temple complex being on the extreme southeastern edge of the habitation areas and immediately adjacent to a low-lying (water filled?) swale. In both cases, water may have acted as a spiritual barrier and assisted in maintaining its ritual purity (cf. Hall 1976, 1979). While not as distinct, similar isolation could be argued for the Range RML-2 and Florence Street mortuary components.

The Range RML-2 node represented the first example of a specialized site focused on religious ceremonialism in the rural countryside. As I argued above, it appeared linked to a community facility (see previous discussion of RML-1) concerned with political and social power and represented an early fused form of what later became two distinct entities (i.e., the *civic node* and the *ceremonial node*). It was distinct from the later Stirling forms, however, for although it contained evidence of ritual activity, no structures were present that could be categorized as "temples." RML-2's small buildings and massive "world renewal" pit contained ritual materials, including killed vessels, exotics, and ritual plants such as red cedar and tobacco. The complex provided extensive evidence of use in community feasting (with a high 0.60 bowl to jar ratio, figure 6.2) and renewal ceremonies such as those historically associated with Green Corn ceremonialism. However, one aspect of this component that should be noted was the absence of any related mortuary activities.

The Lohmann Priest-Morturary *ceremonial node* as expressed at the BBB Motor site reinforces our perception that status and rank differences were becoming prevalent within Lohmann society about Cahokia. This isolated mortuary complex contained the remains of at least eight (and probably more) individuals buried in two recognizable groups (moiety divisions?). Although without any obvious distinctions or markings of high status in mortuary accompaniments, the placement of these individuals within a specialized facility connoted a noncommoner status. The inclusion of both adults and children reinforced the concept of an ascribed status for the individuals buried there; however, the absence of high-status grave goods indicated that status was moderate. The two buildings seemed to represent a domicile (for a guardian?) and a community building with benches (for group ceremonies?). The complex continued the Lohmann nodal pattern of having a high to moderate bowl to jar ratio (0.30, figure 6.2). A striking aspect of this component was the extremely high pit volume to structure area ratio (0.50, figure 6.3). It suggested that subterranean storage of materials at the site was given a high priority.

As Milner (1984a) points out in his review of Mississippian burial patterns, this facility was unique in the American Bottom and was very different from the usual nonelite early Mississippian burial context. Noting the resemblance to elite charnel house-temple pairings in Mississippian towns, he suggests this may have represented a midrange elite burial area. I have interpreted this facility as a low-ranking elite mortuary repository, given its specialized nature and the restricted number of burials. Based on my later arguments that this mortuary site was an important link in consolidating and integrating rural dispersed villages, the buried individuals may have represented the ruling members of a local low-status lineage. The absence of blatantly high-status burials may reflect the movement of lead elite burials to hierarchically superior centers for interment. Likewise, commoners must have been interred in other, less specialized locations. It may also have served as a location for group mortuary activities and, possibly, for the specialized storage of elite sacred, ritual, or status materials.

I have reasoned that the Lohmann component was likely the residence of the priests/attendants, who seemed to be a necessary adjunct as guardians to many ethnohistorically documented temple and mortuary complexes (e.g., see table 6.3 and DePratter 1983: table 5). These guardians had various duties, including tending the sacred fire, restricting access by nonelite to the complex, and ritual mortuary activities. Such individuals were usually resident at the temple. The priest-mortuary component assemblage stressed the mortuary and associated community-centered activities with its high number of serving bowls and utilitarian vessels, structures with benches (which may have indicated either community-centered ritual use *or* service as storage for community remains), and high density of general "domestic" debris. The emphasis in this component more strongly resembled those in which Seeman (1979: 44-45) documented a propensity for mortuary ritualism to be associated with feasting and community food redistribution. To some extent this would explain the more functional utilitarian appearance of the component. Such activities would probably have been related to a lineage level of ritualism.

The Lohmann priest-mortuary ceremonial node was important in demonstrating the extension into the rural areas of status differentiation and its differential mortuary practices that indicated the separation, even in death, of some segments of the rural populace. The presence of such practices among the rural Mississippian populations clearly reflected their presence in the well-established centers in the American Bottom (cf. Fowler 1991). It is important to note, however, that in this component the emphasis was, like the contemporary civic/ceremonial nodes, on community activities. It is also apparent that the appearance of the rich fertility symbolism that marked the Stirling phase had not yet become an important focus of elite integrative manipulation. The Lohmann rural scene saw the spread of the framework for centralized control with the appearance of the nodal sites and priest-mortuary complexes in the countryside about Cahokia. There was, however, still a strong current of community/local control during that time. This situation was to change drastically in the subsequent Stirling phase.

The transition from the Lohmann to early Stirling use of the BBB Motor site saw alterations in the nature and function of the ritual activities. While one finds the repeating of the earlier Lohmann organizational and spatial pattern of structures, features, and burials, that pattern became more complex with the introduction of the "Birger Courtyard" and specialized structures. High status and specialized ritual paraphernalia now dominated the assemblage, with little evidence of community activities, as reflected in the limited assemblage confined to highly specialized and exotic ceramic vessels. The epitome of this ritualism was the presence of two stone fertility idols—the Birger and Keller figurines—and hallucinogenic plants. The presence of limited domestic materials indicated that a few religious practitioners, probably priest specialists, were resident. The site appears to have been abandoned after the ritual destruction of some artifacts and the burning of the structures.

The BBB Motor Stirling component represented primarily a temple facility with an emphasis on ritual activities, based on the artifactual evidence of ceramics and figurines, revolving about fertility as well as the mortuary aspect. The Stirling mortuary program seemed generally similar to that of the previous Lohmann phase. There were two distinct rows of burials as well as another small group to the side, which suggested two to three prehistoric social distinctions were present. The burial of adults and infants argues for a status program based on ascriptive values. There was clear evidence for the defleshing and processing of some burials, and a more complex mortuary program was indicated by the presence of a specialized "grave house."

The complex bore a strong resemblance to Southeastern temple complexes. Accounts exist indicating that many of the historic temples had at least two rooms: one contained the sacred fire, the other ritual paraphernalia and burials. In the BBB Motor site Stirling *ceremonial node* this division took the form of two structures, with Structure 52 containing the sacred fire and Structure 87 containing the ritual paraphernalia and, perhaps, curated burials. The charnel/mortuary aspect of both the BBB Motor site Stirling and Lohmann components seems well supported by the presence of the burials and the grave house. While little skeletal material was found on the structure floors, this was not unusual since preservation of such bone would be unlikely. The presence of the grave house and the scraped and cleaned human bone may indicate that postmortem processing of bodies had occurred at the site. Curation of remains may have been the purpose of the benches in Lohmann Structure 16. There appears to have been little status differential expressed in the burial program in either the Stirling or Lohmann components. It is possible that high-status members' remains would have been transferred to mound centers for final interment and thus would not be found at the site.

As interpreted, the late Stirling phase Sponemann temple complex included, at a minimum, a temple (Structure 282), sacred fire enclosure (Structure 248), and elite storage facilities (at least Structure 180/259) plus, perhaps, a number of special activities structures, all in association with an elite residential compound. In this case the temple and storage facility bordered the northern edge of a formal plaza, the sacred fire enclosure the eastern edge, and perhaps sheds or screens the southern side. There is strong confirmation from the artifactual assemblage (e.g., certainly from the Ramey Incised ceramics and the elaborate figurines) and specialized structures that this ceremonial complex had symbolic associations with "world renewal" or Green Corn ceremonialism. One attribute that was not present was that relating to burial or mortuary ritual.

The association of the temple, the sacred fire, and agricultural fertility is well documented for such groups as the Natchez and the Caddo, with the rites including blessing of the seeds, offerings of first fruits, and rain, general fertility, and sun adoration (DePratter 1983: 139-140; Witthoft 1949). In this regard, the fires in Structures 52 and 248 were unique when compared to other hearth examples, with their contents being limited to twigs, branches, and corn cobs and kernels—perhaps the offering of first fruits? I have argued in the past that the central focus of much of the Stirling component symbolism (1982, 1989, 1995) revolved about fertility—a point reinforced by the stone idols recovered. The presence of stone idols imbued with agricultural symbolism in temples has been reported historically among southeastern groups, with the classic description provided by Peter Martyr, based on a description of rites from a South Carolina native (Swanton 1922: 43-44):

> In the courtyard of this palace, the Spaniards found two idols as large as a three-year-old child, one male and one female. These idols are both called *Inamahari* and have their residence in the palace. Twice each year they are exhibited, the first time at the sowing season, when they are invoked to obtain successful result for their labors. . . . Thanksgivings are offered to them if the crops are good; in the contrary case they are implored to show themselves more favorable in the following year.

> The idols are carried in the procession amidst pomp, accompanied by the entire people. . . . At daybreak the people assemble, and the king himself carries these idols, hugging them to his breast, to the top of his palace, where he exhibits them to the people. He and they are saluted with respect and fear by the people, who fall upon their knees or throw themselves on the ground with loud shouts. The king then descends and hangs the idols, draped with feather mantles and worked cotton stuffs, upon the breasts of two venerable men of authority. . . . the men escort the idols during the day, while during the night the women watch over them, lavishing upon them demonstrations of joy and respect. The next day they were carried back to the palace with the same ceremonies with which they were taken out. If the sacrifice is accomplished with devotion and in conformity with the ritual, the Indians believe they will obtain rich crops, bodily health, peace.

It is also necessary to consider the mundane artifacts one might encounter in a temple–mortuary complex. As pointed out in the Benchley summary, such items would include "sacred objects and treasures"—one culture's "treasures" may be another's "trash." It has been amply illustrated that sacred objects and treasures (as recognized by archaeologists) abounded at the BBB Motor and Sponemann sites. More interesting is the "debris," especially that recovered from the large Features 110 and 125, located in Structure 87 and the floor in Structure 282. As discussed, these structures appeared to be the most likely candidates for the role of temples at the sites. The presence of what we might interpret as "nonritual" debris in Structures 87 and 282 does not rule out the possibility that they functioned as temples. DePratter has documented (1983: 119 ff.) that, historically, temples often literally bulged with chiefly exotica—ranging from "fancy" items such as pearls, crystals, copper, crowns of skins, and feathers to the more "utilitarian" skins, shoes, and trade goods.

The materials in such temples seemed to have been a potpourri of material goods from the sacred to the mundane. Adair (1930: 84) noted that the temple is the depository of consecrated vessels and holy utensils (as one might expect). He also pointed out (1930: 87-88) that it contained much more when he recounted that after the new fire ceremony, in which the priest wears new moccasins, "they [i.e., moccasins] are laid up in the beloved place, or holiest [i.e., the temple], where much of the like sort, quietly accompanies a heap of old, broken earthen ware, conch shell, and other consecrated things." It would seem, then, that the debris associated with the American Bottom temple complexes was not entirely out of place.

Temple–mortuary complexes also appear to have been long-lived facilities that were periodically cleaned and renewed. The evidence has already been presented to suggest that the Stirling ceremonial nodal structures were maintained and utilized for a number of years, perhaps as many as three or four decades (cf. Pauketat 1989). Part of the temple's spiritual renewal, as quoted by Benchley above, may have included the annual replacement of the wall mats. As suggested earlier, such a procedure would have kept a structure clean and fairly free of vermin, thus allowing it to be used for a much longer period of time. It may be that such periodic cleanings and renewals of the temple were represented at BBB Motor by the burned mud dauber nests and in the deliberate reexcavations and refilling episodes of Feature 125. At the Sponemann site, such practices may have been reflected in the rebuilt walls and renewed floors in Structure 282, the community debris pits (Features 716 and 183), and the sequential reuse of pits (Feature 716) or their purification (Feature 208).

Little evidence exists related to Moorehead and Sand Prairie phase nodal ceremonial sites and, consequently, we have a poor understanding of rural ceremonialism during the latter part of the rule of Cahokia. It was not until we reached the early Sand Prairie phase floodplain mortuary sites (Milner 1983a, 1984a; Emerson et al. 1983) that there was evidence of continued centralized community activities in the countryside. These charnel houses bespoke community ritualism focused on mortuary activities, and the excavated cemeteries suggest an egalitarian social and political regime for the local population. There appears to be little resemblance of such charnel houses to the previous ceremonial regimes, based on a hierarchically organized set of functionaries focusing on fertility symbolism. There seems to be little doubt that during the Sand Prairie phase the reach of Cahokia into the countryside was feeble at best.

IMPLICATIONS

In this discussion I have tried to demonstrate the presence of a hierarchical structure that existed in the Mississippian countryside about Cahokia between A.D. 1050 and 1350. Going beyond simply identifying the presence of this organizational structure I have tried to present some interpretive context, within reasonable social parameters, that can be derived from the data. I have argued that instead of an undifferentiated panorama of American Bottom rural settlement one has a setting presenting an extremely complex, but well differentiated, political, social, and religious infrastructure.

Furthermore, I believe that the understanding of this complex hierarchical structure can provide political, social, religious, and economic insights into the internal organization and functioning of Cahokia itself. Yet, while I stress the changes in social, religious and political realms, as I discussed earlier, the physiography of the American Bottom, as well as perhaps a changing environmental context, is the stage on which the Mississippian drama was played. I will discuss all of these parameters in the broader context of the conclusions of this volume.

The onset of the Lohmann phase saw the first changes in the hierarchical structure of the landscape about Cahokia with the appearance of status differences and evidence for specialized civic and religious facilities. I have identified three distinct forms of hierarchical settlements on the rural Cahokia Lohmann phase landscape. These include a *nodal household,* a *civic-ceremonial node,* and a *priest-mortuary ceremonial node.* During the Lohmann phase the countryside provided the evidence for the first hints of status/ wealth differentials among the rural populations. No longer was the rural architecture simply the uniform residences of egalitarian, subsistence horticulturists. We now see evidence at a *nodal household* expressed in control over maize storage facilities and exotic/wealth artifacts.

Lohmann leader-commoner distinctions seemed to be marked by limited differential access to stored and exotic goods, as signified at the JUL-3 household. Rural functionaries had some control expressed in the first appearance of specialized substantial maize storage facilities. Storage simply for comestible purposes seemed unlikely because of the limited size of the storage containers. More likely was the storage and control of seed stock for the upcoming season. We should be cognizant, however, of Kelly's (1990b) earlier recognition of the possible ritual connotations of such limestone-floored areas and not too easily accept a facile sacred-profane functional dichotomy for such facilities. Whether the purpose of this storage was for religious, coercive, or humanitarian goals is irrelevant since its function would have been the same: control over the subsistence future of members of the community.

Lohmann phase political, social, and religious activities were community-oriented and made their debut in rural settlements with the appearance of "council houses" and "renewal" ceremonials at *civic/ceremonial nodes* and low-ranking elite mortuary facilities at *ceremonial nodes*. Such activities may have created the first recognizable specialized functionaries, although such recognition was difficult via unusual residential or artifactual patterns. Given the isolation of the Range and BBB Lohmann nodes from nearby households, some resident "guardians" would have been necessary if the sites contained community stores or the remains of revered ancestors. At BBB Motor there was an example of a "guardian's" residence; however, RML-1's one possible residential structure appeared dramatically out of proportion when compared with the many specialized buildings such as the "community house" and storage facilities. There appeared to be little development of residential architecture or facilities for an associated entourage at the Range *civic/ceremonial node,* seemingly indicating that no sizable populations were resident. Consequently, the creation of these specific civic/ceremonial and mortuary nodes was not simply the grafting on of specialized facilities to some preexisting residential complex but rather the construction of entirely new functional types of sites.

The Stirling florescence was marked by the creation of numerous specialized facilities and the appearance of their attendant functionaries throughout the rural areas. There are now three distinct examples of Stirling phase *civic nodes* and two *ceremonial nodes,* including a *temple–mortuary ceremonial node* and *ceremonial node.*

One specific circular wall-trench facility at the Julien *civic node* provided interesting insights into the shifting power base in rural areas between the Lohmann and Stirling phases. This facility was roughly equivalent in size to the limestone-floored "granaries" associated with the Julien Lohmann *nodal household* although it is also within the range of some of the smaller excavated sweat houses. The lack of *any internal evidence* of fires or hearths argues against its being a sweat house, and Milner's original identification (Milner with Williams 1983) of this as a possible community storage building seems reasonable. This identification as an early Stirling storage facility suggests a possible transition of nodal authority from a Lohmann phase base of stored comestibles or seeds indicating civic and/or economic power to one emphasizing ceremonial/religious authority marked by the appearances of Stirling phase sweat houses. It was apparent in the Julien *civic node* that the storage facility was one of the earlier constructions that fell into disuse and was later superimposed by a large wall-trench structure. The presence of the sweat house may have either been contemporaneous with the storage building or, perhaps, appeared during the later part of the *civic node's* occupation. This may mark an important transition of the rural power base near the beginning of the Stirling phase. One of the key markers for Stirling *civic nodes* was the presence of one or more sweat houses. (For a discussion on circular buildings/sweat houses see Mehrer 1988: 155-158; Hanenberger and Mehrer 1998.) The introduction of this ceremonial and/or religious phenomenon into the *civic nodes* represented a significant shift in both the definition and the role of the local leadership toward an alignment with sacred power.

Just as the existence of the Stirling *civic node* strongly indicated the presence of a specialized political leader with a power base linked to the religious realms of ritual purity, the rural temple, mortuary, and fertility *ceremonial nodes* argued emphatically for the emergence of religious and mortuary specialists. In some cases this may have meant the cessation of previous trends. If I have correctly interpreted the coexistence of "renewal" symbolism (i.e., fertility activities) and civic authority in RML-2 and RML-1 in the Lohmann phase nodes, then Stirling *civic nodes* marked the emergence of elite specialization in the exercise of power. In fact, perhaps the single most defining attribute of the Stirling rural landscape was the elaboration of elite roles into at least three recognizable functions as political, religious, and mortuary specialists. Given the nature of the occupation and utilization patterns at the Stirling rural nodes examined, I would argue that these were separate "roles" filled by different individuals (an observation that certainly has ethnographic validity). This social complexity as reflected in architecture, material culture, and symbolism was unmatched in either previous or subsequent periods. The dominant theme emphasized by the Stirling phase elites bespoke the importance of the spiritual realm of fertility and life *and* the importance of its representatives on earth.

By the late Stirling phase, the nature of the rural ritual activities as represented at the Sponemann site took a dramatic new focus that shifted the symbolic emphasis from mortuary to fertility ritual, perhaps simply completing the transition that started in the late Lohmann phase. The isolation of the Sponemann late Stirling phase temple complex differed from that of the two earlier examples. BBB Motor was physically as well as symbolically separated from surrounding habitation areas. The temple complex at Sponemann, on the other hand, while on one extreme of the habitation area, was only about 50 m from what appeared to be a somewhat typical contemporaneous Stirling residential area. Moreover, the Sponemann temple complex may also have had an associated elite residential complex associated with it. This bespoke a different pattern of religious interaction during this latter period.

There was also a great elaboration in the late Stirling ritual paraphernalia and specialized structures and features associated with the Sponemann temple complex. Not only were such items as Ramey Incised ceramics and stone fertility figurines used, but also a diversity of other items were used such as beakers, miniature beakers, effigy bottles and conch shell jars, crystals, hoe caches, and other ceramic and lithic artifacts. The ritual emphasis on red cedar and several medicinal plants continued from previous periods, but tobacco now appeared in a ritual context. Perhaps the most striking change was the proliferation of specialized structures for storage, food preparation, manufacturing, purification, and habitation. From the great number of build- ings within the Sponemann ceremonial complex, it was clear that a number of attendants, including perhaps local elites and priests, were present.

This form of ritual center also had implications for comprehending changes in rural political and social integration. Since Green Corn type fertility cer- emonies functioned primarily as rites of intensification, their presence indi- cated a high level of community activity and integration. The increased emphasis on such rites may well have created the need to synthesize the ritual temple complexes of the late Stirling with surrounding inhabitants and replace to some degree the physical separation of ritually significant complexes with a more symbolic one. I would maintain that such com- plexes might have served as both ritual and political centers of integration for rural populations. This would be especially apparent if those late temple complexes had an elite residential compound associated with them.

Our data are very limited from the Moorehead and Sand Prairie phases; however, there is sufficient information to suggest some possible trends in the development of Cahokian rural political hegemony. The only example of community organization that we currently know from the Moorehead countryside was from the Julien site where our sample reflected the shift from a sacred/religious structure to one again emphasizing a community- centered (i.e., local) base.

Although I have not attempted to disentangle the Moorehead residential compounds, the extensive reuse of a building site and the presence of large structures with ancillary buildings may have indicated the presence of high-status individuals near the community building. The appearance of the Julien "men's house," suggesting local community rather than more distant hierarchical power, harkened back to earlier Lohmann phase systems. The rapid disappearance of the specialized architecture of the previous Stirling phase sweat lodges and temple–mortuary complexes was striking and denoted the organizational change that swept the rural areas at that time. The reappearance of community structures at small rural nodes, coinciding as it did with the disappearance of the religious architecture, indicated the decline of the sacral/religious power base of the previous phase and the reemergence, or perhaps simply renewed dominance, of local community-based political and social forms of power.

The final dissolution of Cahokian power over the countryside was reflected in archaeological evidence from the Sand Prairie phase. During this phase there appeared to be no obvious central nodes of political power in the rural area. High-status houseclusters such as JUL-11 may have represented late Moorehead-early Sand Prairie nodes. If so, they most closely resembled the pattern reflected in the Moorehead houseclusters and reflected the continuance of a trend of houseclusters toward increasing architectural heterogeneity. Also increasing was the presence of prestige/wealth material goods; JUL-11, for example, included cached hoes and Ramey knives, exotic minerals, a flint clay pendant, whelk shell, a galena bead, and an extensive ceramic inventory.

Completely absent from the Sand Prairie phase archaeological record were features such as sweat houses or community-centered social and/or political structures. Evidence, however, of community-centered activity was not absent but, rather, was redirected or refocused on community-centered rural mortuary facilities such as the East St. Louis cemetery or the Florence Street charnel structure and cemetery. These cemeteries may have had some associated ancillary structures (e.g., Structures 60 and 61 at Florence Street), but the evidence for such a phenomenon is unclear at present. These isolated community-centered cemeteries substantiated that significant organizational shifts had been made in Mississippian society. Not only did the attributes of hierarchical political and religious domination seem to have been severely diminished, but the evidence for differentiated ascribed social status as reflected in mortuary patterns seemed reduced.

As I noted earlier in chapter 2, a number of attributes in the material world can be seen as reflecting the waxing and waning of political and ideological power. These included architecture, mortuary practices, and prestige/wealth goods.

The architectural evidence for power demonstrated a shift from politically and religiously based power during the Lohmann phase to a hierarchically based power structure at the beginning of the Stirling phase. It appears there was a return to locally exercised power in the Moorehead and Sand Prairie phases. These trends were reflected in the community council houses of the Lohmann phase, the specialized civic and ceremonial nodes of the Stirling phase, and the community men's houses and cemeteries of the Moorehead and Sand Prairie phases. Rural nodal mortuary patterns also indicated that the rise of local elites and specialized functionaries reached a peak in the Lohmann and Stirling phases with selective low-ranking elite cemeteries and associated structures. These same trends were parallelled by the co-appearance of prestige/wealth artifacts and *sacra*.

There was some indication that surplus control may have been a factor in the early power of Lohmann elites and, given the possible storage facilities at Stirling nodes, may have continued into that phase. However, only in the case of the Lohmann phase do we have evidence suggesting that specialized storage facilities were involved. The presence of specialized political and religious nodes and paraphernalia during the Stirling phase indicated that ideology and coercive power were the primary forces involved in social control at that time.

Not all distributions of artifacts were such clear indicators of patterns. One series of items appears to be diametrically opposed to the above evidence and, instead, reflects the increasing "wealth" of later Mississippian rural folks. This was clear from an examination of the distribution of "exotic" minerals at the Julien site (Milner with Williams 1984: 196). The distribution of these materials across the Stirling, Moorehead, and Sand Prairie phases indicated that only 25% of the Stirling structures contained exotics. In the subsequent two phases, 66.7% and 75% of the structures, respectively, contained exotics. The distribution of hematite, galena, and fragmentary quartz crystals per structure in each phase, respectively, was 0.67, 4.67, and 6.0.

The Stirling phase, with 0.67, was strikingly low in terms of these exotics when compared to the subsequent two phases. The reason for this low index was the total lack of hematite in the Stirling component. In the case of flint clay, mica, marine shell, and copper, the pieces per structure for each of the phases was given as 0.25, 1.00, and 0.25. The Julien Stirling phase structures contained a cross section of the exotic materials, with the interesting exception of hematite, but in no case was there any concentration of such goods within the site. In fact it should be noted that the relative density of the exotics for this phase was actually less than in the two subsequent phases. A similar pattern was found by Trubitt (1996) in her investigations of shell at Cahokia—the amount of shell available increased through time with a maximum in the Moorehead and Sand Prairie phases.

This pattern can be interpreted as a directly inverse indicator of the power of Cahokia over the countryside. Pauketat (1992, 1996) recently provided an insightful contextual model and analysis of Cahokian elite manipulation of local goods to augment their power. He argues that the elite transformed local materials, via their control of craftspeople, into symbols of value which could be redistributed to their retainers among local elites and nonelites. (Such a pattern would not be out of keeping with Frankenstein and Rowlands' [1978: 76–77] assertion that in a prestige goods economy domestic wealth items are devalued and restricted to minor social transactions while foreign wealth objects are formalized to serve as elite sumptuary items.) A similar concept may have been implemented in the control and distribution of both local and exotic raw materials such as hematite, galena, limonite, and quartz crystals. In such instances the power of the material may have been enhanced by its association and transference by elite patrons. Therefore, even though such materials as hematite could be collected in the locality, their "power" may have been controlled by the elite who were essential in the transfer. In other words, only "exotics" that were obtained from the elite truly had symbolic value. In such a case the pattern displayed in the Julien households makes sense in that the limited presence of exotics during the Stirling phase indicates the firm control by the elite on resource distribution or, at least, on their sanctification. With the decline of elite power, rural access to such symbolic power increased with a maximum access, in some instances, appearing in Sand Prairie components; that access indicated the complete collapse of hierarchical control. Additional support for such an interpretation can also be found in the use of grave goods in rural mortuary sites (e.g., contrast the virtual absence of mortuary items with low-ranking elite burials at BBB Motor with the abundance of items recovered from the later Florence and East St. Louis cemeteries).

ORGANIZING THE COUNTRYSIDE

In the previous sections I have detailed the various forms of rural nodal sites and discussed some implications that changes in these forms through time may have for understanding Cahokian rural political, social, and religious organization. In concluding this discussion I would like to touch briefly on how I envision the countryside organized within the Cahokian polity.

The concept of the "dispersed village" was introduced into Mississippian settlement terminology through Brian Butler's research in the Black Bottom around the Kincaid site in southern Illinois. Essentially, such a village included "a closely spaced group of one or more hamlets and accompanying farmsteads" (Butler 1977: 256) that was spatially separate from similar groups and was assumed to represent the lowest level of sociopolitical community within the society. Additionally, he accepted Riordan's (1975: 115-122) recognition of nodal sites within such dispersed villages that "fulfilled basic integrative functions in binding the individual farmsteads into a larger network. These functions may have included various religious, ceremonial, and redistributive activities" (Butler 1977: 560-561). Essentially, the presence of such dispersed villages argues for the existence of possible additional organizational levels within Mississippian hierarchical settlement beyond mound centers (i.e., figure 4.1b). This argues for an increased elaboration and diversity of settlements outside of the mound centers and could be considered evidence of increasing levels of sociopolitical complexity.

The dispersed villages are seen as the elemental political and economic units within hierarchically constituted political and economic systems. In the commonly accepted interpretation of the Cahokian settlement system, fourth-line settlements were viewed as being directly attached to a second- or third-line community. In such a system, the farmsteads were associated in a one-to-one relationship to the town (cf. figure 4.1a). In a dispersed village settlement system, the basic level of relationships was directed sequentially between farmsteads, civic nodal sites, and ceremonial nodes (cf. figure 4.1b). In other words, the household units were integrated with one another via local ceremonial nodes and their attendant ceremonialism and social/political relationships formed through the local leadership at the nodal point level. It was at this level that interaction occurred and relationships were maintained with hierarchically superior communities.

With such a system operating during the Mississippian period in the American Bottom, one might suggest that much of the population was dispersed across the landscape. Sites such as Cahokia could be conceived of as having populations consisting of high-status lineage members and their associated retainers such as religious and political (perhaps also craft) specialists. In such a system the political history and power of Cahokia could be viewed as a series of fluctuations that corresponded with the ability of the elite to integrate the dispersed population into a cohesive whole. In the four-century history of Cahokia one would expect many variations in the degree of integration, resulting in increases and decreases in the extent of Cahokia's influence.

This picture corresponds more closely to those of southeastern chiefdoms as well as chiefdoms the world over (cf. Anderson 1994). The monumental constructs at mound centers were the archaeological reflection of periods of high levels of integration, while low levels were probably characterized by the absence of public constructions. There may have been a direct relationship between the amount of mound construction activities at first, second, and tertiary mound centers and their political power. During periods when Cahokia's power was at its zenith, public construction may have been concentrated at that site to the exclusion of the smaller centers. Conversely, during periods when Cahokia was less influential, the increased power of secondary mound centers may have been reflected in a rise of public construction. Throughout all of this, the dispersed villages existed as the units of allegiance, integration, and control for the rural populace.

The appropriateness of this model of American Bottom Mississippian settlement can be examined from a number of perspectives. The combination of faunal and botanical data recovered from household units indicated that they may have been occupied year-round (e.g., Jackson and Hanenberger 1990; Milner with Williams 1983, 1984; Milner et al. 1984). In the past it had been suggested that such households were only seasonally occupied by families moving between the towns and scattered household units. This pattern of seasonal movement was not supported by the majority of the archaeological evidence, although some apparently short-term occupations were present (cf. Finney 1993). In general, this indicated that populations of the centers and the dispersed villages were two discrete groups. This decreases the possibility of social integration between centers and the household units on the basis of part-time occupation by families in both places. Unfortunately, a lack of archaeological investigations and evidence regarding nonmound centers does not allow us to address the relationship of rural dispersed villages with such entities.

If one examines the distribution of fourth-line communities throughout the adjacent bluffs and bottomlands of the American Bottom region, it is evident that some were quite far from centers. Given what is known of historic Southeastern groups and inferences concerning Mississippian groups, the role of ceremonialism and ritual was a frequent and important integrating force in the lives of the social group. An annual or even semiannual trip to a secondary center did not fulfill the needs of a population that was dependent on almost a daily need to maintain a balance between purity and pollution. Given our knowledge of the relationship of present-day peasant or rural populations to religious centers, it is hard to envision the household units establishing a sense of community with a somewhat distant mound center. I think that the basic definition of community for a Mississippian rural family was a group of households integrated via nodal sites with their community meeting houses, sweat houses, storage structures, local leaders, and temple–mortuary complexes. This dispersed village pattern can be seen as the basic integrative unit of political/social/religious activities. From this perspective, the Cahokian settlement hierarchy could simply be conceived of as consisting of five, rather than four, levels.

As has been recorded for the historic Southeast (Swanton 1946; Hudson 1976), and in fact, throughout much of the Eastern Woodlands (cf. Green 1977; Woods 1987; Smith, ed. 1978), this pattern of dispersed settlements was the preferred pattern. Towns were specialized in function, serving primarily as the habitations of the elite (i.e., the religious/political leaders, their lineage, and the support community). They also served as the focal point for the social group. There is evidence suggesting that such communities and/or chiefdoms were not all large-scale entities. Creek chiefdoms ranged in size from a single town or settlement to many, but the critical factor was that they possessed their own ceremonial center (Hudson 1976: 237). Adair (Hudson 1976: 211) records a number of Chickasaw chiefdoms that were restricted in size. One covered an area of one by six miles, another one by four miles, and a third (which may have been several affiliated chiefdoms) an area one to two miles wide by ten miles long. This suggests that incipient political consolidation may have arisen from the earlier Emergent Mississippian villages and hamlets. Such small scattered settlements, in turn, may have been the origin of some of the later Mississippian villages and smaller mound centers. The evidence for this pattern of dispersed settlements is widespread in the literature. Unfortunately, few data deal with the various levels of political organization or religious activity that might have been associated with such a settlement pattern.

DISCUSSION

This study has revealed new and previously unrecognized settlement patterns in the Cahokian countryside. The fourth-line communities defined by Fowler's modeling of surface collection data have now been replaced with a complex pattern of multiple, functionally differentiated sites that shift throughout the political history of Cahokia. It is possible to recognize a complex web of organizational relationships within the rural areas. During the entire Mississippian occupation of the floodplain of the American Bottom, the landscape was dotted with farmsteads and special-purpose structures. These formed the basal level of all Mississippian settlements. Even at this level, however, we can see the differentiation that appeared in the form of *nodal households* that represented the introduction of ranking into rural Cahokia. Such household nodes served both as the residences of rural functionaries and as local gathering places. In the instances of rural settlements in the American Bottom, instead of being directly articulated to mound centers, I have argued that this dispersed population was sequentially articulated into *dispersed villages* through nodal sites. The epitome of this organizational pattern was seen in the *civic/ceremonial nodes* of the Lohmann and *civic* and *ceremonial nodes* of the Stirling phases.

Furthermore, I suggest the *priest-mortuary* and *temple-mortuary ceremonial nodes* may have served as an integrating mechanism for surrounding rural dispersed villages. These ceremonial centers may have been the center for a *ritual district* and served as locations for low-ranking elite ceremonies to propitiate agricultural deities and as mortuary facilities for the local elite lineage. These *ritual districts* may have been linked directly to ceremonial complexes at the major mound centers (figure 4.1b right).

There is little basis for reconstructing the nature of the political relationship between such rural elite and the rulers of Cahokia. It seems reasonable, however, to suggest that rural elite must have been directly appointed to their positions by the Cahokian paramount. There is evidence from ethnohistoric and ethnographic accounts (e.g., Swanton 1946; Hudson 1976 and references cited therein) that hierarchical southeastern native societies retained numerous elite "offices" such as these into the historic period. Excellent examples of such complex organizations of offices is documented by Scarry (1992) for the Apalachee and by Wyckoff and Baugh (1980) for the Caddoan Hasinai. Such research documents the existence of individual positions such as chiefs, subchiefs, elders, priests, and advisers who had diverse assigned political, social, and religious duties and responsibilities. These individuals gained their positions through both achieved and ascribed attributes such as war honors, age, moral character, wisdom, kin affiliation, religious experience, or other such mechanisms. While the specific mechanisms that prehistoric Cahokian elite used to select the rural officials who organized the rural population cannot be determined, historic analogies suggest appointments would have been made on the basis of the relatedness of the candidates to the elite lineages, clan affiliation, and personal accomplishments.

The demonstration of the complexity of the organizational structure of the Cahokian rural countryside begs two questions: (1) what was the nature of the center-rural political and religious relationship? and (2) what are the implications of this relationship for understanding Cahokia's internal organization?

In most current interpretations the Cahokian rural populace is represented as moderately stable residential groups of fairly self-sufficient subsistence farmers. As I have demonstrated, this perspective obscures critical settlement variability that contains important insights into rural organizational structure.

One product of such interpretations was Saitta's (1994) proposal that Cahokian political relationships were governed by "communalism." He (Saitta

Cahokia and the Archaeology of Power

1994: 205-206) portrayed this as a nonexploitive interaction between commoners and elites in which it was proper to view the producers as extracting
surplus from themselves as members of a communal entity to pay elites to
perform the activities and ceremonies seen as necessary to perpetuate society. The assumption that Cahokians avoided nonexploitive situations is based
on the observation that small communities appeared to have access to ad-
equate health, foodstuffs, pigments, exotic ceramics, marine shell, and other
items that might be considered signs of wealth or status. Saitta's assumption
that elite exploitation (more accurately read *power over* here) must have been
reflected in the material deprivation of the commoners seems overdrawn.
Cahokian elite were able to commit the labor of their fellow citizens to
massive public works (on a scale that dwarfed others in North America), to
differentiate themselves in elaborate mortuary displays that subsumed extensive wealth and took the lives of many of their citizens for sacrifice; they
were able to recreate the rural and urban social and settlement patterns and
to separate themselves from the world of the commoners by inhabiting a
sacred landscape. The Cahokian elite clearly exerted extensive power over
the daily existence of the common people—no amount of "the good life"
for the commoners could obscure that point.

It could be argued that what was being observed in Cahokia was the
imposition of hegemony in the "guise of communalism" (Pauketat and
Emerson 1996). People are usually full partners and participants in their
own subordination (Foucault 1978); this is as true for the "dominators" as
for the "dominated." Elite emergence is generally undertaken with the full
support of the masses; however, the total economic exploitation and deprivation of the masses by the elite are not the automatic results of such a
process. These modern attempts to "empower" the prehistoric masses by
posing them as "controllers" and "donators" of their surplus labor surely is a
subterfuge worthy of those long-departed Cahokian elites.

The inherent danger in overemphasizing rural population continuity and
stability is that one can mistake them for "autonomy," as Mehrer (1988) did
in modeling the Mississippian rural political landscape. He (1988: 140-141)
suggested that the relative economic self-reliance of family farmsteads, especially during the Stirling phase, indicated a pattern of "substantial independence." Conceptually, this independence was reflected in rural populations
"pulling themselves up by their own bootstraps"—a process in which they
"developed private storage facilities, maintained relatively isolated positions
on the landscape, and developed a hierarchy among themselves based on the
civic and mortuary ceremonialism that helped them integrate as a community" (Mehrer 1988: 151). Carried to its logical extent, such communities
would not even be part of the Cahokian settlement system. I find this pic-

ture incongruous within the context of the small areal extent of the American Bottom and the power of the hierarchically organized Cahokian polity. While there is reason to accept the long-term economic stability of the rural populations based on the agricultural potential of the landscape and the patterned reuse of some building sites, this does not translate into political or ceremonial independence. This approach also overemphasizes the importance of the economic sphere at the expense of political and religious factors. The organization of the countryside should be more appropriately viewed as the result of the direct imposition of an organizational structure by the elite of Cahokia as I argue throughout this text.

What evidence is there that centralized coercive and ideological power rather than independent imitation was the motivating factor for the structural modifications we saw in the rural archaeological record? Perhaps the strongest argument we possess is the nature of hierarchical governments, their penchant for control, concern for security and boundaries, and general intolerance for "nonconformist" groups. I believe that the hierarchical nature of the Cahokia polity can be accepted as a given, based on the existing evidence of the archaeological record. Consequently, I assume that, in keeping with the known attributes of such societies and forms of government, the Cahokia chiefly elite emphasized centripetal control of surpluses, labor, religion, and trade. Such polities do not tolerate "independent groups" within their boundaries since these groups present direct threats to the ruling elite and possibly even compete for local leadership. The question, when examining the rural populace associated with such a polity, is not whether it was "independent" or "dependent," but rather, to what degree were they controlled by the centralized elite and how did that control vary through space and time? I will briefly examine some of these issues below.

In visualizing the Cahokian political countryside, one must first establish its spatial parameters. In general I am discussing scattered Mississippian rural sites spread across the northern portion of the American Bottom. The Range site was the most southern of the known nodal centers discussed in this volume (and it may have been under the control of the Pulcher Mound center rather than Cahokia per se; cf. Kelly 1993); it lay less than 20 km from Monks Mound, the center of the Cahokian polity. Interestingly this is still 10 km less than the maximum distance (30 km, i.e., a one-day walk) that most researchers (e.g., Hally 1993) agree would have formed the limits of practical transport and travel in pedestrian, chiefly societies. The majority of American Bottom farmsteads, ceremonial nodes, and civic centers excavated to date lie much closer to Cahokia. Given the extensive known water routes through the floodplain, these sites would have been easily accessible by dugout from the mound centers. This was not a situation where the rural populace thrived in splendid independent isolation, protected by difficult terrain or long distances from centralized control.

If, as has been suggested by Milner (1990) and myself (Emerson 1991b), the American Bottom was often a politically unstable environment due to possible conflicts between various mound centers and clashing elite factions, the existence of independent rural populations seems untenable. Such populations would swiftly have been eliminated or incorporated into one of the contending polities. DePratter (1983), in reviewing southeastern native chiefdoms, found that similar hostile relations resulted in each chiefdom being surrounded by a buffer zone that served as a "no-man's land" between competing polities. These barriers, as well as elite desire for control, would have tended to produce a centripetal effect on rural populations, drawing them toward the political centers and greater elite control and protection.

The distribution of wealth and status items in the rural nodes indicated a close affiliation with the source of such goods. Pauketat and I (1991; Emerson 1989) have argued that the distribution of Ramey Incised pottery was related to centralized "rites of intensification" controlled by elite at various mound centers. Such an interpretation was implied by the symbolic unity of the ware, its distributional pattern, and history of manufacture. Furthermore, the movement of such prestige/wealth items as marine shell, hematite, galena, crystals, and exotic/ritual ceramics implied center-rural relationships that hinged on trade, reciprocity, or status. Perhaps the most telling status artifacts were the stone goddesses associated with the rural ceremonial nodes. Stylistically, these figurines showed a great homogeneity that suggested they were crafted by a limited number of artisans, most likely associated with the Cahokian elite. The distribution of these important cult objects could only have been via a Cahokian hierarchy. This movement of important status items out into the countryside also indicated the existence of facilitating interaction networks, probably most closely linked to political and religious power between the center and the rural leaders.

The very picture of a continuing stable rural population independent of the mound centers can be questioned. As noted earlier in this section there was a dramatic shift in population density and distribution associated with the Mississippian emergence. The late Emergent Mississippian period was characterized by an increase in village size and density and a decrease in corresponding dispersed rural populations (cf. Kelly 1990a, 1990b). There is good reason to suspect that the Emergent Mississippian–Middle Mississippian transition was marked by a dramatic depopulation of rural areas as populations become nucleated in the new larger town centers (cf. Kelly 1992; Pauketat 1991, 1994). In such cases, there is reason to question whether the late Emergent Mississippian rural populations and the subsequent Lohmann rural populations in the immediate Cahokia locality were, indeed, the same groups or whether the Lohmann countryside was not created anew by repopulation from the centers. The occupation of the countryside may not have been as continuous or as stable as some would like to think. In fact, as I have argued earlier, there is good reason to assume that the Lohmann reoccupation of the countryside was a specific goal of the Cahokian rulers in order to increase agricultural production. Such an increase would have been necessary to supply the increased population of Cahokia with sufficient foodstuffs to support them.

A powerful argument for centralized control within the Cahokia-based polity was the demonstrated synchronism of change between Cahokia and the rural nodes. I discuss this at length in chapter 9, but briefly preview that coverage here. I have noted previously (Emerson 1991b) that one of the remarkable phenomena of the Middle Mississippian emergence was the appearance of a homogeneous material world. The stylistic uniformity of the Lohmann phase ceramic assemblages, religious practices, architectural styles, and organizational patterns swept away the heterogeneous, disparate world of the late Emergent Mississippians. This phase was marked by the first large-scale appearance of elite-associated architecture, monuments, fertility cult symbolism, and distinct mortuary patterns representing direct and subtle working of Cahokian power (cf. Foucault 1979). This interaction also included the steady flow of ceramics and other prestige/wealth goods to the rural nodes. At the very least this transformation bespoke a cultural unity at Cahokia and the rural areas.

This trend toward uniformity continued in marking phase shifts both at Cahokia and in the rural nodes. The onset of the Stirling phase at Cahokia was heralded by the increased emphasis on elite monument construction and the area-wide adoption of the trappings of the fertility cult (Ramey symbolism and stone goddesses). In the rural areas the construction of ceremonial nodes dedicated to both elite mortuary and elite fertility ceremonies and the existence of civic political nodes indicated strong central influences at this time.

The Moorehead decline was poorly understood at Cahokia but was clearly reflected in a decrease of monumental construction. This decrease in power was also reflected in the rural areas with the disappearance of Stirling phase civic and ceremonial nodes and their replacement with community-based "men's houses." Even greater disparity was reflected in the Sand Prairie phase with no evidence of Cahokian centralized power present in the countryside. The rural populations seemed to consist of scattered farmsteads whose communal activities centered on mortuary complexes.

At this point, I would like to return to the earlier question:"What are the implications of this center-rural relationship for understanding Cahokia's internal organization?"As related in earlier discussions (chapter 2) concerning hierarchical societies, one of the key factors in assessing their degree of "centrism" hinges on the amount of horizontal variation present in individual hierarchical levels (Johnson 1973, 1978; Wright 1969, 1977; Wright and Johnson 1975). I have documented the diachronic and functional shifts in nodal settlement forms through the Mississippian period in the American Bottom. If one accepts that rural organization was a direct reflection of centrist relations with Cahokia, then these variations should provide insights on the political structure of Cahokia.

As we currently understand Cahokia, at the height of its power during the Lohmann and Stirling phases, there may have been three administrative levels represented by mound centers. These levels would have included a paramount chief at Cahokia, secondary chiefs at the secondary multiple mound centers, and a lower tertiary set of elite at single mound centers. It must be recognized, however, that there is virtually no evidence to arrange these mound centers in such a hierarchical relationship beyond diminishing mound group size. In many cases it is not even possible to determine if these centers were occupied contemporaneously. Equally unknown are the social, religious, and political networks that may have linked the centers.

It is only when one moved to the smaller Mississippian sites that firm evidence became available with which to examine social, political, and religious relationships. Fowler recognized a "fourth-level" hierarchy comprising nonmounded villages, farmsteads, and hamlets. In this research, I have replaced that vision with a rural landscape that is shown to be functionally and organizationally complex and that involved dispersed villages linked through civic and ceremonial nodes. I have also suggested there was another level of integration of dispersed villages into rural ritual districts; if this was so, it would indicate a rural hierarchical complexity in the Cahokian system that went far beyond that identified in other southeastern prehistoric polities.

If one follows current taxonomic thinking on social typology, the suggestion of these multiple hierarchical levels and the evidence for functional variation within levels would preclude Cahokia's categorization as a paramount chiefdom.This is especially true if my identification of the functional differentiation of civic and ceremonial nodes is correct for the Stirling phase countryside.This identification of extensive horizontal and vertical diversity in the hierarchical decision-making levels would seem to fly in the face of Wright's (1984: 42) assertion that chiefly societies are not "internally specialized in terms of different aspects of the control process." In fact, such functional specialization falls within the standard "state" definition as "specialized government" (i.e., Wright 1977: 383).

To the question of whether Cahokia might best be "typed" as a chiefdom or a state, I might appropriately respond with the common phrase: "If you ask a meaningless question you will surely get a meaningless answer." Interpretive attempts based on social typology can produce many such answers. Directed study of Cahokian political structure has been hampered and the goals obscured by many researchers' adherence to a typological approach in the classification of societies. De Montmollin (1989: 11-16), in a useful critique of the misguided thinking that social typologies generate in the characterization of ancient political organization and structure, demonstrated that such approaches operate at a high level of abstraction that obscures critical synchronic and diachronic variability within societies. Such abstractions often reify society and eliminate from consideration intragroup diversity, cooperation, and conflict—surely critical factors in understanding political structure.

Most distressing, however, is the tendency in such approaches for the identification and "typing" of ancient societies to become an end in itself. Such a goal may be based upon the unsubstantiated belief that variables used to distinguish social types are causally related and covary. Consequently, such research assumes that if the presence of one variable can be documented, the presence of the inferred variables can be assumed. Examples of such presumptions abound in Cahokian interpretations. However, there is extensive documentation (cf. De Montmollin 1989: 14-15; Feinman and Neitzel 1984; Spencer 1987; Upham 1987) indicating that the variables used to define societal types (e.g., chiefdoms or states) do not necessarily *covary*. The search to identify ancient Cahokian political structure and organization through the identification of its societal type is rejected here as a viable or fruitful research strategy.

What is most important is that the above evidence indicates that the Cahokian hierarchical organization was among the most complex known in North America and certainly was the most complex in the Eastern Woodlands. The identification of extensive horizontal diversity (a la Lightfoot) at the lowest level of hierarchical organization within the Cahokian polity at its peak, the functional differentiation of managerial tasks within the lowest settlement levels, and the evidence for the mobilization of comestibles have important implications for our understanding of various models for interpreting the past. It is only by detailed studies such as this that we can begin to unravel the complexity of prehistoric political organization in the Mississippi River Valley and move beyond chiefdom and state typologies.

7

The Cahokian Symbolic World

As Gramsci has shown, persuasion is as critical a factor as force in the construction of hegemonic control. This persuasion may take the form of a dominant ideology that shapes and naturalizes a society's vision of the cultural and natural worlds surrounding it. In the hands of the elite, this ideological vision seeks to ensure the reproduction of the social and political order. Earle (1987, 1991) proposes that this reproduction is accomplished through the symbolic representations of sacred landscapes, individual and warrior power, and the community-centered re-creation of ceremonial presentations of powers to the elite by cosmic forces. It is apparent then that to understand the control and domination of their society by the Cahokian elite, we need to elucidate their ideological base.

I begin that process of understanding Cahokian ideology by examining the ritual behavior and symbolic system implicit in the material assemblages of Cahokia Middle Mississippian sites, especially focusing on symbolically rich temple sites. Two types of symbolic materials have provided great insights into Mississippian religion and ideology—stone figurines and sacred vessels. Based on the common themes derived from these sources, it is evident that, during Cahokia's era of supremacy, much of its religious ideology was linked to fertility and Under World motifs. Underlying all such themes, however, was the presence of a world view dominated by a dualistic, quadripartitioned universe that revealed itself in a number of mediums. It is within this context that, in the following chapter, I explore the material expressions of this symbolic system in the countryside and its utilization by the elite to dominate and rule the rural populace.

Over the decades, research on Cahokia has shown that these prehistoric peoples had few links with the Algonquian Indian peoples the first Europeans encountered in the area (cf. Emerson and Brown 1992). Cahokian culture, with its complex political and social organization, religious beliefs, and horticultural basis, is more appropriately seen as part of the same cultural milieu as the late prehistoric and historic chiefdoms encountered by early Europeans in the southeastern United States. This similarity indicates that in attempting to understand the symbolism and structuration of the ancient inhabitants of Cahokia we are not limited to the recovered archaeological data; a rich world of documentation from early Eastern Woodland native inhabitants promises to enrich and expand our understanding of the Cahokian symbolic repertoire. An essential bulwark of my arguments and interpretations in this work is acceptance of the validity of the ethnohistoric and ethnographic evidence from Eastern Woodlands native groups as a source of insight into Mississippian iconography and religion. I am confident that it is a valid approach and one supported by a long history of successful implementation by archaeologists in the eastern United States. As Vernon J. Knight, Jr., states:

> Within an historical perspective, the theme of previous investigations of these issues by Swanton [numerous works], Waring [1968; Waring and Holder 1945], and Howard [1968] was a demonstration of the importance of the diachronic link from Mississippian archaeology to the ethnohistorical record of the Southeastern Indians. These investigators found positive links between historically recorded ritual, icons, and myths on the one hand, and Mississippian ritual features and icons on the other. They concluded, from different perspectives and attending to different data, that historical Southeastern aboriginal religion was in essence a debased form of a uniform religious complex which reached its peak in Mississippian times, and that historical manifestations could therefore be used to make inferences about the ancestral forms known to archaeology. (Knight 1981: 127)

More recent scholars have elaborated and refined the earlier approaches to provide a greater depth and breadth of interpretation of Mississippian iconography and ritual. In this regard I would cite as examples the research of Robert L. Hall (e.g., 1976, 1977, 1979, 1985, and especially 1989 and 1991), Knight (1981, 1986, 1989a, 1989b), Prentice (1986a), Brown (1976a, 1985), Kelly (1984; Kelly et al. 1990), Phillips and Brown (1978), Fortier (1991c), Emerson (1982, 1983, 1989, 1995), and Pauketat and Emerson (1991). These more detailed studies have not only served to validate the relationship between the archaeological and ethnohistoric records but have also shown the widespread nature of many of the involved iconographic, ritual, and belief systems.

In dealing with an uneven and diverse ethnohistoric record, the problem lies in identifying the core-shared iconographic structure as distinguished from individual group variation. This problem can be amplified by interclass variation (e.g., elite versus commoner) within a regional context. Confusion of regional details and variation with broader patterns of meaningful structuration can seriously hamper our understanding of Mississippian symbolic patterning. Useful sources to direct one from the idiosyncratic particulars to the broader patterns include now classic studies of Southeastern Indians by Hudson (1976), in which he presents a synthetic overview of the cosmological system of the native tribes (albeit with strong Cherokee overtones), and Howard's (1968) and Waring's (1968) examinations of the Southeastern Ceremonial Complex. In addition, I have discussed elsewhere, in detail (Emerson 1989), the subtleties and ramifications of interpreting the symbolic context of the Cahokian belief system.

STONE GODDESSES

A number of Middle Mississippian stone figurines of the highly artistic Cahokia style (cf. Emerson 1983) were recovered from the American Bottom (cf. Emerson 1982), and they provide unique insight into aspects of Cahokian symbolism. The most spectacular and contextually certain examples of these figurines came from the BBB Motor and Sponemann Stirling phase rural ceremonial sites. These figurines are unmatched in their symbolic content and their potential value in exploring the Cahokian spiritual world.

Both the BBB Motor and Sponemann figurines first appeared to be made of reddish brown bauxite, the closest source for which was Arkansas (see discussions in Emerson 1982, 1983, 1989, 1995: 329-330; Prentice 1986a). However, early descriptions of American Bottom stone figurines identified them as made from "fireclay" (e.g., see notes on file at the Missouri Historical Society made by Gerald Fowke at the accessioning of the B&O figurine in the late nineteenth century). Fireclay, or more correctly in geological terms, "flint clay," is a local material in southeastern Missouri (McQueen 1943) that closely resembles bauxite in color, texture, and workability. Samples from east-central Missouri appear megascopically indistinguishable from the material used to manufacture the Birger figurine.

Although past attempts to source the material have provided ambiguous results (i.e., James Gunderson quoted in Jackson et al. 1991: 277-279), our recent efforts have been successful. Using X-ray diffraction and step-dissolution inductively coupled plasma analysis, Hughes and Emerson (1995, 1996) were able to demonstrate that the material the figurines were manufactured from was Missouri "flint clays" from sources located in several counties near metropolitan St. Louis. Use of this local material for the manufacture of American Bottom figurines was in keeping with a pattern in which much

American Bottom Mississippian trade with this area occurred in galena (Walthall 1981), Crescent Quarry cherts (McElrath 1983), and ceramics (Milner et al. 1984; Kelly 1991b).

The BBB Motor Site Figurines

Two flint clay figurines are associated with the Stirling temple area of the BBB Motor Site. The Birger sculpture (figure 7.1) depicts a kneeling or squatting female on a circular base (variously described in detail in Emerson 1982, 1989, 1995). Her left hand rests on the head of a serpent, and her right hand holds a hoe with which she tills the serpent's back. The feline-headed serpent, lying curled about the woman's knees, is a stylized rendering of a puma *(Felis concolor)*. On the woman's back is a flat, square pack held in place by a strap wrapped around her shoulders.

The serpent's body bifurcates and is transformed into vines with fruits that run diagonally up her back and over her left shoulder. Although the carver took some artistic license with the fruits, it is clear they are gourds or squash. More recently, Gayle Fritz, based on her extensive and ongoing research with *Cucurbita,* made a compelling argument (1994) that the fruit is the hitherto unrecognized *Cucurbita argyrosperma.* Fritz's identification of this species in Ozark sites and Mississippian iconography indicated ongoing contacts between the Southwest and the Central Mississippi Valley in the late prehistoric period.

The Keller figurine (described in detail in Emerson 1982, 1989, 1995) represents a female kneeling on a rectangular base (figure 7.2). Her forehead depicts cranial deformation, and her long, straight hair is pulled back behind her ears and hangs down her back to below the waist. The lower portions of her body are covered with a short wraparound skirt that ends just above the knees. The figure is kneeling on a series of contiguous rectangles, some with vertical lines enclosed in shallow arcs on their upper portions. These items have been interpreted as ears of corn. In front of the woman is a rectangular, boxlike object; the lower part is composed of vertical rods, and the upper portion is smoothed, slightly rounded, and loaf shaped. I originally interpreted this object as a metate, based on a possible analogy with the Figure at Mortar figure pipe from Spiro. The presence of additional examples from the Sponemann site suggests that a basket motif is a more likely explanation. Along the right side of the basket rests a vertical object that has been broken off on its upper surface. This likely represents a plant stalk base, possibly maize, that emerges from the corncob base on which it rests. The stalk then presumably rises, to be grasped by the right hand of the figure. From there

Figure 7.1 Birger Figurine; ca. 20 cm in height (Photo by Linda Alexander, used with permission of the Illinois Transportation Archaeological Research Program).

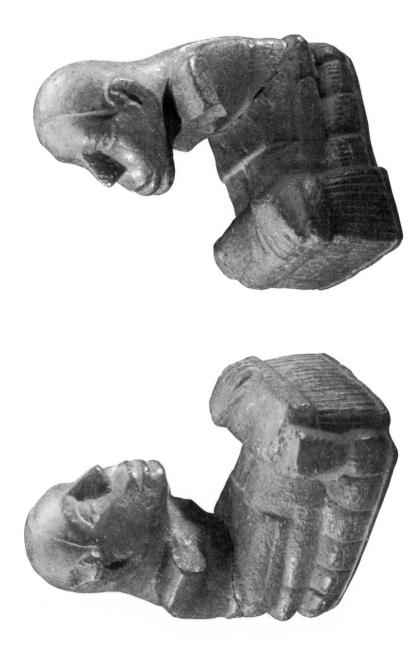

Figure 7.2 Keller Figurine; ca. 13 cm in height (Photo by Linda Alexander, used with permission of the Illinois Transportation Archaeological Research Program).

Cahokia and the Archaeology of Power

it sweeps back to attach to the side of the head, just above the ear, where there is a broken area.

This interpretation of the attributes from the Keller figurine is supported by traits observed in the McGehee figure pipe recovered near the mouth of the Arkansas River. Perino (1971: 117) described it as a kneeling male figure holding stalks of corn or sunflowers. I had the opportunity to examine this pipe briefly at the Cottonlandia Conference. While I cannot comment in detail until a more thorough study can be made, the figure does represent a kneeling individual with hands outstretched on the ground. From each palm a plant stalk grows up and over the figure's shoulders where the stalks are attached. Such a depiction suggested that what the Keller figure grasps in its right hand may be the base of a plant stalk that reaches up and attaches at the broken area on the right temple. This association of female deities with vegetative growth is a dominant one in the Cahokia figurines and appears clearly depicted in the Keller, Birger, Willoughby, Sponemann and, perhaps, the Schild pieces.

The Sponemann Site Figurines

The Sponemann site late Stirling component contained the deliberately shattered remains of at least three flint clay figurines that show evidence of deliberate destruction. A total of 533 pieces have been identified, 509 of which were recovered from the temple, Structure 282. Despite the prehistoric burning and fragmentation of the specimens, analysts were able to reconstruct major portions of three figurines, labeled the Sponemann, Willoughby, and West figurines. The following discussion is based on information from Fortier's (1991b) detailed descriptions and my personal examination of photographs and the actual figurine fragments.

The Sponemann figurine (figure 7.3) represents the head, upper torso, and arms of a female. The carving of this specimen was of high quality and many of the features are reminiscent of the Birger figurine, especially its detailed facial features. Other features include unornamented ears, a necklace, breasts with nipples, possible gourds or pack on the back, and a headband or turban (or more likely a tumpline?). The individual's arms are outstretched, with palms up. From each palm a plant stalk arches upward to the side of the figure's head (a la the McGehee figurine). While the specific plant species are uncertain, they may represent sunflowers or corn.

The most complex specimen recovered is the Willoughby figurine (figure 7.4). It also represents a highly fragmented and incomplete female with only portions of the head, upper torso, and lower body present. The upper torso includes obvious breasts, detailed facial features, an unornamented ear,

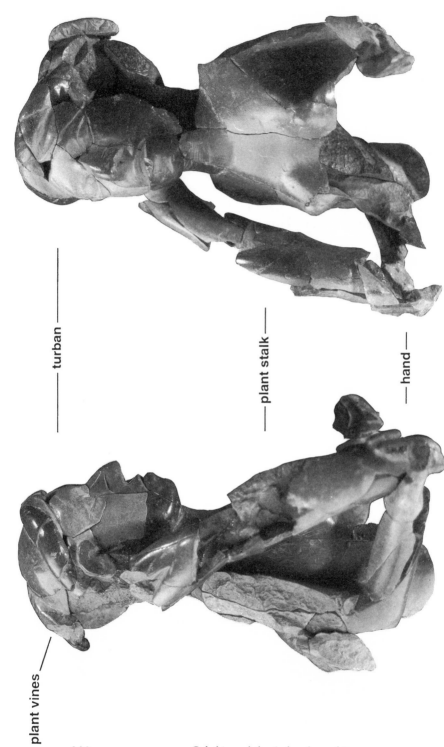

turban

plant stalk

hand

plant vines

Figure 7.3 Sponemann Figurine; ca. 15 cm in height (Photo by Linda Alexander, used with permission of the Illinois Transportation Archaeological Research Program).

Cahokia and the Archaeology of Power

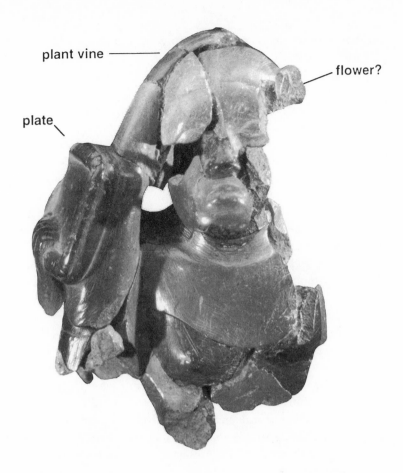

plant vine ————

flower?

plate

Figure 7.4 Willoughby Figurine; ca. 10 cm in height (Photo by Linda Alexander, used with permission of the Illinois Transportation Archaeological Research Program).

hands holding rectangular "vessels," and branching plant vines. The rectangular "vessels" might be dishes associated with ethnohistorically reported Green Corn ceremonialism (Fortier 1991b: 285) or may represent rectangular stone "paint" palettes similar to those recovered from the Moundville area.

The lower torso includes a rectangular basket and lower leg portions wrapped in a skirt. In the Willoughby basket the engraved panels are both horizontal and vertical, strongly suggesting woven cane(?) construction. Yet the cover of this basket is smooth and undecorated like that of the Keller figurine. As Fortier (1991b: 285) indicated, it seems that such a basket would also have a realistically portrayed woven cover. This leaves us again with a question as to the nature of the item being shown—perhaps the symbolic motif of cloud and rain I suggested earlier for Keller (Emerson 1982: 10) did play some role in this portrayal.

The snake motif plays a dominant role in the West figurine fragments (figure 7.5) that have been assembled. In this case, the figurine segments depict an apparent female with a rattlesnake coiled on her head and consist of: "(1) a human head with a snake coiled around it, forming a kind of head turban; (2) a front and back torso piece with a small right breast and back ornament, perhaps a portion of backpack; and (3) a complex of snake heads (n = 2) and a large [tail] rattle, all of which are sculpted in the round and attached to the left side of the head piece" (Fortier 1991b: 290). The snake depicted in this figurine does not in any way resemble the feline-headed serpent of the Birger figurine, but it is a specific portrayal of the rattlesnake, including its triangular head and its tail rattles. As the snake coils on the figure's head, it closely resembles "turbans" present on other figurines, suggesting a possible correlation (Fortier 1991b: 290). One of the other fragments depicts a snake head held in a human hand, perhaps representing a situation similar to that in the Birger figurine.

Because of the fragmented condition of the specimens (Fortier 1991b: 290-302), 120 worked pieces could not be associated with a specific figurine, but they contained important information on Mississippian symbolic motifs. These included recognizable sections of vines, plant stalks, baskets, torsos, snake-gourds, and other miscellaneous items. At least two other basket forms similar to that depicted on the Keller figurine were present. Two fragments may be decorated gourd or backpack motifs. Also recovered was a small fragment showing the lashings on a stone hoe virtually identical to the Birger figurine hoe.

Related Images

A number of stone figures showed a demonstrable thematic relationship to the BBB Motor and Sponemann site figurines. These included the striking "Figure at Mortar" pipe from the Great Mortuary at Spiro (Brown 1976b: 251), the more abstract Schild site pipe (Perino 1971: 119) from the Lower Illinois River Valley, the Svehla effigy elbow pipe (Emerson 1996), and the McGehee figure found on the Arkansas River (Perino: 1971: 117).

The Figure at Mortar effigy (Burnett 1945: 12-13, plates VII, VIII, IX) depicts a kneeling figure on an oval base (figure 7.6). Although gender is not depicted, the lack of earplugs and the task being performed—grinding corn—suggested to Burnett a female figure. There may be some frontal deformation, but it is not as well defined as in the Keller figure. The hair is pulled tightly behind the ears, to the back of the neck. The ears are clearly shown

Cahokia and the Archaeology of Power

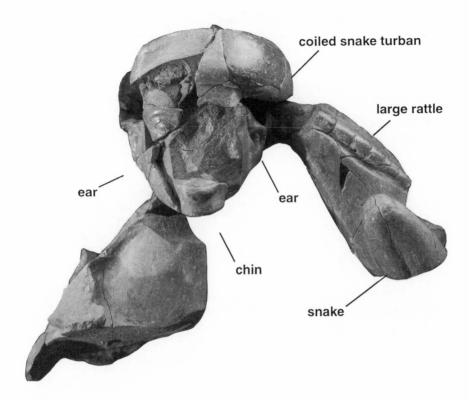

coiled snake turban

large rattle

ear

ear

chin

snake

Figure 7.5 West Figurine; face ca. 8 cm in height (Photo by Linda Alexander, used with permission of the Illinois Transportation Archaeological Research Program).

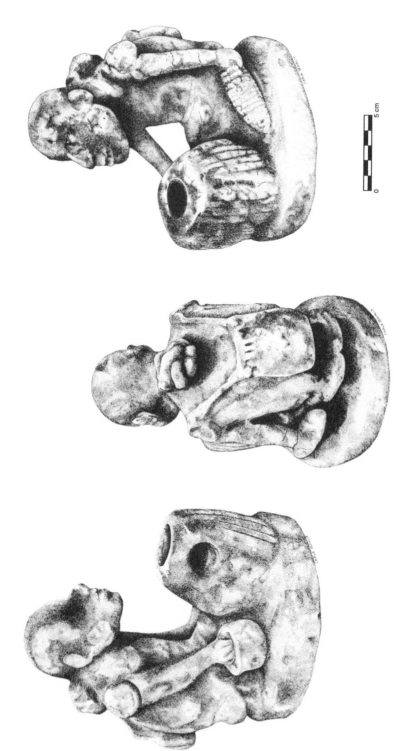

Figure 7.6 Figure at Mortar Figure Pipe (after Emerson 1989, Figure 5).

Cahokia and the Archaeology of Power

and have no ornaments attached. Like the Birger figure, this effigy wears a rectangular backpack that contains protruding vertical rods. It is not possible to determine how, or even if, the figure is dressed. Since there appears to be no definition of legs, we can hypothesize that she may be wearing a skirt. Her lower legs are folded back under her, and her toes point toward each other.

In her right hand she holds a rounded grinding stone, while in her left hand she grasps the end of a carefully depicted ear of corn. In front of her, resting on the base, is a large rectangular, boxlike object with slightly bowed sides. These sides are incised to represent vertical rods. The top of this box and its right-hand side are drilled to form the bowl and stem insertion point for a pipe (which were probably added later, per Emerson 1983, 1989).

Thematically, the Figure at Mortar effigy is reasonably close to the Keller figurine. Both depict females involved with handling maize and some form of container. They also share many stylistic similarities such as facial depiction, hairstyle, posture, and skill of artistic execution. The one obvious difference between the two figures is the addition of the pack to the Figure at Mortar effigy and its absence in the Keller figurine. The resemblance of the pack to that found on the Birger figurine has already been mentioned. As is implied by the figure's name, Burnett interpreted the boxlike object as a mortar. Based on the similarity to the Keller figure and other examples, it may represent a basket or similar container.

Another stone effigy of interest was a flint clay pipe recovered with a Mississippian burial (in association with a Ramey jar and an effigy hooded bottle) at the Schild site, Greene County, Illinois, in the Lower Illinois River Valley (Perino 1971: 117-118). This effigy is highly schematic in execution (figure 7.7), and its interpretation is more subjective than that of either the Keller or the Figure at Mortar effigy. It shows a kneeling human wearing a short wraparound skirt. The gender of the figure is not indicated, but based on the skirt and the lack of ear ornaments (both of which appear to be limited to females), it is probably female. Ears are faintly portrayed on the sides of the head, and the hair is described as hanging "vertically in a rectangular pack located between the shoulder blades" (Perino 1971: 117). The figure has her left hand raised to her breast while her right arm runs down her body and ends in a large bulbous protrusion that does not resemble a hand. The effigy figure sits on a long rectangular base. Behind it is a round pipe bowl, about which is coiled a serpent with its tail on the right and its head on the left. The serpent's head is large, bulbous, and devoid of features.

This effigy is thematically related to the Figure at Mortar and the Keller figurine and is, in effect, an expression of the same symbolic themes as the Birger and West figurines. In light of the Keller, Birger, Sponemann,

Figure 7.7   Schild Figure Pipe; ca. 14 cm in height (Perino 1971).

Cahokia and the Archaeology of Power

Willoughby, West, and Figure at Mortar effigies, the importance of the Schild figurine is apparent, and its motifs become clear. It can be seen that the right hand is similar to the hands of the Figure at Mortar and the Keller figurine, both of which grasp agricultural items. Or this may be an alternative version of the Birger figurine in which the fruit emanates from the "human" figure rather than from the serpent.

It is, after all, with the Birger and West figurines that the Schild figurine has its greatest affinity in terms of motifs. All have kneeling females associated with snakelike creatures. Bearing this in mind, it does not seem unreasonable to suggest that the hooklike object over the shoulder of the Schild figurine is the equivalent of the short-handled hoe in the hand of the Birger female figurine. In fact, it seems, given the nature of the implement, that the normal carrying position for such a hoe would be over the shoulder.

A number of other American Bottom Mississippian stone figures also contain some of the motifs discussed above. The Macoupin Creek Figure pipe (formerly called the Piasa Creek Figure pipe, Emerson 1982: 13-15; Farnsworth and Emerson 1989) represents a kneeling male shaman with a gourd rattle in one hand and possibly a snake or snakeskin around his neck. The gourd as rattle (i.e., snake) also appears in the Rattler Frog pipe (Emerson 1982: 33). Although in another medium, two pottery effigy hooded bottle fragments that have a snake-person association have been recovered from Cahokia. One, collected by Bill Fecht (1960), is described as having a rattlesnake coiled upon a person's head, its tail draped down the side. A similar bottle fragment, with two serpents depicted, is reported as having been recovered from near the Jondro Mound (Fecht 1960).

Another interesting facet of the snake-person association has been discovered recently (Emerson 1996) in a specimen originally part of the Sutter collection and may be from the Cahokia site itself or from the immediate surrounding area. The specimen, the Svehla effigy elbow pipe (11 cm in length and 6 cm in height; figure 7.8), is made of a hard, fine-grained, pinkish igneous (rhyolite?) material. It depicts the head of an individual (gender unknown) with a rattlesnake coiled atop it. The large triangular head of the snake rests on the coils, while the tail and rattles wrap down along the neck of the individual. The similarities of motifs on the Svehla pipe, the West figurine, and the Cahokia hooded bottles are apparent.

SYMBOLIC THEMES EXPRESSED IN THE EFFIGIES

I (Emerson 1989, 1995, 1997b) have presented the argument that these figurines, with their depiction of females, agricultural products, and serpents, represented aspects of the Under World and fertility symbolism. A

Figure 7.8 Svehla Pipe; ca. 6 cm in height (Photo by Kenneth Farnsworth, used with permission of the Illinois Transportation Archaeological Research Program).

composite overview of the mythological and symbolic aspects of serpent motifs has been presented elsewhere in detail (Emerson 1989, 1995), based on Hudson (1976), Swanton (1946), and a number of other ethnohistorical works. Briefly, the serpent motif among the Indians of the Eastern Woodlands was presumably of great antiquity and continued down to historic times, when ethnohistorical documents demonstrated that the peoples of the Southeast were very much concerned with the serpent in both its natural and its supernatural states.

The serpent was a creature both feared and admired. Of all the snakes, the rattlesnake was the "chief," and it is this species that was most commonly depicted in the mythology and the iconography. The serpent was an Under World creature in both its natural and its supernatural states. It was, therefore, associated with the attributes of lightning, thunder, rain, and water; with power over other plants and animals; and with seasons dominated by agricultural pursuits and fertility ceremonialism, both deeply connected with the Under World (Hudson 1976).

In Southeastern symbolism, the characteristics of the serpent were transferred to the serpent monster, a composite beast associated with the Under World. This Under World was the dwelling place of monsters, danger, and

Cahokia and the Archaeology of Power

evil; but conversely it is the source of water, fertility, and power against evil. A common form of Under World monster was the Cherokee "Uktena." This water-dwelling creature has the scaly body of a large serpent with rings or spots, deer antlers on its head, and bird-like wings. The Uktena was a terrible monster, and even to gaze upon it would destroy not only the viewer but his family as well. Yet the scales of this creature (especially the Ulunsuti from its forehead) were the source of overwhelming power if one could obtain them.

Symbolic and iconographic representations of Under World creatures were rampant in prehistoric Mississippian and Caddoan art (e.g., Hamilton 1952; Phillips and Brown 1978; Howard 1968; Fundaburk and Foreman 1957). The depiction of serpents and serpent monsters revealed that snake motifs appeared in combination with talons, birds, men, ambiguous creatures, and felines. In some cases, the depictions were clearly of the Uktena monster. A striking example of the feline-headed serpent, similar to the Birger serpent, was portrayed on an earlier stone disk from Issaquena (Phillips and Brown 1978: 137–38).

The serpent creature portrayed in the Birger sculpture, with its feline head and snake body, was related to the water monsters of the historic Southeast. It is possible that it represented the Uktena or the closely related Water Panther. The resemblance to the Uktena was strengthened by the circular white spots on the Birger serpent's body. These spots were natural inclusions in the stone and may have been selected for by the carver. The presence of spots or circles was common on the Spiro serpent monster/snake depictions (Phillips and Brown 1978), and in historic mythology such spots were one of the attributes of the Uktena.

In the sources on Southeastern mythology, attributes of the various water monsters were not clearly defined or separated. Consequently, it is irrelevant to attempt to associate the Birger serpent with a specific monster. For the purpose of interpretation, it is sufficient that the association of the Birger serpent with the category of underwater monster is established. As a class of creatures, underwater monsters were closely related to water, rain, lightning, and fertility. These associations were also commonly attributed to serpents. The serpent monster/snake motif was clearly strong in the Birger, West, Schild, and Svehla effigies. Another association with the rattlesnake was effected through metaphor. The Birger serpent's body bifurcates and produces two vines from which gourds hang. Gourd rattles were common in the Eastern Woodlands, and the analogy of gourd rattle/rattlesnake is clear. In a reverse situation, one finds that gourd rattles often had snake rattles attached to them, perhaps in an attempt to transfer the power of the serpent to the rattle. This supernatural aspect was strong, and rattles (gourds) were virtually a hallmark of the shaman or priest throughout the Southeast (cf. Prentice 1986b: 112-114; references therein)

The relation of the figurines' motifs to the concept of agricultural cycles is interesting. The hoe, in combination with the vines and gourds emerging from the Birger serpent monster's body, was a rendering of the natural process of regeneration using agricultural motifs. Although in a more schematic form, this same agricultural motif was postulated for the Schild, Willoughby, and Sponemann figurines. The agricultural motif is the primary one in the Figure at Mortar and the Keller figurine. The Figure at Mortar effigy, taken at face value, depicts a woman grinding corn, while the Keller, McGehee, Willoughby, and Sponemann effigies are concerned with the procreation of corn and sunflower(?) plants. These plant and agricultural motifs were especially significant because of their rarity in other Mississippian iconography.

The central figure in each effigy is a female. While women often were influential in Southeastern groups, this social importance was poorly reflected in most elite Mississippian iconography (e.g., at Spiro). The place of women in elite art was also reflected in their general absence in Southeastern myths, at least in central roles. There is, however, one very important exception to this generality: the dominance of the female figure in the important Corn Mother myths (Witthoft 1949). It was more than fortuitous coincidence that the Cahokian effigies, females immersed in agricultural motifs, have been recovered from Mississippian period sites in an area that surely was imbued with the ubiquitous female Corn Mother motifs and mythology.

Prentice (1986a), in a thorough compilation of relevant Native American symbolism from ethnohistoric, ethnographic, and archaeological sources, supports the Birger figurine identification as a Mississippian Earth Mother figure. Specific correlations noted "relate the Shawnee Earth-Mother concept, and the eastern Woodland Earth-Mother concept in general, with the symbolism expressed in the Birger figurine ... [and] include the wearing of a short skirt, association with the great monster serpent, the giving of plants to humankind (most notably corn, pumpkins, and tobacco), use of the tumpline, the giving of the sacred bundles to humankind (sacred bundles were normally carried on the back with a tumpline), and association with death concepts" (Prentice 1986a: 254).

Perhaps Prentice's (1986a: 254) most important point was the overlapping and polysemous nature of the symbolic world and "how notably the death goddess, the lunar goddess, the 'Old Woman,' and the 'Grandmother' deities of the eastern Woodland share each other's traits and merge in their identifying characteristics." This led him to follow Hultkrantz (1957) in arguing that these "deities" are but facets of the Earth Mother, a concept that

I, too, would endorse. In fact, it became clear that many of the same sets of traits were also repeated in the other figurines recovered from the BBB Motor and Sponemann sites and that these represented other facets of the Earth Mother myth. The Keller figurine shows a female in a short skirt holding a plant stalk, with corncobs and basket; the Sponemann figurine depicts a female wearing a turban (tumpline?) and backpack(?) with plants emerging from her palms; the Willoughby figurine displays a female in a short skirt, with plant vines around her head, kneeling in front of a basket with "plates" in her hands; the West female figurine is wrapped with serpents and is wearing a backpack; and the miscellaneous Sponemann site fragments include segments of baskets, snakes, vines, backpacks, and a hoe that are associated with the figurines recovered from the site.

The similarity of these figurines' traits with those referenced by Prentice in correlating the Birger figurine with the Earth Mother are obvious. To reinforce the correlation one might note that the basket and backpack motifs are interchangeable as "containers" for transporting such things as "souls," seeds, and bones; and the basket's vertical rods motif can be easily related to the backpack "rods"—again with similar interpretations as lightning, rain, bones, and arrows. In these later figurines the emergence of the "corn" plants from the female's hands/body represents variations on the Corn Mother myth. (The detailed verification for these associations and others can be found in Prentice 1986a; Witthoft 1949 and references included therein.) In fact, I believe that, given the variation in motif representation between the figurines, the Birger, Schild, and West figurines represent the Earth Mother in all of its facets, while the Keller, Sponemann, and Willoughby figurines may represent more limited aspects.

Prentice's (1986a) compilation has been extremely helpful in reinforcing the link between eastern Woodland native mythology and late prehistoric symbolism. His examination of these sources has also provided extensive symbolic references that played an important role in interpreting American Bottom Mississippian figurines, and his specific conclusions regarding the Birger figurine are worth repeating here because of what I believe is their wider applicability to Middle Mississippian cosmology:

> I believe the Birger figurine to be an expression of the Earth-Mother concept—the goddess of life and death, creator of people and plants. With her help the "Earth Serpent," symbol of death and the Under World, provides the agricultural crops that humans need. On her back the goddess carries the pack or sacred bundle that is the symbol of fertility goddesses.

> The pack may be symbolic of rain, fertility, the source of knowledge, and the power of deities. It may contain human bones or the souls of men and

women in the process of being returned to the land of the living. It may also contain the first seeds of the plants given by the fertility goddess to humankind.

The vines may be the symbols of animal and plant fertility; or they may be symbolic of the UnderWorld origin of humans and the equation of people with plants. Two vines may symbolize the bifurcated road to the land of the dead . . . or the twin sons of the earth goddess.

The gourds may be symbols of the deity's mythical garden, or may represent the number of seeds given each person on earth. They may be symbolic of female fertility as they were among the Alabama Indians where squashes were equated with female breasts. . . ; they may be symbolic of the squash medicine that cured diseases; or they may be symbolic of the return of dead souls in gourd containers, equating human life with plant life.

The Mississippian view of the world was that of a closed and enduring system. In this cosmological system humans were equated with plants, and, just as seeds bring forth new life in the spring, so are the souls of the dead reborn in children. At the heart of this system lay the Earth-Mother, the goddess of life and death. It was a system of order and balance. (Prentice 1986a: 262-263)

These effigies illustrate the productivity of considering Mississippian iconography and symbolism through a thematic approach. There can be little doubt that these figures were visual presentations of varied aspects of a single symbolic theme that embodied a linked set of beliefs concerning the relationship of fertility, serpents, horticulture, and a female supernatural being.

SACRED CERAMICS

Many of the symbolic themes depicted in the stone figurines can also be seen in the trailed designs present on a set of sacred vessels known to archaeologists as Ramey Incised ceramics (Emerson 1989, 1995). These vessels are moderate-sized, sharp-shouldered jars with low rims and dark smudged surfaces (i.e., Griffin 1949). In the archaeological lore of Cahokia, Ramey Incised has been subject to multiple interpretations; however, most recently, Pauketat and I (1991; Emerson 1989) have presented an argument that those ceramics were intimately tied to fertility symbolism and to elite-commoner interaction at Cahokia.

The bases for such conclusions were studies I undertook earlier of American Bottom Ramey Incised form, distribution, and design (Emerson 1981, 1989, 1995). These studies included a descriptive-formalistic aspect using the principle of design symmetry to characterize Ramey motifs (Emerson 1981, 1995: 348-365). The principle of symmetry in basic element description has been discussed for archaeological use by Shepard (1948) and was first applied to Ramey ceramics by Griffith (1962, 1981).

The analyses revealed nine categories of basic design elements and their elaborations (I-IX): chevron (I), arc (II), trapezoid (III), scroll 1 (IV), scroll 2 (V), wing (VI), spiral (VII), forked eye (VIII), and circle (IX). Some divergent designs tended to be combinations of certain basic elements or portions of basic elements combined with others of a like nature. Those designs were placed in Categories X-XII.

Category X represents a combination of Category III trapezoids with Category VII spirals (Xa), with a scroll or wing form (Xb-c), or with a Category IX circle. Category XI appears to represent linked Category IV scroll 1, Category VI wing, and perhaps Category VII spiral motifs. Category XII is a combination of Category V scrolls with Category I chevron forms. The basic elements and their various elaborations are shown in figure 7.9.

This basic quantification and description of Ramey motifs provided some of the first reliable information on design types and distribution. The quantification of the design elements from Cahokia and eight outlying sites showed (Emerson 1995: figure 44) that fully 60.8% of the elements in the sample came from Cahokia, with the next largest number from the outlying sites of Julien (10.6%) and Mitchell (11.5%). In general, motifs appear to be fairly evenly distributed across the sites examined. Of the 45 design motifs quantified (figure 7.9), 69% appeared at Cahokia. No distinct pattern of similarity was apparent in the 31% of the motifs absent at Cahokia. Because of the small size and fortuitous nature of the sample examined, I do not believe there is significance in any intersite variation noted in symbol presence or absence. This suggests a uniform system for the distribution of Ramey vessels across the American Bottom.

The co-association of basic design motifs with one another could be recorded for only 48 examples (figure 7.9c). These associations took two forms; 48% involved the association of identical basic elements, while 52% involved the association of different elements. If one considered the element associations as a whole, two major pairings were observable: one pairing was Category XIa-type combinations, comprising Categories IV and VI (22.9%); and 20.8% of the pairings involved Categories IIIa and VII elements. Other minor groupings consisted of Category II elements (14.6%) and pairs of Category I (10.4%).

This research represented the first quantification of Ramey symbol homogeneity. Such a quantification is essential to my subsequent arguments

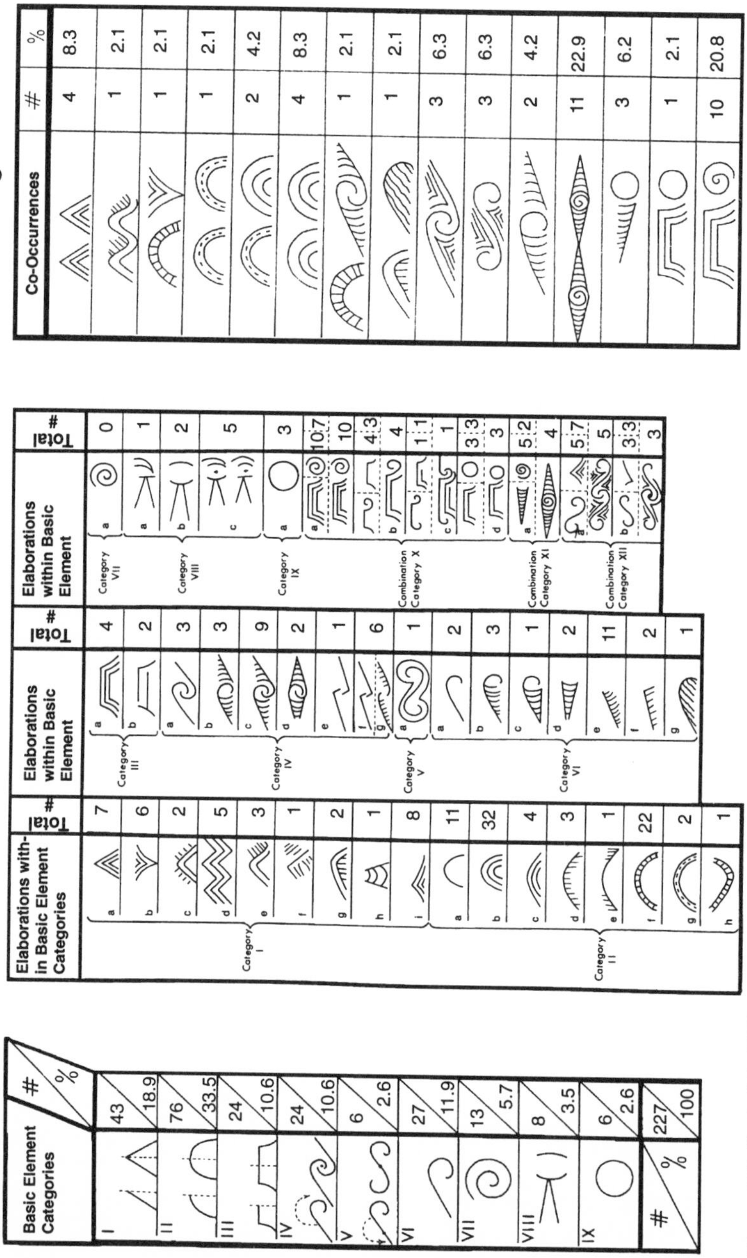

Figure 7.9 Basic Motif Elements, Elaborations, and Co-occurrences on Ramey Incised Ceramics from the American Bottom: (a) basic elements (b) basic elements elaborations (c) basic elements co-occurrences.

(a) Basic Element Categories

Category	#	%
I	43	18.9
II	76	33.5
III	24	10.6
IV	24	10.6
V	6	2.6
VI	27	11.9
VII	13	5.7
VIII	8	3.5
IX	6	2.6
# / %	227	100

(b) Elaborations within Basic Element Categories

Category	element	Total #
I	a	7
	b	6
	c	2
	d	5
	e	3
	f	1
	g	2
	h	1
II	a	8
	b	11
	c	32
	d	4
	e	3
	f	1
	g	22
	h	2
III	a	4
	b	2
IV	a	3
	b	3
	c	9
	d	2
V	e	1
	f	6
	g	1
VI	a	2
	b	3
	c	1
	d	2
	e	11
	f	2
VII	a	0
VIII	a	1
	b	2
	c	5
IX	a	3
Combination Category X		10:7, 10
		4:3, 4
		1:1
		3:3, 3
Combination Category XI	a	5:2, 4
	b	5:7, 5
Combination Category XII		3:3, 3

(c) Co-Occurrences

#	%
4	8.3
1	2.1
1	2.1
1	2.1
2	4.2
4	8.3
1	2.1
1	2.1
3	6.3
3	6.3
2	4.2
11	22.9
3	6.2
1	2.1
10	20.8

that the symbolic theme was homogenous and tightly focused and that it presented an interpretable pattern. While I do not want to discuss symbolic connotations in detail at this juncture, it is useful to present some broad statements about symbolic patterning. For example, of motifs within Categories I-IX that can be considered as examples of basic elements, a full 63.7% relate to the chevron-arc (Categories I-II). Not only were such motifs likely to be related to the sky-arch/bird/Upper World continuum, but they also have an Under World/fertility association. One of the most interesting aspects of this study has been to show that the Upper World and Under World are not mutually exclusive but may have been linked through a specific set of symbols.

The other dominant symbolic motifs revolved about the scroll/spiral/circle and represented 27.8% of those recorded here. Again, symbolically, I believe these were primary Under World/serpent/water motifs. Two minor symbol motifs were the forked eye (4.5%, Category VIII) and the trapezoid (3.4%, Category III). In the first instance the forked eye is assumed to have had a "Thunderer" association, while the trapezoid is an earth/mound symbol.

It is the extreme homogeneity of the Ramey symbolic system, with more than 90% of the symbols falling into two closely related groups, that is so remarkable. As Pauketat and I argued (1991), the Ramey symbols represent a visual portrayal of a tightly integrated Cahokian cosmos. This "oneness" is reinforced by the combination categories (X-XII) that documented the close association of what might be seen as unrelated symbols. Based on formal analysis alone, there was no reason to argue for the association of the chevron, scroll, and trapezoidal forms. Each, stylistically, could be seen as a separate and distinct symbolic form. Yet, it was exactly the linkage of these disparate symbols that is presented in the combination categories (i.e., trapezoid with scroll [Category X] and scroll with chevron [Category XII]). The linkages are also visible in the co-occurrence of design elements, documented in figure 7.9, which also portray the overall pattern found on Ramey Incised jars.

Ramey Symbolism

Comparisons and analogies with the beliefs and archaeology of early natives of the Eastern Woodlands provide abundant clues to the symbolic themes inherent in the Ramey motifs. Here I will briefly discuss major symbolic patterns apparent in the Cahokian data (for a fuller discussion and justification see Emerson 1989, 1995: 374-387).

Several schematic curvilinear motifs appear in the Ramey designs, including arcs, spirals, circles, and to some extent, scrolls. A series of interpretations has been proffered for these designs, but perhaps the most intriguing was put forward by Phelps (1970: 91), who saw them as symbolic of water in its many manifestations and ultimately tied to the Under World. In the same vein, Hall (1973: 2) postulated that on Ramey vessels "the scroll design and 'feathered' curvilinear designs seem to represent water either directly or through association with the spiral of a marine shell. The arch designs seem to represent water by association with rain and the rainbow." Hall's suggestions of the arc's rainbow symbolism is supported by Howard's (1968) association of the rainbow with portions of Busk ceremonialism. This "sky" association is strengthened by the possibility of the rays (IId–e) and ladders (IIf–g) connotating the "sky arch or arch"—a notion "virtually synonymous with the notion of an Upper or Sky World" (Pauketat and Emerson 1991: 928).

The spiral/scroll motifs contribute significantly to our understanding of Mississippian symbolism. The spiral motif appears among historic Southeastern groups in a number of diverse associations. Hudson (1976: 405), for example, notes that in many dances the spiral movement about a central fire represented the serpent/Under World in opposition to the sun (a central fire)/Upper World. The serpent/spiral relationship and the opposition of these symbols to the fire/sun symbols is common in the Southeast (Hudson 1976). The spiral/scroll/circle motifs are part of the same symbolic theme and include the columella of the highly valued marine shells. Also, for the Southeast, marine shell cups are closely associated with black drink ceremonialism and life/fertility symbolism (Milanich 1979).

The implications of the spiral/serpent relationship for Southeastern cosmology are far-reaching since the serpent motif is integrated with the symbolism of the Under World. The thematic content of this system stems directly from the conceptual dualism prevalent in Southeastern mythology: the opposition of the Upper World characterized by the sun (and fire) and the Under World of serpents/monsters (and water).

A number of partial scroll forms have the interesting attribute of vertical lines suspended from them (categories IV and VI in figure 7.9b). Hall called these "feathered" scrolls and suggested that the representation was similar to that of the plain scrolls and spirals. I have interpreted (Emerson 1995:380–382, figure 47) these design elements as wing/bird symbols and related them to the bird-man motifs from the Southeast. Given the relationship of the falcon figure/bird motif with the feathered-scroll element, they can also be tied to the closely related motif of the forked eye (Category VIII, figure

7.9b). Given this intertwining of the forked-eye, bird, and feathered-scroll motifs, it is appropriate that they be discussed in conjunction.

The most commonly accepted symbolic association for the falcon-impersonator figure and forked-eye motif has been warfare. This is based both on ethnohistorical data and on the natural attributes of the peregrine falcon (Howard 1968: 43–45; Brown 1975: 19–22; Hudson 1976: 128–129). It appears that the falcon may have served as the model for the monster birds in the Southeast, such as the Cherokee Tlanuwa, which killed men with their sharpened breasts (Howard 1968: 43–44). In general, in the Southeastern symbolic system, birds (particularly the falcon) were identified with the Upper World through the association of the weeping-eye motif with the "eye of the Thunderbird, from which lightning flashes, with its water association" (Hall 1973: 2). They were closely related to the great spirits of the Upper World, which (in the case of the Cherokees) included the Sun, the Moon, the great Thunder (Kanati), and Corn (Selu). That was the world of structure and order.

Two major themes may be associated with the feathered-scroll, forked-eye, and falcon-man motifs. One theme is aggressive warfare, and the other is water symbolism, which dwells on fertility as depicted by rain, thunder, and lightning. The Thunderer role is particularly interesting when taken in conjunction with the other dominant motifs of serpent/water/Under World. The Thunderer is a creature of the Upper World who contests the forces of the Under World as epitomized by the serpent (e.g., Hall 1977: 501–502). Yet both the serpent and the bird are symbolically tied to rain, lightning, and thunder; they are oppositions bound through water symbolism.

At Spiro, Brown (1975) opted for the warfare aspect of the falcon impersonator based on association of design elements (weapons, acts of violence, aggressive postures, etc.). Given the eleventh- and twelfth-century context and the associations of the material from the American Bottom area (and the scarcity of symbols of the warlike falcon-impersonator role), the forked-eye and feathered-scroll motifs seem to be associated more closely with the Thunderer/Upper World. Perhaps the spiral curvature and interlocking scroll of the feathered scrolls is an artistic expression of the linking of the water symbolism of the Thunderer and the serpent. There is strong evidence from the Spiro iconography that supports the association of the Thunderer (as bird-man) with serpents (as water motif). Phillips and Brown (1978: 128–129) have pointed out that the figures in the Spiro bird-man depictions have some of the attributes of serpents, and similar associations are present at Etowah. Significant evidence supports the bird-water association through the use of serpent attributes.

Category III motif elements have been called trapezoids here, based on their resemblance to that form. The analogy that is most appropriate is probably with truncated, stepped platform mounds. Some Southeastern ceramics and modeled vessels display "stepped" motifs. Phelps (1970: 97) has suggested a similar association. In ethnohistorical documents and as extrapolated from the archaeological data, the temple mound symbolizes the centrality of the temple to group integration, solidarity, and welfare (cf. Knight 1989b). It is the single most important religious expression of the group and, in turn, is intimately associated with the community elites. It is reasonable to assume that the elite lineages or families are closely related to the Upper World (as is the case, for example, with the Natchez Suns). This is further attested to by the association of the elite with platform mounds and the general association of the chief's house with raised platform mounds in the Southeast, linking temple and temple mounds with the Upper World.

This association is in keeping with general themes in Southeastern symbolic systems. Temple mounds, because they are composed of "earth," are also intimately tied to the Under World (cf. Knight 1989b). It is interesting that the trapezoid motif is commonly associated with spirals or circles (figure 7.9b, Category X, and figure 7.9c). The relationship may be expressed symbolically in the intertwining of the trapezoidal element (the mound motif) and the spiral element (the water/serpent motif). That coupling of motifs may express the importance of the temple/mound in attaining the all-important rain, critical in an agricultural society.

This section has presented data from ethnohistorical, ethnographic, and archaeological sources that contribute some insights into the nature of the symbolic elements found on Cahokian sacred vessels. I have been able to demonstrate thematic associations for a number of motifs that focus primarily on Under World and Upper World water symbolism. The validity of these motif-symbolism associations is based on the premise that there is an underlying unity to the symbolic systems of the Indians of the Eastern Woodlands. At a thematic level, the symbolic systems of southeastern and plains/prairie zones are particularly useful in understanding those of the Mississippian peoples.

Sacred Vessels and Ritual Performance

Archaeologically, one can define Ramey Incised as a distinctive ceramic type that possesses a recognizable constellation of attributes related to form, paste, design, and such. It is possible to place it approximately in time and to map its spatial distribution. What has been difficult to comprehend is its contextual meaning in Mississippian society—to produce an explanation that can adequately reconcile a number of seemingly disparate and some-times contradictory facts concerning its occurrence and nature.

The recovery of a concentration of Ramey ceramics in the special con-texts of the BBB Motor site and the ritual area at the Sponemann site pro-vided an opportunity to reevaluate the role of Ramey Incised pottery in Mississippian society. Symbolically, the Stirling component at the BBB Motor site represents a ritual complex associated with both mortuary and life con-tinuity ceremonies, while Sponemann is closely associated with fertility ac-tivities in Cahokian society. The close association of Ramey symbolism with this complex is clear evidence that it is part of the ritual and symbolic para-phernalia of this culture. In interpreting Ramey Incised it has been sug-gested that Ramey pottery was a ritual ware associated with the preparation of medicines or the distribution of comestibles in the ceremonial cycle of the Mississippian peoples of the American Bottom (Emerson 1989, 1995:365-374; Pauketat and Emerson 1991).

This interpretation reflects the association of symbolic designs on the Ramey vessels with an ideological complex that involved fertility and life forces. Historically, such concepts were expressed in agricultural and so-cially integrating ceremonies such as the Green Corn Ceremonies. Such ritualism was pervasive in the Eastern Woodlands (Witthoft 1949). Although their specific content and form are not known, it is not unreasonable to see an integrating mechanism of Mississippian society at this time as probably including a number of socioreligious ceremonies that occurred at various times throughout the year. Such ceremonies were presumably centralized, probably in mound centers, to reinforce the community's solidarity with the elite hosts. Such festivals might bring together several rural communities at the mound center to which they owed allegiance and which were, in turn, tied ritually to Cahokia. A part of the ritual of such ceremonies was the manufacture of the semisacred symbolic Ramey Incised ceramics. It appears that their manufacture may have been limited to specific times of the year, and they were produced only in limited numbers, probably by potters who were associated with each specific lineage/community ritual group.

More recently Pauketat and I (1991) have elaborated on our understand-ing of the "use" of Ramey Incised ceramics as a mediator in Cahokian elite-commoner interactions. Succinctly, we argued for the use of Ramey symbolism within the context of "rites of intensification" which are "calendrically based, community-focused rites that play a critical role in the resolution of cosmological discontinuities in the annual ritual sequence . . . [that] are based on community-wide participation, which requires a sym-bolic text both highly visible and understandable to the masses. This text, we contend[ed], is Ramey iconography" (Pauketat and Emerson 1991: 919-920).

The rites of intensification are assumed to be those associated with the pan-Eastern Woodlands Green Corn ceremonialism—for which evidence is plentiful in Cahokia Mississippian culture. We argue that, during such festivals, the widespread distribution by the elite of both these vessels and their message reinforced and naturalized political centralization and elite supremacy.

MISSISSIPPIAN WORLD STRUCTURING

If there was a single overriding theme in the cosmology of the Southeastern Indian groups, it was the organization of the natural and supernatural worlds into dualistic categories that often were expressed as sets of oppositions (for example, the opposition of Upper World and Under World). The dualistic organizational framework in Mississippian symbolism suggests that some of the concepts Levi-Strauss (1963: 132-163) used in his investigation of dualistic organization are applicable here. One could point to the organization of the BBB Motor site components as an example of dualistic structure, and that structure also can be seen in the courtyard organization patterns of some of the other sites described here. The plans of the larger Mississippian temple towns, with their central precincts, can be seen as composite dualistic sets or, perhaps, as examples of "concentric structure."

It is also possible to see Levi-Strauss's third form of dualism, triadic structure. Among the Southeastern Indians, most efforts were directed toward striking a balance between the Upper World and the Under World. Although humans could not affect the intrinsic powers of the Upper and Lower Worlds, it was possible to mitigate their impact in this world. This symbolic system can be seen as embodying a triadic structure that included the Upper and Lower Worlds and the world of people. As Hudson (1976) has noted, much of the concern among the Southeastern groups focused on how to maintain the separation of the Upper and Lower Worlds and to avoid the resulting pollution if they became mixed.

The structuration of the Mississippian world in dualistic sets opens wider parameters for understanding the cultural milieu that we are investigating; these parameters involve the four-cornered world and the critical importance of the cosmic cardinal points. The quadripartite cosmos is quite literally all pervasive, both specifically in Middle Mississippian and generally in North American Indian symbolism; here I will cite only a few obvious examples such as the mythological cardinal directions, the circle and cross, or the mound and plaza complex. Recognizing that Mississippian peoples, historic Southeastern groups, and many other groups in North America appear to have organized their world (at least in some aspects) within a framework of oppositions and quadripartition allows one to use that framework as a descriptive, and perhaps modeling, device. My specific concern in this analysis is the productiveness of using the dualistic or quadripartite model to describe and understand Mississippian symbolism.

As a basis for examining the dualistic, quadripartitioned world of the Mississippian, we can again look to Ramey Incised symbolism—perhaps, as we have argued, as a map of the Cahokian cosmos (Pauketat and Emerson 1991). Above, I have discussed the conceptualization of the motifs used on Ramey ceramics. Now we can explore the organizational parameters that dictate their placement. Pauketat (Pauketat and Emerson 1991) recognized a distinction between "center elements" that rotate about a central point and "adjunct elements" that alternate with center elements or focus on an implicit point. This distinction becomes critical to a further interpretation of Ramey "meaning."

In reexamining the Upper World-Lower World dichotomy the discussion becomes one in which the center elements may represent the Upper World and the adjunct elements may represent Lower World symbols. Yet, as always, there is the possibility of polysemy in Ramey symbolism. I have emphasized the Lower World motifs on Ramey pottery, yet Upper World symbolism was also present, and it will be briefly treated here. Many researchers recognize the importance of native fire/sun symbolism iconography, and it is possible that the Ramey central scroll motifs may reflect some aspect of sun symbols; however, there is clearly an intertwined Under World facet in the serpent. The sky arch is also closely associated with the Upper World, and motifs that reflect this may be the ladder, the concentric arch, and perhaps the chevron. The Thunderbird is present in such icons as chevrons or weeping eyes. The essential concept here is that

> most Ramey Incised motifs contain morphological qualities of other motifs and appear to blend together. . . . While center and adjunct elements may have symbolic meanings all their own, motifs are probably subordinate to and better equipped within a higher level of meaning. (Pauketat and Emerson 1991: 929)

> The motifs on Ramey Incised vessel rims are actually components of a single *design field,* the entire exterior surface of the vessel's inslanted rim (Griffith 1981: 7). Ramey Incised vessel design fields depict a unified decorative theme. This theme consists of a quadripartite division of space, each quadrant containing a center and/or a multilayered adjunct elements. . . . The quadripartite design field may be characterized by the same motif in each quadrant or by two opposing sets (cf. Hudson 1976: 317-318) . . . This design

field unity suggests a common theme (or themes) was being conveyed by Ramey design in a nonarbitrary, and, indeed, highly redundant manner." (Pauketat and Emerson 1991: 929)

A centered quadripartite world view is hardly a new perspective in the American Bottom. At least four centuries earlier such patterns are recognizable. In the American Bottom, villages had attained a four-sided organization (i.e., laid out about a central courtyard) by the Late Woodland Patrick phase (A.D. 600-700). During this phase, Kelly (1990b: 85-86) documents the appearance of an arrangement of four specialized, limestone-lined ceremonial pits arranged in a rectangular pattern facing a village square, and he notes their similarities to later historic Southeastern Indians' quadripartition of the world. It is in the subsequent Dohack phase (A.D. 750-850), however, that we first see the classic expression of quadripartitioning in the creation of the village post-pit complexes. These features, located in the center of the community square, consist of four rectangular pits arranged in a square surrounding a central post or rectilinear structure (Kelly 1990b: 88-89).

Kelly (1990b: 92) notes that, "[t]he overall configuration of Dohack phase communities and their central corporate facilities also appears to embody certain symbolic elements that underlie Mississippian belief systems. The central fourfold pit complexes, often accompanied by a central post, could well reflect the initial emergence of the cross-in-circle complexes, incorporated as part of the community plan, with the central community square feature complexes symbolic of the 'cross' within a 'circle' of houses."

He further relates the presence of elite structures, fire, and above and below ground facilities to the historic "fire-sun-deity" and "upperworld-lowerworld" dichotomy.

This quadripartition pattern continues in various forms to emerge full bloom with the appearance of Middle Mississippian culture at A.D. 1050. The emergence of the rectangular plaza surrounded by mounds reflects a large-scale reenactment of this pattern (e.g., the construction of Cahokia's Grand Plaza; Dalan 1997) while the presence of a similar site organization in the countryside indicates the pervasiveness of this theme. In fact, the four-sided platform mound may have graphically portrayed the cosmos as "earth-islands," as imaged in the Muskogean belief that the world was flat-topped and four-sided (Knight 1989b: 287). Knight (1989b) has further tied the mound icon to earth symbolism involving the earth "navel," Green Corn ritualism and fertility, and world renewal, effectively linking it to the central focus of Cahokian belief systems (and illustrating an ideal example of a Foucaultian heterotopia).

SUMMARY

By A.D. 1050 a dominant cosmology in the American Bottom depicted a quadripartite universe balanced between a dualistic conception of Upper and Lower World forces; the roots of that universe were deeply embedded in the area and extended back into Late Woodland times. This universal quadripartitioning of space was rendered forcefully in the creation of the Cahokian sacred elite landscape with its four-sided plazas and mounds and was recreated across the countryside in smaller versions at lower level elite sites. At a reduced scale, it appears on the iconography of sacred vessels and in other art of the Cahokian people.

Most striking, however, was the existence an all-pervasive concept of a dualistic universe intimately associated with the Upper and Lower Worlds of historically described southeastern Indian cosmologies. That cosmology was overwhelmingly portrayed in the available Cahokian iconography of sacred vessels and stone figurines. An important basis of Cahokian ideology has been shown to be associated with the Under World forces of procreation, fertility, water, agriculture, and in various guises, a female earth goddess. Even more important, an argument has been put forward that the control and effective manipulation of this "fertility cult" ultimately played an important role in the rise and consolidation of elite power. This subject will be explored in more detail in the next chapter when I deal with rural material manifestations of Mississippian ideology and the relationship to the emergence of local cults.

8

Cahokian Rural Cults

de materialibus ad immaterialia
(Twelfth-century comment by Abbot Suger on his reconstruction of the
Abbey Church of St.-Denis, in Panofsky 1979: 62.)

I presume that the ritual behavior and symbolic system of the Cahokian
people are implicit in the assemblages of rural Middle Mississippian sites
around Cahokia. Those assemblages reflected strong evidence for the dominance of fertility symbolism in the rural temples and mortuary sites. In addition, it was possible to identify a number of specialized sites that I interpret
as representing the presence of rural religious practitioners, perhaps as members of a centralized ruling elite. This congruence of symbolic and settlement data suggests that a Cahokian "fertility cult" is recognizable from the
archaeological record. The rise and fall of this rural cult were ultimately tied
to Cahokia's period of dominance and suggest that it represented a deliberate manipulation of deeply embedded fertility ideology by the elite to consolidate their power.

The archaeological and ethnohistoric evidence discussed in the last chapter is brought to bear here on the symbolic implications of the BBB Motor
and Sponemann sites: their assemblages of stone figurines, Ramey pottery,
burials and grave goods, exotic lithics, botanical remains, and spatial organization represent classic examples of American Bottom, Stirling-phase symbolism and structure. An exploration of the unique context of this ritualistic
material and its symbolic implications also expands our interpretations of
the Middle Mississippian belief system as manifested within the rural settlements and shows that these religious beliefs were integrated into a pattern of
elite power and domination over the rural populace. Such an approach pro-

vides new insights not only into Cahokia's countryside, but also into the nature of Cahokia itself.

SYMBOLS OF POWER

A series of items recovered in moderate numbers from Mississippian sites in the Midwest are associated with religious beliefs, based on archaeological context and ethnohistorical analogy. I have presented the evidence for the spectacular stone figurines and sacred vessels earlier. There are a number of more common materials discussed here that, in the proper context, can be seen as markers of power. These include engraved sherds, pigments, exotic minerals, and crystals. Such items were part of the assemblage from the BBB Motor and Sponemann temple sites, as well as a number of other more commonplace Mississippian sites.

An engraved Bird-Man sherd recovered from a refuse pit in the BBB Motor Lohmann priest-mortuary component had human heads with falconoid attributes engraved on both its polished, dark-slipped, exterior surface and its interior surface. Similar motifs were found in the Cahokia area in the past on the Cahokia (Ramey) tablet reported by Peet in 1891 and on sherds recovered from the area of Mound 34 by Perino (1959). In the case of the latter two sherds, Phillips and Brown (1978: 172; Brown 1989: 196-197) were confident enough of their similarity to the Spiro material to assign the heads to Spiro artistic schools.

The function of such engraved sherds is unclear, and they are rare in the Cahokia area. The often sloppy execution seems to indicate that they may have been folk magic amulets, and the engraving may originally have been done on broken sherds. However, Wilson (1996), in a review of such engravings, has been able to show they were primarily associated with Lohmann-phase sites that often had special political/religious functions. He argues that they, as much as the later more formal Ramey symbolism, were important mediums for getting the elite's message to the masses.

Several exotic minerals recovered from the sites were used ethnohistorically, and very likely also in Mississippian ceremonialism, in a magicosymbolic context. These items included mica, red ocher/hematite, galena, limonite, and quartz crystals. Mica presumably was valued for its light-reflecting qualities and generally workable sheet form. It was traded throughout the Southeast and was apparently highly valued, considering that it was offered to de Soto along with copper when he was sojourning in sixteenth-century South Carolina (Hudson 1976: 110). The examples of mica recovered from the BBB Motor site were all confined to the interior pits of the temple. Of the 16 pieces, 9 were pierced, as if by a needle, indicating that they had at one time been sewn to some type of fabric or hide. In this context it may be noted that in the Southeast mica often was associated with the scales of the serpent. This association was strengthened at the BBB Motor site through the presence of other serpent symbolism.

Both red ocher/hematite and galena cubes were recovered from a number of sites. These items were used primarily to produce pigments. It was common practice among Southeastern groups to paint the body with elaborate, many-colored designs during certain ceremonies (Hudson 1976: 380). Ground galena produces a white pigment and red ocher a red pigment, and both were used for this purpose (Lawson 1966[1709]: 51). In addition, red ocher was often found coating pottery, shell artifacts, various lithic tools, and other items. The supposed supernatural powers of hematite varied among Southeastern groups (Hudson 1976). A few pieces of limonite have been found occasionally and may have been used to produce pigments.

Some of the most interesting items recovered from the BBB Motor site excavations were a number of quartz crystals. The most impressive was a well-formed piece 10 cm long and 14 cm in circumference, weighing 278.4 g. It was found in the west wall trench of Structure 16. One other quartz crystal was found in a Lohmann refuse pit. A small crystal was in the fill of a wall trench, Feature 149, in the screened area. In the Stirling temple-mortuary area a medium-size crystal and another small fragment were recovered from a burial pit. All the quartz crystals showed some signs of battering on several of their facet junctures. The large Structure 16 crystal had a red impurity visible on one of its surfaces. The Sponemann temple structure contained a small quartz crystal.

Quartz crystals were a source of power (Hudson 1976: 356–357), and as a consequence, they were a required part of a shaman/priest's paraphernalia; however, they were also commonly found in the possession of adult men. Those crystals were associated with the powerful monster, the Uktena. The small crystals were seen as the scales of the Uktena. The most powerful crystal of all was the Ulunsuti, which came from the crest on the forehead of the Uktena (Hudson 1976: 357). Mooney and Olbrechts (1932) recorded that if one looked into an Ulunsuti one could see a whitish fluid or a vein of blood (cf. the red stain in the large crystal from the BBB Motor site Structure 16). Mooney (1900: 297-298) presented a Cherokee tale that indicated such a crystal was kept hidden in an earthen vessel buried in the ground, fed with blood, and buried with the owner.

Many of the themes in the Cherokee myth could be seen clearly in the archaeological deposit of crystals at the BBB Motor site. Given the spectacular appearance and the red impurity in the Structure 16 crystal, it does not stretch the evidence to interpret it as a powerful Ulunsuti. Finding this most powerful magical crystal at the BBB Motor site was in keeping with the nature of the area. Most of the crystals were in locations that suggest deliberate hiding places (wall trenches) or burials (with their owners). As Hudson (1976: 168) pointed out, this was consistent with the nature of crystals, which were Under World objects and must be kept underground. The presence of five such quartz crystals in the rather limited Lohmann and Stirling components, along with the mica, galena, red ocher, and limonite, was not in itself proof of the ritual nature of the BBB Motor site, since all these items have been recovered from other types of Mississippian settlements (Milner et al. 1984), but the concentration of items known to have symbolic significance (as well as practical magical and semisacred ceremonial and decorative uses) at the BBB Motor site is important.

The ethnobotanical remains at the BBB Motor site have been analyzed in detail by Whalley (1982, 1984, n.d.). Her work demonstrated that for the most part the plants used at the site were typically those recovered from Mississippian habitation sites in the region. Such remains include nuts, maize, and the starchy seed complex (goosefoot, maygrass, and erect knotweed). There were, however, significant deviations from this pattern in the amount of red cedar recovered and in the unique presence of jimsonweed. A virtually identical pattern was present in Parker's (1991) analysis of the Sponemann Stirling ceremonial area.

Red cedar was absent or was found only in minute quantities in most Mississippian occupations in the American Bottom. However, at the BBB Motor site red cedar fragments constituted 12.2% of identifiable wood, and at Sponemann 27.4%. It has been well documented that red cedar was viewed as a sacred wood by many Southeastern, Eastern Woodland, and Plains groups (Bowers 1965; Douglas 1976; Densmore 1928; Dorsey 1894; Mooney 1900; Mooney and Olbrechts 1932; Hudson 1976). Its importance to Mississippian elites was demonstrated by their use of red cedar to construct the burial litters associated with the high-status Lohmann phase burials in Mound 72 at Cahokia (Fowler 1991); in the construction of elite mortuary facilities at the Cemetery Mound E-1 of the East St. Louis Group (Kelly 1994); in Mississippian cemeteries at the Range site (John Kelly, personal communication 1996); as markers in the Cahokia Woodhenge (cf. Smith 1992); in litter poles and effigies at Spiro (Brown 1966); perhaps in litter poles of the Natchez Great Sun (cf. Radin 1927: 207); and most important, in the restriction of its use to the rural ceremonial nodes at the Range, BBB Motor, and Sponemann sites.

The cosmological ramifications of red cedar ca. A.D. 1000 has been documented most fully by Douglas (1976: 224-239) in his attempt to understand a Mississippian-influenced Late Woodland ceremonial complex in eastern

Illinois. He found the symbolic connotations and associated uses of red cedar to be varied, although remarkably consistent in overall precepts. It was used by native peoples as a purifying smoke or incense to cleanse the body, soul, and sacred precincts, and cedar boughs were similarly used in ceremonies and structures to ward off impure or evil forces. Because of its red wood, cedar was associated with the color red and, consequently, with blood, fire, and water. This "red" affiliation gave cedar a strong connection with fire, and it was commonly used in the "sacred fire." Cedar was also associated with water and life forces as the "ever-lasting" tree (noting its evergreen qualities). When included as a component in tools, weapons, or structures, it endowed them with great magical powers. Douglas argues (1976: 233-235) that cedar was a mediator for humankind between earth-sky and partook of sky-fire-sun attributes to protect humans against the supernatural earth/water forces (which often bespoke an Under World association). These attributes accounted for cedar's uses as a purifying agent with fire and in poles as links reaching the sky (i.e., that which wards off Under World forces). Red cedar's presence as a purifying fumigant and as structural members in the BBB Motor, Sponemann, and Range RML-2 context strengthens such an interpretation as a critical protective force in rituals that required participant involvement with the Under World forces of water and fertility.

More surprising was the recovery of carbonized *Datura stramonium* (jimsonweed) from the BBB Motor site Feature 125 in the temple structure. That same feature also contained the largest amount of red cedar and a large number of exotic items discussed earlier. Ingested *Datura* produced delirium, intoxication, hallucinations, and other symptoms, including death (Goodman and Hilman 1955: 534-535; Lewis and Elvin-Lewis 1977: 419).

In her review of aboriginal uses of *Datura* in the Western Hemisphere, Whalley (n.d., 1984) found extensive documentation for Mexico, South and Central America, and the North American Southwest, but few examples from the eastern Woodlands. It appeared that among the Virginia and North Carolina Algonquian groups *Datura* was commonly used as an external medicine and was recognized as producing delirium if taken internally (Hoffman 1964; Speck 1944; Lawson 1966). Whalley (n.d.) speculated that *Datura* may have been one of the ingredients used in the medicine associated with the Huskenaw initiation ceremony of some East Coast Algonquians. Hudson (1976: 332, 532) suggested that the "tobacco" pellets given to the intended sacrificial victims in the Natchez mortuary ceremonies may have been *Datura,* the leaves of which superficially resembled tobacco. The presence of carbonized seeds of *Datura* in secure context in a ceremonial feature within a temple structure clearly indicated that the plant was a deliberate inclusion with religious/ritual connotations. Whether the *Datura* was being used as a medicinal plant or to achieve a state of hallucination is not known.

Although strangely missing at the BBB Motor site, tobacco seeds *(Nicotiana rustica)* were present in many of the ritual structures and features at the Sponemann site ceremonial complex (Parker 1991: 316). Tobacco is an interesting narcotic since it has both mundane and ritual uses, yet it seldom appeared in any quantity in American Bottom archaeological sites. Rather than reflecting any prehistoric scarcity, such lack of evidence for tobacco use from an archaeological context is no doubt a result of the difficulty in recovering the minute seeds (which were only an incidental inclusion since it was the leaves that were used), as well as a fact of preservation. Ethnohistoric accounts from many sources document the ritual use of tobacco leaves as a purifying and partly hallucinogenic vehicle. Its ritual use in the Mississippian period for similar purposes is suggested by the presence of pipes and carbonized specimens in ritual sites.

CAHOKIAN RURAL WORLD STRUCTURING

In the previous chapter I illustrated the importance of the cosmological organization of the natural/supernatural worlds into dualistic categories expressed as oppositions in the Mississippian world. My earlier recognition of the presence of a dualistic organizational framework in Cahokian Mississippian symbolism is briefly reiterated and expanded here to discuss the evidence from the rural ceremonial nodes. This cosmology also involved the presence of a four-cornered world that formed a quadripartite cosmos pervasive in North American Indian symbolism; here I will cite only obvious Middle Mississippian examples, such as the circle and cross and the mound and plaza complex. We recognized the application of that framework of oppositions and quadripartition in the rural countryside.

How was this dualistic quadrilateral world reflected in the rural countryside? I have already addressed, in terms of specific sites, the presence of magicoritual items at rural centers, the evidence of fertility ceremonialism, courtyard organization, marker posts, Ramey Incised vessels, ritual plants, and specialized architecture. The Upper World-Lower World aspects of symbolism reflected in Green Corn ceremonialism pervaded rural nodal sites. But what was more fascinating was the organizational pattern reflected in such sites. While, to some extent, the placement of these small sites was dictated by the long, linear ridges they were built on, there was still sufficient flexibility in site layout to incorporate symbolic themes. For example, the spatial organization of structures and features at the BBB Motor site exemplified the dualistic nature of the Lohmann and Stirling phase components. I suggested that the dualistic spatial organization also was reflected in a functional, as well as a chronological, division between the two components. The temple-mortuary complex could have been characterized as a special status ritual-religious area, while the priest-mortuary complex, though also ritualistic, tended to suggest a community-centered use. I believe that the two sequential complexes represented the continuation and implementation of a spatial and functional ritual, as well as chronological, dualism.

Many of the Stirling rural centers present a similar picture in patterning. The layout of the Sponemann site reflected a familiar organizational pattern, with ritual structures laid out around a courtyard that opened to the northwest. An identical layout of structures about a northwestern-opening courtyard was found at Labras Lake. The Julien Stirling civic node was more difficult to interpret, but the courtyard there appeared to open to the northeast, while the Range nodal site comprised two clusters of structures on the northeastern and southwestern sides of a courtyard. These rural centers were also often set off from the surrounding areas through the use of the topography. For instance, the BBB Motor site's ritual status was enhanced by its physical, and presumably spiritual (cf. Hall 1976), separation from the surrounding land by a barrier of water and marshes. The Sponemann, Julien, Range, and Labras Lake nodes were isolated from surrounding buildings and often situated on the highest land form. I suggest that the rural plan of some of these nodes was a miniature (microcosm of sacred macrocosm a la Tilley 1991) reflection of the larger mound and plaza center concept with its courtyard layout, ritual structures, adherence to directional orientations, symbolic content, and spatial and "spiritual" isolation or islands.

Over the years, research has demonstrated that Mississippian culture was concerned with the concept of directional orientation. Ethnohistorically, Southeastern groups such as the Creeks and Cherokees were known to have associated colors, certain spirits, and a series of social values and personal attributes with the cardinal directions. Similar values have been documented for other groups in the Eastern Woodlands (cf. Douglas 1976). As Hudson (1976: 132) has commented, these attributes often took the form of opposites. Prehistorically, there is good evidence from the archaeological data that site organization and mound construction may have been based on specific orientations in the Mississippian cultures. We know that many of the ceremonial structures and areas among the historic groups were organized in terms of direction (e.g., see Reed 1969).

Most groups laid out their square grounds along the cardinal directions, with the buildings facing north, south, east, and west. This system was not absolute, however; the Creeks often oriented the corners of their square grounds to the cardinal directions, so the buildings were placed at 45-degree angles to the cardinal points (i.e., along the semi-cardinal points). In fact, Douglas has described in great detail a similar pattern of semicardinal orientation for the Late Woodland Collins (ca. A.D. 1000) ceremonial site in east central Illinois. Douglas (1976: 257-269), using extensive ethnographic and ethnohistoric data, argued that the prehistoric native world view at this time conceived of a four-quartered world in which the primary axis ran northwest to southeast, with a second divisor running northeast to southwest. This created four diamond-shaped quarters to the north, east, west, and south. In such a world, north was linked to east and south to west, spiritually. A semicardinal orientation of many of the religious and political sites discussed in this text seems apparent. At the same time, however, it appeared that the primary center at Cahokia reflected a different organizational plan—one keyed to the cardinal directions (cf. Fowler 1989). Such a difference may suggest that hierarchical levels were oriented on the basis of different symbolic parameters. The spatial organization and contents of these rural sites represented the organization of the Mississippian world view in microcosm. The site layouts suggested adherence to an overall plan that reflected the dualistic quadripartite nature of the symbolic world in the cosmology of the builders.

One cannot discuss dualism in Mississippian and historic Southeastern cultures without some reference to its possible association with the social organization of the group. Hudson's discussion of the social organization of Southeastern Indians (1976: 184-257) will be the major source for this discussion. One of the essential units of the kinship system appeared to be the matrilineage, consisting of a group of related individuals who traced their ancestry from a known female. Such groups often lived in the same area, practiced joint ownership of property, and shared certain ceremonial rights and obligations (Hudson 1976: 189). A higher level of organization was achieved through clans (cf. Knight 1990), which consisted of a number of lineages that claimed descent from a common mythical ancestor. Such clans apparently were spread over a wide area and were present in all the associated towns. The ceremonial/ritual function of such clans varied historically, but they were known to be exogamous. The extant data indicate that such clans were the single most important social entity in Southeastern groups.

The system portrayed above was also flexible enough to be manipulated to allow for expansion and division of the lineages. There was evidence that when lineages became too large or had internal conflicts they might split. Lineages were of varied sizes, and one might occasionally find small lineages linking themselves to larger ones in the interests of self-preservation. This usually involved an exogamous relationship. Such alliances were often fragile and frequently dissolved, with subsequent realignment of relationships (Hudson 1976: 196).

Divisions within Creek towns were along lineage lines. Very often the resulting moieties split into "white" and "red" divisions, each with different social, political, and ceremonial obligations. Such moieties were sometimes exogamous. Hudson (1976: 237) suggested that the dual organizational pattern was very old in the Southeast and in the past probably was based on a division into moieties of clans within a chiefdom. How does this relate to the Cahokia Mississippian countryside? One line of argument on rural organization has focused on nodal sites as critical central nodes to maintain unity and control. In such instances, the social units being integrated may have consisted of either segments of a single lineage or different lineage groups. For example, the dualistic organization seen in the division of the Stirling temple and Lohmann priestly areas at the BBB Motor site and in the internal division of each component may have reflected kinship or political variation. It is intriguing to consider that the different grave orientations and their division into two clusters may have had social connotations. If the temple-mortuary complex there served to integrate different lineages occupying a number of dispersed villages, it is possible to interpret the division of graves as representing moiety differences, while the different grave orientations within each unit reflected lineage affiliation. At this point, of course, discussion along such lines is only speculative.

MIDDLE MISSISSIPPIAN CULTS

Mississippian iconography has long been of interest to archaeologists. In the past, most discussions have incorporated such symbolic representations into the context of the Southern Cult (cf. Galloway, ed. 1989). All too often, the analysis of the Southern Cult has been based on a trait list approach, with all its inherent problems (Brown 1976a). Brown has suggested that the idea of a single ideological cult—that is, the Southern Cult—should be replaced by a more appropriate model of an interregional interaction sphere coextensive with the distribution of complex Mississippian cultural systems (1976a: 115, 1985, 1989). He goes on to suggest that the most productive approach would be to view the cult data from the standpoint of the "structural and organizational features of panregional art styles and on the cultural context of specialized artifacts" (1976a: 131).

Given the existence of regional Mississippian cultural systems, one would expect to see this regionalism reflected in the symbolic systems. Thus, while the same set of symbolic themes pervaded all Mississippian cosmology, the degree of elaboration of these themes was likely to vary from region to region. I have argued previously that such a unique fertility symbolic theme can be recognized within the Cahokian symbolic world (cf. Emerson 1989).

Brown believed that much of Spiro Mississippian symbolism could be "directly related to three organizational networks of social power operating in the Mississippian hierarchical society"; furthermore, "as symbols the artifacts and art motifs relate to prestige structures based on the sanctity of power in chiefdom-type societies" (1976a: 126). These three organizational networks were represented by groups of traits that included cult paraphernalia, especially weapons associated with warfare; falcon representations associated with another aspect of warfare; and the mortuary temple complex that reaffirmed the sanctity of the elite. He summarized these sets of artifacts/symbols as follows (after Brown 1976a: 126-127):

The first set was made up of prestige items, including cult paraphernalia and symbolic representations in other mediums. In this category one finds nonutilitarian weapons. "It is undoubtedly significant to understanding the processes for maintaining Mississippian systems that weapons are conspicuous prototypes to sociotechnic artifacts and their derivative decorative symbols. Moreover these weapon-derived cultural forms are found overwhelmingly in specialized settings, frequently associated with burials of the elite dead. This connection of military symbolism with the elite reinforces rather emphatically the social significance that warfare has in confirming prestige" (Brown 1976a: 126).

The second set consists of the falcon, falcon impersonator, and associated symbols, which formed the conceptual core of the cult. These were symbols of aggression and war and were thus associated with military operations. The role of war captain was directly associated with hawk symbols at Spiro (Brown 1976a: 127).

The third category was associated with "upholding the sanctity of chiefdoms." These symbols were present in the temple-mortuary complex and included mortuary figurines, skeletal art motifs, human masks and maskettes, and head pots. Brown (1976a: 127) noted that items associated with this set would be the rarest because of their specific link to a specialized building. These items were seldom found in graves. The symbolism they depicted is rarely used in the iconography.

Brown (1975) has elaborated on the mortuary temple complex model as it is manifested at Spiro. Willoughby (1932) was the first to recognize the temple-mortuary complex as an entity, based on his research at Etowah. His description was expanded by Antonio Waring (Williams 1968: 58-62), and Brown refined it in his Spiro research (1975: 11-17). Waring's development of the concept was based primarily on the Natchez analogue and the archaeological data from Etowah, Moundville, and Fatherland. Waring saw the important aspects of the complex as consisting of high-status burials preserved in a temple in association with the tribal cult figures. An additional facet of the mortuary/temple complex was its role in honoring the ancestors of the leading families. Brown developed this idea using the Spiro data and suggested that "the mortuary amounts to a cult headquarters from which the politically significant descendants of the honored dead draw ideological power. This power was principally manifest in their capacity to mount successful war parties and in their authority to manage the distribution of food and other critical resources" (Brown 1975: 15).

Although not directly associated with the mortuary/ancestral cult house, the mortuary complex contained extensive symbolic representations of warfare at Spiro (Brown 1975: 19-23). These included the falcon motif, falcon impersonator, weapons and symbolic weapon depictions, and occasional scenes of violence. Brown (1975: 23) suggested that much of the "political power vested in the elite is due to, and maintained by, military prowess or, at least, managerial effectiveness in warfare." In terms of thematic symbols, the mortuary/ancestral cult and warfare seemed to represent the major concepts at Spiro.

However, in a significant later reevaluation of these schema, Brown (1985) shifted his perspective to recognize a differing set of images that may best be conceived of as pan-Mississippian "cults" related to ancestor veneration, fertility symbolism, and chiefly iconography. In such a system, ancestor veneration was materialized in the existence of an ancestral mortuary/charnel house, shrine ancestor statuary, and skull-and-bone motifs (i.e., items generally associated with his previously related third category of "chiefly authority").

Chiefly iconography is primarily signaled by the chiefly litter, the chunkee player and game, and the falcon impersonator. In this case, I believe Brown sought to consolidate in this chiefly category both of his previously conceived cult and warfare-related "networks" (i.e., Brown 1976a) to emphasize the political and warfare aspects of chiefly power. He recognized the conceptualization of the serpent and fertility cults in Cahokian figurines such as the Birger, West, and Keller images; serpent variants; and the important underwater panther or monster.

Of special interest was Brown's dramatic perception of the interaction of these cults. He stated (1985: 129): "Two antithetical social forces were at work in Mississippian societies: autonomy versus centralized political autocracy. The interests and aspirations of each were represented by the fertility cults of the populace on the one hand and the ancestor cults organized by the elite on the other. Standing, as it were, with a leg in each camp was the military cult of the falcon, which commanded the allegiance of major segments of the masses, but was firmly under the control of the elite."

Knight (1986), in an elaboration of a similar view, attempted an outline of Mississippian religious institutional organization utilizing the concept of "the formal articulation of two powerful and complementary cult organizations into a structure of dyadic type. . . ." He saw this pairing of a cult of nobility and a cult of fertility in Mississippian religion as participating in a worldwide precedence of such cult linkages (cf. Turner 1969). *Sacra* (i.e., artifacts argued to represent the nobility) were those with warfare and cosmological images. The manipulation and possession of such items were likely limited to members of "privileged unilineal descent groups."

The fertility cult *sacra* were symbolized for Knight (1986: 678-679) by that magnificent Mississippian icon, the platform mound. I find his connections of this "earth island" with fertility symbolism singularly compelling and worth repeating in full:

> Evidence in support of this contention consists of (1) Muskogean terminology for mounds, having cognates and associations metaphorically tying them to a native earth/autochthony symbolic nexus; (2) a historically traced connection between mound platform addition and communal "green corn" ceremonialism, the latter oriented to concepts of earth, agriculture, and purification; (3) Muskogee and Choctaw traditions that discuss mound-building ritual in the context of symbolic burial, purification, and the placation of earth powers; and (4) the quadrilateral, flat-topped configuration of the mounds themselves, probably connoting the southeastern cosmological concept of earth as a discrete, flat-surfaced entity oriented to the four world quarters.

Temple statuary is identified as a third set of Mississippian *sacra* that was presumably associated with ancestor and/or mortuary cults. Knight (1986: 679) specifically eliminates the Birger and Keller type figurines from such a category, and I presume he was referring to examples of what have generally been labeled the Tennessee-Cumberland style (Webb and DeJarnette 1942; Emerson 1983) that seem to have death/ancestor imaging.

Perhaps Knight's most important insight, however, regarding the ancestor/mortuary cult was his recognition of the presence of an "organized priesthood." While extensively documented in the ethnohistoric literature, few researchers have dealt in a meaningful way with the role or the importance of such priests, shamans, or "jugglers." Most have assumed that these individuals were minor players in the native power structure or that such minor roles were incorporated into the existing nobility. Knight (1986: 681), using documented accounts, noted that such priests were responsible for "the maintenance of temples and ossuaries, administration of mortuary ritual, the maintenance of sacred fires and responsibilities connected with their supernatural aspects, and the preparation of ritual medicines. The roles of priests intermeshed with both chiefly practice (especially mortuary) and with community rites of intensification. [They] . . . were occupationally specialized ritual groups . . . restricted in membership to certain age graded and normally gender bound initiates."

The relationship between these various Mississippian cults is proposed to resemble a "dyadic structural type," with the chiefly warrior cult being opposed by the communally based fertility cult, and the ancestor/mortuary priesthood playing a pivotal role as mediator. Such a scenario is similar to that outlined above by Brown (1985), in which he saw the dialectic opposition of the nobility cult to the fertility cult; however, in that case, the mediator came in the guise of a warrior cult. Both stress the intrinsic conflict within the system of Mississippian cults. To a large degree, this is due to the social connotations that were presumed to be carried by each cult. The cult of the nobility carried with it implications of restricted membership, most likely based on kin ties and associations of *power over* the actions of others. Such a cult focused on creating spiritual, social, and spatial *distance* between social groups. The fertility cult, on the other hand, was conceived of as community-centered by its very nature. Wallace (1966: 87), in fact, noted that leadership positions in such types of cults were usually not filled by nobility but rather by civil authorities who had a wide range of other duties. The iconography of such cults delved into the very symbolic core and deeply held values of the social group to promote unity—often, as I have held here, through rites of intensification.

In this study I find that the role of the fertility cults was the dominant force in rural Cahokia life. To a large degree this reflects earlier perspectives in which Brown noted that categories of symbols appeared in specific contexts, concurring with Griffin (1952) that the frequency and diversity of *sacra* were related directly to the site type and its position in the settlement hierarchy. As I commented previously (Emerson 1989: 82), rural symbolism and iconography may not completely reflect Cahokian elite ritual, yet there must have been a link between the two realms.

CAHOKIA SYMBOLISM

In previous sections I have attempted to deal with a number of material items and their possible symbolic associations. In this summary I will make an effort to derive themes from these disparate symbols. A number of qualifying statements should be presented delimiting both the extent and the depth of this interpretation. The emphasis will be on the material recovered from the rural ceremonial nodes of a dispersed village. How well these "rural" nodes reflected the Cahokia system is unknown, but there was obviously a strong connection between the two. Since these ceremonial complexes were located on the outskirts of the main center, one might have expected to recover only a segment of the ritual and symbolic paraphernalia associated with the total Mississippian symbolic system. In fact, if ceremonial and civic complexes and their attached symbolism were directly associated with a social group, such as a lineage, clan, or moiety, they may have been specialized. We know from historical accounts that certain social groups possessed special ritual/ceremonial privileges and obligations. Some of the symbolic content of the sites could be specific to the social group using the ceremonial center.

Let me stress again at this point that the symbolic associations of many of the elements were based on information from ethnohistorical/ethnographic documents of historic Southeastern Indian groups and occasionally of Plains and Prairie groups. In addition, I have relied heavily on the data available from the rich iconography of the Spiro site and their interpretation. It has been my contention from the outset that such analogues are valid and useful in gaining insights into Mississippian iconography. The levels of interpretation being sought are broad. I am using symbols to seek basic themes that pervaded American Bottom Mississippian ritualism during the eleventh and early twelfth centuries. I make no attempt to give design elements or motifs specific, rigid meanings; instead, I use their common symbolic content to define basic symbolic themes.

As at Spiro and a number of other Mississippian centers, there seemed to be sufficient evidence for the temple-mortuary cult. The Range, BBB Motor, and Sponemann sites are the only known examples of a rural ceremonial temple-mortuary complex that were not at a major ceremonial mound center. However, all were located in proximity to such centers. In addition, minimal evidence exists for an ancestor cult, and more important, warfare symbolism was virtually nonexistent in the early Cahokia countryside.

The major theme in such rural sites as Range RML-2, Sponemann, and BBB Motor was concerned with the broad conceptualization of fertility. I have discussed the symbolic representations of this theme in detail in previous sections. In summary, the delineation of the interwoven themes of the Under World and fertility is based on the dominance of the serpent/spiral motifs in conjunction with the less well represented Thunderer/bird motifs. The association of the serpent/spiral motifs with water and fertility has been discussed at length and will not be repeated here. It might be worthwhile, however, to review briefly my interpretation of the forked-eye/wing motifs as Thunderers rather than as symbols of war, as at Spiro. At Spiro elite burials, falcon impersonators, weapons, and so forth constituted a tightly inter-woven set of symbols that could justifiably be seen as warfare motifs. The bird motifs in the Cahokia sphere were of an entirely different type. Wing motifs were mainly confined to Ramey Incised ceramic symbolism, which may have been closely integrated with the agricultural ceremonialism cycle. The forked eye appears in a similar context. There were no elaborate falcon-impersonator symbols or weapons (symbolic or otherwise).

This is not to say that warriors and warfare did not exist at Cahokia. The massive arrowpoint caches in Mound 72, the possible sacrificed captives, the presence of arrowpoints, the massive rebuilt palisades all were suggestive of conflict and the importance of warriors. What is important, however, is the lack of a known Cahokian symbolic repertoire of warfare. Of the organiza-tional networks and cults Brown and Knight defined, those with strong military connotations were symbolically absent, the temple-mortuary com-plex was present in an attenuated and modified form, while fertility symbol-ism was a dominant theme. This reaffirmed the regional and temporal variability of Mississippian iconography and ceremonialism and suggested that, at least in this time and place, fertility ideology was dominant.

The major symbolic themes at the rural sites such as Range RML-2, BBB Motor, and Sponemann were associated with water and thus with fertility and the Under World. The theme of fertility may have been associ-ated with the broader topics of renewal, regeneration, life cycles, and life continuation. Such themes and symbolic associations would have been in keeping with the nature of the temple-mortuary complex at the BBB Mo-tor site and the temple/ceremonial Sponemann site in their function as im-portant nodal sites for agricultural ceremonialism (as seen in the figurines and the Ramey symbolism).

The different emphasis within the Spiro mortuary complex and the re-ported American Bottom sites likely reflected the different social status, hi-erarchical position, and function of the two groups involved. As previously shown, the Spiro complex functioned to reaffirm the primacy of the elite and to reinforce their values. The temple-mortuary and ceremonial com-plexes at the rural sites, on the other hand, were attached to a dispersed village of "commoners" and low-ranking elites. The primary concern of this community was probably subsistence production and the control of the forces that influenced it. One should not expect to find elaborate sumptuary items dedicated to glorifying the ruling elite at a small local temple com-plex. (Although it is clear that such iconography also reminded the com-moners that it was the elite they had to thank for maintaining control of the cosmos.)

This raises the issue of an elite economy in which exotic artifacts were exchanged to maintain the elite hierarchical supremacy—this created a pan-Mississippian elite that was removed from the common masses (i.e., Frankenstein and Rowlands's prestige economy, 1978). To some researchers, the artifacts of the Southeastern Ceremonial Complex (SECC) represented such a material world (e.g., Brown et al. 1990; Peregrine 1992; various papers in Galloway, ed. 1989). But where is the SECC at Cahokia? In general, excavations have not been carried out in high-ranking elite Cahokian mortuary facilities that one would expect to be major repositories of such items. However, evidence for the presence of the Southeastern Ceremonial Complex, or at least contact with groups that practiced it, was indicated by a number of engraved ceramic vessels, ceramic fragments, and shells showing relationships to the Spiro Braden style (Brown 1989: 193-198). The recovery of a sandstone tablet with a falcon dancer on it, associated with a burial under the east lobe of Monks Mound (Williams 1972: 75-77, figure 7), has also been attributed to the SECC. Regardless of these artifacts, evidence for the presence of SECC materials at Cahokia has been unusually limited (Brown and Kelly 1996).

Considering that there is evidence of contact with the Southeast and Caddoan regions, in terms of both ceramic and lithic exotic material at Cahokia, the lack of SECC material is perplexing. It is doubly so when one considers there is considerable evidence that regional sites were actively participating in what could be referred to as a "pre-SECC" complex (cf. Hall 1991; Kelly 1991a). This is the Long Nosed God Horizon, as defined by Williams and Goggin (1956). Hall (1991) has documented the spread and occurrence of these icons across the Upper Mississippi River Valley. While only a limited number of Long Nosed God Masks have been found in the American Bottom, such masks were plentiful at northern sites that show Mississippian influence, such as the Lower Illinois River Valley, the Spoon River Mississippian, Aztalan, and the Diamond Bluff area.

In the Central Illinois River Valley, Conrad (1989) thoroughly documented the extensive nature of the SECC materials associated with the Spoon River and La Moine Mississippian groups. These items included such traits as human sacrifice; massive stone effigy pipes; cross-shaped buildings; large chert blades, swords, and maces; copper-covered wooden blades; various SECC motifs; and the Peoria Eagle Plate. Importantly, Conrad has been able to demonstrate the appearance of the SECC-related traits at about A.D. 1050 and their continuance into the fifteenth century. All of this indicated that the American Bottom area was very likely participating to some degree in the SECC as early as the Stirling phase and continuing as late as the early Sand Prairie phase. The limited presence of SECC material at Cahokia itself was probably a result of the vagaries of sampling the large site, especially the absence of data from the mounds of the central precinct area.

At Cahokia itself, the evidence from excavations in Mound 72 (Fowler 1991) indicates that the elite of the Mississippian society were willing to dispose of raw material and retainers to affirm their status. This elite burial contained large numbers of grave goods, but there was limited deposition of military items or symbols. The grave goods consisted mainly of large amounts of raw material or caches of manufactured items. Recently, based on his research with Cahokian site material, Pauketat (1992, 1996) demonstrated that just such a manipulation of often local raw materials was a powerful tool in the hands of the Cahokian elite and was central to maintaining their positions in the hierarchy. As mentioned previously, this elite control of raw materials was also reflected in the countryside. However, it is clear that the focus of elite cult symbolism of inner Cahokia may have been very different from the earthly fertility iconography of its rural settlements.

RURAL CULTS

Both Brown (1985: 103-104) and Knight (1986: 675-676) have sought to facilitate our comprehension of Mississippian religion and ritualism by introducing the concept of the "cult," to a large degree following Turner's (1964, 1969, 1974) lead. "Cult institutions . . . [are defined as] a set of rituals all having the same general goal, all explicitly rationalized by a set of similar or related beliefs, and all supported by the same social group" (Wallace 1966: 75, as cited in Knight 1986). Each cult may also be expected to have a series of symbols or *sacra* associated with it, including "representational art, artifacts, and icons that by inference appear to have been charged with conventional supernatural meanings, in the context of ritual activity or display" (Knight 1986: 675; Turner 1964).

What are the implications of this approach in understanding Cahokian religion and ritual? First, the recognition of cults is essential to our study of Cahokian iconography because it establishes a basis for studying as a composite of separates what might initially appear as a unitary monolith. Religions are composed of multiple cults (i.e., they are pluralistic) (Knight 1986). This is critical to understanding and identifying the sets of *sacra* and establishes the critical nature of secure archaeological context, something I have taken great pains to do in this text. Another facet of this pluralistic approach is to realize that each cult has its own developmental history and that cults may or may not covary as they wax and wane. Conversely, cults may be in accord with or in opposition to one another. It is important to note, as above, that the motives, symbolism, and ritual of the Cahokian elite operated on a different plane from the leadership at the small rural ceremonial centers of dispersed villages. Cults should not automatically be conceived of as integrative mechanisms; they may just as easily serve as divisive mechanisms (e.g., for political reasons [cf. Eister 1974]).

The recognition of cults and *sacra* is also essential to distinguishing between religious symbolism and structure. If Wallace was correct in his correlation of a "cult" with a "social group," then it is important to confine one's research to an appropriate level within a hierarchical society such as was present at Cahokia. As Brown (1985) and Griffin (1952) noted earlier, symbolic content may change with hierarchical level. However, at the same time, as is clear from our previous discussions, symbolic messages appeared to pervade all levels of society. It is at this point that these elements become useful in distinguishing "cult" from "structure." In our case, this means not confusing the structural principles of dualism and quadripartition with the cult *sacra* of fertility and world renewal. The issue here is that all-pervasive factors leading to the dualistic and quadripartitioning structuration of Cahokian society cross-cut the pluralistic cults; they were organizing principles of a worldview and were not restricted to any social group or class. Consequently, the structuration of Mississippian space was as accurately reflected in the massive quadrilateral platform mounds and rectangular plaza on Cahokia's Grand Plaza as in the quadrilateral courtyards and structure organization of the small rural ceremonial centers.

Yet there appeared to be a dialectical relationship between two cult forms that was universal in its appearance: the poised conflict between an elite cult of the nobility and a cult of the earth, of fertility, of the masses (cf. Turner 1974: 185, 1969: 99). This dichotomy might have been seen in Mississippian life as Brown's distinction between chiefly iconography and the serpent and fertility cults or Knight's iconic warfare/cosmogony and platform mound complexes. The identification of these distinct cults was primary to establishing and understanding their relationship.

One of the difficult tasks that faced us was deriving some measure of power relationships between the hierarchical levels in Mississippian society. Here I will suggest that the relative strength of these cults, as illustrated in the rural areas, was one such subjective measure. The "relative strength" of the cults could be recognized and defined in the appearance and variation in the material world of an "architecture of power" and the associated "artifacts of power." These were clear manifestations of centralized elite domination in the countryside. Specifically, the ability of the elite to expropriate and control the fertility symbolism and rituals at rural centers was a direct measure of their control over the rural population, and the symbolic expropriation and manipulation of the fertility cult by the elite was most marked in Stirling times.

It is useful then, in order to provide some insights into the greater spectrum of Mississippian elite domination through religion, to examine the developmental history of one such cult within the context of small Middle Mississippian rural centers around Cahokia. Religious symbolism by no means originated with the onset of the Mississippian period in the American Bottom. Kelly (1990a: 129-130) has documented the presence of the courtyard, central post and four pits, and four quarters motifs by about A.D. 800, which he interpreted as representing the cross-in-circle. Such an association was strengthened by connections to a ceremonial structure with multiple hearths along one side of the square. He suggested a "fire-sun-fertility" symbolic content for this complex. This association was continued and expanded during the late Emergent Mississippian period (cf. Kelly 1990a, 1990b) with circle-and-cross motifs, with Green Corn-related renewal ceremonies, and with the appearance of the large plazas bordered by elite structures in large villages. It is useful to note, however, that this ceremonial architecture was confined to larger Emergent Mississippian villages and did not manifest itself at smaller rural sites.

The onset of the Lohmann consolidation saw the first appearance of ceremonial construction in the rural countryside. That was one of the clearest indicators that the elite consolidation of power at Cahokia had reached out into the countryside to re-create it in a new and very different way. The restructuring of rural patterns was reflected in building an "architecture of power," one that indicated an imposed pattern of site layout and construction and suggested centralized control. This was most apparent at the Range site where the civic/ceremonial node included two sets of structures around a central courtyard. This center (RML-1) included a large (ca. 58 m) multiwalled, single-post, community-centered gathering structure with interior benches and cooking areas; two large rectangular wall-trench structures; and two earlier smaller structures. The wall-trench structures appear to represent both residential and storage facilities. They were separated from RML-2 by a large open space.

The latter complex contained two large rectangular structures between which lay a large rectangular pit. That feature complex demonstrated a clear pattern of being associated with fertility and "world renewal" ceremonies. Structure 4379 contained a number of ceramic vessels, some of which were ceremonially killed. A key feature for interpreting this complex, however, was Feature 2770. This massive centrally located pit contained more than thirty ceramic vessels, some of which were ceremonially broken. In addition, exotic items such as a discoidal, shell hoes, beads, a hematite abrader, multiple grinding and abrading tools, and bifacial tools were present. Critical in interpreting the function of this pit was the extensive presence of both red cedar and tobacco. Hanenberger (Hanenberger and Mehrer 1998), in noting that Feature 2770 was the only Lohmann pit to contain red cedar, tobacco, effigy bowls, ceremonially killed vessels, shell objects, and engraved sherds, suggested a ceremonial connection. The presence of large concentrations of magicoritual items in this Lohmann complex was another sign of the transformation of the countryside. There was absolutely no precedent among earlier Emergent Mississippian rural sites for such an accumulation of exotica.

I think such a connection was present at RML-2 and that its correlation with Green Corn fertility ceremonialism was also apparent and demonstrated in the presence of a large ceremonial "world renewal" pit containing ritual artifacts and plants. This Lohmann ceremonial complex also displayed some interesting attributes concerning rural fertility cults at that time. It appears to have served as a special facility where community activities were carried out, perhaps the residence of individuals trained to conduct such rituals. The community nature of the ceremony was reinforced by the presence of the large community structure at RML-1 and suggested the participation of many individuals in such rituals. The community nature of the activities may also be adduced from the presence of possible food(?) storage facilities, such as in the Structure 32 complex. The appearance of community food storage facilities at these Lohmann sites was another attribute that distinguished them from previous Emergent Mississippian sites. This is the first instance we have of the control of comestibles by a subset of the community. If the evidence from the ethnographic record is appropriate here, the individuals associated with performing these rituals might have been drawn from the local dispersed village civic leadership and, consequently, should not be considered specialists. It would also indicate that RML-1 and RML-2 may have served a more generalized use during their lifetimes, being places of both civic and ritual meetings and not restricted to only cult activities. This may explain the presence of the massive community structure, which could have functioned as a council house for the local leaders on a year-round basis.

A similar community-centered atmosphere was present in the late Lohmann priest-mortuary ceremonial node at the BBB Motor site. The structures indicate that, while one may possibly have served as a residence for a local priest/shaman, the other, with its internal benches, appears to have had a group use. While the Lohmann phase might have seen the appearance of mortuary specialists, perhaps an actual priesthood as Knight's model would suggest, mortuary ritual appeared to have community-centered aspects that involved groups of individuals. The BBB Motor Lohmann mortuary complex also seems to indicate in the countryside the presence of low-ranking elite with an ascribed membership. Whether these individuals were a minor lineage segment of the ruling elite at Cahokia or a "superior" lineage segment of the rural population is not clear. Interestingly, few blatant symbolic referents existed in this mortuary complex, and the only connection to the fertility cult per se was the medium of death.

As in most discussions of cultural change in the American Bottom, a dramatic shift could be seen in rural ceremonial complexes with the beginning of the Stirling phase. At least three specialized nodal complexes can be distinguished during this period—a temple-mortuary ceremonial node, civic nodes, and a Green Corn ceremonial node. There was at least some evidence to suggest there may have been a chronological shift in the use and emphasis of these rural centers.

The most common and best known Stirling phase rural centers are the classic civic nodes at sites such as Labras Lake, Julien, or Range. Those centers typically included residential, storage, and other specialized buildings in association with purification sweat houses. I believe that these Stirling phase sites represent local civic nodes from which political control was exerted over the surrounding households. Typically such nodes were centrally and accessibly located within a dispersed village and contained both residences and specialized storage and/or cooking facilities. While the presence of such facilities bespoke either the existence of storage or "feasting" activities that exceeded those of the local inhabitants, they were not on the community scale, such as recognized at the Range Lohmann phase RML-1 and RML-2 complex. In fact, no community-scale "architecture" existed at these sites. There is little evidence of cult activity such as noted at either the earlier Range Lohmann civic-ceremonial node or the later BBB Motor or Sponemann ceremonial nodes. While it is clear that their inhabitants had access to the standard magicoritual materials and vessels, missing was any evidence of Green Corn ceremonialism, such as "renewal dumps" or the critical red cedar wood.

The unique feature associated with all these civic nodes was the presence of the sweat houses—clearly of ceremonial function but not for large-scale, community-centered use. The permanence of their construction demonstrated that such sweat houses were critical and constant aspects of nodal activities, but their small size proved that only a limited number of individuals had access to them. Such a role and access may have been restricted to the local leader and a few selected, respected elders. As I noted earlier, the concept of ritual purity was central to Southeastern native beliefs and also was valid on a wider scale through the Eastern Woodlands. It is critical to understand that this "purity" was not simply a ritual aspect of cult activities but was an aspect of everyday actions; the cleansing of the body and spirit through emetics, incenses, fasting, or sweating was essential before important activities took place or decisions were made. Consequently, sweat houses were an integral part of political and ritual life (however, they seemed absent in our well-documented fertility cult ritual sites).

I find a similar situation existed regarding the isolated temple-mortuary ceremonial node at the BBB Motor site (i.e., a specialized rather than community-oriented function). The two structures were specialized rather than generalized, with one serving as a facility for the sacred fire and the other as a temple. While I suggested it was possible that mortuary specialists may have been developing during the Lohmann phase, I believe the Stirling component at the BBB Motor site indicated the existence of a full-time, organized mortuary priesthood, probably in residence at the temple. The developing complexity of the ritual paraphernalia, hallucinogenic medicines, mortuary ceremonialism (as evidenced by the grave house and corpse manipulations), and the elaborate organizational pattern of the site indicated such activities were in the hands of trained specialists. The isolated site location, size, and layout also indicated that these ceremonies were not community oriented, or at least not for public participation. An additional argument for the presence of a specialized priesthood at this time was the recovery of shaman figurines and depictions from the graves of individuals (e.g., the Macoupin Creek Figure Pipe [Farnsworth and Emerson 1989] or the Rattler Frog Figure Pipe [Emerson 1982]) who may have been priests (Emerson 1990).

The site evidence indicated that there was a fusion of fertility and mortuary cult symbolism from the previous Lohmann phase. Religious fertility paraphernalia was totally absent from the earlier adjacent "ancestral" Lohmann priest-mortuary complex, yet it was an integral part of the Stirling phase temple-mortuary complex. As in the Lohmann phase, the mortuary complex also suggested the presence in the countryside of low-ranking elite, with an ascribed membership; whether those individuals were a lineage segment of the ruling elite at Cahokia or a "superior" lineage segment of the rural population was not clear. Regardless of their social position, however, those individuals possessed a definable connection to the fertility cult symbolism.

The development of fertility cult ritual and symbolism reached its climax in the rural areas with the late Stirling Sponemann ceremonial node. In that case, a large fertility cult complex existed, complete with multiple specialized buildings that included a temple structure, storage buildings, ritual activity buildings, sacred fire enclosure, "world renewal" dumps, benches, isolated wall trenches, and, perhaps, a large accompanying set of high-status residences. There we would find a rich accompanying assemblage of such items as ritual plants, vessels, cult figurines, and exotic artifacts. It was similar to the BBB Motor site temple area, but with a complete absence of mortuary facilities. I think there can be little doubt that Sponemann was staffed by religious specialists who were part of a permanent priesthood. However, similar to the BBB Motor site's ritual zone, I do not see any evidence for the encouragement of large-scale public participation. The organization, location, and layout suggested attempts to limit access rather than facilitate it.

What does this imply for rural Mississippian political and cult organization during the Stirling phase? It strongly argues for a breakup of the Lohmann pattern in which we saw a division between a civic/cult leader operating from a community/cult power base and an emerging mortuary priesthood. The Stirling civic sites, such as Labras Lake or Range, with a virtual absence of cult paraphernalia or symbolism, indicated the emergence of local political leadership, with a political rather than a cult basis. On the other hand, at that time, a highly organized and specialized mortuary and cult priesthood appeared at sites such as BBB Motor and Sponemann, in close proximity to Cahokia. Moreover, such sites did not seem to have been community-oriented, as one might predict in the case of fertility cults; instead they were restricted in accessibility. This suggests that ritual access may have been limited to the rural elite—certainly a seemingly inappropriate role for cults that characteristically acted to integrate a dispersed community. However, it is in keeping with the suggestion that many of the Stirling phase symbols (e.g., Ramey Incised [Emerson 1989; Pauketat and Emerson 1991]) served as much to naturalize the dominance of the elite as to integrate the social classes. To preview my later arguments I will suggest that this phenomenon was the result of the elite expropriation of the fertility cult as part of their centralization of power and their increased consolidation of the rural population.

Initiation of the Moorehead and Sand Prairie phases resulted in significant changes in ritual and religious activity in the countryside. No demonstrable organized cult activities were recognizable in the excavated Moorehead rural sites. The only community structure was the "men's house" from Julien, and while it contained magicoritual materials and artifacts, there was no indication it served as a cult facility. Kelly (1984) has suggested that Wells Incised plates now played an important role in American Bottom ritual. If that is so, it represented a shift in Cahokian symbolic referents since these plates carried unambiguous sun symbols. While such sun symbolism was not new at Cahokia, its dominance would certainly indicate a re-emphasis in ritual direction.

By the onset of Sand Prairie times, cult activity focused on mortuary practices as demonstrated in the community-centered, bounded cemeteries of dispersed villages such as Florence Street (Emerson et al. 1983) or East St. Louis Stone Quarry (Milner 1983a). Nonmortuary organized cult symbolism was apparently absent at that time. The disappearance of cults may simply have reflected the total breakdown of all large-scale, organized social functions that appeared to have represented the end of hierarchical Mississippian society within the area.

9

Conclusions

THE MISSISSIPPIAN LANDSCAPE

The American Bottom floodplain possessed a diversity of opportunities for Middle Mississippian horticulturalists. It was an environment that could provide rich yields of cultivars and natural foods, or it could produce devastating floods that would destroy a community's entire food supply. It was a land of sloughs, oxbow lakes, wet prairies, forests, long ridges interspersed with wet swales, with occasional, sizable areas of high, dry bottomland.

It was an ever-shifting landscape that was exploited primarily through a system of settlement dispersion across its variable physiography. Small agricultural settlements were spread across the valley to take advantage both of their immediate surrounding for gardens and of nearby larger dry plots for community(?) agricultural fields. The placement of large nucleated centers was also probably significantly influenced by concerns for high land above the usual flood levels. Such a pattern may have been exacerbated at times in the American Bottom of rising water-levels, either due to regional climatic shifts and/or the Mississippians' over-utilization of their immediate surroundings.

Across this landscape I have identified remnants of a complex Middle Mississippian hierarchical settlement system that reflected the waxing and waning of Cahokian *power over*. The mechanism for delineating such power rests on identifying the appearance of and variations in an "architecture of power" and "artifacts of power." At the peak of this Cahokian *power over*, in place of undifferentiated rural settlements, I have shown the presence of widely dispersed subsistence farmsteads and special-purpose sites articulated through a series of civic/ceremonial and civic nodes to create a functional political unit whose internal cohesiveness may have been encouraged by kin ties as well as by the presence of elite control of supernatural and natural resources. These units have been described as dispersed villages, and they, in turn, may have been consolidated into ritual districts through the presence of regional rural ceremonial religious nodes. Such nodes may have been fertility cult centers and often served both as elite mortuary sites and as centers for Green Corn and "world renewal" rituals.

I have also postulated that this rural organization was a direct product of Cahokian elite intervention. At the end of the Emergent Mississippian period, the countryside about the great mound center of Cahokia was emptied of its rural populations, presumably because these people moved to larger nucleated centers. With the onset of the Lohmann phase, a new system of dispersed farmsteads and controlling nodal centers was superimposed across this depopulated landscape. Such nodal centers, linked to mound centers, could be recognized because they possessed, for the first time in the rural areas, an architecture and artifacts of power (e.g., community food storage, sacred ceramics, exotica, world renewal facilities, and council houses). Their officials presumably were directly appointed by and served at the pleasure of the paramount chief. I have argued, given the large Lohmann and Stirling phase populations at Cahokia, that this rural organization was designed to intensify the production and mobilization of staples to support the centers. Consequently, a significant aspect of Cahokian Lohmann and Stirling phase power can be related to the ability of the elite to mobilize rural populations through both coercive and ideological means, and as I have demonstrated in this study, the traces of this power were observable in the material world.

Furthermore, in reviewing the political and functional articulation of sites in Mississippian settlements within the region, I have been able to define two very different systems that I have identified as "direct" and "sequential" articulation. Systems that featured direct articulation of functionally undifferentiated rural sites with their respective mound centers, such as the Powers phase of Missouri, Harn's model for the Central Illinois River Valley, or Fowler's model for Cahokia, can be seen to be politically "simpler" and less complex than those societies that were sequentially articulated. These latter political systems, which possessed functionally differentiated rural sites with specific political and religious aspects, indicated a more complex organizational pattern for such a polity as a whole. This suggests, for example, that the Kincaid political system with its dispersed villages may have been qualitatively more complex than the Powers phase system of undifferentiated rural sites, even though both could be seen as traditional Mississippian temple towns surrounded by small rural sites. Another instance of the interpretive value of this insight was provided by the Central Illinois River Valley.

In this case, the initial intrusion of Mississippian peoples in the valley was marked by the presence of a sequentially articulated settlement system, ca. A.D. 1050. The appearance of this complex system in a "frontier" area inhabited by small Late Woodland groups strongly supports Conrad's argument (1991) that there was a direct influx of Cahokian people and their political organization into the valley. As these Mississippian groups evolved and developed, they quickly shifted their organizational pattern to one that can best be described as direct articulation—more appropriate with the ongoing "devolution" of the complexity of the local political and social system.

The delineation of such systems of hierarchical complexity as represented by patterns of sequential articulation is contrary to traditional perspectives on identifying hierarchical levels and classifying complex societies. The previously described fourth-line sites of Cahokia have been demonstrated to include much internal horizontal functional differentiation and, perhaps, an additional vertical hierarchical level of sequential articulation. Such a series of hierarchical levels exceeds those identified at all known late prehistoric societies in the eastern United States. In addition, I believe there is evidence in the Stirling phase rural nodes of loci of specialized political and religious functionaries; these could be interpreted, perhaps, by social taxonomists as marking the presence, in Wright's terms (1977: 383), of a "specialized government" (i.e., one that saw the institutionalization of non-kin forms of leadership and *power over*).

So what was Cahokia—a chiefdom or a state? As I have discussed previously, such typologically framed questions do not bring understanding to the issue of Cahokian political organization. At its height, Cahokia may have had some characteristics of an incipient state that died "aborning." During its historical political trajectory, Cahokia, at one point, was likely a "simple" chiefdom; later probably a sacral paramount chiefdom, perhaps on the verge of becoming a state; and, in its final decline, perhaps a simple chiefdom again. But these labels do not inform us in and of themselves. What this study has addressed is the question of specifics. At each point in its complex development, how were Cahokian politics and society organized, how and when did this take place, how does this resemble other known examples of the rise of complex societies, and how does this example correlate with the theoretical literature on the development of such societies?

In the American Bottom the rural sites appear to have been part of a sequentially articulated mode of settlement that included functionally differentiated site types such as farmsteads, civic/ceremonial centers, civic nodes, and ceremonial complexes. These special sites were recognized by identifying the presence of an architecture and artifacts of power that symbolized centralized Cahokian control. Such nodal sites served as centralizing political and religious centers to politically and religiously organize the rural populations.

As has been observed (Lightfoot 1984: 23), the elaboration of functions and responsibilities within a horizontal decision-making hierarchical level is a way to greatly increase "the amount and diversity of information" a polity can manage. The wide range of functional activities represented within Cahokia's rural sites may represent just such a strategy by the centralized elites. A series of changing rural settlement forms can be observed through time that reflects major shifts in the political and religious power of Cahokia. Analysis of these rural patterns has provided a number of insights into Cahokia itself.

CAHOKIA AND THE COUNTRYSIDE

In previous discussions I have described the evidence relevant to the organization of the rural populations about the Middle Mississippian center of Cahokia for the one-half millennium between A.D. 925 and A.D. 1375. In doing this, I have concentrated on the applicability of architectural, artifactual, and settlement information to create political and religious models of behavior, to understand *mentalistic* patterning in the material world. Here I wish to expand on that point of view to outline the relationship that existed between the Cahokian central polity and the surrounding countryside. I intend to explore the "fit" (cf. table 9.1) between my perceptions of the chronological development of rural political and religious organization against a model of internal Cahokian development posed by Timothy Pauketat (1991). Pauketat (1991: 302-330) has constructed an elegant scenario portraying the consolidation, sacralization, and dissolution of elite power at Cahokia. His work is the first major attempt by a scholar to comprehend the internal development of the polity in terms of combined social, political, and economic agendas based on extensive analysis of Cahokian archaeological data and, consequently, is of great utility in analyzing rural events.

From A.D. 925 to A.D. 1050, both the rural and Cahokian landscapes were dominated by the presence of Emergent Mississippian social groups characterized as kin-based, lineage-level societies. Recognized by archaeologists as participating in at least two separate traditions (Kelly 1990a), their settlements were typically organized in courtyard clusters of small single-post, basin houses. Such communities ranged from small, isolated farmsteads to large, plaza-organized villages, with village size increasing through the period as a whole (cf. Kelly 1990a: 130-136). American Bottom researchers increasingly accept that such communities were associated with a series of simple chiefdoms. Pauketat sees a similar trend at Cahokia, al-

Table 9.1 Summary of Cahokia and Rural Change in the American Bottom
(*Hall 1991; †Cahokia: Pauketat and Lopinot 1997; Rural: Milner 1986. Densities expressed in person/km^2)

Phase/Chronology[*]	Population[†]	Settlement	Organization/Symbols
Emergent Miss. A.D. 925–1050	Cahokia Pop.: 1,382–2,768 Cahokia Density: 768–1,538 km^2 Rural Density: unknown	Cahokia and rural areas: Plaza villages, hamlets, and some farmsteads	Cahokia and rural areas: Shared quadripartite world view, some elites, simple chiefdoms
Lohmann A.D. 1050–1100	Cahokia Pop.: 10,218–15,327 Cahokia Density: 5,676–8,515 km^2 Rural Density: unknown	Cahokia: Md. 72, mounds and plaza, crafts and population nucleation Rural: civic/cerem. and mortuary nodes and farmsteads-dispersed villages	Cahokia: Sacred landscape and elite differentiation, collaborative chiefdom Rural: Fertility ceremonies, agricultural intensification, central political control
Stirling A.D. 1100–1200	Cahokia Pop.: 5,166–7,204 Cahokia Density: 2,870–4,002 km^2 Rural Density: 124 km^2	Cahokia: Pop. nucleation, crafts, post-circles, rotundas, monumental construct. Rural: Civic, ceremonial, mortuary and Busk nodes with farmsteads Dispersed villages	Cahokia: Sacred Chiefdom, intensification of previous trends, Ramey Incised Rural: Sweat lodges, fertility cult, Ramey Incised, figurines, priestly and political offices, intensified agriculture
Moorehead A.D. 1200–1275	Cahokia Pop.: 2,999–4,498 Cahokia Density: 1,666–2,499 km^2 Rural Density: 47 km^2	Cahokia: Declining continuity of material culture and monuments Rural: Communal nodes and farmsteads Dispersed villages?	Cahokia: Decline Rural: Disappearance of central organization with only communal nodes present, some fertility symbolism
Sand Prairie A.D. 1275–1350	Cahokia Pop.: Unknown Rural Density: 18 km^2	Cahokia: Little evidence of activity, reduced residential area Rural: Mortuary nodes and farmsteads Independent dispersed villages?	Cahokia: Unknown Rural: Mortuary and sun symbolism Fertility cult absent

though he suggests some economic variation may have occurred, with Cahokian residents less involved in farming and hunting, perhaps beginning an ever-increasing dependence on external supplies or tribute. The rural and Cahokian evidence demonstrates that late Emergent Mississippian development was *specifically gradual* (i.e., no abrupt archaeologically visible cultural transformation occurred within this period).

The transition to the Lohmann phase, however, is dramatically visible in the rural countryside. For unknown reasons, near the end of the Emergent Mississippian period a select few of the clustered villages underwent an abrupt consolidation of power and population to become major mound centers (e.g., Cahokia and Pulcher), while most others disappeared. Those were replaced by a complex system of small, dispersed farmsteads, nodal households, and small nodal community civic/ceremonial nodes. The depopulation of the countryside and its re-creation in a new Lohmann phase vision was a major marker for the historical appearance of a Cahokian centralized elite power base.

The Lohmann shift at Cahokia was also marked, but less so than in the rural areas. This is probably related to the nature of the archaeological data base, which is more extensive and continuous for central Cahokia than for isolated rural sites. However, Kelly (1997) notes that the large-scale construction, such as the Grand and West plazas, and possibly the East Plaza, suggests that transition may have been more abrupt than previously believed. Pauketat interprets the early Lohmann evidence as suggesting continuity with the Emergent Mississippian lifestyle, but the phase itself represented "a qualitative political-economic shift and restructuring of social organization . . . [which] is inferred to be the political consolidation of a complex chiefdom" (1991: 307).

That transformation was marked by the breakup of previous household courtyard patterns, a shift in architectural construction, a dramatic increase in both local and exotic item densities within Cahokia, large-scale expansion/creation of a "sacred landscape" through public construction activities, and a significant population increase (table 9.1). There is also the first blatant evidence for the existence of an elite with absolute control over (i.e., the emergence of hegemonic *power over* [see earlier discussions of social control]) multiple material and human resources. This is most dramatically reflected in the multiple burials and associated human sacrifices and material offerings recovered from Mound 72 (Fowler 1991). Such large-scale and spectacular ceremonial burial events provide the first conclusive evidence for the formation and existence of an elite that truly became a "different people"—people whose superior position was supported by both mythology and ideology. Perhaps, as suggested by Wright (1984) and Sahlins (1963,

Cahokia and the Archaeology of Power

1977, 1981), that elite elevation occurred through a complex process of political, marriage, and conflict patterns that encouraged elite dispersion. Such elite dispersion may be reflected in the appearance for the first time of rural elite settlements in the Lohmann phase.

The archaeological evidence, in general, from this phase signals the "physical and social transformation of Cahokia" and has direct implications for center-rural relationships (Pauketat 1991: 310-311). Calculations by Pauketat and Lopinot (1997) suggest that population densities, as reflected in excavated areas of Cahokia, may have undergone a fivefold to tenfold increase from the Emergent Mississippian period through the Lohmann period, and that increase could have been accomplished only by rural populations relocating into the central core area. Clearly some persuasive or coercive force served as the vehicle to encourage this movement of formerly scattered groups to Cahokia.

What were the implications of such a relocation of population for the countryside? There was not only a shift in population, but a dramatic restructuring of social and political interaction afterward: "The centralization of the population from the surrounding floodplain (and uplands) . . . enable[d] the Cahokia elites to reshape the social landscape of the rural countryside . . . the centralization of people also would have amounted to the centralization (or the articulation) of the social networks of these former peripheral subgroups (now relocated at Cahokia), giving the high-ranking Cahokia subgroups full and direct access to low-ranking networks along with indirect access to the rural farmer as he or she socially was linked into these networks" (Pauketat 1991: 310).

The Emergent Mississippian to Lohmann transition in the rural areas was an interesting one. Just when it appeared that there was a steadily increasing consolidation of multiple Emergent Mississippian villages with their plaza complexes, the transition was in many places apparently "short-circuited"— this "short-circuiting" was undoubtedly caused by the pre-emption of local power created by the emergence of nearby simple chiefdoms. As we now understand the archaeological record, *a population consolidation at centers occurred during the Lohmann phase in conjunction with a subsequent elite-organized dispersion of rural populations.* Both the nucleation of population and the concurrent reorganization and dispersal of immediate rural populations were in the hands of the Cahokian elite. This patterned rural dispersal can be related to an increasing elite need for efficient and intensified use of the floodplain topography (as discussed earlier) for agricultural production in response to demands by a centralized political elite (a la Drennan 1988; Smith 1978a; Pauketat 1991: 320-321). It is critical, however, to recognize that the dispersion did not bring into play a direct articulation system of settlement (as might be suggested by the "household autonomy" concept of Mehrer 1988; Mehrer and Collins 1995; Pauketat 1991: 320), but rather a sequential articulation mode (see chapter 4) as one might reasonably expect in a complex hierarchical society. The Cahokian elite did not leave the organization of their rural food producers to chance but created a specific, centrally controlled political and religious organization to ensure that foodstuffs were produced and transmitted to Cahokia in an orderly manner.

It is the rural organizational "networks" and their material manifestations in architecture and artifacts that I have sought to identify throughout this work and that, to a large degree, I have identified with the phenomenon of dispersed villages. The Lohmann phase countryside was dominated by single food-producing households, in stark contrast to preceding times; yet not all was rural anomie or chaos as one might suggest. There is convincing evidence for the internal organization (or to use Pauketat's term, networks) of the countryside through a series of community religious and civic centers such as were present at the Lohmann component at the Range site. This Lohmann rural civic/ceremonial node, marking the first appearance of specialized, rural religious and political facilities (an architecture of power), suggests that the combined power of Green Corn ceremonialism and community political activities played a central role in rural networks and that the local Cahokian-derived, kin-based leadership controlled both spheres of power. One can see this development as derived from the Emergent Mississippian patterns of leadership, as evidenced in late period villages that showed combined religious and political attributes. Rural leadership patterns may have continued unabated into the Lohmann phase, although the actual ruled population dispersed across the landscape. The creation of specialized architectural and artifactual symbols of power, however, indicates that the ultimate power base resided elsewhere and descended from above rather than growing out of local kin ties. Also, the existence of specialized rural mortuary facilities for local leaders and their families, such as at the BBB Motor site, supports the belief that there was continued social distance between the local low-ranking ruling elites and the resident commoners.

The centralization of ritual and the sacralization of power were other attributes of evolving control in chiefly societies, and Pauketat (1991) first recognized these attributes at Cahokia with the onset of the Stirling phase (although they were clearly incipient in the earlier Lohmann phase). He argues that the Lohmann phase political consolidation may have been based on a series of "collaborative chiefships" minus the absence of any evidence (primarily iconographic) for a paramount chief or ruling class. Such evidence (Pauketat 1991: 323-324) appears, however, in the early Stirling phase in the form of Ramey iconography and the construction of monumental

symbols of elite authority, such as the woodhenges and mound constructions and reconstructions (instruments for the exercise of elite power a la
Foucault). Pauketat (also Smith 1992) notes the correlation of the appearance of the ritual woodhenges (as cosmic ritual devices?) with that of Ramey
iconography and its cosmic symbolism. These ritualistic devices bespeak an
elite concern with aspects of fertility symbolism that resulted in their incorporation into elite cosmography and ritualism (i.e., Emerson 1989; Pauketat
and Emerson 1991).

The development and transformation of fertility symbolism and ritual is
worth examining here in some detail because it provides clear insights into
the transformation of rural and Cahokian relationships. I have discussed the
importance of oppositions and the quadripartite and dualistic structuring of
the world in the belief systems of eastern North American native populations and the role this played in the pre-Mississippian and Mississippian world
view. Late Emergent Mississippian and Lohmann symbolism and ritual suggest the presence of local community-based ritualism involving this world
structure in conjunction with an all-encompassing concept of fertility and
life renewal symbolism, especially in the context of agricultural fertility.
Elite symbolism at this time is ambiguous, although the high-status burials
in Mound 72 indicate a concern for control of exotic materials and for
chunkee ritualism with some emphasis on warfare-related items. Artifactual
fertility symbolism appears absent, but John Kelly (personal communication
1996) has made the intriguing observation that the mass sacrifice of young
females of child-bearing age in Mound 72 may have been seen as a metaphor for fertility.

Pauketat's contention that the Stirling phase was characterized by the
sacralization of the elite and the presence of a divine chief seems to be borne
out by the iconographic, settlement, and political evidence. The appearance
of Ramey Incised ceramics as an elite-produced ware coincided with this
event. Pauketat and I (1991) have argued that Ramey iconography was a
symbiosis of Under World and Upper World symbols and was, in fact, a
symbolic portrayal of the cosmos and of elite-commoner relationships. It
was a visible reminder of the elite control of the cosmos, distributed through
the most essential of commoner rites—those dealing with agricultural fertility. The elite control of "rites of intensification" was an essential part of
elite consolidation of power during the Stirling phase, especially during the
early Stirling.

Elite control, as manifested in the Stirling phase rural communities, supports the model of centralized divine/political consolidation. This phase
marked the appearance of numerous specialized rural religious, mortuary,
and civic architectural facilities and reflects a dramatic increase in hierarchi-

cal elaboration through the development of a system of specialized religious and civic officials. Not only did distinctive architectures and artifacts of power come into the countryside, but they were accompanied by a transformation of rural sites into sacred landscapes using the same structural principles as those at the mound centers (Foucault 1986). At present, the only type of Lohmann phase centralizing forces recognized in the rural areas consists of community political and fertility ritual sites indicating a joint role for rural leadership. The Stirling phase saw the development of political civic nodes, mortuary-temple ceremonial sites, and temple-fertility ceremonial centers. Each of these nodes reveals the presence of distinctive attributes suggesting functional variation and specialization. I have argued that these sites and other information also indicate the presence of specialized Middle Mississippian functionaries, including at a minimum an organized priesthood, mortuary specialists, and political leaders.

The Stirling phase represents the total expropriation of power, both civic and religious, from the commoners. The sacralization of the landscape, elaboration of "powerful" architecture, and sheer magnitude of sacred and symbolic exotica reached a peak at this time. Rural political control was dominated by dispersed nodal civic centers. The temple-mortuary ceremonial centers demonstrated a tremendous elaboration and consolidation of rural wealth and an ever-increasing social distance between low-ranking elites and commoners. The late Stirling temple-fertility ceremonial complex holds no evidence of widespread community activities, but does seem to indicate an elaborate ceremonial ritualism that may have, by then, been confined to the local elite population. The ultimate symbols of elite control may be represented by the presence of the exotic and beautifully crafted Earth Mother figurines at rural fertility temples—surely such items must have come into the local community via elite largess.

A primary reason the elite were successful in the use of the Ramey iconography and the accompanying ideology was because they expropriated and manipulated the symbols of the folk cosmology. Basic fertility symbolism most often is an intrinsic part of the folkways of agriculturalists. The formal incorporation of this cosmology into an elite-mediated symbolic system was part of the transfer and centralization of power that characterized the Stirling elites. Elite control of that cosmology and iconography was demonstrated by the limited production and distribution of Ramey Incised and red goddesses through rural nodal centers with their specialized architectural power. The breaking down of that control, as shown in the end of Ramey symbolism and the disappearance of the specialized Stirling nodal centers, may have marked the return of some symbolic *power to* the rural dispersed villages, or at least the increasing failure of the elite to be discerned as cosmological mediators.

Yet, as the fetters apparently grew tighter about the members of the Cahokian polity, recent researchers have also documented the signs of disintegration. To a great extent, disintegration is inherent in chiefly politics (cf. Anderson 1994), with the persistent clash of elite subgroups vying for power. It is suggested that internal elite factional disputes may have been a possible cause for some Stirling phase movement of groups out of the American Bottom area into the northern periphery (Emerson 1991a, 1991b). Collins (1990) produced additional evidence of internal subgroup reorientations in Cahokia, and Pauketat (1991: 324–326) observed decreasing access to exotic goods by some subgroups. This indicates that, while sacralization of the central elite may have increased ritual authority and power, it actually may have seen some diminution of centralized political *power over* (cf. Pauketat 1991: 326). However, the increased complexity of the organizational structure of the rural areas did not suggest that this relaxation of central *power over* had any real effect on the commoners who were tightly controlled by the rural elite subgroups.

Another factor that may have played a role in the disintegration of the center was the inherent stability of the rural population organization. Once established, those dispersed communities provided a stable, kin-based rural organization that was not easily influenced by political developments in the center. This would indicate that there may have been a definite time lag between events in the center and their reflection in the rural landscape. I think the creation of an organized stable rural population may ultimately have been a major factor in the decentralization process. Such external, semi-independent, low-ranking elite political structures could have been destabilizing, even threatening to central elite control. They are clear examples of the hegemonic exercise of *power to*. In a similar Natchez analogue, the Great Sun lived in the central ceremonial complex with "control" over a number of villages (that were very similar, if not identical, to our dispersed villages). The Great Sun's authority was constantly being thwarted (e.g., Swanton 1911: 208 ff.) by low-ranking elite suns to the extent that the Grigra, White Apple, and Jenzenaque villages were hostile to his French allies and became allies with the English. Even tribute was denied at times. There was a continuing dialectic between the centers and their rural countryside and a marked continuity in the rural areas *despite* the breakdown of the centers.

As a political process, the decline of Cahokia was neither unique nor unusual within the diachronic context of eastern North American or, in fact, worldwide hierarchically organized societies. Pauketat (1991: 326–327) provides a scenario of decline that emphasizes the alienation of the paramount elite from the practical matters of political reality, with increasing factionalization of other high elite groups leading down a slow path to polity morbidity. Evidence he has gathered from Cahokia indicated decreases in the Moorehead phase populations, integration, structure diversity, and exotics, although conversely, one can trace continuance of the elite "symbols" through most of this phase. The final Cahokian decline, when it came during the early Sand Prairie phase, was total.

The countryside mirrors this pattern of decline, but as always, the transitions are sharper there since our observational windows are smaller and more limited. The break with the complex, rural Stirling phase bureaucratic structure was total and complete—in an archaeological instance all the specialized facilities and elites disappeared. The rural Moorehead pattern suggests a return to a simpler way—that of community leadership that lacked obvious political or religious specialists. Specialized architecture from that time period was confined to the presence of what seems most appropriately termed a "community men's house" at Julien, with a possible community storage building. There was an interesting shift, however, in domestic lifestyles with the appearance of larger structures and, at least in my subjective evaluation, increasing access to, and quantities of, both local and foreign exotics (also Milner with Williams 1984; Trubitt 1996).

For most researchers, the Sand Prairie phase within the American Bottom represents the aftermath of Cahokian decline. Within the rural areas, archaeological evidence is limited to the isolated households and associated complex community cemeteries. Again there is some perception that domestic access to raw materials was comparable to that of the previous phase and much increased over rural Stirling domestic access. There is a real indication that mortuary ceremonialism had become the central organizing premise in the Sand Prairie "community," while evidence of even communal forms of political organization was missing.

CAHOKIA AND THE COSMOS

Previous research has amply demonstrated the presence of a recognizable pre-Middle Mississippian world-quarters and fertility symbolism during the Emergent Mississippian period (Kelly 1990a, 1990b). Kelly (1990b: 92 ff.) argues that the presence of elite or temple structures, circle-and-cross symbolism, Upper and Under World conceptions, and renewal ceremonies can be identified in the archaeological record as early as the Dohack phase (A.D. 750-850), and these continued unabated up to the Mississippian emergence. This symbolic system emerged as a significant force in Cahokia during the Lohmann phase. Initial analysis of the BBB Motor stone figurines (Emerson

Cahokia and the Archaeology of Power

1982, 1984, 1989; Prentice 1986a) provided extensive iconographic evidence for the appearance of a Cahokian Earth Mother cult. This has been supported by the additional evidence supplied by the Sponemann site figurines (Jackson et al. 1991). I have suggested that a number of these figurines, such as the Keller, Sponemann, and Willoughby depictions, are also symbolic of aspects of the Earth Mother.

The symbolism of these figurines is supported by the interpretation of the extensive Ramey iconography that also speaks of Under World and Upper World symbolism. These lines of evidence are also encouraged by the broader cultural symbolism of earthen mounds, the quadripartite world, and plaza organization.

Furthermore, it has been observed that this fertility symbolism complex was most assuredly part of the cultural milieu of the elite and the commoners (i.e., a society-wide, shared cult, as evidenced by its presence in Emergent Mississippian village context); but with the onset of the Stirling phase, this cult was appropriated and manipulated by the elite as a tool to dominate the commoners. That expropriation of the fertility cult by the Cahokian elite during the Lohmann-Stirling transition was a major ideological tool in creating and sanctifying elite sacredness and consolidating elite *power over* through mediation of such symbols as Ramey Incised. The manipulation of fertility cosmology through a system of "rites of intensification" and associated symbols of authority served to naturalize the inherent social inequality that was a major hallmark of Stirling life.

How close was that fertility cult to that which is historically referred to as the Green Corn ceremonialism? The archaeological evidence indicates it was very close and was well within the range of variation reported historically (cf. Witthoft 1949). Howard (1968: 80-88) and Witthoft (1949) specifically investigated ritual, ceremonial, and symbolic connotations of the Green Corn rituals. Those Green Corn ceremonialism attributes that may be reflected in the archaeological record include the use of square grounds or courtyards, often renewed and purified, around which shelters were built; comprehensive renewal activities such as cleaning houses, breaking and discarding artifacts, and new fire ceremonies; burning animal and plant offerings; manufacturing ceremonial vessels; holding "going to water" ceremonies; invoking Earth/Corn Mother mythology; fasting and feasting; and employing color symbolism.

In the previously detailed analysis of sites included within this study I demonstrated in many instances the occurrence of the above traits (also see Fortier 1991c: 340-348 who discusses in detail such attributes at the Sponemann site). These included archaeological evidence for sacred fires; world-renewal features with ceremonially killed artifacts and plants; extensive use of red cedar for purification; presence of hallucinogenic and emetic drugs such as tobacco and jimsonweed; red color symbolism; plaza/court-yard organization and the four-sided world; manufacture of ceremonial Ramey pottery; Corn Mother mythology; and directional symbolism. This evidence indicates a strong pattern of cosmological and iconographic conti-nuity from at least A.D. 1000 (and probably earlier), within both Middle Mississippian culture and the Eastern Woodlands as a whole.

INTERPRETING HEGEMONY IN THE CAHOKIAN PAST

The past was not inherently different from the present. It was not a world filled with mechanistic societies that responded only to the external forces of nature or in which members functioned as cogs in a machine. It was an actor-filled world in which individuals responded, within the context of the complex interactions of their natural and cultural world, to their fellow actors and their society. It was a world in which individuals were motivated by ideas, thoughts, values, and beliefs within a cultural context. That world was accessible because it was structured. In this work I have provided docu-mentation of that structured archaeological past—a past in which the po-tentialities of the material world are seen "as constituting a symbolic, active communicative field" (Shanks and Tilley 1987: 95). I argue that an approach in which we recognize the material world as a form of discourse that, con-sequently, *must* be structured in order to fulfill its role is useful in under-standing the past. As observed earlier, this insight is not restricted to a structuralist approach but one that is universal in all approaches to studying the past. Structure provides the framework in which culture and society operate.

The Cahokian Mississippian world was one of structure and constraints; a stratified society inhabited by diverse factions of varying status; a society of inequality and domination; a society faced with both external and internal stresses; a society driven to transformation. It was a society that provides the researcher with the opportunity to examine structural stress, the develop-ment of hegemonic forces, the appropriation of power, and the role of ide-ology in reproduction and transformation within a diachronic setting.

The Cahokian cosmos is here depicted as a four-sided place of oppositions present in their world in the material images they created. That quadripartite world was reflected in their greatest icon, the platform mound; in the great mound and plaza designs; in the organization of their smallest ritual centers; in the central post and pits complex; in the cosmic wood circles; and even in the ceramic designs displayed on their ritual pottery. It was a cosmology that also revolved about sets of dualisms—of oppositions. Their world revolved about the Upper and Under Worlds as reflected, for example, in their stone fertility figurines and the elaborate cosmological iconography of their art.

This constructed sacred world served as a medium for both the dispersal and imposition of social power. It was at one and the same time architectural, hierarchical, and functional (Foucault 1979; Tilley 1991: 311)—the operationalization of power. It represented the timeless sacred world as opposed to the transient world of the people; and the inhabitants of this world, by right, were set apart as superior. It represented a Mississippian heterotopia in which the incompatible world of the sacred was brought to this world, where those from this world could, on certain occasions, penetrate through ritual the sacred world beyond (cf. Foucault 1986). But more than anything, it represented the ongoing, overwhelming operation of *power over* by society's leaders.

Yet, as I have discussed, that cosmology and its structural implications existed in the pre-Mississippian world—it was not a product of the Mississippian culture or society. The remarkable aspect of this situation was the context in which the Cahokian elite manipulated this world view to re-create the cosmos to support their hegemonic position.

The late Emergent Mississippian and early Mississippian worlds appear to have been ones of inequality, ones in which certain strata of society had inherent rights and access to privileges and material goods denied most members of the group. The inhabitants also appear to have recognized the same cosmological structure that pervaded earlier and later times. Yet there is no evidence that a great dichotomy existed within these groups. The "elite" structures identified by Kelly (1990a, 1990b) in Emergent Mississippian villages were larger, strategically located in ritual space, and may have been associated with some specialized facilities; however, elites were not yet set apart from the majority of the population through the use of *"luxuries as weapons of exclusion,"* or spatial positioning, or isolation in a *"sacred landscape."* Society had not yet crossed the threshold that served forever to differentiate its members. As many others have argued, I believe the key to that door lies in ideology.

Late Emergent Mississippian power was expressed as a dichotomy of earthly and political forces within a community setting. There appears to be no evidence from sites such as Range, where there are large population clusters from this period, that political or ritual power was manifested apart from the community. What little ritualistic "construction" that we did recover appeared in the context of the community as a whole. While pre-Mississippian symbolic systems are neither abundant nor decisive, it appears that a vision of a quadripartite world with sun-fertility symbolism can be supported (Kelly 1990a, 1990b). Given the virtually universal association of world renewal and fertility beliefs with the communities as a whole and with commoners especially (i.e., Wallace 1966; Turner 1969), it is safe to assume that a similar correlation held true in the American Bottom. Such an ideology was critical in the reproduction of society.

With the transition to the Lohmann phase, that pattern was transformed with the first(?) construction of platform mounds (and plaza complexes?). Such a transformation of the landscape is a classic example of elite manipulation of ideology to create a community-centered, community-constructed "sacred landscape" (cf. Earle 1987, 1991; Foucault 1979, 1986) that forever confirmed the aloofness of the elites and their special relationship with the cosmos. Those constructed landscapes were the cosmos brought to earth by the elite.

In the rural areas that ideology was reflected in the appearance of specialized nodal centers—miniature heterotopian replications of the greater cosmos within their social sphere. The increasingly hierarchical organization of the society, leading to spatial and social division of individuals, reinforced the internal systemic stress already present. It is clear that early elite *sacra,* as manifested in the Lohmann phase Mound 72, was focused on both local and exotic prestige goods, suggesting that interregional elite trade and access was an important avenue of prestige (cf. Peregrine 1992). At Cahokia, however, the presence of a prestige economy was linked to the process of increasing the differentiation of the elite from the masses rather than as a tool for creating such differentiation per se (contra Peregrine 1992). There is evidence now apparent in the archaeological record for the origins of the process by which the elite co-opt the structure of the cosmos. That event was signaled by the first large-scale construction of "cosmic" landscapes (i.e., a cosmic geography portrayed on earth). An intrinsic part of that action was the increasing association of the elite with the cosmic landscape and an increasing disassociation of commoners from such sacred areas.

The transformation of societal relations became complete with the onset of the Stirling phase. In the tradition of the Lohmann phase, elite separateness continued to be affirmed, both in life and spiritually. Elite domination of all ceremonial aspects of Cahokian society was complete with the imposition of elite-controlled rural temple-mortuary, civic-ceremonial, and temple-ceremonial centers. As I said earlier, the figurines and Ramey Incised iconography are the keys to understanding this transition. The Ramey symbols not only represented cosmic unity, but also reflected elite control of the cosmos. What more fitting emphasis of this control than to distribute such symbols of their superiority within the context of elite-orchestrated "world renewal" and fertility "rites of intensification"? The usurping of both the cosmic landscape and the fertility-world renewal ritualism totally alienated the commoners from the cosmos. Only through the brokerage of the elite could they have access to spiritual or earthly sustenance. The elite hegemony was complete.

Yet, as all things pass, so too did the elite of Cahokia. Within a century of their rise to dominance they had fallen, and the cosmos was no longer theirs. The collapse of elite dominance of the cosmos is aptly reflected in the demise of their iconography as well as in the associated political trappings. Why and how that fall came is unknown, but when it came it was so complete that never again were there lords in Cahokia.

REPRISE

In the previous sections of this work I have examined in detail aspects of the hierarchically organized Middle Mississippian society at Cahokia during the eleventh to fourteenth centuries after the birth of Christ. The purpose of this investigation was, by examining a specific prehistoric society, to understand better the relationship of hegemonic forces in the rise of early complex societies. In chapter 2, I provided the theoretical basis through which material remains could be used to reveal insights into the existence of hegemonic forces in the past. Subsequently, I established a number of research goals that involved the study of architecture, settlement, and symbolism to understand elite hegemony. Here I will briefly revisit these research approaches and describe their value in revealing information about the past.

Following up on Lightfoot's identification of an "architecture of power," I was able to demonstrate that rural Cahokian settlements possessed specific architectural correlates to both political and ideological power. Those reflecting political power included civic-ceremonial nodes marked by storage units, ritual sweat lodges, community men's houses, and council houses. The importance of ideology was seen in the presence of priest-mortuary and temple-mortuary complexes containing burials, temples, and priest houses, and in community nodal cemeteries. Furthermore, I have shown that the degree of Cahokian elite power in the rural areas was demonstrated in the Late Emergent Mississippian depopulation of the countryside and its repopulation by centrally controlled Lohmann phase Mississippians and in the variations within this rural architecture of power. These changes of power can be synchronized with shifts of power at Cahokia.

I also examined the distribution of "artifacts of power" through the patterns of diachronic and synchronic variation at rural sites of "power" to gauge their relationship with patterns of variations in the architecture of power. It soon became apparent that rural centers of power differed little in access to those items that were pervasive through the Cahokia sphere. Those items included hematite, galena, shell objects, crystals, limonite, mica, and copper that, to a lesser or greater degree, were present in many households. Other artifacts such as earspools, shell and galena beads, pendants, Ramey knives, projectile point caches, or discoidals were less frequently encountered in all contexts, and their significance was not clear. It was apparent that the ubiquity of such items was higher in rural nodal sites than in rural farmsteads. We also can recognize that there were a few unique materials that *were* symbolic signifiers. They included flint clay figurines, engraved sherds, certain ceramic vessels such as Ramey Incised pots, and ethnobotanical materials from red cedar, jimsonweed, and tobacco plants.

This study has re-emphasized what every archaeologist knows—one cannot interpret artifacts without a comprehensive understanding of their associations and context. *The association and concentration of the above artifact types within an architecture of power give the assemblage meaning.* These artifacts become symbolically significant within a context that included ceremonial killing of vessels, "world renewal" pits, marker posts, courtyards, council houses, and sweat lodges. In order to comprehend the significance of artifacts that may have functioned as artifacts of power, it was necessary to segregate those elements of ideological power from those concerned with coercive, political power. For example, in the instance of ideological power, artifactual symbols played a much stronger part in defined power. It is in ideology that one observes the presence of hallucinogens, purifying red cedar, stone goddesses, sacred vessels, houses of the dead, and other such cosmic items. In the Middle Mississippian realm, political power was less obviously reified in the rural areas, although there is some impression that political nodes were marked by above-average concentrations of exotic materials. The key to recognizing political power rests firmly within the area of architectural features such as courtyards, sweat houses, marker posts, storage features, and accessory domiciles. In the case of both ideological and political power, the overall structure of the site, its architecture, and associated artifacts provide the interpretation of hegemonic force.

There was more to the architectural and ideological patterns in rural Cahokia than variation in buildings and artifacts. Those have been shown to be manifestations of an underlying structure in Middle Mississippian society. That structure represented the social reification of the cosmic landscape (i.e., the four-cornered universe). It pervaded the material world and, based on the ethnohistoric record, was equally prevalent in the social and ideological spheres. We saw its first representation in the small courtyards and four central pits and post in the Emergent Mississippian villages from whence it was expropriated to form the cosmic landscape in the temple mound and plaza complex of the large elite centers. In periods of Cahokian domination the sacred courtyard with its associations was exported to the new rural nodal centers as a sign of power. The elite expropriation of the universe was also reflected in the symbolism of the Ramey Incised vessels, the cult of the red goddesses and the fertility rites of the commoners.

Importantly, this research has shown that it is possible to recognize, via the material record, the structure of a prehistoric society and to examine the manipulation of that inherent structure by elites to facilitate and naturalize their use of power. I have also shown that such policies have a "life expectancy" that is visible in the past. Elite confiscation of the universe appeared to have been short-lived, and when it collapsed, it created a dramatic shift in the very structure of Middle Mississippian society that resulted in a diminishing of both the depiction of cosmic landscapes and the fertility cults of the powerful.

A final word is appropriate on the ongoing dialogue between scholars on the role of political control versus ideology in the formation of elite power bases. Both political and ideological power were present and active in the hands of the Cahokian elite during the imposition of control over the local Middle Mississippian societies. I have been able, in the archaeological record, to identify and correlate synchronic relationships and diachronic shifts in the material manifestations of both ideological and coercive power. It is clear that a significant focus of this power was on the intensification of the rural production and mobilization of agricultural staples to support the nucleated centers. There is little clear evidence, however, for the precedence of one factor over the other in the formation of the Cahokian polity. There is circumstantial evidence in the late Emergent Mississippian period and early Lohmann phase to suggest that the conceptualization and control of ideological power was developing at a faster pace than strategies to effectively manage and maintain elite political control. However, it is difficult to envision that the lords of Cahokia rose to the heights without total hegemonic control over the masses.

References Cited

Abercrombie, N., S. Hill, and B. Turner
    1980   *The Dominant Ideology Thesis.* George Allen and Unwin, London.

Adair, J.
    1930   *The History of the American Indians.* Ed. S. C. Williams. Watauga Press, Johnston City.

Althusser, L.
    1977   *For Marx.* New Left Books, London.

Anderson, D. G.
    1986   Stability and Change in Chiefdom-Level Societies: An Examination of Mississippian Political Evolution on the South Atlantic Slope. Paper presented at 43rd Annual Southeastern Archaeological Conference, Nashville.
    1990a   *Political Change in Chiefdom Societies: Cycling Changes in the Late Prehistoric Southeastern United States.* Ph.D. dissertation, University of Michigan, Ann Arbor. University Microfilms, Ann Arbor.
    1990b   Stability and Change in Chiefdom-Level Societies: An Examination of Mississippian Political Evolution on the South Atlantic Slope. In *Lamar Archaeology,* ed. M. Williams and G. Shapiro, pp. 187-213. University of Alabama Press, Tuscaloosa.
    1994   *The Savannah River Chiefdoms: Political Change in the Late Prehistoric Southeast.* University of Alabama Press, Tuscaloosa.

Anderson, J.
    1969   A Cahokia Palisade Sequence. In *Explorations into Cahokia Archaeology,* ed. M. Fowler, pp. 89-99. Illinois Archaeological Survey Bulletin No. 7, Urbana.

Bareis, C. J.
    1976   *The Knoebel Site, St. Clair County, Illinois.* Circular 1. Illinois Archaeological Survey, Urbana.
    1981   An Overview of the FAI-270 Project. In *Archaeology in the American Bottom,* ed. C. Bareis and J. Porter, pp. 1-9. Depart-

ment of Anthropology Research Report 6, University of
Illinois at Urbana-Champaign.

Bareis, C. J., and J. W. Porter
   1984   Research Design. In *American Bottom Archaeology*, ed. C. Bareis
          and J. Porter, pp. 1-14. University of Illinois Press, Urbana.

Bareis, C. J., and J. W. Porter (editors)
   1984   *American Bottom Archaeology.* University of Illinois Press, Urbana.

Barker, A. W., and T. R. Pauketat (editors)
   1992   *Lords of the Southeast: Social Inequality and the Native Elites in
          Southeastern North America.* Archaeological Papers, No. 3,
          American Anthropological Association, Washington, D.C.

Bartram, W.
   1958   *The Travels of William Bartram: Naturalist's Edition.* Ed. F. Harper.
          Yale University Press, New Haven.

Benchley, E.
   1974   *Mississippian Secondary Mound Loci: A Comparative Functional
          Analysis in a Time-Space Perspective.* Ph.D. dissertation, University
          of Wisconsin-Milwaukee. University Microfilms, Ann Arbor.

Benton, M.
   1981   "Objective" Interests and the Sociology of Power. *Sociology*
          15(2): 161-184.

Berres, T. E.
   1984   *A Formal Analysis of Ceramic Vessels from the Schlemmer Site (11-S-
          382): A Late Woodland/Mississippian Occupation in St. Clair
          County, Illinois.* Unpublished Master's thesis, Department of
          Anthropology, Western Michigan University, Kalamazoo.

Black, G. A.
   1967   *Angel Site: An Archaeological, Historical, and Ethnological Study.* 2
          vols. Indiana Historical Society, Indianapolis.

Blitz, J. H.
   1993   *Ancient Chiefdoms of the Tombigbee.* University of Alabama Press,
          Tuscaloosa.

Bloch, M.
   1989   From Cognition to Ideology. In *Ritual, History and Power:
          Selected Papers in Anthropology*, by M. Bloch, pp. 106-136.
          London School of Economics, Monographs on Social Anthro-
          pology 58.

Bourdieu, P.
  1977   *Outline of a Theory of Practice.* Cambridge University Press,
          Cambridge.

Bowers, A. W.
  1965   *Hidatsa Social and Ceremonial Organization.* Bulletin 94. Bureau
          of American Ethnology, Washington, D.C.

Brackenridge, H. M.
  1962 [1814]   *View of Louisiana Together with a Journal of a Voyage up the
          Missouri River, in 1811.* Quadrangle Books, Chicago.

Brandt, K. A.
  1972   American Bottom Settlement. Paper Presented at the 37th
          Annual Meeting of the Society for American Archaeology, Bal
          Harbour.

Brown, J. A.
  1965   *The Prairie Peninsula: An Interaction Area in the Eastern United
          States.* Unpublished Ph.D. dissertation, Department of Anthro-
          pology, University of Chicago, Chicago.
  1966   *Spiro Studies: The Graves and Their Contexts,* vol. 2. Second Part
          of the Second Annual Report of Caddoan Archaeology. Spiro
          Focus Research, Norman.
  1975   Spiro Art and Its Mortuary Context. In *Death and the Afterlife in
          Pre-Columbian America,* ed. E. Benson, pp. 1–32. Dumbarton
          Oaks Research Library and Collections, Washington, D.C.
  1976a The Southern Cult Reconsidered. *Midcontinental Journal of
          Archaeology* 1: 115–135.
  1976b *Spiro Studies: The Artifacts,* vol. 4. Second Part of the Third
          Annual Report of Caddoan Archaeology. Spiro Focus Research,
          Norman.
  1985   The Mississippian Period. In *Ancient Art of the American Woodland
          Indians,* ed. D. Penny, pp. 93–145. Harry N. Abrams, New York.
  1989   On Style Divisions of the Southeastern Ceremonial Complex:
          A Revisionist Perspective. In *The Southeastern Ceremonial
          Complex,* ed. P. Galloway, pp. 183–204. University of Nebraska
          Press, Lincoln.

Brown, J. A., and J. E. Kelly
  1996   Cahokia and the Southeastern Ceremonial Complex. Revised
          draft of paper presented at the 50th Southeastern Archaeological
          Conference, Raleigh, North Carolina. Ms. in possession of
          authors.

Brown, J. A., R. A. Kerber, and H. D. Winters
  1990   Trade and the Evolution of Exchange Relations at the Beginning of the Mississippian Period. In *The Mississippian Emergence,* ed. B. Smith, pp. 251-280. Smithsonian Institution Press, Washington, D.C.

Burnett, E. K.
  1945   *The Spiro Mound Collection in the Museum.* Heye Foundation Contributions of the Museum of the American Indian. New York.

Butler, B.
  1977   *Mississippian Settlement in the Black Bottom, Pope and Massac Counties, Illinois.* Ph.D. dissertation, Southern Illinois University at Carbondale. University Microfilms, Ann Arbor.

Caldwell, J. R.
  1961   Untitled paper presented at the Annual Meeting for the Central States Anthropological Society, Bloomington.

Campbell, T.
  1981   *Seven Theories of Human Society.* Clarendon Press, Oxford.

Carneiro, R. L.
  1981   The Chiefdom: Precursor of the State. In *The Transition to Statehood in the New World,* ed. G. Jones and R. Krautz, pp. 39-79. Cambridge University Press, Cambridge.

Chang, K.
  1958   Study of Neolithic Social Grouping: Examples from the New World. *American Anthropologist* 60(3): 298-334.
  1967   Major Aspects of the Interrelationships of Archaeology and Ethnology. *Current Anthropology* 8(3): 227-243.

Chang, K. (editor)
  1968   *Settlement Archaeology.* National Press Books, Palo Alto.

Chase, A. F., and D. Z. Chase
  1992   Meso American Elites: Assumptions, Definitions, and Models. In *Mesoamerican Elites: An Archaeological Assessment,* ed. D. Chase and A. Chase, pp. 3-18. University of Oklahoma Press, Norman.

Chase, D. Z., and A. F. Chase (editors)
  1992   *Mesoamerican Elites: An Archaeological Assessment.* University of Oklahoma Press, Norman.

Chisholm, M.

  1962 *Rural Settlement and Land Use.* Hutchinson, London.

Chmurny, W.

  1973 *The Ecology of the Middle Mississippian Occupation of the American Bottom.* Ph.D. dissertation, University of Illinois, Urbana. University Microfilms, Ann Arbor.

Coe, M., and K. Flannery

  1964 Microenvironments and Mesoamerican Prehistory. *Science* 143: 650-654.

Cole, F., R. Bell, J. Bennett, J. Caldwell, N. Emerson, R. MacNeish, K. Orr, and R. Willis

  1951 *Kincaid: A Prehistoric Illinois Metropolis.* University of Chicago Press, Chicago.

Cole, F., and T. Deuel

  1937 *Rediscovering Illinois.* University of Chicago Press, Chicago.

Collins, J. M.

  1990 *The Archaeology of the Cahokia Mounds ICT-II: Site Structure.* Illinois Cultural Resources Study No. 10. Illinois Historic Preservation Agency, Springfield.

Collins, J. M., and M. L. Chalfant

  1993 A Second-Terrace Perspective on Monks Mound. *American Antiquity* 58(2): 319-332.

Conkey, M.

  1989 The Structural Analysis of Paleolithic Art. In *Archaeological Thought in America,* ed. C. Lamberg-Karlovsky, pp. 135-154. Cambridge University Press, New York.

Conrad, L. A.

  1989 The Southeastern Ceremonial Complex on the Northern Middle Mississippian Frontier: Late Prehistoric Politico-religious Systems in the Central Illinois River Valley. In *The Southeastern Ceremonial Complex: Artifacts and Analysis,* ed. P. Galloway, pp. 93-113. University of Nebraska Press, Lincoln.

  1991 The Middle Mississippian Cultures of the Central Illinois River Valley. In *Cahokia and the Hinterlands,* ed. T. Emerson and R. Lewis, pp. 119-156. University of Illinois Press, Urbana.

Conrad, L. A., and T. E. Emerson

  1974 1973 Excavations at the Orendorf Site (11F1284). *Illinois*

Association for the Advancement of Archaeology, Quarterly Newsletter 6(1): 1-2.

Cordy, R.
  1981 *A Study of Prehistoric Social Change: The Development of Complex Societies in the Hawaiian Islands.* Academic Press, New York.

Dalan, R.
  1992 *Landscape Modification at the Cahokia Mounds Site: Geophysical Evidence of Cultural Change.* Ph.D. dissertation, University of Minnesota, Minneapolis.
  1997 The Construction of Cahokia. In *Cahokia: Domination and Ideology in the Mississippian World,* ed. T. Pauketat and T. Emerson, pp. 89-102. University of Nebraska Press, Lincoln.

Dalton, G.
  1977 Aboriginal Economies in Stateless Societies, In *Exchange Systems in Prehistory,* ed. T. Earle and J. Ericson, pp. 191-212. Academic Press, New York.

De Montmollin, O.
  1989 *The Archaeology of Political Structure: Settlement Analysis in a Classic Maya Polity.* Cambridge University Press, New York.

Densmore, F.
  1928 Uses of Plants by the Chippewa Indians. *Bureau of American Ethnology, Annual Report* 44: 275-397. Washington, D.C.

DePratter, C. B.
  1983 *Late Prehistoric and Early Historic Chiefdoms in the Southeastern United States.* Ph.D. dissertation, University of Georgia. University Microfilms, Ann Arbor.

Dickens, C.
  1893 *American Notes.* MacMillan and Sons, London.

Dorsey, J. O.
  1894 A Study of Siouan Cults. *Bureau of American Ethnology, Annual Report* 11: 351-544. Washington, D.C.

Douglas, J.
  1976 *Collins: A Late Woodland Ceremonial Complex in the Woodfordian Northeast.* Ph.D. dissertation, University of Illinois. University Microfilms, Ann Arbor.

Douglas, M., and B. Isherwood
  1979   *The World of Goods: Towards a Theory of Consumption.* Allen Lane,
         New York.

Drennan, R. D.
  1988   Household Location and Compact Versus Dispersed Settlement
         in Prehispanic Mesoamerica. In *Household and Community in the
         Mesoamerican Past,* ed. R. Wilk and W. Ashmore, pp. 273-293.
         University of New Mexico Press, Albuquerque.

Drennan, R. D., and C. A. Uribe
  1987   Introduction. In *Chiefdoms in the Americas,* ed. R. Drennan and
         C. A. Uribe, pp. vii-xix. University Press of America, Lanham.

Drennan, R. D., and C. A. Uribe (editors)
  1987   *Chiefdoms in the Americas.* University Press of America, Lanham.

Dreyfus, H. L., and P. Rabinow
  1983   *Michel Foucault: Beyond Structuralism and Hermeneutics.* 2nd ed.
         University of Chicago Press, Chicago.

Dupre, G., and P. Rey
  1973   Reflections on the Pertinence of a Theory of the History of
         Exchange. *Economy and Society* 2(2): 131-163.

Durkheim, E.
  1933   *The Division of Labor in Society.* The Free Press, New York.

Earle, T. K.
  1987   Chiefdoms in Archaeological and Ethnohistorical Perspective.
         Annual Review of Anthropology 16: 279-308.
  1989   The Evolution of Chiefdoms. *Current Anthropology* 30: 84-88.
  1991   The Evolution of Chiefdoms. In *Chiefdoms: Power, Economy, and
         Ideology,* ed. T. Earle, pp. 1-15. Cambridge University Press,
         Cambridge.

Eckholm, K.
  1977   External Exchange and the Transformation of Central African
         Social Systems. In *The Evolution of Social Systems,* ed. J.
         Friedman and M. Rowlands. Duckworth, London.

Eister, A. W.
  1974   Religious Institutions in Complex Societies: Difficulties in the
         Theoretic Specification of Functions. In *The Social Meanings of
         Religions,* ed. W. Newman, pp. 71-79. Rand McNally, Chicago.

Eliade, M.

    1954   *The Myth of the Eternal Return or, Cosmos and History.* Princeton University Press, Princeton.

Emerson, T. E.

    1981   The BBB Motor Site. Ms. on file, FAI-270 Archaeological Project, Department of Anthropology, University of Illinois at Urbana-Champaign.

    1982   *Mississippian Stone Images in Illinois.* Circular No. 6. Illinois Archaeological Survey, Urbana.

    1983   The Bostrom Figure Pipe and the Cahokian Effigy Style in the American Bottom. *Midcontinental Journal of Archaeology* 8: 257-267.

    1984   The Stirling Phase Occupation. In *The BBB Motor Site,* by T. Emerson and D. Jackson, pp. 197-321. University of Illinois Press, Urbana.

    1989   Water, Serpents, and the Underworld: An Exploration into Cahokian Symbolism. In *The Southern Ceremonial Complex: Artifacts and Analysis; The Cottonlandia Conference,* ed. P. Galloway, pp. 45-92. University of Nebraska Press, Lincoln.

    1990   Representations of Shamans/Priests in Mississippian Stone Art. Paper presented at a symposium entitled "Symbolism of the Upper Mississippi Valley, A.D. 900-1500." Dickson Mounds Museum, Lewistown.

    1991a The Apple River Mississippian Culture of Northwestern Illinois. In *Cahokia and the Hinterlands,* ed. T. Emerson and R. Lewis, pp. 164-182. University of Illinois Press, Urbana.

    1991b Some Perspectives on Cahokia and the Northern Mississippian Expansion. In *Cahokia and the Hinterlands,* ed. T. Emerson and R. Lewis, pp. 221-236. University of Illinois Press, Urbana.

    1992   The Mississippian Dispersed Village as a Social and Environmental Strategy. In *Late Prehistoric Agriculture: Observations from the Midwest,* pp. 198-216. Studies in Illinois Archaeology 8, Illinois Historic Preservation Agency, Springfield.

    1995   *Settlement, Symbolism, and Hegemony in the Cahokian Countryside.* Ph.D. dissertation, University of Wisconsin-Madison. University Microfilms, Ann Arbor.

    1996   The Svehla Effigy Elbow Pipe and Spud: Mississippian Elite Sacra from the Sutter Collection. *Tennessee Anthropologist* 21(2):124-131.

1997a Reflections from the Countryside on Cahokian Hegemony. In *Cahokia: Ideology and Domination in the Mississippian World,* ed. T. Pauketat and T. Emerson, pp. 167–184. University of Nebraska Press, Lincoln.

1997b Cahokia Elite Ideology and the Mississippian Cosmos. In *Cahokia: Domination and Ideology in the Mississippian World,* ed. T. Pauketat and T. Emerson, pp. 190–228. University of Nebraska Press, Lincoln.

Emerson, T. E., and J. A. Brown

1992   The Late Prehistory and Protohistory of Illinois. In *Calumet and Fleur-de-Lys: Archaeology of Indian and French Contact in the Midcontinent,* ed. J. Walthall and T. Emerson, pp. 77–128. Smithsonian Institution Press, Washington, D.C.

Emerson, T. E., and D. K. Jackson

1984   *The BBB Motor Site.* University of Illinois Press, Urbana.

1987a The Edelhardt and Lindeman Phases: Setting the Stage for the Final Transition to Mississippian in the American Bottom. In *The Emergent Mississippian: Proceedings of the Sixth Mid-South Archaeological Conference,* June 6–9, 1985, ed. R. Marshall, pp. 172–193. Cobb Institute of Archaeology, Occasional Papers 87-01. Mississippi State University, Mississippi State.

1987b *The Marcus Site.* University of Illinois Press, Urbana.

Emerson, T. E., and R. B. Lewis (editors)

1991   *Cahokia and the Hinterlands: Middle Mississippian Cultures of the Midwest.* University of Illinois Press, Urbana.

Emerson, T. E., and G. Milner

1981   The Mississippian Occupation of the American Bottom: The Communities. Paper presented at 26th Annual Midwest Archaeological Conference, Madison.

1982   Community Organization and Settlement Patterns of Peripheral Mississippian Sites in the American Bottom, Illinois. Paper presented at 47th Annual Society for American Archaeology, Minneapolis.

1988   Internal Structure, Distribution, and Relationships Among Low-Level Mississippian Communities in Illinois. Paper presented at 53rd Annual Meeting of the Society for American Archaeology, Phoenix.

Emerson, T. E., G. Milner, and D. Jackson
   1983   *The Florence Street Site.* University of Illinois Press, Urbana.

Emerson, T. E., and W. I. Woods
   1990   The Slumping of the Great Knob: An Archaeological and
         Geotechnic Case Study of the Stability of a Great Earthen
         Mound. In *Adobe 90 Preprints of the 6th International Conference
         on the Conservation of Earthen Architecture,* ed. N. Agnew, M.
         Taylor, A. Balderrama, and H. Houben, pp. 219-224. Getty
         Conservation Institute, Los Angeles.

Esarey, D., and T. R. Pauketat
   1992   *The Lohmann Site: An Early Mississippian Center in the American
         Bottom.* University of Illinois Press, Urbana.

Esarey, M. E.
   1983   *Report of Archaeological Testing at the East St. Louis Stone Company
         (11-S-468) and the LaBras Lake (11-S-299) Sites in FAI-255
         Borrow Pit 32, St. Clair County, Illinois.* Midwest Archaeological
         Research Center, Illinois State University, Normal.

Fallers, L. A.
   1973   *Inequality: Social Stratification Reconsidered.* University of Chicago
         Press, Chicago.

Farnsworth, K. B., and T. E. Emerson
   1989   The Macoupin Creek Figure Pipe and Its Archaeological
         Context: Evidence for Late Woodland–Mississippian Interaction
         Beyond the Northern Border of Cahokian Settlement.
         Midcontinental Journal of Archaeology 14(1): 18-37.

Fecht, W. G.
   1960   Cahokia Mounds Serpent Pottery. *Central States Archaeological
         Journal* 7(1): 34-35.

Feinman, G., and J. Neitzel
   1984   Too Many Types: An Overview of Sedentary Prestate Societies
         in the Americas. In *Advances in Archaeological Method and Theory,*
         vol. 7, ed. M. Schiffer, pp. 39-102. Academic Press, New York.

Finney, F. A.
   1985   *The Carbon Dioxide Site.* University of Illinois Press, Urbana.
   1993   Spatially Isolated Structures in the Cahokia Locality: Short-
         Term Residences or Special-Purposes Shelters? In *Highways to
         the Past: Essays in Honor of Charles J. Bareis,* ed. T. Emerson, A.

Fortier, and D. McElrath, pp. 381-392. Illinois Archaeology, vol. 5 (1&2).

Ford, R. I.
1974   Northeastern Archaeology: Past and Future Directions. In *Annual Review of Anthropology,* ed. B. Siegal, pp. 385-413. Annual Reviews, Inc., Palo Alto.

Fortier, A. C.
1985   *The Robert Schneider Site.* University of Illinois Press, Urbana.
1991a   Features. In *The Sponemann Site 2* by D. Jackson, A. Fortier, and J. Williams, pp. 49-124. Department of Anthropology, University of Illinois at Urbana-Champaign, FAI-270 Archaeological Mitigation Project Report 83.
1991b   Stone Figurines. In *The Sponemann Site 2,* by D. Jackson, A. Fortier, and J. Williams, pp. 277-303. Department of Anthropology, University of Illinois at Urbana-Champaign, FAI-270 Archaeological Mitigation Project Report 83.
1991c   Interpretation. In *The Sponemann Site 2,* by D. Jackson, A. Fortier, and J. Williams, pp. 339-348. Department of Anthropology, University of Illinois at Urbana-Champaign, FAI-270 Archaeological Mitigation Project Report 83.

Fortier, A. C., T. O. Maher, and J. A. Williams
1991   *The Sponemann Site (11-Ms-517): The Emergent Mississippian Sponemann Phase Occupations.* Department of Anthropology, University of Illinois at Urbana-Champaign, FAI-270 Archaeological Mitigation Project, Report 82.

Foucault, M.
1978   *The History of Sexuality: An Introduction, vol. I.* Vintage Books, New York.
1979   *Discipline and Punish: The Birth of the Prison.* Vintage Books, New York.
1986   Of Other Spaces. *Diacritics* 16: 22-27.

Fowler, M. L.
1969   Middle Mississippian Agricultural Fields. *American Antiquity* 34: 365-375.
1972   The Cahokia Site: Summary and Conclusions. Paper Presented at the 37th Annual Meeting of the Society for American Archaeology, Bal Harbour.
1974   Cahokia: Ancient Capitol of the Midwest. *Addison-Wesley Module in Anthropology* 48: 3-38.

1978   Cahokia and the American Bottom: Settlement Archaeology. In *Mississippian Settlement Patterns,* ed. B. D. Smith, pp. 455-478. Academic Press, New York.

1989   *The Cahokia Atlas: A Historical Atlas of Cahokia Archaeology.* Studies in Illinois Archaeology, No. 6, Illinois Historic Preservation Agency, Springfield.

1991   Mound 72 and Early Mississippian at Cahokia. In *New Perspectives on Cahokia: Views from the Periphery,* ed. J. B. Stoltman, pp. 1-28. Prehistory Press, Madison.

Fowler, M. L., and R. L. Hall

1972   *Archaeological Phases at Cahokia.* Illinois State Museum Research Series, Papers in Anthropology, No. 1. Springfield.

1975   Archaeological Phases at Cahokia. In *Perspectives in Cahokia Archaeology,* ed. M. Fowler, pp. 1-14. Illinois Archaeological Survey Bulletin No. 10, Urbana.

Frankenstein, S., and M. Rowlands

1978   The Internal Structure and Regional Context of Early Iron Age Society in Southwestern Germany. *Bulletin of the Institute of Archaeology of London* 15: 73-112.

Freimuth, G. A.

1974   *The Lunsford-Pulcher Site: An Examination of Selected Traits and Their Social Implications in American Bottom Prehistory.* Master's thesis, Department of Anthropology, University of Illinois at Urbana-Champaign.

Friedman, J., and M. Rowlands

1977   Notes Towards an Epigenetic Model of the Evolution of "Civilization." In *The Evolution of Social Systems,* ed. J. Friedman and M. Rowlands, pp. 201-276. Duckworth, London.

Fried, M. H.

1967   *The Evolution of Political Society.* Random House, New York.

Fritz, G. J.

1994   Precolumbian *Cucurbita argyrosperma* ssp. *argyrosperma* (Cucurbitaceae) in the Eastern Woodlands of North America. *Economic Botany* 48(3): 280-292.

Fundaburk, E. L., and M. D. Foreman

1957   *Sun Circles and Human Hands: The Southeastern Indians, Art and Industries.* E. L. Fundaburk, Luverne, Alabama.

Galloway, P. (editor)

1989   *The Southeastern Ceremonial Complex: Artifacts and Analysis.*
University of Nebraska Press, Lincoln.

Gibbon, G.

1974   A Model of Mississippian Development and Its Implication for
the Red Wing Area. In *Aspects of Upper Great Lakes Archeology,*
ed. E. Johnson, pp. 129-37. Minnesota Prehistoric Archaeology
Series No. 11. Minnesota Historical Society, St. Paul.

1989   *Explanation in Archaeology.* Basil Blackwell, Oxford.

Giddens, A.

1979   *Central Problems in Social Theory.* Macmillan Press, London.

Goldman, I.

1970   *Ancient Polynesian Society.* University of Chicago Press, Chicago.

Goodman, L. S., and A. Hilman

1955   *A Pharmacological Basis of Therapeutics.* Macmillan, New York.

Gramsci, A.

1971   *Selections from the Prison Notebooks of Antonio Gramsci.* Trans. Q.
Hoare and G. Smith. International Publishers, New York.

Green, T. J.

1977   *Economic Relationships Underlying Mississippian Settlement Patterns
in Southwestern Indiana.* Ph.D. dissertation, University of Indiana, Bloomington. University Microfilms, Ann Arbor.

Green, W., and R. L. Rodell

1994   The Mississippian Presence and Cahokia Interaction at
Trempealeau, Wisconsin. *American Antiquity* 59(2): 334-359.

Gregg, M.

1975a *Settlement Morphology and Production Specialization: The Horseshoe
Lake Site, A Case Study.* Ph.D. dissertation, University of
Wisconsin-Milwaukee. University Microfilms, Ann Arbor.

1975b A Population Estimate for Cahokia. In *Perspectives in Cahokia
Archaeology,* ed. M. Fowler, pp. 126-136. Illinois Archaeological
Survey, Bulletin No. 10, Urbana.

Griffin, J. B.

1949   The Cahokia Ceramic Complexes. In *Proceedings of the Fifth
Plains Conference,* assembled by J. Chample, pp. 44-58. Laboratory of Anthropology, Notebook No. 1. University of Nebraska, Lincoln.

1952   Culture Periods in Eastern United States Archaeology. In *Archaeology of Eastern United States*, ed. J. Griffin, pp. 352-364. University of Chicago Press, Chicago.

1984   Observations on the FAI-270 Project. In *American Bottom Archaeology*, ed. C. Bareis and J. Porter, pp. 253-261. University of Illinois Press, Urbana.

1985   Changing Concepts of the Prehistoric Mississippian Cultures in the Eastern United States. In *Alabama and the Borderlands*, ed. R. Badger and L. Clayton, pp. 40-63. University of Alabama Press, University.

Griffin, J. B., and V. H. Jones

1977   The University of Michigan Excavations at the Pulcher Site in 1950. *American Antiquity* 42(3): 462-488.

Griffith, R. J.

1962   *Ramey Incised Pottery.* Master's thesis, Department of Art, Southern Illinois University-Carbondale.

1981   *Ramey Incised Pottery.* Circular 5, Illinois Archaeological Survey, Urbana.

Hall, E. T.

1966   *The Hidden Dimension.* Doubleday, Garden City.

1968   Proxemics. *Current Anthropology* 9: 83-108.

Hall, R. L.

1966   Cahokia Chronology. Paper presented at the annual meeting of the Central States Anthropological Society, St. Louis.

1967   The Mississippian Heartland and Its Plains Relationships. *Plains Anthropologist* 12: 175-183.

1972a   Pottery Representing Some Ceramic Periods at Cahokia. Sketches prepared for distribution at the annual meeting of the Society for American Archaeology, Bal Harbour.

1972b   Chronology and Phases at Cahokia. Paper Presented at the 37th Annual Meeting of the Society for American Archaeology, Bal Harbour.

1973   An Interpretation of the Two-Climax Model of Illinois Prehistory. Paper presented at 9th International Congress of Anthropological and Ethnological Sciences, Chicago.

1975a   Chronology and Phases at Cahokia. In *Perspectives in Cahokia Archaeology*, ed. M. Fowler, pp. 15-31. Illinois Archaeological Survey, Bulletin 10, Urbana.

1975b Some Problems of Identity and Process in Cahokia Archaeol-
       ogy. Paper Prepared for the Proceedings of the Advanced
       Seminar Reviewing Mississippian Development held at the
       School for American Research, Santa Fe.
1976   Ghosts, Water Barriers, Corn and Sacred Enclosures in the
       Eastern Woodlands. *American Antiquity* 41(3): 360-364.
1977   An Anthropocentric Perspective for Eastern United States
       Prehistory. *American Antiquity* 42: 499-518.
1979   In Search of an Ideology of the Adena-Hopewell Climax. In
       Hopewell Archaeology: The Chillicothe Conference, ed. D. Brose and
       N. Greber, pp. 259-278. Kent State University Press, Kent.
1980   Labras Lake C-14 Dates. In *Investigations at the Labras Lake Site,*
       pp. 366-406. Department of Anthropology, University of
       Illinois at Chicago Circle.
1985   Medicine Wheels, Sun Circles, and the Magic of World Center
       Shrines. *Plains Anthropologist* 30: 181-193.
1989   The Cultural Background of Mississippian Symbolism. In *The
       Southeastern Ceremonial Complex,* ed. P. Galloway, pp. 239-278.
       University of Nebraska Press, Lincoln.
1991   Cahokia Identity and Interaction Models of Cahokia Mississip-
       pian. In *Cahokia and the Hinterlands,* ed. T. Emerson and R.
       Lewis, pp. 3-34. University of Illinois Press, Urbana.

Hally, D. J.
1993   The Territorial Size of Mississippian Chiefdoms. In *Archaeology
       of Eastern North America: Papers in Honor of Stephen Williams,* ed.
       J. Stoltman, pp. 143-168. Archaeological Report No. 25,
       Mississippi Department of Archives and History, Jackson.

Hamilton, H. W.
1952   The Spiro Mound. *Missouri Archaeologist* 14: 1-276.

Hanenberger, N. H., and M. W. Mehrer
1998   *The Range Site 4 (11-S-47): Mississippian and Oneota Occupations.*
       University of Illinois Press, Urbana. (In Press)

Harn, A. D.
1967   Dickson Mounds: An Evaluation of the Amateur in Illinois
       Archaeology. *Earth Science* 20(4): 152-157.
1971   An Archaeological Survey of the American Bottoms and Wood
       River Terrace. In *Archaeological Surveys of the American Bottoms*

and Adjacent Bluffs, Illinois, part 2. Reports of Investigations, No. 21, pp. 19-39. Illinois State Museum, Springfield.

1975   Cahokia and the Mississippian Emergence in the Spoon River Area of Illinois. *Transactions of the Illinois State Academy of Science* 68(4): 414-434.

1978   Mississippian Settlement Patterns in the Central Illinois River Valley. In *Mississippian Settlement Patterns,* ed. B. Smith, pp. 233-268. Academic Press, New York.

1980   Comments on the Spatial Distribution of Late Woodland and Mississippian Ceramics in the General Cahokia Sphere. *Discovery* 1: 17-26.

1994   *Variation in Mississippian Settlement Pattern: The Larson Settlement System in the Central Illinois River Valley.* Illinois State Museum Reports of Investigations, No. 50. Springfield.

Helms, M. W.

1979   *Ancient Panama: Chiefs in Search of Power.* University of Texas Press, Austin.

1988   *Ulysses' Sail: An Ethnographic Odyssey of Power, Knowledge, and Geographical Distance.* Princeton University Press, Princeton.

1996   Why Maya Lords Sat on Jaguar Thrones. Paper presented in Material Symbols: Culture and Economy in Prehistory, Thirteenth Annual Visiting Scholar Conference, Center for Archaeological Investigations, Southern Illinois University, Carbondale.

Hirth, K.

1992   Interregional Exchange as Elite Behavior: An Evolutionary Perspective. In *Mesoamerican Elites: An Archaeological Assessment,* ed. D. Chase and A. Chase, pp. 18-29. University of Oklahoma Press, Norman.

Hodder, I.

1982   Theoretical Archaeology: A Reactionary View. In *Symbolic and Structural Archaeology,* ed. I. Hodder, pp. 1-16. Cambridge University Press, Cambridge.

1984   Archaeology in 1984. *Antiquity* 58: 25-32.

1985   Postprocessual Archaeology. In *Advances in Archaeological Method and Theory,* vol. 8, ed. M. B. Schiffer, pp. 1-26. Academic Press, New York.

1991   *Reading the Past.* 2nd ed. Cambridge University Press, Cambridge.

1992   *Theory and Practice in Archaeology.* Routledge, London and New York.

Hodder, I. (editor)
  1982   *Symbolic and Structural Archaeology.* Cambridge University Press, Cambridge.

Hoffman, B. G.
  1964   John Clayton's 1687 Account of the Medicinal Practices of the Virginia Indians. *Ethnohistory* 11: 1-40.

Holley, G. R.
  1989   *The Archaeology of the Cahokia Mounds ICT-II: Ceramics.* Illinois Cultural Resources Study 11. Illinois Historic Preservation Agency, Springfield.
  1995   Microliths and the Kunnemann Tract: An Assessment of Craft Production at the Cahokia Site. *Illinois Archaeology* 7 (1 & 2): 1-68.

Holmes, W.
  1903   Aboriginal Pottery of the Eastern United States. *Bureau of American Ethnology, Annual Report,* 1-237. Washington, D.C.

Howard, J. H.
  1968   *The Southern Ceremonial Complex and Its Interpretations.* Missouri Archaeological Society Memoir 6, Columbia.

Hudson, C.
  1976   *The Southeastern Indians.* University of Tennessee Press, Knoxville.

Hughes, R. E., and T. E. Emerson
  1995   Preliminary Sourcing of Cahokia Middle Mississippian Flint Clay Figurines. Paper presented at the Annual Meeting of the Southeastern Archaeological Conference, Knoxville.
  1996   Sourcing of Cahokia Middle Mississippian Flint Clay Figurines. Poster paper presented at the 30th International Symposium on Archaeometry, University of Illinois, Urbana.

Hultkrantz, A.
  1957   *The North American Indian Orpheus Tradition.* Ethnological Museum of Sweden, Monograph Series, Publication 2. Stockholm.

Iseminger, W. R., T. R. Pauketat, B. Koldehoff, L. S. Kelly, and L. Blake
    1990   *The Archaeology of the Cahokia Palisade: The East Palisade Investiga-
            tions.* Illinois Cultural Resources Study 14. Illinois Historic
            Preservation Agency, Springfield.

Jackson, D. K.
    1991   Ceramics. In *The Sponemann Site 2 (11-Ms-517): The Mississip-
            pian and Oneota Occupations,* by D. Jackson, A. Fortier, and J.
            Williams, pp. 125-215. FAI-270 Archaeological Mitigation
            Project Report 83, Department of Anthropology, University of
            Illinois at Urbana-Champaign.
    1992   Oneota in the American Bottom. In *The Sponemann Site 2: The
            Mississippian and Oneota Occupations* (11-Ms-517), by Douglas
            K. Jackson, Andrew C. Fortier, and Joyce A. Williams American
            Bottom Archaeology FAI-270 Site Reports Vol. 24:383-391.

Jackson, D. K., and T. E. Emerson
    1983   Mississippian Sand Prairie Phase Habitation Component. In *The
            Florence Street Site,* by T. Emerson et al., pp. 179-219. University
            of Illinois Press, Urbana.

Jackson, D. K., and N. H. Hanenberger
    1990   *Selected Early Mississippian Household Sites in the American Bottom.*
            University of Illinois Press, Urbana.

Jackson, D. K., A. C. Fortier, and J. A. Williams
    1991   *The Sponemann Site 2 (11-Ms-517): The Mississippian and Oneota
            Occupations.* FAI-270 Archaeological Mitigation Project Report
            83. Department of Anthropology, University of Illinois at
            Champaign-Urbana.

Johnson, G. A.
    1973   *Local Exchange and Early State Development in Southwestern Iran.*
            University of Michigan, Museum of Anthropology, Anthropo-
            logical Paper No. 37. Ann Arbor.
    1978   Information Sources and the Development of Decision-Making
            Organizations. In *Social Archaeology Beyond Subsistence and
            Dating,* ed. C. Redman, M. Berman, E. Curtin, T. Langhorne,
            N. Versaggi, and J. Wanser, pp. 87-112. Academic Press, New
            York.

Kelly, J. E.
    1980   *Formative Developments at Cahokia and the Adjacent American
            Bottom: A Merrell Tract Perspective.* Unpublished Ph.D. disserta-

tion, Department of Anthropology, University of Wisconsin.

1984 Wells Incised Plates: Their Context and Affinities with O'Byam Incised. Paper Presented at the Paducah Ceramic Conference, Paducah, Kentucky.

1987 Emergent Mississippian and the Transition from Late Woodland to Mississippian: The American Bottom Case for a New Concept. In *The Emergent Mississippian: Proceedings of the Sixth Mid-South Archaeological Conference,* June 6-9, 1985, ed. R. Marshall, pp. 212-226. Cobb Institute of Archaeology, Occasional Papers, pp. 87-101. Mississippi State University, Mississippi State.

1988 Archaeological Investigations of the East St. Louis Mound Center: Past and Present. Paper Presented at the Midwest Archaeological Conference, Urbana.

1990a The Emergence of Mississippian Culture in the American Bottom Region. In *The Mississippian Emergence,* ed. B. Smith, pp. 113-152. Smithsonian Institution Press, Washington, D.C.

1990b Range Site Community Patterns and the Mississippian Emergence. In *The Mississippian Emergence,* ed. B. Smith, pp. 67-112. Smithsonian Institution Press, Washington, D.C.

1991a Cahokia and Its Role as a Gateway Center in Interregional Exchange. In *Cahokia and the Hinterlands,* ed. T. Emerson and R. Lewis, pp. 61-80. University of Illinois Press, Urbana.

1991b The Evidence for Prehistoric Exchange and Its Implications for the Development of Cahokia. In *New Perspectives on Cahokia* ed. J. Stoltman, pp. 65-92. Prehistory Press, Madison.

1992 The Impact of Maize on the Development of Nucleated Settlements: An American Bottom Example. In *Late Prehistoric Agriculture: Observations from the Midwest,* ed. W. Woods, pp. 167-197. Studies in Illinois Archaeology No. 8. Illinois Historic Preservation Agency, Springfield.

1993 The Pulcher Site: An Archaeological and Historical Overview. In *Highways to the Past: Essays on Illinois Archaeology in Honor of Charles J. Bareis,* ed. T. Emerson, A. Fortier, and D. McElrath. *Illinois Archaeology* 5(1 & 2): 434-451.

1994 The Archaeology of the East St. Louis Mound Center: Past and Present. *Illinois Archaeology* 6(1 & 2): 1-57.

1997 Stirling Phase Socio-Political Activity at East St. Louis and Cahokia. In *Cahokia: Domination and Ideology in the Mississippian World,* ed. T. Pauketat and T. Emerson, pp. 141-166. University of Nebraska Press, Lincoln.

Kelly, J. E., F. A. Finney, D. L. McElrath, and S. J. Ozuk
  1984a Late Woodland Period. In *American Bottom Archaeology,* ed. C.
         Bareis and J. Porter, pp. 104-127. University of Illinois Press,
         Urbana.
Kelly, J. E., A. C. Fortier, S. J. Ozuk, and J. A. Williams
  1987   *The Range Site: Archaic Through Late Woodland Occupations.*
         University of Illinois Press, Urbana.

Kelly, J. E., S. J. Ozuk, D. K. Jackson, D. L. McElrath, F. A. Finney, and D.
  Esarey
  1984b Emergent Mississippian Period. In *American Bottom Archaeology,*
         ed. C. Bareis and J. Porter, pp. 128-157. University of Illinois
         Press, Urbana.

Kelly, J. E., S. J. Ozuk, and J. A. Williams
  1990   *The Range Site 2: The Emergent Mississippian Dohack and Range
         Phase Occupations.* University of Illinois Press, Urbana.

King, F. B.
  1984   *Plants, People, and Paleoecology.* Illinois State Museum, Scientific
         Papers 20. Springfield.

Knight, V. J., Jr.
  1981   *Mississippian Ritual.* Ph.D. dissertation, University of Florida.
         University Microfilms, Ann Arbor.
  1986   The Institutional Organization of Mississippian Religion.
         American Antiquity 51(4): 675-687.
  1989a Some Speculations on Mississippian Monsters. In *The Southeast-
         ern Ceremonial Complex,* ed. P. Galloway, pp. 205-210. Univer-
         sity of Nebraska Press, Lincoln.
  1989b Symbolism of Mississippian Mounds. In *Powhatan's Mantle,* ed.
         P. Wood et al., pp. 279-291. University of Nebraska, Lincoln.
  1990   Social Organization and the Evolution of Hierarchy in South-
         eastern Chiefdoms. *Journal of Anthropological Research* 46(1): 1-
         24.

Koldehoff, B.
  1989   Cahokia's Immediate Hinterland: The Mississippian Occupation
         of Douglas Creek. *Illinois Archaeology* 1(1): 69-81.

Larrain, J.
  1979   *The Concept of Ideology.* University of Georgia Press, Athens.

Lawson, J.
  1966[1709] *A New Voyage to Carolina.* 1966 Facsimile Reprint, Readex
         Microprint.

Leone, M.
   1986   Symbolic, Structural, and Critical Archaeology. In *American Archaeology, Past and Present,* ed. D. Meltzer, D. Fowler, and J. Sabloff, pp. 415–438. Smithsonian Institution Press, Washington, D.C.

Lesure, R.
   1996   The Meaning and Uses of Valuables in Formative Period Mesoamerica. Paper presented in Material Symbols: Culture and Economy in Prehistory. Thirteenth Annual Visiting Scholar Conference, Center for Archaeological Investigations, Southern Illinois University, Carbondale.

Levi-Strauss, C.
   1963   *Structural Anthropology.* Basic Books, New York.

Lewis, W. H., and M. Elvin-Lewis
   1977   *Medical Botany: Plants Affecting Man's Health.* John Wiley, New York.

Lightfoot, K. G.
   1984   *Prehistoric Political Dynamics: A Case Study from the American Southwest.* Northern Illinois University Press, De Kalb.

Lightfoot, K. G., and S. Upham
   1989   Complex Societies in the Prehistoric American Southwest: A Consideration of the Controversy. In *The Sociopolitical Structure of Prehistoric Southwestern Societies,* ed. S. Upham et al., pp. 3-30. Investigations in American Archaeology, Westview Press, Boulder.

Lopinot, N. H., and W. I. Woods
   1993   Wood Overexploitation and the Collapse of Cahokia. *In Foraging and Farming in the Eastern Woodlands,* ed. C. Scarry, pp. 206-231. University Press of Florida, Gainesville.

McConaughy, M. A.
   1991   The Rench Site Late Late Woodland/Mississippian Farming Hamlet from the Central Illinois River Valley: Food for Thought. In *New Perspectives on Cahokia: Views from the Periphery,* ed. J. Stoltman, pp. 101-128. Monographs in World Archaeology No. 2. Prehistory Press, Madison.

McElrath, D. L.
   1983   Mississippian Chert Exploitation: A Case Study from the American Bottom. Paper Presented at the Annual Meeting of the Society for American Archaeology, Pittsburgh.

McQueen, H. S.

    1943   *Geology of the Fire Clay Districts of East Central Missouri.* Missouri
             Geological Survey and Water Resources, Second Series, vol. 28.
             Rolla.

Marcus, G. E.

    1983   "Elite," as a Concept, Theory, and Research Tradition. In *Elites:*
             Ethographic Issues, ed. G. Marcus, pp. 7-27. University of New
             Mexico Press, Albuquerque.

    1992   The Concern with Elites in Archaeological Reconstructions:
             Mesoamerican Materials. In *Mesoamerican Elites: An Archaeologi-*
             cal Assessment, ed. D. Chase and A. Chase, pp. 292-302. Univer-
             sity of Oklahoma Press, Norman.

Marcus, G. E. (editor)

    1983   *Elites: Ethographic Issues.* University of New Mexico Press,
             Albuquerque.

Marx, K., and F. Engels

    1989   *The German Ideology.* International Publishers, New York.

Mason, R. J., and G. Perino

    1961   Microblades at Cahokia, Illinois. *American Antiquity* 26: 553-
             557.

Mehrer, M.

    1982   *A Mississippian Community at the Range Site (11-S-47), St. Clair*
             County, Illinois. FAI-270 Archaeological Mitigation Report 52,
             Department of Anthropology, University of Illinois at Urbana-
             Champaign.

    1988   *The Settlement Patterns and Social Power of Cahokia's Hinterland*
             Households. Unpublished Ph.D. dissertation, Department of
             Anthropology, University of Illinois, Urbana.

    1995   *Cahokia's Countryside: Household Archaeology, Settlement Patterns,*
             and Social Power. Northern Illinois University Press, De Kalb.

Mehrer, M. W., and J. M. Collins

    1995   Household Archaeology at Cahokia and Its Hinterlands. In
             Mississippian Communities and Households, ed. J. Rogers and B.
             Smith, pp. 32-57. University of Alabama Press, Tuscaloosa.

Milanich, J. T.

    1979   Origins and Prehistoric Distribution of Black Drink and the
             Ceremonial Shell Drinking Cup. In *Black Drink: A Native*

American Tea, ed. C. Hudson, pp. 83–119. University of Georgia Press, Athens.

Miller, D.
  1985   *Artifacts as Categories.* Cambridge University Press, Cambridge.

Miller, D., M. Rowlands, and C. Tilley
  1989   Introduction. In *Domination and Resistance,* ed. D. Miller et al., pp. 1–26. Unwin Hyman, Boston.

Miller, D., and C. Tilley
  1984   Ideology, Power and Prehistory: An Introduction. In *Ideology, Power and Prehistory,* ed. D. Miller and C. Tilley, pp. 1–15. Cambridge University Press, Cambridge.

Miller, D., and C. Tilley (editors)
  1984   *Ideology, Power and Prehistory.* Cambridge University Press, Cambridge.

Milner, G. R.
  1981   *The Julien Site (11-S-63): An Early Bluff and Mississippian Multicomponent Site.* FAI-270 Archaeological Mitigation Project Report 31, Department of Anthropology, University of Illinois at Urbana–Champaign.
  1982   *Measuring Prehistoric Levels of Health: A Study of Mississippian Period Skeletal Remains from the American Bottom, Illinois.* Unpublished Ph.D. dissertation, Department of Anthropology, Northwestern University, Evanston.
  1983a *The East St. Louis Stone Quarry Site Cemetery.* University of Illinois Press, Urbana.
  1983b Mississippian Sand Prairie Phase Mortuary Complex. In *The Florence Street Site,* by T. Emerson et al., pp. 220–302. University of Illinois Press, Urbana.
  1984a Social and Temporal Implications of Variation Among American Bottom Mississippian Cemeteries. *American Antiquity* 49(3): 468–488.
  1984b Human Skeletal Remains from the BBB Motor Site. In *The BBB Motor Site,* by T. Emerson and D. Jackson, pp. 395–397. University of Illinois Press, Urbana.
  1986   Mississippian Period Population Density in a Segment of the Central Mississippi River Valley. *American Antiquity* 51(2): 227–238.
  1987   Cultures in Transition: The Late Emergent Mississippian and Mississippian Periods in the American Bottom, Illinois. In *The*

*Emergent Mississippian: Proceedings of the Sixth Mid-South Archaeo-
logical Conference,* June 6-9, 1985, ed. R. Marshall, pp. 194-211.
Cobb Institute of Archaeology, Occasional Papers 87-101.
Mississippi State University, Mississippi State.

1990 The Late Prehistoric Cahokia Cultural System of the Mississippi River Valley: Foundations, Florescence, and Fragmentation. *Journal of World Prehistory* 4(1): 1-43.

Milner, G., and T. E. Emerson
1981 The Mississippian Occupation of the American Bottom:The
Farmsteads. Paper presented at the Midwestern Archaeological
Conference, Madison.

Milner, G. R., T. E. Emerson, M. W. Mehrer, J. A. Williams, and D. Esarey
1984 Mississippian and Oneota Period. In *American Bottom Archaeology,* ed. C. Bareis and J. Porter, pp. 158-186. University of
Illinois Press, Urbana.

Milner, G. R., S. C. Pullins, and R. Paine
1998 Burial Groups. In *The Range Site 4 (11-S-47): Mississippian and
Oneota Occupations.* University of Illinois Press, Urbana. (In
Press)

Milner, G., with J. Williams
1983 *The Turner and DeMange Sites.* University of Illinois Press,
Urbana.
1984 *The Julien Site (11-S-63).* University of Illinois Press, Urbana.

Moffat, C. R.
1991 Mississippian in the Upper Kaskaskia Valley: New Data from
Lake Shelbyville and New Interpretations. In *Cahokia and the
Hinterlands,* ed. T. Emerson and R. Lewis, pp. 239-256. University of Illinois Press, Urbana.

Mooney, J.
1900 Myths of the Cherokee. Bureau of American Ethnology,
Nineteenth Annual Report, Part 1. Washington, D.C.

Mooney, J., and F. M. Olbrechts
1932 *The Swimmer Manuscripts, Cherokee Sacred Formulas and Medicinal
Practices.* Bulletin 99. Bureau of American Ethnology, Washington, D.C.

Morgan, H. L.
1881 *Houses and House Life of the American Aborigines.* Contributions to
Ethnology, U.S. Geological Survey, Washington, D.C.

Muller, J.
    1978   The Kincaid System: Mississippian Settlement in the Environs of a Large Site. In *Mississippian Settlement Patterns,* ed. B. Smith, pp. 269–292. Academic Press, New York.

Munson, P. J.
    1971   An Archaeological Survey of the Wood River Terrace and Adjacent Bottoms and Bluffs in Madison County, Illinois. In *Archaeological Surveys of the American Bottoms and Adjacent Bluffs, Illinois,* pp. 3–17. Illinois State Museum, Reports of Investigations No. 21.

Neitzel, R. S.
    1965   *Archaeology of the Fatherland Site: The Grand Village of the Natchez.* American Museum of Natural History Anthropological Papers 51(1), New York.

O'Brien, P.
    1972a   Urbanism, Cahokia, and Middle Mississippian. *Archaeology* 25(3): 88–197.
    1972b   *A Formal Analysis of Cahokia Ceramics from the Powell Tract.* Illinois Archaeological Survey, Memoir 3, Urbana.
    1989   Cahokia: The Political Capital of the "Ramey" State? *North American Archaeologist* 10(4): 275–92.
    1993   Cultural Taxonomy, Cross-Cultural Types, and Cahokia. In *Highways to the Past: Essays on Illinois Archaeology in Honor of Charles J. Bareis,* ed. T. Emerson, A. Fortier, and D. McElrath. *Illinois Archaeology* 5(1 & 2): 481–497.

O'Brien, P., and W. McHugh
    1987   Mississippian Solstice Shrines and a Cahokian Calendar: An Hypothesis Based on Ethnohistory and Archaeology. *North American Archaeologist* 8(3): 227–247.

Ortner, S. B.
    1984   Theory in Anthropology Since the Sixties. *Comparative Studies in Society and History* 26: 126–166.

Panofsky, E. (editor, translator, and annotator)
    1979   *Abbot Suger on the Abbey Church of St.-Denis and Its Art Treasures.* 2nd ed., by Gerda Panofsky-Soergel. Princeton University Press, Princeton.

Parker, K. E.

1991   Archaeobotany. In *The Sponemann Site 2,* by D. Jackson, A. Fortier, and J. Williams, pp. 305-324. FAI-270 Archaeological Mitigation Project Report 83. Department of Anthropology, University of Illinois at Urbana-Champaign.

Parsons, J. R.

1971   *Prehispanic Settlement Patterns in the Texcoco Region, Mexico.* Museum of Anthropology Memoir 3. University of Michigan, Ann Arbor.

1972   Archaeological Settlement Patterns. *Annual Review of Anthropology* 1: 127-150.

Pauketat, T. R.

1989   Monitoring Mississippian Homestead Occupation Span and Economy Using Ceramic Refuse. *American Antiquity* 54: 288-310.

1991   *The Dynamics of Pre-State Political Centralization in the North American Midcontinent.* Unpublished Ph.D. dissertation, Department of Anthropology, University of Michigan, Ann Arbor.

1992   The Reign and Ruin of the Lords of Cahokia: A Dialectic of Dominance. In *Lords of the Southeast: Social Inequality and the Native Elites of Southeastern North America,* ed. A. Barker and T. Pauketat, pp. 31-52. Archaeological Paper No. 3, American Anthropological Association. Washington, D.C.

1993   *Temples for Cahokia Lords: Preston Holder's 1955-1956 Excavations of Kunnemann Mound.* Museum of Anthropology, Memoir No. 26, University of Michigan. Ann Arbor.

1994   *The Ascent of Chiefs: Cahokia and Mississippian Politics in Native North America.* University of Alabama Press, Tuscaloosa.

1996   Specialization, Political Symbols and the Crafty Elite of Cahokia. *Southeastern Archaeology.* (In Press)

Pauketat, T. R., and T. E. Emerson

1991   The Ideology of Authority and the Power of the Pot. *American Anthropologist* 93: 919-941

1996   The Production of Hegemony and Mississippianism in the Guise of Communalism. Invited paper presented in Material Symbols: Culture and Economy in Prehistory. Thirteenth Annual Visiting Scholar Conference, Center for Archaeological Investigations, Carbondale.

Pauketat, T. R., and T. E. Emerson (editors)
   1997   *Cahokia: Domination and Ideology in the Mississippian World.*
          University of Nebraska Press, Lincoln.

Pauketat, T. R., and B. Koldehoff
   1983   Emerald Mound and the Mississippian Occupation of the
          Central Silver Mound Creek Valley. Paper presented at Mid-
          western Archaeological Conference, Iowa City.

Pauketat, T. R., and N. H. Lopinot
   1997   Cahokian Population Dynamics. In *Cahokia: Domination and
          Ideology in the Mississippian World,* ed. T. Pauketat and T.
          Emerson, pp. 103–123. University of Nebraska Press, Lincoln.

Pauketat, T. R., and W. I. Woods
   1986   Middle Mississippian Structure Analysis: The Lawrence Primas
          Site (11-Ms-895) in the American Bottom. *Wisconsin Archeologist*
          67(2): 104–127.

Peebles, C. S.
   1987   Moundville from 1000 to 1500 AD as Seen from 1840 to 1985
          AD. In *Chiefdoms in the Americas,* ed. R. Drennan and C. Uribe,
          pp. 21–42. University Press of America, Lanham, Maryland.

Peebles, C., and S. Kus
   1977   Some Archaeological Correlates of Ranked Societies. *American
          Antiquity* 42: 421–448.

Peet, S. D.
   1891   The Cahokia Tablet. *The American Antiquarian* 13(1):58–59.
          Chicago.

Peregrine, P. N.
   1992   *Mississippian Evolution: A World System Perspective.* Prehistory
          Press, Madison.

Perino, G.
   1959   Recent Information from Cahokia and Its Satellites. *Central
          States Archaeological Journal* 6(4): 130–138.
   1971   The Mississippian Component at the Schild Site (no. 4),
          Greene County, Illinois. In *Mississippian Site Archaeology in
          Illinois I: Site Reports from the St. Louis and Chicago Areas,* pp. 1–
          148. Illinois Archaeological Survey, Urbana.

Pettit, P.
   1977   *The Concept of Structuralism: A Critical Analysis.* University of
          California, Berkeley.

Phelps, D. S.
  1970 Mesoamerican Glyph Motifs on Southeastern Pottery. *Transactions of International Congress of Americanists,* vol. 2: 89-99. Thirty-Eighth Session, Munich, August 1968.

Phillips, P., and J. A. Brown
  1978 *Pre-Columbian Shell Engravings from the Craig Mound at Spiro, Oklahoma.* Part 1 (paperback ed.). Peabody Museum Press, Cambridge.

Plog, F., and S. Upham
  1983 The Analysis of Prehistoric Political Organization. In *The Development of Political Organization in Native North America,* ed. E. Tooker and M. Fried, pp. 199-213. American Ethnological Society, Washington, D.C.

Porter, J. W.
  1964 *Thin Section Descriptions of Some Shell Tempered Prehistoric Ceramics From the American Bottoms.* Southern Illinois University Museum Lithic Laboratory, Research Report 7. Carbondale.
  1969 The Mitchell Site and Prehistoric Exchange Systems at Cahokia: A.D. 1000+-300. In *Explorations into Cahokia Archaeology,* ed. M. Fowler, pp. 137-164. Illinois Archaeological Survey Bulletin No. 7, Urbana.
  1974 *Cahokia Archaeology as Viewed from the Mitchell Site: A Satellite Community at A.D. 1150-1200.* Unpublished Ph.D. dissertation, Department of Anthropology, University of Wisconsin.
  1981 FAI-270 Project: Background. In *Archaeology in the American Bottom,* ed. C. Bareis and J. Porter, pp. 9-26. Department of Anthropology Research Report 6, University of Illinois at Urbana-Champaign.
  1984 Concluding Remarks. In *American Bottom Archaeology,* ed. C. Bareis and J. Porter, pp. 241-252. University of Illinois Press, Urbana.

Prentice, G.
  1986a An Analysis of the Symbolism Expressed by the Birger Figurine. *American Antiquity* 51: 239-266.
  1986b The Origins of Plant Domestication in the Eastern United States: Promoting the Individual in Archaeological Theory. *Southeastern Archaeology* 5(2): 103-119.

1987   Marine Shells as Wealth Items in Mississippian Societies. *Midcontinental Journal of Archaeology* 12(2): 193-223.

Price, B. J.
1981   Cultural Materialism: A Theoretical Review. Manuscript available from the author.

Price, J. E.
1978   The Settlement Pattern of the Powers Phase. In *Mississippian Settlement Patterns,* ed. B. Smith, pp. 201-232. Academic Press, New York.

Price, J. E., and J. B. Griffin
1979   *The Snodgrass Site of the Powers Phase of Southeast Missouri.* Museum of Anthropology, Anthropological Paper 66. University of Michigan.

Radin, P.
1927   *The Story of the American Indian.* Boni and Liveright, New York.

Reed, N. A.
1969   Monks and Other Mississippian Mounds. In *Explorations into Cahokia Archaeology,* ed. M. Fowler, pp. 31-42. Illinois Archaeological Survey Bulletin 7, Urbana.

Reed, N. A., J. W. Bennet, and J. W. Porter
1968   Solid Core Drilling of Monks Mound: Technique and Findings. *American Antiquity* 33: 137-148.

Riordan, R.
1975   *Ceramics and Chronology: Mississippian Settlement in the Black Bottom, Southern Illinois.* Ph.D. dissertation, Southern Illinois University at Carbondale. University Microfilms, Ann Arbor.

Sahlins, M. A.
1958   *Social Stratification in Polynesia.* University of Washington Press, Seattle.
1963   Poor Man, Rich Man, Big-Man, Chief: Political Types in Melanesia and Polynesia. *Comparative Studies in Society and History* 5: 285-303.
1977   The State of the Art in Social/Cultural Anthropology. In *Perspectives in Anthropology 1976.* Special Publication of the American Anthropological Association 10. Washington, D.C.
1981   *Historical Metaphors and Mythical Realities.* University of Michigan Press, Ann Arbor.
1985   *Islands of History.* University of Chicago Press, Chicago.

Saitta, D. J.
   1994   Agency, Class, and Archaeological Interpretation. *Journal of Anthropological Archaeology* 13: 201-227.

Sanders, W. T.
   1972   Population, Agricultural History and Societal Evolution in Mesoamerica. In *Population Growth, Anthropological Implications,* ed. B. Spooner, pp. 101-153. MIT Press, Cambridge.

Scarry, J. F.
   1992   Political Offices and Political Structure: Ethnohistoric and Archaeological Perspectives on the Native Lords of Apalachee. In *Lords of the Southeast: Social Inequality and the Native Elites in Southeastern North America,* ed. A. Barker and T. Pauketat, pp. 163-184. American Anthropological Association, Archaeological Paper No. 3, Washington, D.C.

Scarry, J. F. (editor)
   1996   *Political Structure and Change in the Prehistoric Southeastern United States.* University Press of Florida, Gainesville.

Sears, W. H.
   1961   The Study of Social and Religious Systems in North American Archaeology. *Current Anthropology* 2: 223-246.
   1962   The State in Certain Areas and Periods of the Prehistoric Southeastern United States. *Ethnohistory* 9:109-125.
   1968   The State and Settlement Patterns in the New World. In *Settlement Archaeology,* ed. K. Chang, pp. 134-153. National Press Books, Palo Alto.

Seeman, M. F.
   1979   Feasting with the Dead: Ohio Hopewell Charnel House Ritual as a Context for Redistribution. In *Hopewell Archaeology: The Chillicothe Conference,* ed. D. Brose and N. Greber, pp. 39-46. Kent State University Press, Kent.

Service, E.
   1962   *Primitive Social Organization.* Random House, New York.
   1971   *Cultural Evolutionism: Theory in Practice.* Holt, Rinehart, and Winston, New York.
   1975   *Origins of the State and Civilization.* Norton, New York.

Shanks, M., and C. Tilley
   1982   Ideology, Symbolic Power and Ritual Communication: A Reinterpretation of Neolithic Mortuary Practices. In *Symbolic*

and Structural Archaeology, ed. I. Hodder, pp. 129-154. Cambridge University Press, Cambridge.

1987 *Social Theory and Archaeology.* University of New Mexico Press, Albuquerque.

Shennan, S.
1986 Towards a Critical Archaeology? *Proceedings of the Prehistoric Society* 52: 327-338.

Shepard, A. O.
1948 A Symmetry of Abstract Design with Special Reference to Ceramic Description. In *Carnegie Institute of Washington Publication 574,* Contribution 47: 211-292. Carnegie Institute, Washington, D.C.

Skele, M.
1988 *The Great Knob: Interpretations of Monks Mound.* Studies in Illinois Archaeology No. 4. Illinois Historic Preservation Agency, Springfield.

Smith, B. D.
1978a Variation in Mississippian Settlement Patterns. In *Mississippian Settlement Patterns,* ed. B. Smith, pp. 479-503. Academic Press, New York.

1978b *Prehistoric Patterns of Human Behavior: A Case Study in the Mississippi Valley.* Academic Press, New York.

1984 Mississippian Expansion: Tracing the Historical Development of an Explanatory Model. *Southeastern Archaeology* 3(1): 13-32.

1986 The Archaeology of the Southeastern United States: From Dalton to de Soto, 10,000-500 B.P. In *Advances in World Archaeology,* 1-92. Academic Press, New York.

1992 Mississippian Elites and Solar Alignments—A Reflection of Managerial Necessity, or Levers of Social Inequality? In *Lords of the Southeast: Social Inequality and the Native Elites of Southeastern North America,* ed. A. Barker and T. Pauketat, pp. 11-30. American Anthropological Association, Archaeological Paper No. 3.

Smith, B. (editor)
1978 *Mississippian Settlement Patterns.* Academic Press, New York.
1990 *The Mississippian Emergence.* Smithsonian Institution Press, Washington, D.C.

Smith, J.
  1819   *The True Travels, Adventures, and Observations of Captaine John Smith.* Franklin Press, Richmond.

Speck, Frank G.
  1944   Catawba Herbals and Curative Practices. *Journal of American Folklore* 57(223): 37-50.

Spencer, C. S.
  1987   Rethinking the Chiefdom. In *Chiefdoms in the Americas,* ed. R. Drennan and C. Uribe, pp. 369-389. University Press of America, Lanham.

Steponaitis, V. P.
  1983   *Ceramics, Chronology, and Community Patterns: An Archaeological Study at Moundville.* Academic Press, New York.
  1986   Prehistoric Archaeology in the Southeastern United States, 1970-1985. *Annual Review of Anthropology* 15: 363-404.

Stoltman, J. B. (editor)
  1991   *New Perspectives on Cahokia: Views from the Periphery.* Prehistory Press, Madison.

Struever, S.
  1968   Woodland Subsistence-Settlement Systems in the Lower Illinois Valley. In *New Perspectives in Archeology,* ed. S. Binford and L. Binford, pp. 285-312. Aldine, Chicago.

Suhm, D. A., and E. B. Jelks
  1962   *Handbook of Texas Archaeology: Type Descriptions.* Special Publication 1, Texas Archaeological Society, Austin.

Sumner, C.
  1979   *Reading Ideologies: An Investigation into the Marxist Theory of Ideology and Law.* Academic Press, London.

Swanton, J. R.
  1911   *Indian Tribes of the Lower Mississippi Valley and Adjacent Coast of the Gulf of Mexico.* Bureau of American Ethnology, Bulletin 43. Washington, D.C.
  1922   *Early History of the Creek Indians and their Neighbors.* Bureau of American Ethnology, Bulletin 73. Washington, D.C.
  1946   *The Indians of the Southeastern United States.* Bureau of American Ethnology, Bulletin 137. Washington, D.C.

Szuter, C.

1979 *The Schlemmer Site: A Late Woodland-Mississippian Site in the American Bottom.* Master's thesis, Department of Anthropology, Loyola University, Chicago.

Tilley, C.

1982 Social Formation, Social Structures and Social Change. In *Symbolic and Structural Archaeology,* ed. I. Hodder, pp. 26-38. Cambridge University Press, Cambridge.

1991 Michel Foucault: Towards an Archaeology of Archaeology. In *Reading Material Culture: Structuralism, Hermeneutics, and Post-Structuralism,* ed. C. Tilley, pp. 281-347. Basil Blackwell, Oxford.

Trigger, B. G.

1968 The Determinants of Settlement Patterns. In *Settlement Archaeology,* ed. K. Chang, pp. 53-78. National Press Books, Palo Alto.

1978 *Time and Tradition.* Columbia University Press, New York.

Trubitt, M. B. D.

1996 *Household Status, Marine Shell Bead Production, and the Development of Cahokia in the Mississippian Period.* Unpublished Ph.D. dissertation, Department of Anthropology, Northwestern University, Evanston.

Turner, V.

1964 Betwixt and Between: The Liminal Period in *Rites de Passage.* In *Symposium on New Approaches to the Study of Religion,* ed. J. Helm, pp. 4-20. Proceedings of the American Ethnological Society, University of Washington Press.

1967 *The Forest of Symbols: Aspects of Ndembu Ritual.* Cornell University Press, Ithaca.

1969 *The Ritual Process: Structure and Anti-Structure.* Cornell University Press, Ithaca.

1974 *Dramas, Fields, and Metaphors: Symbolic Action in Human Society.* Cornell University Press, Ithaca.

Upham, S.

1987 A Theoretical Consideration of Middle Range Societies. In *Chiefdoms in the Americas,* ed. R. Drennan and C. Uribe, pp. 345-368. University Press of America, Lanham.

Upham, S., K. G. Lightfoot, and R. A. Jewett (editors)

    1989   *The Sociopolitical Structure of Prehistoric Southwestern Societies.* Westview Press, Boulder.

Vogel, J. O.

    1975   Trends in Cahokia Ceramics: Preliminary Study of the Collections from Tracts 15A and 15B. In *Perspectives in Cahokia Archaeology,* ed. M. Fowler, pp. 32-125. Illinois Archaeological Survey Bulletin No. 10. Urbana.

Vogt, E. A.

    1956   An Appraisal of Prehistoric Settlement Patterns in the New World. In *Prehistoric Settlement Patterns in the New World,* ed. G. Willey, pp. 173-182. Viking Funds Publications in Anthropology 23, New York.

    1968   Some Aspects of Zinacantan Settlement Patterns and Ceremonial Organization. In *Settlement Archaeology,* ed. K. Chang, pp. 154-173. National Press Books, Palo Alto.

    1983   Some New Themes in Settlement Pattern Research. In *Prehistoric Settlement Patterns,* ed. E. Vogt and R. Leventhal, pp. 3-20. University of New Mexico Press, Santa Fe.

Wallace, A. F. C.

    1966   *Religion: An Anthropological View.* Random House, New York.

Walthall, J.

    1981   *Galena and Aboriginal Trade in Eastern North America.* Illinois State Museum Scientific Papers, vol. XVII. Springfield.

Waring, A. J.

    1968   The Southern Cult and Muskogean Ceremonial. In *The Waring Papers,* ed. S. Williams, pp. 30-69. Papers of the Peabody Museum of Archaeology and Ethnology 58. Harvard University, Peabody Museum, Cambridge.

Waring, A. J., and P. Holder

    1945   A Prehistoric Ceremonial Complex in the Southeastern United States. *American Anthropologist* 47(1): 1-34.

Watson, P. J., and M. Fotiadis

    1990   The Razor's Edge: Symbolic-Structuralist Archeology and the Expansion of Archeological Inference. *American Anthropologist* 92: 613-629.

Webb, W. S., and D. L. DeJarnette

1942   *An Archaeological Survey of Pickwick Basin in Adjacent Portions of the States of Alabama, Mississippi and Tennessee.* Bureau of American Ethnology, Bulletin 129. Washington, D.C.

Welch, P. D.

1991   *Moundville's Economy.* University of Alabama Press, Tuscaloosa.

Whalley, L.

1982   Plant Remains from the Stirling Component. In *The BBB Motor Site (11-S-595): An Early Mississippian Site in the American Bottom,* by T. Emerson and D. Jackson, pp. 335–349. FAI-270 Archaeological Mitigation Project Report 38, Department of Anthropology, University of Illinois at Urbana.

1984   Plant Remains from the Stirling Phase. In *The BBB Motor Site,* by T. Emerson and D. Jackson, pp. 321–335. University of Illinois Press, Urbana.

n.d.   Ethnohistorical and Ethnobotanical Implications of the BBB Motor Stirling Botanical Materials. Ms. on file at the FAI-270 Mitigation Project, University of Illinois at Urbana-Champaign.

White, L. A.

1959   *The Evolution of Culture.* McGraw-Hill, New York.

Willey, G. R.

1953   *Prehistoric Settlement Patterns in the Viru Valley, Peru.* Bureau of American Ethnology, Bulletin 155. Washington, D.C.

1956   Problems Concerning Prehistoric Settlement Patterns in the Maya Lowlands. In *Prehistoric Settlement Patterns in the New World,* ed. G. Willey, pp. 107–114. Viking Fund Publications in Anthropology 23. Wenner-Gren Foundation, New York.

1983   Settlement Patterns and Archaeology: Some Comments. In *Prehistoric Settlement Patterns,* ed. E. Vogt and R. Leventhal, pp. 445–462. University of New Mexico Press, Santa Fe.

Willey, G. R. (editor)

1956   *Prehistoric Settlement Patterns in the New World.* Viking Fund Publications in Anthropology, No. 23. Wenner-Gren Foundation, New York.

Williams, J. A.

1991   Lithics. In *The Sponemann Site 2,* by D. Jackson, A. Fortier, and J. Williams, pp. 217–276. FAI-270 Archaeological Mitigation

Report 83, Department of Anthropology, University of Illinois at Urbana–Champaign.

Williams, K.
  1972 Preliminary Summation of Excavations at the East Lobes of Mound 38. Paper Presented at the 37th Annual Meeting of the Society for American Archaeology, Bal Harbour.

Williams, R.
  1977 *Marxism and Literature.* Ed. S. Williams. Oxford University Press, Oxford.

Williams, S. (editor)
  1968 *The Waring Papers: The Collected Works of Antonio J. Waring, Jr.* Papers of the Peabody Museum of Archaeology and Ethnology 58. Peabody Museum, Harvard University Press, Cambridge.

Williams, S., and J. M. Goggin
  1956 The Long Nosed God Mask in the Eastern United States. *Missouri Archaeologist* 18(3): 4–72.

Willoughby, C. C.
  1932 Notes on the History and Symbolism of the Muskhogeans and the People of Etowah. In *Etowah Papers: Explorations of the Etowah Site in Georgia,* ed. W. Moorehead, pp. 7–105. Yale University Press, New Haven.

Wilson, G. D.
  1994 Clues to Consolidation: An Update on the Early Cahokia Project's Excavations in the American Bottom. Paper presented at the Southeastern Archaeological Conference, Lexington, Ky.
  1996 Insight Through Icons. *Illinois Archaeology* 8(1 & 2): 23–37.

Winters, H. D.
  1969 *The Riverton Culture: A Second Millennium Occupation in the Central Wabash Valley.* Illinois Archaeological Survey, Monograph 1, Urbana.

Witthoft, J.
  1949 *Green Corn Ceremonialism in the Eastern Woodlands.* University of Michigan Museum of Anthropology Occasional Publication 13. Ann Arbor.

Wittry, W. L.
  1969 The American Woodhenge. In *Explorations into Cahokia Archaeology,* ed. M. Fowler, pp. 43–48. Illinois Archaeological Survey Bulletin No. 7. Urbana.

Wolforth, T. R.
  1989   *Small Settlements and Population Movement in the Mississippian Settlement Pattern*. Unpublished Master's thesis, Department of Anthropology, University of Wisconsin at Milwaukee.

Woods, W. I.
  1987   Maize Agriculture and the Late Prehistoric: A Characterization of Settlement Location Strategies. In *Emergent Horticultural Economies of the Eastern Woodlands*, ed. W. Keegan, pp. 275-294. Occasional Paper No. 7. Center for Archaeological Investigations, Southern Illinois University at Carbondale.

Woods, W. I., and G. R. Holley
  1991   Upland Mississippian Settlement in the American Bottom Region. In *Cahokia and the Hinterlands* ed. T. Emerson and R. Lewis, pp. 46-60. University of Illinois Press, Urbana and Chicago.

Woods, W. I., and D. W. Meyer
  1988   Soil Selection and Management Criteria for Late Prehistoric Midwestern Agriculture. Paper Presented at the 46th International Congress of Americanists, Amsterdam, The Netherlands.

Wright, H. T.
  1969   *The Administration of Rural Production in an Early Mesopotamian Town*. University of Michigan, Museum of Anthropology, Anthropological Papers No. 38. Ann Arbor.
  1977   Recent Research on the Origin of the State. *Annual Review of Anthropology* 6: 379-397.
  1984   Prestate Political Formations. In *On the Evolution of Complex Societies: Essays in Honor of Harry Hoijer 1982,* ed. T. Earle, pp. 41-77. Undena Publications, Malibu.

Wright, H. T., and G. A. Johnson
  1975   Population, Exchange and Early State Formation in Southwestern Iran. *American Anthropologist* 77: 267-289.

Wyckoff, D. G., and T. G. Baugh
  1980   Early Historic Hasinai Elites: A Model for the Material Culture of Governing Elites. *Midcontinental Journal of Archaeology* 5: 225-288.

Wylie, M. A.

1982   Epistemological Issues Raised by a Structuralist Archaeology. In *Symbolic and Structural Archaeology,* ed. I. Hodder, pp. 39-46. Cambridge University Press, Cambridge.

Yerkes, R. W.

1980   The Mississippian Component. In *Investigations at the Labras Lake Site,* pp. 143-264. Department of Anthropology, University of Illinois at Chicago Circle.

1983   Microwear, Microdrills, and Mississippian Craft Specialization. *American Antiquity* 48: 499-518.

1987   *Prehistoric Life on the Mississippi Floodplain: Stone Tool Use, Settlement Organization, and Subsistence Practices at the Labras Lake Site, Illinois.* University of Chicago Press, Chicago.

Index

A

Abercrombie, N., 23

Adair, J., 170, 175, 185

Althusser, L., 24

American Bottom: chronology, 46, 56; Dohack Phase, 222, 260; Fairmount Phase, 46; George Reeves, 155; Jarrot Phase, 46; Lindeman phase, 156; Lohmann Phase, 47, 48-49; Moorehead Phase, 46; Patrick Phase, 46; Sand Prairie Phase, 46, 53; Stirling Phase, 46; physiography, 151-155, 249; and agriculture, 152-153; deforestation, 153; flooding, 151, 153-154, 154-155; population, 50

Apalachee, 16

Architecture of power, 4, 33, 36, 60, 63, 81, 148, 242, 243, 256, 265, 266; as measure of control, 36-38, 39, 249; ideological, 39

Artifacts of power, 4, 5, 33, 38, 39, 242, 249-251, 258, 265, 266; chiefly, 25; international style, 25; of warriors, 25

B

Bareis, C. J., 71

Basket motif, 196, 201, 202, 205, 211

Baugh, T. G., 186

BBB Motor Site, 45, 77, 79, 82, 95, 96, 98, 100-102, 115, 116, 118, 121, 123, 124, 127, 132-135, 147, 153, 156, 162, 163, 166, 167, 169, 170-173, 175, 177, 179, 182, 225-231, 233, 238, 239, 244-247, 256, 260

Benton, M., 19

Black Bottom Mississippian: settlement, 67-69; ceremonial center, 68; dispersed villages, 68; extractive camps, 67; farmsteads, 68;

hamlets, 68; nodal points, 68; settlement system, 68, 70

Black drink, 164, 216

Blitz, J. H., 34

Bourdieu, P., 10, 16, 29

Brandt, K. A., 53

Brown, J. A., 194, 217, 226, 233-235, 237, 239, 241, 242

Built environment, 20, 41, 62; and power, 20, 25. *See also* Architecture of power

Busk, 6, 134, 216. *See also* Green Corn

Butler, B., 68

C

Caddo, 16, 174, 186

Cahokia, 44, 58, 170; and rural organization compared, 190-191, 252-260; blind men and elephant, 1; craft specialization, 51; cultural homogeneity, 51, 59; culture history, 44-54, 59; absence of SECC, 53; Emergent Mississippian, 44, 47; environmental degradation, 59; First-Line settlement, 74; Fourth-Line settlements, 71, 74; dispersed villages, 77-79, 183-186, 249-250; hegemony, 2, 57; instability, 51, 57, 59, 60, 259; models, 1, 4, 46, 54, 55, 56, 191, 251; as redistributional society, 75; Central Political-Administrative Complex, 46; Fowler model questioned, 74-75; in-situ model, 55; integration model, 55; interaction model, 55; migration model, 55; Monks Mound, 43, 44, 188, 240; population, 50, 189; satellite temple towns, 45; Second-Line settlement, 74; stockades, 50, 59; Third-Line settlement, 74

Cahokia Cordmarked, 51-53, 86, 106

Caldwell, J., 55

Carbon Dioxide Site, 82, 83

Ceremonial node, 82, 88, 95, 102, 115, 122-124, 134, 144, 148, 167-175; defined, 83, 159; ethnohistoric evidence, 167-170, 174-175. *See also* Fertility Cult

Chase, A. F., 15

Chase, D. Z., 15

Chickasaw, 185

Chiefdoms: 58; and ideology, 24; collaborative, 35; complex, 18; cycling, 18, 59; definition, 17, 58; in Southeast, 58, 185; leadership, 17, 186; offices, 17; paramount, 18; simple, 18; snowball effect, 58; versus state, 191-192, 251-252

Chmurny, W., 151

Civic node, 82, 102, 106, 111, 115, 136, 140, 148, 164-165; defined, 82, 159

Communalism, 14; at Cahokia, 15; questioned, 187-192, 255; and elite-commoner dichotomy, 15

Communitas, 13, 14

Conrad, L. A., 69, 70, 76, 240

Copper, 34, 111, 147, 168, 175, 181, 226, 240, 266

Courtyards, 66, 155, 165, 242, 261, 266. *See also* Mound and plaza organization; Sacred landscapes

Creek, 170, 185

Crystals, 34, 95, 100, 101, 107, 110, 111, 120, 123, 124, 127, 133, 143, 147, 158, 165, 168, 175, 179, 181, 182, 189, 226-228, 266

Culture. *See* Material culture

D

Datura, 123, 229, 230

De Montmollin, O., 192

DePratter, C. B., 189

Dickens, C., 151

Discoidals, 38, 48, 88, 92, 94, 99, 243, 266

Dominant ideology, 14, 21; and subalternate ideologies, 23; contradictions, 23, 24; definition, 22; false consciousness, 22, 23; functions of, 24. *See also* Ideology

Douglas, J., 228, 229, 232

Douglas, M., 28

Drennan, R. D., 155

Dualism, 193, 216, 220, 221, 223, 230-233, 242, 262

E

Earle, T. K., 24, 35, 193

Earth Mother, 210, 211, 258, 261

East St. Louis Mound Group, 45, 50, 57, 58, 74, 170, 228

East St. Louis Stone Quarry Site, 140, 148, 180, 182, 248

Egalitarian societies, 4, 12; as chimera, 4

Elites: and commoners, 13, 239; and communitas, 13; as rich and powerful, 15; as sacred, 14, 35; at Cahokia, 16; definition, 15; fissioning, 13; in control, 15, 41; intercommunity competition, 14; multi-tiered model, 16; North American evidence,

16; origins, 13; two-tier model, 16

Emerald Mounds, 58

Emergent Mississippian Period, 47, 56, 57, 189; Collinsville Phase, 47; north-south division, 47; rural settlement forms, 155-156, 252-254; Sponemann Phase debate, 47

Engels, F., 22

Engraved sherds, 226

F

FAI-270 Archaeological Mitigation Project, 46-48, 50, 54, 71, 75, 77, 102; and settlements, 76; research design, 75; site-stripping, 76; and B. G. Trigger, 76

Falcon motifs, 216, 217, 226, 234-236, 239, 240

Farmsteads, 68, 160, 184

Females, 147, 205, 207, 210, 257; as Earth Mother, 210-212

Fertility, 157, 172-174, 176, 178, 179, 190, 193, 207-209, 211, 212, 215-217, 219, 222, 223, 225, 229, 230, 234-239, 241-247, 250, 257, 258, 260, 261, 263, 264, 267

Fertility cult, 6, 35, 52; at Cahokia, 35, 40, 59, 258, 260-262. *See also* Fertility; Mississippian cults

Figurines, 195-207, 258, 260, 261, 263, 264, 266; Birger, 196; Figure at Mortar, 202-205; flint clay and, 195-196; Keller, 196-199, 261; Macoupin Creek, 207, 246; McGhee, 199; Rattler Frog, 246; Schild, 205-207; Sponemann, 199; Svehla, 207; West, 202; Willoughby, 199-202

Finney, F. A., 156, 160

Flint clay, 34, 52, 87, 122, 127, 129, 133, 143, 180, 181, 195, 196, 199, 205, 266

Florence Street Site, 81, 82, 121, 141, 144, 145, 146, 148, 167, 169, 170, 180, 182, 248

Forked Eye Motif, 52, 213, 215, 216, 239

Fortier, A. C., 47, 124, 127, 129, 132-134, 194, 199, 201

Foucault, M., 14, 16, 19, 20, 41

Fowler, M. L., 47, 48, 50, 52, 55, 71, 73, 74, 75, 185, 191

Frankenstein, S., 34, 182

Freimuth, G. A., 55

Functionaries: lower-level, 6, 16, 157, 164, 176, 177, 181, 185, 251, 258

G

Galena, 34, 52, 87, 92, 99, 100, 101, 110, 111, 113, 119, 120, 133,

139, 143, 147, 180, 181, 182, 189, 226-228, 266
Giddens, A., 10, 11, 24, 29
Goggin, J. M., 240
Gramsci, A., 4, 21, 193
Green Corn, 6, 90, 94, 125, 129, 134, 157, 164, 167, 171, 173, 179,
201, 219, 220, 222, 230, 236, 243-245, 250, 256, 261. *See also*
Busk; World Renewal
Griffin, J. B., 43, 57, 237, 242

H

Habitus, 3, 11, 29; and individuals, 11
Hall, R. L., 1, 47, 48, 54, 55, 56, 194, 216, 240
Harn, A., 49, 69, 70, 71, 74
Hegemony, 4, 6, 16, 18, 21, 31, 35, 186-188; and coercion, 4, 21;
and elites, 21; and ideology, 4, 21; and resistance, 21, 22; and
social change, 22; and subalternate groups, 21; definition, 21,
22; versus autonomy, 187-188
Hematite, 92, 94, 95, 100, 101, 104-107, 110, 111, 114, 115, 139,
143, 181, 182, 189, 226-228
Hierarchical societies, 5, 16; and inequality, 12; and typology, 16,
191-192; chiefdoms, 17, 188-189; definition, 32; middle-
range societies, 17. *See also* Chiefdoms
Hirth, K., 33
Hodder, I., 10, 25, 29
Hoe motif, 196, 202, 207, 210, 211
Holmes, W., 43
Horseshoe Lake Mound Group, 57
Howard, J. H., 194, 195, 216
Hudson, C., 195, 208, 216, 220

I

Ideology, 18, 22, 24; and cults, 35, 40; and power, 22; as critique of
domination, 24; as naturalizing force, 23, 24, 31, 36; as
reproduction, 24; of equality, 12; Southeastern evidence, 193-
194. *See also* Dominant ideology
Individual: as actor, 9, 11, 21, 27; as locus of reproduction and
transformation, 10
Institutionalized inequality, 4, 13, 14
Isherwood, B., 28

J

Johnson, G. A., 31
Juice presses, 52
Julien Site, 81-84, 86, 102, 111, 112, 115, 123, 133, 135-139, 141, 144, 153, 161, 165, 176-182, 231, 245, 247

K

Kelly, J. E., 46, 47, 48, 50, 54, 55, 194, 222, 243, 248, 254, 257, 260, 263
Kincaid Site, 65
Knight, V. J., Jr., 194, 222, 236, 239, 241, 242, 244
Kunnemann Mound Group, 51
Kunnemann Tract, 51

L

Labras Lake Site, 102, 103, 115, 165, 231, 245, 247
Lathrap, D., 55
Lesure, R., 34, 35
Lightfoot, K. G., 192
Limonite, 87, 92, 99, 100, 101, 111, 114, 226-228
Lohmann Phase, 49, 57; ceramics, 48; construction at Cahokia, 48; external contacts, 49; population, 49; temple towns, 49
Lohmann Rural Settlement, 83-100; civic-ceremonial node, 88-95, 164, 170-171, 243-244; households, 83; nodal household, 83-87, 161; priest-mortuary ceremonial node, 95-101, 171-172, 244; rural organization, 176-177, 254-257
Long Nosed God, 240
Lopinot, N., 50, 52, 153, 154, 253, 255
Lower World. *See* Under World

M

Marcus Site, 16, 156
Marker posts, 84, 87, 89, 92, 96, 99, 103, 106, 108, 111, 112, 115, 116, 124, 125, 132, 157, 156, 230, 266
Marx, K., 22, 24
Mason, R., 51
Material culture, 3, 18, 26; and functionalism, 26, 28; as purveyor of culture, 11, 27; as reflecting social partitioning, 3, 4, 27, 28, 31, 263; as text, 3, 9, 25-28, 30, 33, 36

Mehrer, M. W., 56, 81-83, 86-88, 92, 102, 135, 138, 141, 149, 160, 187

Merrell Tract 15A, 53

Mica, 48, 52, 113, 119, 181, 226, 227, 228, 266

Miller, D., 19, 22

Milner, G. R., 47, 50, 56, 77, 83, 99, 111, 112, 114, 120, 121, 139, 140, 142, 144, 147, 148, 152, 171, 177, 189

Mississippian cults, 233-237; fertility versus ancestor, 235; fertility versus nobility, 236-237; organizational networks, 234-235; priests, 236-237. *See also* Fertility cults

Mississippian culture, 43; defined, 43

Mitchell Mound Group, 50, 57, 74, 76, 170

Monks Mound, 48, 51, 53, 57, 95, 124

Moorehead Phase, 52; ceramics, 52; population, 52

Moorehead rural settlement, 135-140; civic nodes, 136-140, 165, 247; households, 135; nodal clusters, 135-136, 161; rural organization, 179-180, 260

Mound 72, 228, 239, 241, 254, 257, 264

Mound and plaza organization, 39, 41, 57, 170, 220, 230, 231, 262, 266; Emergent Mississippian, 57. *See also* Courtyards; Sacred Landscapes

Mounds Place Incised, 52

Muller, J., 67, 68, 70, 152

Munson, P., 49

N

Natchez, 16, 174, 228, 259

Nodal household, 82, 83, 148, 161; defined, 82, 156

O

O'Brien, P., 55

Omaha, 16

Oneota Culture, 47, 54; Bold Counselor Phase, 54; Groves Complex, 54; Vulcan Phase, 47, 54. *See also* American Bottom, chronology

P

Paradigmatic dimension, 10

Pauketat, T. R., 34, 35, 38, 50-52, 56, 57, 78, 154, 182, 189, 194, 212, 215, 219, 221, 241, 252-257, 259

Perino, G., 51, 199

Pettit, P., 28

Phillips, P., 194, 217

Pochteca, 55

Porter, J. W., 50, 52, 55, 57, 76

Postprocessual archaeology, 2, 3, 16

Powell Plain, 53, 106, 114, 115

Power, 18; and built environment, 20; and individuals, 19; as coercion, 19; as dispositional capability, 19; as freewill, 19; as resource bounded, 19, 31; definition, 19, 20; in society, 19. *See also* Architecture of power; Artifacts of power

Power over, 13, 16, 20, 31, 36, 38, 40, 187, 249, 251, 254, 259, 261, 263; definition, 19, 20

Power to, 258, 259; definition, 19, 20

Powers Fort, 65, 66

Powers Phase, 66, 76; ceremonial center, 67; hamlets, 66; limited-activity sites, 66; villages, 66

Praxis, 3, 9; and domination, 12; as locus of reproduction and transformation, 3, 10, 27; recursive nature of, 30

Prentice, G., 194, 210, 211

Prestige-good economies, 33; and elites, 33; and social relationships, 33; and value, 34, 35; defined, 33; questioned, 33, 34, 181-182

Price, J. E., 65, 66

Pulcher Mound Group, 45, 49, 57, 58, 74, 188, 254

Pulcher Tradition, 48

Q

Quadripartite world, 193, 220-222, 223, 230, 232, 242. *See also* Courtyards; Sacred Landscapes

R

Ramey Incised, 51, 53, 54, 86, 105, 106, 107, 111, 114, 119, 120, 122, 123, 127, 129, 132, 133, 173, 179, 189, 190, 205, 212-222, 225, 226, 230, 239, 247, 256, 257, 258, 261, 262, 264, 266, 267; formal analysis, 212-215; symbolism, 216-218; and rites of intensification, 219-220; bird motifs, 216-217; curvilinear motifs, 216-217; earth mound motifs, 218. *See also* Fertility; Fertility cult; Green Corn

Range Site, 81, 82, 83, 87-90, 93, 102, 106, 108, 110, 111, 115, 133,

148, 153, 155, 164, 165, 167, 169, 170, 177, 188, 228, 229, 231, 238, 239, 243, 245, 247

Red cedar, 94, 100, 101, 123, 124, 127-129, 132-134, 170, 179, 228, 229, 244, 245, 262, 266

Red ochre. *See* Hematite

Riordan, R., 68

Rites of intensification, 179, 189, 219, 220, 237, 257, 261, 264. *See also* Green Corn

Ritual districts, 186

Robert Schneider Site, 82, 102, 133

Rowlands, M., 34, 182

Rural countryside: remade, 41. *See also* Lohmann Phase

S

Sacra, 39, 40, 181, 236, 237, 241, 242, 264

Sacred fire, 119, 121, 123, 124, 129, 229, 237, 246

Sacred landscapes, 4, 25, 40, 263; and elites, 14, 254; as heterotopias, 41, 222, 263. *See also* Mound and plaza organization; Quadripartite world

Sahlins, M. A., 29, 30, 254

Saitta, D. J., 14, 15, 186, 187

Sand Prairie Phase, 53; dispersal, 54; and SECC, 53

Sand Prairie rural settlement, 141-148; households, 141; mortuary ceremonial node, 144-148, 175, 248; nodal housecluster, 135-138; rural organization, 180-181, 260

Scarry, J. F., 186

Schlemmer Site, 156

Screens, 89, 92, 96, 101, 103, 106, 108, 111, 112, 116, 121, 125, 132, 144

SECC. *See* Southeastern Ceremonial Complex

Serpents, 202, 203, 207-210, 212; as Under World motifs, 208-210

Service, E., 17, 75

Settlement, 62; and environment, 62; and information theory, 31; and society, 62, 63; hierarchies, 31, 191; Mississippian, 63-65; as adaptation, 64; dispersal versus nucleation, 64; farmsteads, 64; regional variation, 65-69, 250; systems, 63

Settlement articulation: direct, 5, 250; defined, 71, 73; models, 5, 70-71, 76; community stratification, 73, 74; measures of articulation, 31, 32; population nucleation, 74; social correlates, 76, 250; sequential, 5, 250

Shanks, M., 24

Shell, 94, 106, 138, 143, 175, 179, 180, 181, 187, 189

Smith, B., 43, 63, 65, 66, 151, 152, 154

Snakes. *See* Serpents

Social systems, 10, 12; as recurrent social practices, 12

Southeastern Ceremonial Complex (SECC), 53, 233, 240

Special purpose sites, 156, 160. *See also* Farmsteads

Spiro Site, 226, 228, 234, 235, 238, 239, 240

Sponemann Site, 45, 47, 54, 94, 102, 115, 124, 125, 128, 130, 131, 133, 134, 135, 167, 169, 170, 173, 175, 178, 179, 195, 225-231, 238, 239, 245-247, 261

Spoon River culture, 65; settlement, 69-70; camps, 70; dispersed villages, 70; hamlets, 69; Larson Phase, 70; system, 70, 71; towns, 69

St. Louis Mound Group, 45, 74

Stirling Phase, 49, 51; ceramics, 51; expansion, 49, 59; nucleation, 50; population, 50; temple towns, 49

Stirling rural settlement, 101, 101-133; ceremonial nodes, 124-134, 173-174, 246-247; civic nodes, 102-115, 164-165, 245-246; households, 101-102, 103; rural organization, 177-179, 256-260; temple-mortuary ceremonial nodes, 115-123, 172-173, 246

Structuralism, 3, 25; and material culture, 25, 27; defended, 28

Structuration, 3, 10, 12, 19, 29, 30, 31; and practice, 11

Structure, 10, 12; and history, 29, 30; and synchrony, 11, 29; as framework, 10, 12; failed reproduction, 30; "longue duree," 29, 30

"Structure of the conjuncture," 29

Stumpware, 48, 51, 94, 100, 107, 111

Sumner, C., 23

Swanton, J. R., 194, 208

Sweat houses, 51, 78, 83, 103, 105, 106, 108, 111, 112, 115, 127, 129, 140, 157, 159, 165, 177, 178, 180, 184, 245, 246, 265, 266

Syntagmatic dimension, 10, 12

Systems, 11

T

Theory of practice, 10, 29

Thunderbird, 217, 221

Tilley, C., 19, 24

Tippets Bean Pots, 51-53

Tobacco, 94, 107, 111, 127, 132, 134, 170, 179, 210, 229, 230, 244, 262, 266

Trigger, B. G., 76

Trubitt, M. B. D., 181

Turner–DeMange Sites, 82, 83, 102, 135

U

Uktena, 209; and crystals, 227, 227-228

Under World, 193, 207-209, 211, 212, 215-218, 220, 221, 223, 257, 260, 261, 263

Upper World, 215-218, 220, 221, 257, 260, 261, 263

V

Vogel, J. O., 55

Vogt, E. A., 63

W

Waring, A. J., 194, 195, 234

Weeping eye motif, 52

Welch, P. D., 34

Wells Broad–Trailed plates, 52

Wells Incised Plate, 53, 247

Whalley, L., 228, 229

Willey, G. R., 62

Williams, R., 21

Williams, S., 240

Willoughby, C. C., 261

Winnebago, 16

Wolforth, T., 152, 153

Women. *See* Females

Woods, W. I., 152, 153

World renewal, 94, 119, 170, 173, 222, 250, 264, 266. *See also* Green Corn

Wright, H. T., 17, 31, 191, 251, 254

Wyckoff, D. G., 186

Wylie, M. A., 25, 28

Y

Yerkes, R. W., 51